Securing Cyber-Physical Systems

Scrivener Publishing
100 Cummings Center, Suite 541J
Beverly, MA 01915-6106

Industry 5.0 Transformation Applications

Series Editors: Dr. S. Balamurugan (sbnbala@gmail) and Dr. Sheng-Lung Peng

The increase in technological advancements in the areas of artificial intelligence (AI), machine learning (ML) and data analytics has led to the next industrial revolution "Industry 5.0". The transformation to Industry 5.0 collaborates human intelligence with machines to customize efficient solutions. This book series covers various subjects under promising application areas of Industry 5.0 such as smart manufacturing, intelligent traffic, cloud manufacturing, real-time productivity optimization, augmented reality and virtual reality, etc., as well as titles supporting technologies for promoting potential applications of Industry 5.0, such as collaborative robots (Cobots), edge computing, Internet of Everything, big data analytics, digital twins, 6G and beyond, blockchain, quantum computing and hyper-intelligent networks.

Publishers at Scrivener
Martin Scrivener (martin@scrivenerpublishing.com)
Phillip Carmical (pcarmical@scrivenerpublishing.com)

Securing Cyber-Physical Systems

Fundamentals, Applications and Challenges

Edited by

K. Ananthajothi
Dept. of Computer Science and Engineering, Rajalakshmi Engineering College, Chennai, India

S. N. Sangeethaa
Dept. of Computer Science and Engineering, Bannari Amman Institute of Technology, Tamil Nadu, India

D. Divya
Dept. of Computer Science and Engineering, Jerusalem College of Engineering, Chennai, India

S. Balamurugan
Albert Einstein Engineering and Research Labs, Coimbatore, Tamil Nadu, India

and

Shen-Lung Peng
Dept. of Creative Technologies and Product Design, National Taipei University of Business, Taiwan

Scrivener Publishing

WILEY

This edition first published 2025 by John Wiley & Sons, Inc., 111 River Street, Hoboken, NJ 07030, USA and Scrivener Publishing LLC, 100 Cummings Center, Suite 541J, Beverly, MA 01915, USA

For more information about Scrivener publications please visit www.scrivenerpublishing.com.

Wiley Global Headquarters
111 River Street, Hoboken, NJ 07030, USA

For details of our global editorial offices, customer services, and more information about Wiley products visit us at www.wiley.com.

The manufacturer's authorized representative according to the EU General Product Safety Regulation is Wiley-VCH GmbH, Boschstr. 12, 69469 Weinheim, Germany, e-mail: Product_Safety@wiley.com.

Library of Congress Cataloging-in-Publication Data

ISBN 978-1-394-28773-4

Cover image: Generated with AI using Adobe Firefly
Cover design by Russell Richardson

Set in size of 11pt and Minion Pro by Manila Typesetting Company, Makati, Philippines

Printed in the USA

10 9 8 7 6 5 4 3 2 1

Contents

Preface **xvii**

1 Enhancing Safety and Security in Autonomous Connected Vehicles: Fusion of Optimal Control With Multi-Armed Bandit Learning **1**

K.T. Meena Abarna, A. Punitha and S. Sathiya

1.1 Background 2

1.1.1 Problem Statement 4

1.1.2 Motivation 4

1.2 Related Works 5

1.2.1 Contributions 7

1.2.2 Centralized CRN Scheduling 8

1.2.3 Multi-Armed Bandit (MAB) 9

1.2.4 Bandit Learning with Switching Costs 11

1.3 System Model 12

1.3.1 Resource Spectrum 12

1.3.2 CRs' Spectrum Utilization Schemes 13

1.3.3 CBS Scheduling 13

1.3.4 PUs' Activity 13

1.4 Outcomes 15

1.4.1 Scenario I: Fallen Traffic Signs 15

1.4.2 Scenario II: Traffic Signs Alert by the Road Workers 16

1.4.3 Scenario III: Back/Rotated Traffic Sign Across the Road 17

1.4.4 Scenario IV: Hacking of a Stop Sign at a Four-Way Stop Intersection 18

1.5 Conclusions and Future Enhancement 19

1.5.1 Conclusions 19

1.5.2 Future Directions 21

References 23

2 Secure Data Handling in AI and Proactive Response Network: Create a Physical Layer–Proposed Cognitive Cyber-Physical Security 25
A. Sivasundari, P. Kumar, S. Vinodhkumar and N. Duraimurugan
2.1 Introduction 26
2.1.1 The Role of AI in Cybersecurity 27
2.1.2 Usage of CCPS in IoT 27
2.2 Challenges and Mechanisms 28
2.2.1 Brief Account of Challenges Faced 28
2.2.2 Innovative Mechanisms 30
2.3 Using AI to Support Cognitive Cybersecurity 30
2.3.1 Cognitive Systems 30
2.3.2 AI in IoT 30
2.4 Create a Physical Layer–Proposed CCPS 31
2.4.1 Create a Physical Layer–Proposed CCPS in Healthcare Application 33
2.4.1.1 Privacy-Aware Collaboration 33
2.4.1.2 Cycle Model of CCPS 36
2.4.1.3 Dynamic Security Knowledge Base 36
2.4.2 Method for Secure Data Handling 36
2.5 Road Map of Implementation 38
2.5.1 AI for CCPS-IoT 38
2.5.2 AI-Enabled Wireless CCPS-IoT to Provide Security 39
2.6 Conclusions and Future Enhancement 40
Future Directions 41
References 43

3 Intelligent Cognitive Cyber-Physical System–Based Intrusion Detection for AI-Enabled Security in Industry 4.0 45
V. Mahavaishnavi, R. Saminathan and G. Ramachandran
3.1 Introduction 46
3.1.1 Cyber-Physical Systems 46
3.1.2 Intelligent Cyber-Physical Systems (ISPS) 47
3.1.3 Cognitive Cyber-Physical Systems (CCPS) 48
3.1.4 IDS in Industry 4.0 Using iCCPS 49
3.1.5 AI in iCCPS-IDS 49
3.2 Problem Statement 50
3.3 Motivation 51
3.4 Research Gap 52

3.5 Methodology 53
3.5.1 Training Dataset 54
3.5.2 Information for Assessment and Instruction 54
3.5.3 Model 54
3.5.4 CPS Determined by Cognition Agents 56
3.5.5 Useful Implementation of the Actual Device 57
3.6 Importance and Impact of AI-Based Intrusion Detection in iCCPS in Industry 4.0 59
3.6.1 Need 59
3.6.2 Challenges 60
3.7 Conclusions and Future Directions 60
Future Directions 61
References 63

4 Resilient Cognitive Cyber-Physical Systems: Conceptual Frameworks, Models, and Implementation Strategies 65
R. Manivannan and M.P. Vaishnnave
4.1 Introduction 66
4.1.1 Problem Statement 70
4.1.2 Motivation 71
4.2 Materials and Methods 72
4.3 CCPS Design Challenges 74
4.4 Cyber-Physical Systems Principles and Paradigms 77
4.4.1 CCPS Conceptual Framework 79
4.4.2 CCPS Modeling 81
4.4.3 Other Modeling Issues in CCPS 82
4.5 Conclusions and Future Enhancements 83
4.5.1 Future Enhancements 83
References 85

5 Cognitive Cyber-Physical Security Challenges, Issues, and Recent Trends Over IoT 87
Chinnaraj Govindasamy
5.1 Introduction 88
5.1.1 From IoT to CCPS-IoT 93
5.1.2 Fundamental Cognitive Tasks 94
5.2 Motivation and Challenges 94
5.2.1 Motivation 94
5.2.2 Challenges 95
5.3 Security 96

5.3.1 Physical Layer Attacks 98
5.3.2 Physical Layer Security 99
5.3.3 Main Constituents 100
5.4 Research Gap 102
5.5 An Automatic Security Manager for CCPS Using IoT 103
5.5.1 Combatting Erroneous Estimations 103
5.5.2 Detection and Classification 104
5.6 Conclusions and Future Enhancement 104
Future Enhancement 105
References 106

6 Cognitive Cyber-Physical Security With IoT: A Solution to Smart Healthcare System 109
P. Shanmugam, Mohamed Iqbal M. and M. Amanullah
6.1 Introduction 110
6.1.1 Motivation 112
6.1.2 Need and Contribution 113
6.1.2.1 Need 113
6.1.2.2 Contribution 114
6.2 Medical CCPS with IoT 116
6.2.1 IoT Device for AI Solution 118
6.2.2 Traditional Bio-Modality Spoofing Detection 119
6.2.3 MCPS Using AI Device 119
6.3 Functional and Behavioral Perspectives 120
6.4 Modeling and Verification Methods of MCPS 123
6.4.1 MCPS Modeling Based on ICE 124
6.4.2 MCPS Modeling Based on Component 125
6.5 Artificial Intelligence for Cognitive Cybersecurity 125
6.5.1 Privacy-Aware Collaboration 127
6.5.2 Cognitive Security Cycle Model 127
6.6 Conclusions and Future Direction 128
6.6.1 Conclusions 128
6.6.2 Future Directions 129
References 130

7 Cognitive Cyber-Physical Security with IoT and ML: Role of Cybersecurity, Threats, and Benefits to Modern Economies and Industries 133
P. Anbalagan, A. Kanthimathinathan and S. Saravanan
7.1 Introduction 134
7.1.1 Key Contributions 136

7.1.2 Problem Statement 137
7.1.3 Motivation 138
7.2 CCPS Associated with IoT 139
7.2.1 Reasons in Favor of Cognitive Analytics 140
7.2.2 Analyses of Current Cyber Risk Data 141
7.3 Materials and Methods 143
7.3.1 Role of Cybersecurity in CCPS with IoT and ML 143
7.3.2 ML in Cognitive Cyber-Physical Security with IoT 144
7.3.3 Threats to Modern Economies and Industries 144
7.3.4 Benefits to Modern Economies and Industries 147
7.4 Outcomes 148
7.4.1 AI-Enabled Management Technology and Approach Taxonomy 151
7.4.2 Essential Self-Adapting System Technologies 151
7.4.3 Attack Malware Classifier 151
7.5 Conclusions and Future Direction 152
Future Directions 152
References 154

8 A Safety Analysis Framework for Medical Cyber-Physical Systems Using Systems Theory 157
K. Ananthajothi, K. Balamurugan, D. Divya and T.P. Latchoumi
8.1 Introduction 158
8.2 Background 160
8.2.1 Cyber-Physical Systems 160
8.2.2 Quality-of-Service Issues in CPS 161
8.2.3 Medical Cyber-Physical Systems 161
8.3 The Systems-Based Safety Analysis Observation for MCPS 162
8.3.1 Identification of Critical Requirements in MCPS 162
8.3.2 A Systems Theory–Based Method for Safety Analysis in Medical Cyber-Physical Systems 163
8.3.3 MCPS in Patient-Controlled Analgesia 165
8.4 Improved Wireless Medical Cyber-Physical System (IWMCPS) 166
8.4.1 Level: Data Acquisition 166
8.4.2 Layer: Data Aggregating 167
8.4.3 Level: Storing 167
8.4.4 Level: Action 168
8.4.5 IWMCPS Architectural Research 168
8.4.6 Core of Communications and Sensors 168
8.5 Hazard Analysis on PCA-MCPS 169

8.5.1 System Safety Constraint 170
8.5.2 System Safety Control Structure 170
8.5.3 Identify Unsafe Control Actions 170
8.5.4 Specifying Causes 171
8.6 Conclusions and Future Directions 172
Future Directions 172
References 174

9 Cognitive Cybersecurity and Reinforcement Learning: Enhancing Security in CPS-IoT Enabled Healthcare 177
A. Arokiaraj Jovith, M. Sangeetha, D. Saveetha and S. Antelin Vijila
9.1 Introduction 178
9.2 Methodology 182
9.2.1 Device AI Solutions 182
9.2.2 Detect the Spoofing of Bio-Modality 182
9.2.3 Detect the Spoofing of Bio-Modality Using Machine Learning 183
9.3 Challenges and Mechanisms 183
9.3.1 Challenges 183
9.3.2 Innovative Mechanisms 185
9.4 Cognitive Cyber-Physical Systems and Reinforcement Learning 185
9.4.1 Model Formulation 188
9.4.2 AI in CCPS 189
9.4.2.1 Privacy-Aware Collaboration 192
9.4.2.2 Cognitive Security Cycle Model 192
9.4.2.3 Need 193
9.4.2.4 Cross-Sectoral Techniques 193
9.4.2.5 Actuation and Data Collection 194
9.5 Conclusions and Future Directions 194
9.6 Future Directions 195
References 196

10 Navigating the Digital Landscape: Understanding, Detecting, and Mitigating Cyber Threats in an Evolving Technological Era 199
Manikandan J., Hemalatha P., Jayashree K. and Rajeswari P.
10.1 The Digital Transformation: Shaping Modern Business Dynamics 200
10.2 Impact of COVID-19: Accelerating the Digital Shift 201
10.3 Online Safety Concerns: Navigating the Digital Landscape 202
10.4 Interplay of Digital Technologies: Vulnerabilities and Threats 204

10.4.1 Introduction to Digital Technologies 204
10.4.2 Case Studies and Examples 206
10.5 Rise of Cyber Assaults as a Service: Automating Criminal Activities 207
10.6 Evolving Threat Landscape: Understanding Modern Cyber Attacks 210
10.7 Beyond Conventional Security Measures: The Need for Advanced Defense 211
10.8 Rise of Cyber Assaults as a Service: Automating Criminal Activities 213
10.8.1 Introduction to Cyber Assaults as a Service 213
10.8.2 Automation of Criminal Activities 213
10.8.3 Impact and Implications 214
10.9 Evolving Threat Landscape: Understanding Modern Cyber Attacks 215
10.9.1 Types of Modern Cyber Attacks 215
10.9.2 Implications for Cybersecurity Defense 216
10.10 Beyond Conventional Security Measures: The Need for Advanced Defense 217
10.10.1 Challenges with Conventional Security Measures 217
10.10.2 The Evolution of Advanced Defense 218
10.11 Uncovering Cyber Threats: Patterns, Trends, and Detection Methods 218
10.11.1 Patterns of Cyber Threats 218
10.12 Addressing Advanced Persistent Threats: Challenges and Solutions 220
10.12.1 Introduction to Advanced Persistent Threats (APTs) 220
10.12.2 Challenges Posed by APTs 220
10.12.3 Solutions for Addressing APTs 221
References 222

11 Defense Strategies for Cyber-Physical Systems 225
Rajendran Thanikachalam, T. Nithya, Balaji Sampathkumar and J. Mangayarkarasi
11.1 Introduction 226
11.2 Threat Landscape in CPS 228
11.3 Advanced Defense Strategies 231
11.3.1 Anomaly Detection in CPS 231
11.3.2 Secure Communication Protocols 232
11.3.3 Machine Learning-Driven Defenses 235

11.3.4 Zero Trust Model for CPS 237
11.3.5 Resilience Techniques for CPS 240
11.3.6 Intensive Training and Awareness 241
11.3.7 Conclusion and Future Directions 245
References 245

12 Cybersecurity in the Era of Artificial Intelligence: Challenges and Innovations 249
Ashwini A., H. Sehina and Banu Priya Prathaban
12.1 Introduction to Cybersecurity Analysis 250
12.2 Need for AI in Cybersecurity 252
12.3 Current Cybersecurity Techniques 253
12.4 Role of AI in Cybersecurity 255
12.5 Challenges in AI Enhanced Cybersecurity 256
12.6 Quantum Computing and Post Quantum Computing in Cybersecurity 257
12.7 AI Powered Encryption Analysis 259
12.8 Adaptive Cybersecurity 261
12.9 Overall Analysis of AI in Cybersecurity 262
12.10 Privacy Preserving AI and Cybersecurity 263
12.11 Future Directions and Research Challenges 264
12.12 Conclusion 266
References 266

13 Safeguarding the Virtual Realm: Assessing Cyber Security Challenges and Innovations in Today's World 269
Rajaram P., Rajasekar Rangasamy, R. C. Karpagalakshmi, J. Lenin and S. Muthulingam
13.1 Introduction 270
13.2 Understanding the Motivations Behind Cyber Attacks: Financial, Political, and Military Goals 272
13.3 Types of Cyber Threats: From Viruses to Data Breaches 276
13.4 Impact of Cyber Attacks on Businesses and Governments: Financial and Operational Consequences 278
13.5 Strategies for Cyber Security: Prevention, Detection, and Response 281
13.6 Evolving Threat Landscape: Keeping Pace with Emerging Cyber Threats 283
13.7 Exploring Global Cyber Security Initiatives: Collaborative Efforts and Best Practices 285

13.8 Cyber Security Frameworks: Origins, Evolution, and Effectiveness 286
13.9 Emerging Trends in Cyber Security: AI, Blockchain, and IoT Solutions 288
13.10 Challenges and Limitations of Current Cyber Security Approaches 289
13.11 Future Directions in Cyber Security Research and Development 291
13.12 Conclusion 293
References 293

14 Predicting Android Ransomware Attacks Using Categorical Classification 295
A. Pandiaraj, N. Ramshankar, Mathan Kumar Mounagurusamy, Karakanapati Mrudhula, P. Lahari Sai and Lekkala Likhitha
14.1 Introduction 296
14.2 Background Study 297
14.3 Scope 300
14.4 Experimentation 300
14.5 Methodology 303
14.6 Conclusion 306
References 306

15 Defense Strategies for Cognitive Cyber-Physical Systems in Machine Learning Domain 309
M. Karthiga, N. Sangavi, V. R. Kiruthika, S. N. Sangeethaa, P. Ananthi and S. Vaanathi
15.1 Introduction 310
15.1.1 Background and Motivation 313
15.1.2 Challenges in CPS Defense 314
15.1.2.1 Resource Constraints and Real-Time Demands: Security in a Tight Spot 314
15.1.2.2 Data Security and Privacy: Balancing Protection with User Rights 314
15.1.2.3 Human Factors and Insider Threats: The Weakest Link 315
15.1.2.4 Evolving Threats: A Never-Ending Battle 315
15.2 Literature Review 315
15.3 CPS Security Fears 318
15.3.1 Vulnerabilities Posed in CPS 319

15.4 Secure Approaches for CPS: In Terms of Technology and Attack Perspectives 320
15.4.1 Security Strategies for Various Aspects of Attacks 320
15.5 Issues and Concerns for Ml Protection for CPS 322
15.5.1 ML Model Attacks and the Relevant Measures for Prevention 323
15.5.1.1 Dataset Poisoning Attacks 325
15.5.1.2 Black-Box Attack 327
15.5.1.3 White Box Attack 328
15.5.1.4 Backdoor Attacks 328
15.6 Countermeasures Against Dataset Poisoning Attempts 328
15.6.1 Simulated Poisoning Incidents 329
15.6.2 Countermeasures Against Model Poisoning Incidents 330
15.7 Vulnerability to Privacy 330
15.7.1 Process of Reverse Engineering and API Calls Disclosing Sensitive Data 331
15.8 Membership Inference Assaults 333
15.9 Runtime Disruption Assault 335
15.10 Comparative Investigation 336
15.11 Conclusion and Future Research Directions 338
References 339

16 Cyber-Physical Systems: Challenges, Opportunities, Security Solutions 343
Gopinathan S., S. Babu and P. Shanmugam
16.1 Cyber-Physical Systems 344
16.1.1 Introduction 344
16.1.2 Present Issues on Cyber Security 345
16.1.2.1 Phishing Exploits 346
16.1.2.2 Internet of Things Ransomware 347
16.1.2.3 Strengthened Regulation of Data Privacy 347
16.1.2.4 Cyberattacks Using Mobile Technology 347
16.1.2.5 A Higher Allocation of Resources to Automation 347
16.1.3 CPS –Applications and Research Areas 348
16.2 Cyber Security Challenges 351
16.2.1 Social Media Role in Cyber-Security 352
16.2.2 Cyber-Security Methods 352
16.2.2.1 Access Management and Passphrase Protection 352
16.2.2.2 Verification of Data 352

16.2.2.3 Malicious Software Detectors 353
16.2.2.4 Network Security Barriers 353
16.2.2.5 Antimalware 353
16.3 Integration of Physical and Digital 353
16.3.1 Materials and Procedures 354
16.3.2 Applications 355
16.3.2.1 Financial Sector 355
16.3.2.2 Health Division 355
16.3.2.3 Business Sector 356
16.3.2.4 Industry Sector 356
16.4 Digital Threats to Physical Systems 357
16.4.1 Threats Prioritization 357
16.4.2 Selection of Security Requirements 358
16.5 Industry 4.0 Security 359
16.5.1 Classification of Cyber-Physical Systems and their Pertinent Themes within the Framework of Industry 4.0 360
16.5.2 The Digital Supply System 361
16.5.2.1 The Data Sharing Hazards Associated with the Digital Supply System 361
16.5.2.2 Data Sharing: Granted Access to Information for More Parties 362
16.5.3 Cybersecurity Challenges in Industry 4.0 363
16.6 Evaluation of Risk for CPS 364
16.6.1 Safety Risk Assessment Standards 364
16.6.2 Approaches for Safety Risk Evaluation in CPS 365
16.6.2.1 Analysis of Fault Trees 365
16.6.2.2 Failure Modes and Impacts Evaluation (FMIE) 365
16.6.2.3 The Menace and Operability Approach 365
16.6.2.4 Model-Centred Engineering 366
16.6.2.5 Master Logic Illustration with Objective Tree - Accomplishment Tree 366
16.6.2.6 System Theoretical Accident Model and Procedures (STAMP) is the Foundation for System Theoretic Process Analysis, a Hazard Analysis Method 366
References 366

Index 369

Preface

In the rapidly evolving landscape of technology, the integration of cyber-physical systems (CPS) has become a cornerstone of innovation across various sectors, including healthcare, transportation, and manufacturing. This book aims to illuminate the critical intersection of these systems and cybersecurity, addressing the profound challenges and opportunities that arise in this context. As we navigate the complexities of an increasingly interconnected world, the necessity for robust security measures has never been more pressing. The convergence of the physical and digital realms has introduced unprecedented vulnerabilities, necessitating a proactive and comprehensive approach to securing these essential systems.

This book brings together contributions from esteemed researchers and industry professionals, offering a comprehensive exploration of cognitive CPS, their inherent security challenges, and the latest advancements in safeguarding these systems. Each chapter presents cutting-edge research, frameworks, and methodologies that delve into diverse topics, including the enhancement of safety and security in autonomous vehicles, innovative strategies for secure data handling in artificial intelligence, and resilient frameworks for managing threats in Industry 4.0. The insights provided by the authors not only highlight the current state of the art but also pave the way for future innovations in CPS and cybersecurity.

By addressing critical areas such as intrusion detection, the implications of machine learning in enhancing security, and the integration of IoT in cyber-physical environments, this book aims to equip professionals with the knowledge and tools necessary to confront emerging threats. Our collective goal is to empower researchers, practitioners, and policymakers with actionable insights that enhance the resilience of cyber-physical systems against ever-evolving threats.

Moreover, this book recognizes the importance of interdisciplinary collaboration in tackling the challenges posed by CPS security. As you embark on this journey through the pages of Securing Cyber-Physical Systems:

Fundamentals, Applications and Challenges, we invite you to engage with the material critically and to envision the transformative potential of these technologies. Together, we can foster a secure and sustainable future, ensuring that the integration of cyber-physical systems continues to drive innovation while safeguarding the integrity and safety of our interconnected world. The discourse initiated within these pages is not just an academic exercise but a call to action for all stakeholders in the CPS landscape to actively participate in fortifying our technological foundations against the challenges ahead.

This volume explores the fusion of cognitive computing, AI, and cybersecurity strategies to enhance the safety, security, and resilience of cyber-physical systems (CPS), especially in domains like autonomous vehicles, smart healthcare, Industry 4.0, and IoT.

Chapter 1 introduces a framework combining optimal control and multi-armed bandit learning to secure Autonomous Connected Vehicles from cyber-physical threats. Chapter 2 presents a cognitive cyber-physical security (CCPS) framework for secure data handling in AI and proactive networks using cognitive capabilities at the physical layer.

Chapter 3 develops an AI-enabled intrusion detection system for Industry 4.0, integrating cognitive systems and deep learning to detect sophisticated threats. Chapter 4 focuses on building resilient CCPS by addressing quality of service, cost, and security through robust models, simulations, and system architectures.

Chapter 5 explores cybersecurity challenges in IoT environments and leverages cognitive computing techniques to improve data privacy, scalability, and resilience. Chapter 6 applies CCPS and IoT integration to smart healthcare systems, enhancing patient data security and threat detection through real-time cognitive computing.

Chapter 7 analyzes how machine learning enhances CPS security across modern economies, emphasizing benefits and potential threats in IoT-driven industries. Chapter 8 offers a systems-theory-based safety analysis framework to identify and mitigate risks in medical CPS throughout their lifecycle.

Chapter 9 proposes using reinforcement learning and cognitive cybersecurity to protect CPS-IoT-enabled healthcare systems from evolving threats. Chapter 10 examines evolving cyber threats in the digital era and proposes advanced tools—like blockchain and cloud computing—for building resilient defenses.

Chapter 11 outlines comprehensive CPS defense strategies, including anomaly detection, encryption, machine learning, and Zero Trust models. Chapter 12 reviews AI-driven innovations in cybersecurity, including post-quantum security and blockchain, highlighting the interplay between AI and digital protection.

Chapter 13 assesses global cybersecurity challenges, motivations for attacks, and innovations in defense frameworks and practices. Chapter 14 presents a predictive model using categorical classification to detect Android ransomware, enhancing mobile cybersecurity.

Chapter 15 addresses ML-specific vulnerabilities in CPS, such as data poisoning and privacy breaches, and offers defense strategies validated through simulations. Chapter 16 explores a smart aquaculture system using IoT and data analytics to optimize oxygen levels and shrimp health, advancing sustainable seafood production.

This book is significant, as it addresses the urgent need for solutions to the escalating risks associated with interconnected systems. As technology advances, the potential vulnerabilities of cyber-physical systems grow, making it imperative to understand and mitigate these risks. By providing practical frameworks, methodologies, and insights into innovative solutions, the book contributes to the ongoing discourse on safeguarding CPS—fostering a safer and more secure technological landscape for the future. We extend our gratitude to everyone who helped with this publication, including Martin Scrivener and the team at Scrivener Publishing.

The Editors
August 2025

1

Enhancing Safety and Security in Autonomous Connected Vehicles: Fusion of Optimal Control With Multi-Armed Bandit Learning

K.T. Meena Abarna*, A. Punitha and S. Sathiya

Department of Computer Science and Engineering, Annamalai University, Annamalainagar, Chidambaram, India

Abstract

Communication between vehicles as well as intra-vehicle sensors that include radar and cameras are some of the components that are necessary for autonomous connected vehicles (ACVs) to function properly. This paves ways for both physical as well as cyberattacks, where by an adversary can physically control the ACVs by manipulating the sensor readings. This study proposes a complete control and learning system to protect ACV networks from the physical and the cyberattacks. It has been established that the proposed controller is resistant to physical assaults meant to cause instability in ACV systems. As driverless vehicles become more common, it is crucial to make sure that safety procedures and security safeguards are resilient. The proposed framework makes use of the best control techniques to steer cars through challenging situations while maximizing efficiency and safety. Furthermore, adaptive decision-making in unpredictable and dynamic scenarios—taking into account safety and security restrictions—is made possible by multi-armed bandit learning. The framework attempts to create robust systems that can mitigate cyber-physical threats and guarantee the safe operation of ACVs in a variety of contexts by incorporating various strategies.

***Keywords*:** Autonomous connected vehicles, cognitive cyber-physical systems, cybersecurity, adaptive control, network security, sensor fusion, vulnerability assessment, dynamic environments

**Corresponding author*: abarnakt@gmail.com

K. Ananthajothi, S. N. Sangeethaa, D. Divya, S. Balamurugan and Shen-Lung Peng (eds.) Securing Cyber-Physical Systems: Fundamentals, Applications and Challenges, (1–24) © 2025 Scrivener Publishing LLC

1.1 Background

Traditional manual driving entails using the vehicle's pedals and steering, which can result in dangerous actions in a complex traffic environment and this leads to a variety of accidents related to driving. Reaction time, distractibility, and lack of experience are a few instances of these human flaws. Furthermore, a lot of drivers have a lots of bad driving habits, which adds to the unpredictable driving behaviors that cause traffic jams/congestions and thereby a decline in the traffic system's overall efficiency [1]. In contrast, it is expected that autonomous vehicles (AVs) would either increase the efficiency of roadways or completely reduce accidents that result from human actions or behavior or inactions. Simultaneously, the notion "internet of vehicles" since has gained support for improving the getting together of AVs. Automobiles can exchange a range of datasets through the internet of vehicles, such as sensory inputs, information on locations, and their sensing of their environmental surroundings [2].

Keeping the roads safe has always been of utmost importance. In area of AVs and human-driven vehicles adoption, determining the most effective strategy to lower vehicle-related traffic accidents in today's environment is one of the most actively researched issues. In situations where different factors (such the weather) are constantly changing, AVs are required to make necessary decisions [3]. To minimize the likelihood of collisions, an automobile needs to be able to predict adjacent cars' or objects' actions with sufficient accuracy. All vehicles in a typical traffic scenario are operated by people, and, because of their knowledge and expertise, the people are able to predict with accuracy what other vehicles or nearby objects are likely to do next. Based on this evaluation, everyone who drives instantly modifies their behavior to enhance safety and ensure a free traffic flow [4]. However, in a mixed traffic situation, AVs have to anticipate actions of the human driver upon their perspectives of the road. While driving, the vehicles are allowed through communications such as vehicle-to-infrastructure (V2I) and vehicle-to-vehicle (V2V) to get information regarding the objects that are present in the road. Additionally, by enabling information sharing between AVs and surrounding entities, vehicle-to-everything (V2X) communication contributes significantly to AV decision-making processes, resulting in more safer and more effective driving [5]. An AV's decision-making process could be improved by V2X communications and more specifically V2V communication, and that importance has been highlighted.

The authors have proposed a steering control method based on machine learning (ML) with urban settings coupled with V2X communications to enhance driving. The communication protocols used in vehicular networks, which enable safe communication between vehicles driven by humans and AVs, have been the subject of extensive research. An AV can predict the actions of other objects in the vicinity by exchanging information with other cars and learning about their present driving conditions [6].

These vehicles possess the capacity to precisely identify traffic signs (TSs) and categorize things that are present in the scenario according to their environmental function—a feat mostly made possible by sophisticated ML algorithms—is essential to how they operate. The integrity of these algorithms is a very crucial factor, though. Serious road accidents might result from malicious acts or misinterpretations. Anomalies do exist in most of advanced technology. These flaws could be used by hostile actors to trick autonomous driving systems, which could have a disastrous result. Therefore, to promote AVs' safe incorporation into our transportation system network, a thorough understanding of cyber-physical security is vital, with a particular emphasis on traffic sign recognition (TSR) and object classification (OC) algorithms [7].

In the future, AVs (ACVs) will need to handle a lot of data that is gathered through communication links and sensors. Maintaining the accuracy of this information is essential for smooth flow of traffic and to ensure safe roads [8]. However, autonomous connected vehicles (ACVs) are very much susceptible to cyber-physical attacks because of their reliance on data processing and connectivity. Specifically, an attacker may introduce errors into the ACV at data processing stage, which might lead to accidents or negatively impact traffic flow on the roads [9]. As shown by a practical experiment conducted on a Jeep Cherokee in [10], ACVs are mostly susceptible to cyberattacks that can take over some of its vital functions, such as acceleration and braking. Naturally, an unauthorized person gaining control of an ACV might not only affect the compromised ACV but also hinder other vehicles' flow and result in subpar intelligent transportation system (ITS) performance. This, in turn, encourages an in-depth study into the combined physical and cyber effects of assaults on ACV systems. Cognitive radio networks (CRNs) have emerged as an intriguing model to change the efficiency of spectrum utilization and offer ubiquitous connections for an increasing number of applications [11].

For the purpose of creating and executing effective spectrum sharing mechanisms in CRNs, an essential building piece is the knowledge regarding primary user (PU) activity, or whether the channels are ON/OFF or busy/idle. When assigning a fixed spectrum, the cognitive base station (CBS) queries an external white space database to obtain complete information about the spectrum occupancy of each PU [12]. However, this approach assumes that the data held in the database is always accurate and has not been compromised, which results in increased communication overhead between the database and the CBS.

1.1.1 Problem Statement

The challenge of ACVs is to balance societal integration with technology growth. Many issues need to be resolved as we move toward a time when automobiles are more interconnected and autonomous, in order to guarantee the safe and widespread use of these AVs.

Ensuring the safety of self-driving vehicles in a range of intricate and dynamic contexts is one of the main concerns. Unpredictable situations such as bad weather, construction zones, and encounters with human-driven vehicles, pedestrians, and cyclists are some of the challenges that ACVs must navigate efficiently. Achieving comprehensive safety assurance systems is essential to fostering confidence in autonomous systems' dependability and averting further mishaps or accidents.

Furthermore, it becomes clear that cybersecurity is an important cog in the wheel of deployment of ACV. Vehicles, nowadays, are more susceptible to cyber threats including malware, hacking, and illegal access, owing to their increased connectivity via wireless networks and communication systems. Preventing hostile assaults that could jeopardize vehicle's functionality, passenger safety, or data privacy requires ensuring the integrity and security of ACV systems.

Moreover, there are ethical, legal, and regulatory issues with integrating ACVs into the present transportation system. It becomes essential to set up thorough frameworks that regulate AV operations, accident responsibility, and moral decision-making in dire circumstances. To encourage public acceptance and governmental support for ACVs, it is crucial to strike a balance between innovation and safety, privacy, and societal issues.

To put the safety and well-being of all road users in priority, developing strong safety mechanisms, bolstering cybersecurity, and navigating ethical and regulatory landscapes are all necessary to address the problem statement of ACVs and to ensure their seamless integration into our transportation systems.

1.1.2 Motivation

ACVs are being developed and advanced due to a combination of innovation-promoting factors, societal demands, and technological advancements.

Improvement of Safety: The principal objective of ACVs is to significantly decrease the amount of traffic-related incidents and fatalities.
Effectiveness and Adaptability: Because of ACVs' potential to decongest traffic flow, lessen gridlock, and optimize route planning, they have the potential to completely transform the transportation industry. ACVs can navigate more effectively, resulting in shorter journey times and lower fuel consumption, thanks to their capacity to coordinate and communicate with infrastructure systems and one another.
Accessibility: For people who are too old or disabled who are unable to drive for some other reason, AVs provide more mobility possibilities. ACVs can provide accessibility and independence for a variety of people, including the elderly and those with disabilities, by offering dependable and safe transportation options.
Environmental Sustainability: ACVs have the potential to lessen transportation's negative environmental effects and cut down on greenhouse gas emissions. ACVs can encourage the use of greener energy sources and aid in the effort against climate change by advancing electric and autonomous technologies.
Economic Opportunities: ACVs' development and adoption offer substantial economic prospects in a number of industries cutting across sectors. This includes the establishment of jobs in the fields of AV research, development, production, and maintenance in addition to the introduction of new business models for mobility services and logistics of transportation.
Urban Planning and Infrastructure: ACVs have the power to alter urban environments and have an impact on infrastructure and future city architecture. ACVs can make cities more livable and sustainable by maximizing traffic flow and lowering the requirement for parking slots.
Technological Innovation: Technological advancement in several domains, such as artificial intelligence, robotics, sensor technology, and communication networks, is propelled by the goal of AVs. These developments not only can encourage progress in other industries and fields but also could have wider ramifications than just transportation industry.

ACVs are driven by their potential to drive technological innovation; shape the future of urban development and transportation; and improve safety, efficiency, accessibility, sustainability, and economic prosperity.

1.2 Related Works

Intra-vehicle networks and vehicular communication cybersecurity issues have recently been addressed by a number of security solutions. The controller area network (CAN) of ACVs can be interfered with by long-range wireless assaults on their current security mechanisms, as demonstrated by the authors in [13]. Additionally, the study applied a hidden Markov model to suggest a data analytics solution for the problem of intrusion detection. The security flaws in the current designs for vehicle communication are identified in [14]. Multi-source filters were proposed as a way to protect a vehicle network from the data injection attacks (DIAs). Furthermore, a novel framework that combines two physical metrics from received wireless signals—the angle of arrival and the Doppler Effect—to increase the beacons' credibility was presented. Moreover, in order to combat spoofing and denial of service threats, the proposed a cooperative control method for vehicular platooning [15]. A deep learning technique regarding sensor authentication of signal was developed. A summary of recent work on sophisticated networks that connect intra-vehicle and the intelligent parts of ITS is provided. An overview of wireless communications and cyber physical system security concerns was outlined. Furthermore, for V2I communications, a secure beam shaping technique is presented for centralized radio access networks [16].

Physical safety of ACVs and their optimal controls have been explored in addition to cybersecurity in ITSs. The developers of determined the vehicles controller's primary weaknesses and used intrusion detection algorithm to patch them. For ACV platoons, both decentralized and centralized safe cruise control strategies were proposed. A learning-based strategy for regulating ACV velocity is put forward. Additionally, a robust deep reinforcement learning algorithm safeguards the ACV system from cyberattacks and minimizes their impact on ACV sensors. The fundamentals of safe and secure code sign for ACV systems were examined [17].

Furthermore, it does not offer any strategies to strengthen ACV motion control's resistance against hostile attacks. However, resistance to attacks on intra-vehicle sensors and intervehicle communication are necessary for developing an ideal and safe intelligent transportation system. Furthermore, although offering their security solutions, these previous studies fail to accurately characterize the area of action of an attacker and his goal that is to disrupt physical the ITS. In this situation, interdependence of the objective of the assaulter and his activities by utilizing the cyber-physical will be possible to improve the security solutions. The extant research is deficient in its basic description of physical attacks, such as the one described in the context of the Jeep hijacking scenario, wherein the assaulter seeks to interfere with the performance of an ITS by inducing non-optimality in the speed of a hijacked ACV [18].

The fact that cognitive radios (CRs) must pay a price in terms of lost throughput when they switch from one frequency channel to another because it takes time for the radio to actuate and settle is another important practical aspect of CBS scheduling. According to studies, the channel switching delay in industrial CRs and conventional CRs can vary from 0.224 ms to 160 ms. As a result, channel switching for CRs causes a non-negligible latency that lowers CRN performance and causes throughput loss. Therefore, the channel switching lag that is present in the CBS scheduling problem must be fixed and looked into how it affects the maximum throughput that can be achieved on the network [19].

A significant portion of the current literature has embraced optimization-based techniques and the limitation factor as costs of channel switching. Nevertheless, the results of the aforementioned methods are either intuitive or prone to specific limits, and the conceptual assurances regarding the effectiveness of the same in the global approaches are not easily accessible [20].

For the recommended scheduling mechanism, each channel is assigned to a CR for the transmission of data at each time slot. There is a cost of switching for every CR in the form of throughput being decreased whenever the CBS decides to employ an alternate set of channels that is completely different to previous time slot. With a time-decaying parameter that is based on Bernoulli stochastic process, we permit the CBS to change the slate in order to manage the costs associated with channel switching. It was demonstrated that, by using efficient channel switching, this approach prevents excessive throughput loss. Ultimately, at the conclusion of every time interval, each CR sends the achieved throughput to the CBS that is used by the CBS to alter its learning parameters.

1.2.1 Contributions

This paper's primary contribution is a thorough analysis of the coupled cyber-physical security issues and their resolutions in the networks of ACV that is expressed as follows:

- An ideal safe controller is initially proposed in order to optimize the flow of traffic and reduce the chance of collisions of vehicles by duly adjusting the rate of movement of distance and distance between the ACVs. This addresses not only the safety but also the optimality of an ACV system. As far as we are aware, this research will be the first to look at an ACV network physical attack and demonstrate demonstrated the recommended control system could maximize ACV systems' stability and defense against physical threats, such the one that occurred in the scenario involving the hijacking of a Jeep.

- The first proposed method for DIA detection determines the ideal threshold value for sensors that already presented with the ACV state. By applying such a threshold, the proposed method is demonstrated to effectively identify DIAs in contrast to baseline situations that merely employ a Kalman filter for the state estimate. This method works especially well in situations where some of the state variables of the ACV are known *a priori*.
- The proposed MAB algorithm optimizes the sensor fusion process of the ACV by employing an algorithm known as upper confidence bound and calculates a regret value based on and referred to as Mahalanobis distance between an *a posteriori* forecast and the sensor data.

Furthermore, it is demonstrated that the proposed methods for DIA identification are able to mitigate the impact of DIAs on the ideal ACV network spacing and velocity. Comparing the proposed optimal safe controller against existing state-of-the-art methods, simulation results demonstrate that it has superior safety, optimality, and robustness against physical attacks. Furthermore, our findings demonstrate that the proposed DIA detection techniques exceed Kalman filtering performances in terms of cyberattacks mitigation. As a result, the proposed modifications strengthen ACV networks' resistance to DIAs.

1.2.2 Centralized CRN Scheduling

In these works, a collection of CBS scheduling heuristic algorithms was obtained by solving a non-linear integer programming issue. Each CR is supposed to be permitted to transmit on various channels. The optimization problem's constraints were relaxed and the channel assignment process was made simpler owing to this assumption. Nevertheless, there is no available theoretical performance guarantee for the scheduler. Current research is unable to provide suitable frameworks that meet the traffic needs of the CRs while accounting for performance loss caused by channel switching latency, despite several advancements in the development of CBS scheduling mechanisms.

Prior studies have looked into CBS scheduling in relation to channel switching costs. As an alternative, our proposal is to utilize an online learning strategy that guarantees the theoretical performance of the proposed algorithms. This method prevents adding unnecessary costs by appropriately constraining the switching of channels and decreasing the inevitable overhead.

For the purpose of generating efficient and successful CBS scheduling algorithms, understanding PU activity (ON/OFF status) is another essential component. Previous research endeavors either presume that the activity of PUs is constant and available in predetermined or utilize established statistical models to simulate the occupancy status of PUs. The conventional two-state Markov chain, also known as the Gilbert-Elliott represent, is commonly used in these works to represent PUs activity. The PUs' state transition probabilities are estimated through the application of maximum likelihood estimation techniques. Generalized Pareto distributions have also been used in the recent work for estimation of the PUs occupancy sequence in both short and long times. The technique adaptively adjusts to the changing behavior of the PU by dynamically estimating the sample sequence's necessary length. Nonetheless, the low forecast accuracy persists in the estimation accuracy as assessed by this method's confidence level.

1.2.3 Multi-Armed Bandit (MAB)

MAB is an online learning game that is one of the most basics. In each of the round, the player (or learner) selects one activity from a list of K options and considers the reward that goes with the selected arm. Every round's reward may be non-stochastic, also known as adversarial, or stochastic. Because the PUs' behaviors are thought to deviate from any statistical distribution, we concentrate on non-stochastic settings in this study. In the MAB problems, the player's objective is to keep empirical regret at a minimum discrepancy between the player's total reward and the highest aggregate reward for every arm in retrospect. If the number of rounds played is a sublinear function of the player's regret, then we say that the player is learning. In the context of researching clinical trials introduced the issue of multi-armed bandits, which was later made more commonly popularized. The subject was initially examined in the pioneering work in a non-stochastic environment. The Exploration and Exploitation algorithm, a well-known Exponential Weights method, is derived from earlier research on the Hedge algorithm and the Weighted Majority algorithm. An explanation of the proposed TSR and OC algorithmic structure is provided in Figure 1.1, especially in the areas where they have trouble making

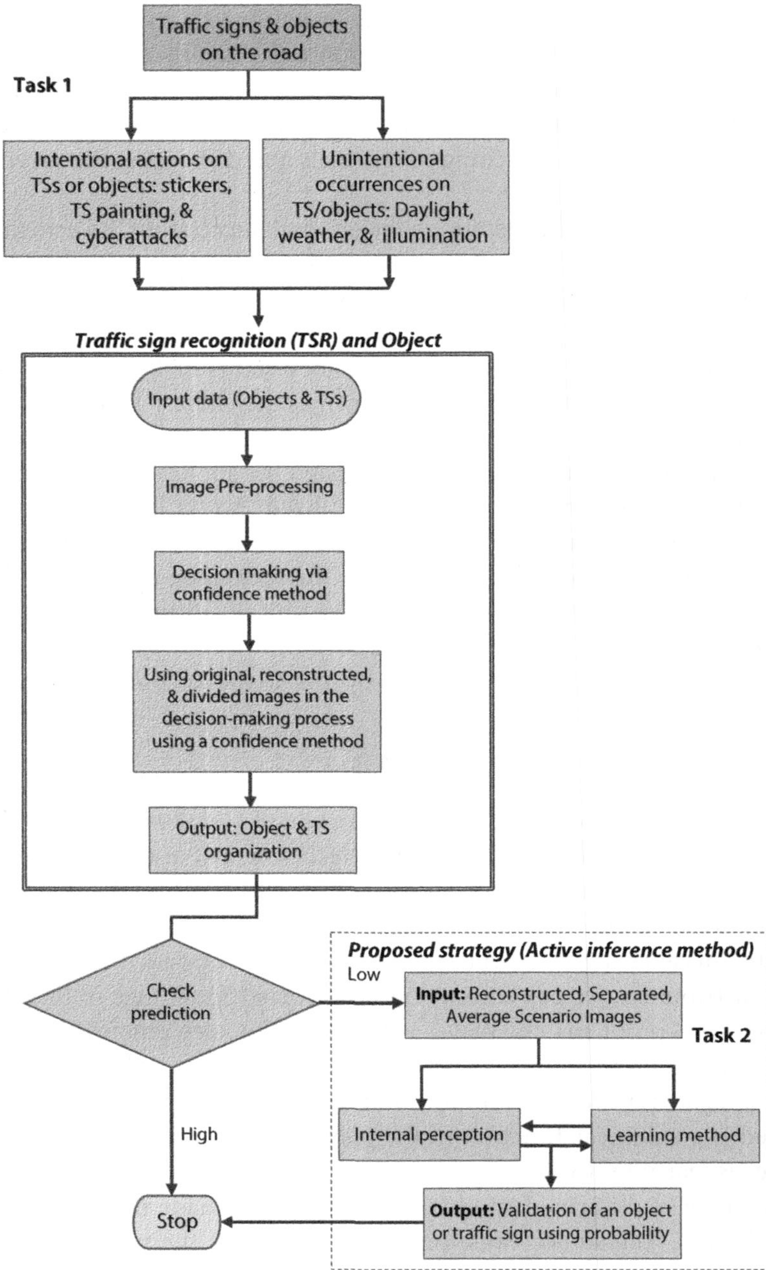

Figure 1.1 A proposed framework considering the ActInf method in abnormal scenarios to enhance the prediction.

precise predictions. By using context awareness of anomalous occurrences, the ActInf model improves prediction accuracy.

1.2.4 Bandit Learning with Switching Costs

This technique has also been used to apply user mobility management in communication systems. In terms of learning as soon as the feedback setting of semi-bandit is combined with the mini-batching method switching

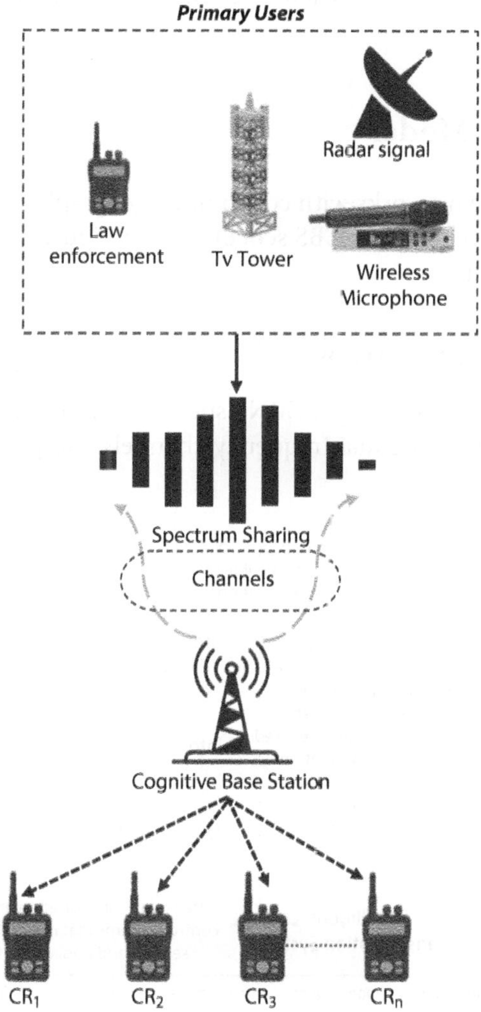

Figure 1.2 Application scenario of cognitive base station (CBS) scheduling for cognitive radios (CRs).

costs of semi-bandit width is produced, its regret yields the same sequence as this piece of work. Such an environment may require analysis, which influences the learning parameters shown in Figure 1.2.

The CBS is required by application-wise mini-batching to choose the identical channels of frequencies for a predetermined amount of time. However, our method delivers secure CRNs in addition to bringing robustness to the systems of communication by adopting randomness in determining whether or not to switch the transmission channels. By utilizing such framework with the setting of semi-bandit may lead to collisions in subsequent arm selections when selecting numerous arms with varying mini-batch sizes.

1.3 System Model

Smaller cognitive networks with constrained geographic coverage are usually the focus of centralized CBS scheduling. In Figure 1.3, the application scenario is shown.

1.3.1 Resource Spectrum

It is assumed such as the target CRN's spectrum resource is divided into K non-overlapping orthogonal frequency channels. Despite the PUs having

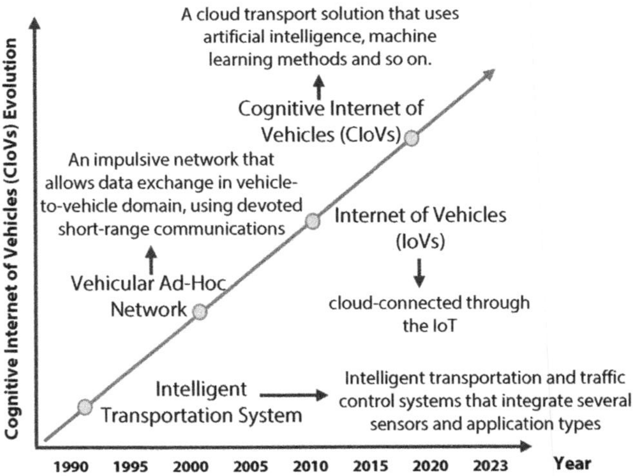

Figure 1.3 Evolution of cognitive internet of vehicles (CIoVs).

a license for the channels, the CBS scheduler is used to share them with unlicensed CRs in order to maximize spectrum use.

1.3.2 CRs' Spectrum Utilization Schemes

The CRs in networks can adopt three distinct strategies to share the spectrum with the PUs. 1) Underlay: On the pre-conditions that till the PU side's interference level is manageable, this method permits simultaneous CR and PU broadcasts. 2) Overlay: In this method, the signal codebooks of PUs provide the CRs access, enabling the CRs to know about spectrum use in advance. 3) Interweave: In this method, as long as the PUs are not in use, the CRs are allowed to detect the frequency channels and use them for data transfer. In this study, we address the interwoven spectrum sharing solution for our CBS scheduling problem. Readers who are interested in learning more about these paradigms should consult.

1.3.3 CBS Scheduling

The CBS chooses a group of channels and allocates a CR to each channel during each time slot. If, at that particular time slot and channel, the PUs' signal is absent (OFF status), then the CRs detect the channel assigned and data is sent across it.

1.3.4 PUs' Activity

CBS scheduler is unaware of the state of PUs activity information, i.e., whether the state is "ON/OFF" or "busy/idle" state, *a priori* or any statistical distribution is followed by it. Stated differently, the occupancy of spectrum of the PUs is thought to be non-stochastic and uncertain. Subsequently, an online learning algorithm is employed by the CBS that is inbuilt in it, which are proposed in this research, to acquire knowledge of the PUs' activities and strategically arrange the transmission channels for the CRs.

It is still not possible to completely eliminate road casualties, despite substantial progress in automation and connection. Ninety percent of traffic accidents are the result of human oversight, according to recent research, with driving faults and driver errors being the main contributing factors. Some typical factors that lead to accidents include driving when fatigued, overspreading, and obstructions in one's line of sight, as shown in Figure 1.4.

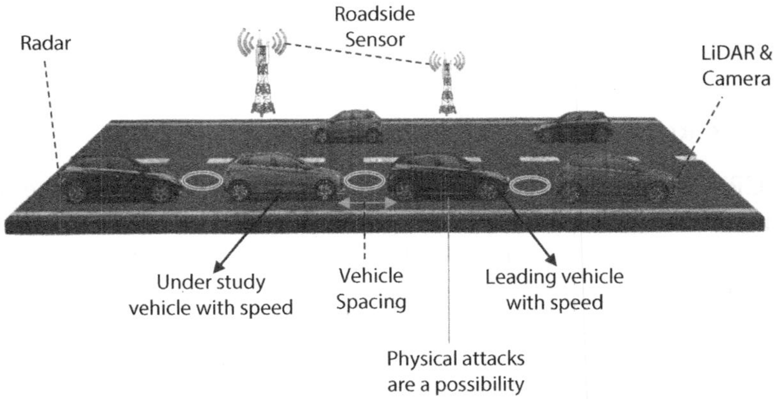

Figure 1.4 Illustration of the considered ACV system model.

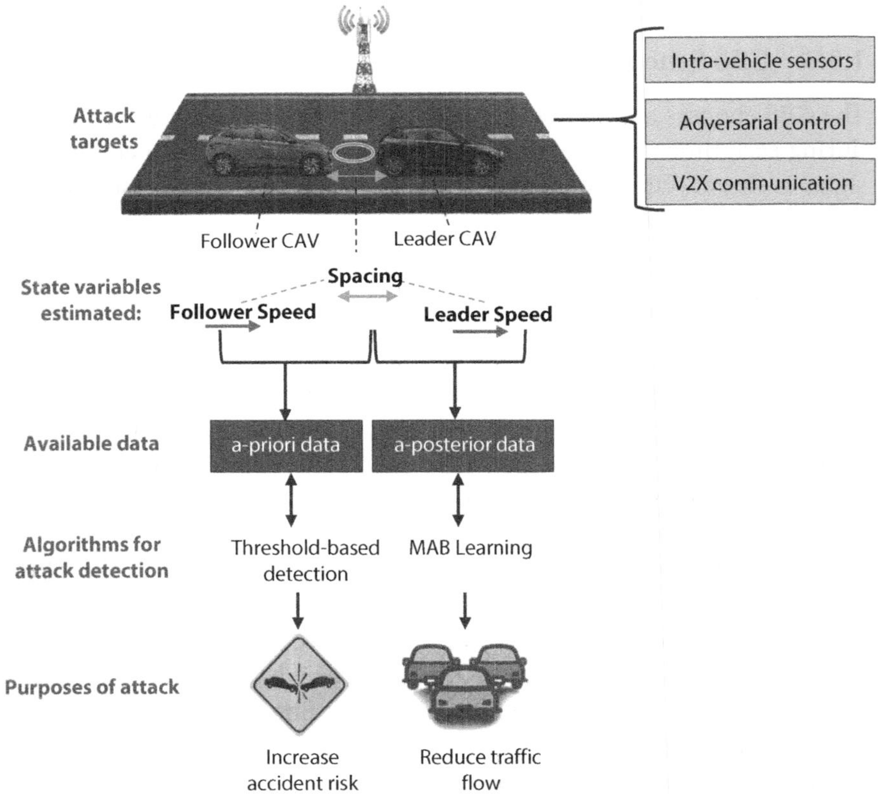

Figure 1.5 Cyber security threats and attack detection in connected autonomous vehicles.

A linear transformation to change the previously mentioned from a continuous to a discrete system paradigm was used because ACVs have discrete temporal sensor readings.

As seen in Figure 1.5, addressing these three issues necessitate an in-depth dissection of the dependencies that exist between the physical and cyber aspects of system of ACV. The identification of ACV systems' vulnerabilities to physical and cyberattacks is aided by such interconnected cyber-physical researches. As a result, we are able to determine the best controller that reduces the possibility of mishaps and create cyber-attack detection strategies that consider the ACVs' system cyber characteristics as well as the possibility of eliminating collisions in ACV present networks to a minimum. In contrast to the research, take into account the ACV systems' physical properties when creating DIA detection methods.

1.4 Outcomes

1.4.1 Scenario I: Fallen Traffic Signs

A fallen TS, namely, the STOP sign, is one of the scenarios that causes trouble for TSR using ML techniques. For an AV (eco vehicle), as exemplified in Figure 1.6, especially the one colored in green, predicting possible roadside situations still remains a difficult task. When using all available current observations, the TSR system is unable to predict events like a toppled TS. As a result, its precision in identifying or predicting the intended TS is impaired. Furthermore, the LiDAR capabilities, radar, and vision of the ego vehicle are depicted in Figure 1.7.

In the event that a sign of this kind has not been experienced during training, traditional models may be unable to identify such missing sign. Nonetheless, the ActInf model can be used as an alternative by including

Figure 1.6 Scenario I.

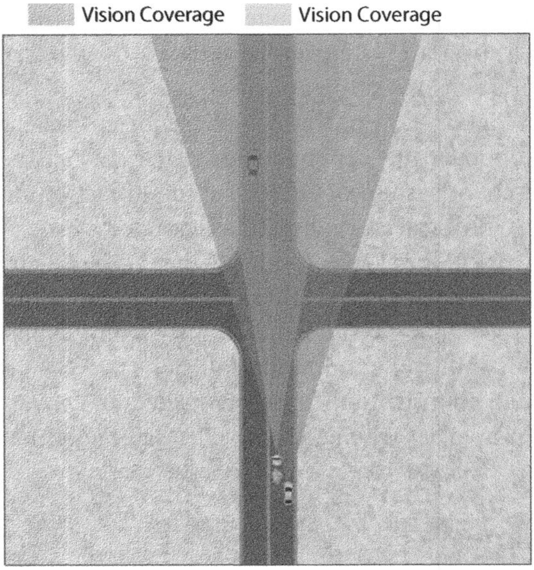

Figure 1.7 LiDAR capabilities of vehicles.

actions of other road users such as partial observations, abrupt stops, or cautious driving close to the crossing, which enables for figuring out of the possibility that STOP sign is exhibited even in situations where it may not be clearly visible. This approach anticipates possible future behaviors in addition to responding to the current surroundings. For instance, it can deduce that stopping is necessary even in the absence of a clearly visible STOP sign if it notices other vehicles reducing the speed at the crossing and people looking either side of the road at a frequent pace. This implies that the ActInf equipped car would deduce the need to stop and drive cautiously in order to ensure safety when it notices unexpected behavior from other cars as well as pedestrians. As a result, it adapts to real-time changes effectively and does not need a lot of retraining for every new scenario.

1.4.2 Scenario II: Traffic Signs Alert by the Road Workers

The illustration below portrays a road crew issuing an emergency alert and asking to follow their directions. There is a roadside speed limit sign (TS) that restricts the speed limit to 65 mph to let traffic to proceed on the route, as seen in Figure 1.8. However, a road crew member displays an alternate TS to indicate fresh directions because there is are barriers present on the way ahead. In an emergency, it is imperative that all drivers

Figure 1.8 Scenario II.

follow the workers' instructions without any deviation; unfortunately, an AV cannot adapt to this kind of forecasted shift. The obligation of drivers is to obey new conditions irrespective of whether barriers are present or absent from the road. For ML algorithms that deal with this problem, this situation can be confounding, and a TSR model is unable to predict the correct TS with a high degree of accuracy. The ego vehicle is fully equipped with sensors to have a full coverage, yet it is unable to determine the right direction. An AV can make utilize the ActInf framework to effectively figure out these situations wherein a roadwork personnel use different TSs to guide traffic. The automobile keeps track of an imaginative model (which is generated by it) of the environment that consists of the likelihood of coming across road repairs and the corresponding signage. When this observation detects a road employee displaying a sign, it refreshes and modifies the assumption state. Taking into account the existing circumstances (for example, continuous construction and restrictions on usage of lanes), the automobile forecasts the TS most likely to be held by the road employee next based on the updated beliefs. As a result, the automobile decides on next course of action (such reducing the speed down or moving from one lane to another), which will reduce the difference that exists in its forecasts and actual happenings. Because it can continually improvement in its predictions based on feedback, this technique easily outperforms typical ML models and enables more adaptable and context-aware decision-making.

1.4.3 Scenario III: Back/Rotated Traffic Sign Across the Road

A TS back or a TS turned to the other side of a junction is explained by this scenario (Figure 1.9). If the same analysis is applied, then this might resemble "fallen TS." To take a good action, the information regarding its

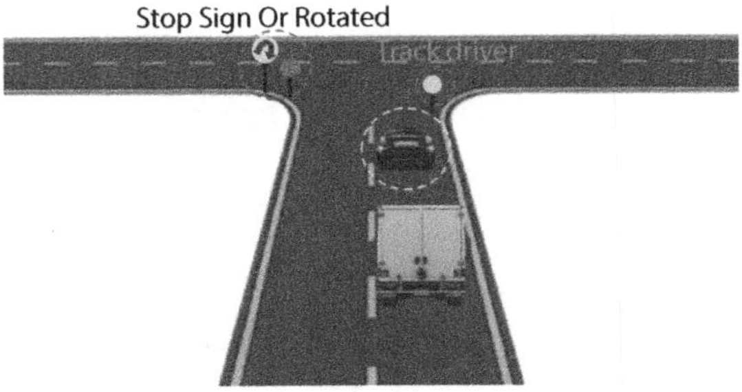

Figure 1.9 Scenario III.

environmental settings has to be acquired by the ego vehicle. However, due to the lack of linguistic or CXI interpretation from the signs, ML algorithms are unable to predict the TSs. Based on the intersection context, the vehicle uses the ActInf model to figure out whether it is a STOP or YIELD sign. It slows down as a result, getting ready for both of the situations. When it draws near, it recognizes the STOP sign and comes to a halt. In some cases, the TSR model can make an accurate prediction based on unique TS shapes, like the STOP sign. Among other things, most of the time, its effectiveness declines because certain numerals have different shapes and some have similarities. Additionally, these unusual cases are not included in the driving scenarios dataset that currently exists, which may result in errors when using traditional ML models.

1.4.4 Scenario IV: Hacking of a Stop Sign at a Four-Way Stop Intersection

An attacker can alter the STOP sign by encroaching it, rendering the ego vehicle incapable of identifying the proper sign. A variety of deceptive signals (TSs) can be employed by the attacker to get the AV to change directions from the optimal path into other cars and wreck them on the road. When it comes to road junctions, there is a chance that every single car could get into an accident. Because it is not integrated with the surrounding entities' environmental dynamics, the TSR algorithm ability is clearly limited in its capacity to forecast signs. Nevertheless, employing an ActInf model—which integrates incomplete observational data—provides a stronger defense against cyberattacks. Its improved prediction ability originates from its capacity to integrate data observed from nearby cars, their individual driving patterns in the same lane, and the surroundings of a four-way crossroads. Therefore, even if the data presented contradicts

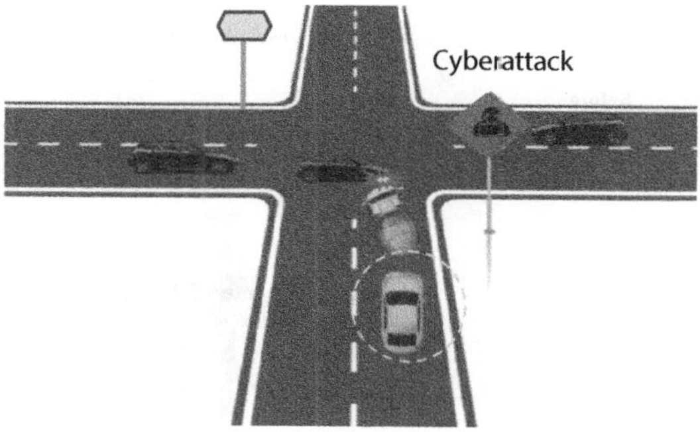

Figure 1.10 Scenario IV.

this forecast, based on model generated by it, the vehicle expects to see a STOP sign. The car decides to stop after cross-referencing its prediction with additional sensor data rather than depending just on the changed visual signal, perhaps preventing an accident. The car then modifies its internal model to take sign manipulation into consideration, strengthening its defenses against future attempts of this nature shown in Figure 1.10.

The confidence level bar in Figure 1.11 displays the highest and lowest likelihood of a forecast made utilizing a correct value. This picture has three numbers of tables that display mapping of matrices between observations and dormant states. Each table shows observations and concealed states as rows and columns, respectively. It is noteworthy that multiple concealed conditions and observations might be identified, and these charts are merely sample matrices for assessing the probability values at different phases. The first step describes a situation where an AV has just crossed into a street and is unaware of its surroundings.

1.5 Conclusions and Future Enhancement

1.5.1 Conclusions

In a nutshell up, the creation and application of ACVs have great potential to transform transportation infrastructure all over the world. With improvements in infrastructure, safety, and technology, ACVs provide revolutionary advantages in a number of domains. To fully utilize ACVs and minimize related challenges, a few important factors must be taken into account. Safety is still the top priority, to start. Sturdy safety assurance systems need to be put in place to guarantee ACVs will operate dependably

Before exploring the environment

	Local Area	Highway	Campus	Intersecting Road
30	40	40	40	40
60	40	40	40	40
Incoherent 1	40	40	40	40
Incoherent 2	40	40	40	40

After the partial scan

	Local Area	Highway	Campus	Intersecting Road
30	90	40	80	60
60	40	90	20	30
Incoherent 1	40	40	40	40
Incoherent 2	40	20	40	40

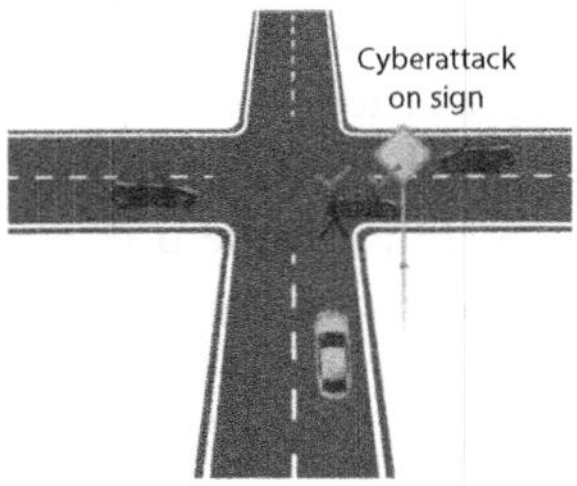

After the Comprehensive scan

	Local Area	Highway	Campus	Intersecting Road
30	100	0	100	100
60	0	100	0	0
Incoherent 1	0	0	0	0
Incoherent 2	0	0	0	0

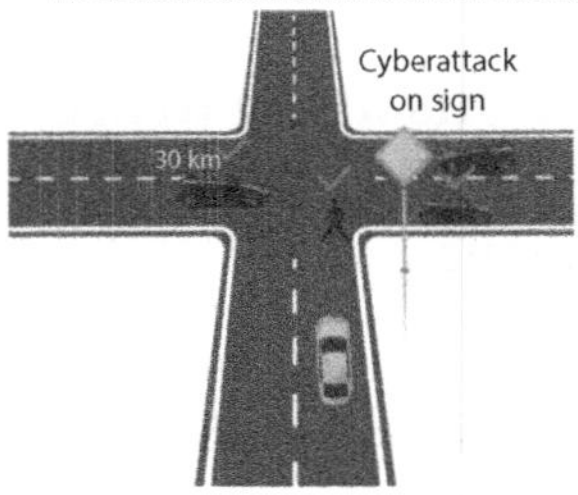

Figure 1.11 ACVs' sample learning process.

in a variety of dynamic situations. To reduce risks and avoid accidents, this entails thorough testing, validation, and continued improvement of autonomous systems.

Cybersecurity is a serious issue as well, which follows suit. Because ACVs are susceptible to cyberattacks, strong cybersecurity measures are required to protect against malware, hacking, and illegal access. To safeguard passenger safety, data privacy, and the integrity of ACV systems, stronger cybersecurity measures and secure communication networks are necessary. Moreover, regulatory frameworks need to be evolved to meet the distinct challenges that ACVs provide. To control AV operations, liability in the event of an accident, and moral decision-making in critical situations, precise rules and regulations are required. Policymakers, industry stakeholders, and researchers must work together to create comprehensive regulatory frameworks that strikes a balance between the safety and societal concerns we well as balancing innovation.

Furthermore, the general acceptability and credibility of ACVs are very crucial for their mass adoption. To address concerns about autonomy, privacy, and ethical consequences, it is imperative to engage stakeholders and maintain transparency and education. Gaining the confidence of the public necessitates proving the dependability, safety, and social advantages of ACVs via transparent discussions and on road application. To enable the integration of ACVs into current transportation networks, investments in infrastructure and urban planning are also required. This entails creating intelligent infrastructure to facilitate the smooth operation of ACVs and enhance traffic flow, including as designated lanes, more stations for charging, and robust communication networks.

In conclusion, even though the development of ACVs has advanced significantly, more work, creativity, and funding are required to get over lingering obstacles and fully utilize the promise of autonomous and networked mobility. Adopting autonomous cars (ACVs) has the potential to transform transportation, improve mobility, and build more sustainable and habitable cities for future generations by tackling safety, cybersecurity, political, and social issues.

1.5.2 Future Directions

When we look ahead, a number of exciting new avenues for the development and incorporation of ACVs into our transportation networks become apparent:

Enhanced Autonomous Capabilities: Ongoing research and development will concentrate on creating ACVs more intelligent and autonomous.

This includes innovations in sensor technology, artificial intelligence, and ML that makes it possible for ACVs to navigate complicated surroundings more reliably and effectively.

Interoperability and Standardization: In order to facilitate smooth communication and coordination between various ACVs and infrastructure systems, future initiatives will put a priority on developing interoperability standards and protocols. The scalability, compatibility, and interoperability of ACV technology among various manufacturers and legal systems will be facilitated by standardization efforts.

Mobility as a Service (MaaS): MaaS will become more popular, and ACVs will be essential in delivering shared, on-demand mobility solutions. Users will have access to more practical and efficient transportation options while lowering traffic and environmental impact through integration with ride-sharing services, public transportation, and other mobility services.

Urban Air Mobility (UAM): The growth of ACVs beyond the transportation at ground level is to include urban air mobility through aerial vehicles. In order to facilitate the broad deployment of autonomous flying vehicles for the transportation of people and goods in urban contexts, future directions in UAM will concentrate on addressing regulatory, infrastructure, and safety requirements.

Sustainability and Electrification: ACVs and sustainability initiatives will be closely related in the future, with an increasing focus on electrification and zero-emission technologies. Developments in battery technology, improvement in infrastructure for charging, and integration of renewable energy sources will hasten the shift to more environmentally friendly and sustainable modes of transportation.

Human–Machine Interaction: Innovative methods of human–machine interaction in ACVs, like as augmented reality interfaces, gesture detection, and natural language processing, will be the subject of future research. Widespread deployment of ACVs will depend on improving the user experience and guaranteeing the comfort and confidence of passengers.

Ethical and Legal Frameworks: Future efforts will concentrate on creating moral guidelines and legal rules to handle intricate liability and moral dilemmas as ACVs get more independent. Deliberations around moral judgment, responsibility, and assigning responsibility will influence the creation and application of ACVs in practical situations.

Rural and Remote Applications: Although a lot of attention has been paid to urban settings, future research will also examine how ACVs might be used in remote and rural locations. To fully realize the benefits of autonomous transportation in these areas, specific difficulties including poor infrastructure, severe weather, and greater distances will need to be addressed.

To summarize, in order to fully achieve the promise of autonomous and connected mobility in influencing the future of transportation, future directions in the development and integration of ACVs will require more breakthroughs in technology, adopting acceptable regulation, creating infrastructure, and public acceptance. ACVs have the power to completely transform the way we move people and things by tackling new problems and embracing creative possibilities. This will result in more accessible, effective, and sustainable transportation networks for the coming generations.

References

1. Ahmad, J., Zia, M.U., Naqvi, I.H., Chattha, J.N., Butt, F.A., Huang, T., Xiang, W., Machine learning and blockchain technologies for cybersecurity in connected vehicles. *Wiley Interdiscip. Rev.: Data Min. Knowl. Discov.*, *14*, 1, e1515, 2024.
2. Chougule, S.B., Chaudhari, B.S., Ghorpade, S.N., Zennaro, M., Exploring Computing Paradigms for Electric Vehicles: From Cloud to Edge Intelligence, Challenges and Future Directions. *World Electr. Veh. J.*, *15*, 2, 39, 2024.
3. Latchoumi, T.P., Parthiban, L., Balamurugan, K., Raja, K., Vijayaraj, J., Parthiban, R., A Framework for Low Energy Application Devices Using Blockchain-Enabled IoT in WSNs, in: *Integrating Blockchain and Artificial Intelligence for Industry 4.0 Innovations*, pp. 121–132, Springer International Publishing, Cham, 2023.
4. Tuncal, A. and Ufuk, E.R.O.L., Integrating Unmanned Aerial Vehicles in Airspace: A Systematic Review. *J. Aviat. Res.*, 6, 1, 89–115, 2024.
5. Sun, H., Poskitt, C.M., Sun, Y., Sun, J., Chen, Y., ACAV: A Framework for Automatic Causality Analysis in Autonomous Vehicle Accident Recordings, 2024, arXiv preprint arXiv:2401.07063.
6. Chen, X., Deng, Y., Ding, H., Qu, G., Zhang, H., Li, P., Fang, Y., Vehicle as a service (VaaS): Leverage vehicles to build service networks and capabilities for smart cities. *IEEE Commun. Surv. Tutorials.*, 26, 2048–2081, 2024.
7. Balamurugan, K., Latchoumi, T.P., Satla, S., Machining Studies on AlSi7+ 63% SiC Composite Using Machine Learning Technique, in: *Metal Matrix Composites*, pp. 139–166, CRC Press, Boca Raton, Florida, USA, 2023.
8. Parthiban, L., Latchoumi, T.P., Balamurugan, K., Raja, K., Parthiban, R., Cognitive Computing for the Internet of Medical Things, in: *Integrating Blockchain and Artificial Intelligence for Industry 4.0 Innovations*, pp. 85–100, Springer International Publishing, Cham, 2023.

9. Liu, S., Li, Y., Guan, P., Li, T., Yu, J., Taherkordi, A., Jensen, C.S., FedAGL: A Communication-Efficient Federated Vehicular Network. *IEEE Trans. Intell. Veh.*, 9, 3704–3720, 2024.
10. Huang, C.J., Cheng, H.W., Lien, Y.H., Jian, M.E., A Survey on Video Streaming for Next-Generation Vehicular Networks. *Electronics*, *13*, 3, 649, 2024.
11. Gao, J., Xu, X., Qi, L., Dou, W., Xia, X., Zhou, X., Distributed Computation Offloading and Power Control for UAV-Enabled Internet of Medical Things. *ACM Trans. Internet Technol.*, 3, 1–22, 2024.
12. Wu, J., Jin, J., Wu, C., Challenges and Countermeasures of Federated Learning Data Poisoning Attack Situation Prediction. *Mathematics*, *12*, 6, 901, 2024.
13. Retzlaff, C.O., Das, S., Wayllace, C., Mousavi, P., Afshari, M., Yang, T., Holzinger, A., Human-in-the-Loop Reinforcement Learning: A Survey and Position on Requirements, Challenges, and Opportunities. *J. Artif. Intell. Res.*, *79*, 359–415, 2024.
14. Antil, H., Mathematical Opportunities in Digital Twins (MATH-DT), 2024, arXiv preprint arXiv:2402.10326.
15. Evgenidis, N.G., Mitsiou, N.A., Koutsioumpa, V., II, Tegos, S.A., Diamantoulakis, P.D., Karagiannidis, G.K., Multiple Access in the Era of Distributed Computing and Edge Intelligence, 2024, arXiv preprint arXiv:2403.07903.
16. Anca, M. and Anca, M., Learning Long Chain of Actions through Hierarchical Reinforcement Learning. *Distances*, *1*, 1, 2024.
17. Wang, F., Liu, Y., Liu, K., Wang, Y., Medya, S., Yu, P.S., Uncertainty in Graph Neural Networks: A Survey, 2024, arXiv preprint arXiv:2403.07185.
18. Kedys, J., Tchappi, I., Najjar, A., UAVs for Disaster Management-An Exploratory Review. *Procedia Comput. Sci.*, *231*, 129–136, 2024.
19. Nkenyereye, L., Nkenyereye, L., Ndibanje, B., Internet of Underwater Things: A Survey on Simulation Tools and 5G-Based Underwater Networks. *Electronics*, *13*, 3, 474, 2024.
20. Kedziora, D.J., Musial, K., Gabrys, B., AutonoML: Towards an Integrated Framework for Autonomous Machine Learning. *Found. Trends® Mach. Learn.*, *17*, 4, 590–766, 2024.

2

Secure Data Handling in AI and Proactive Response Network: Create a Physical Layer–Proposed Cognitive Cyber-Physical Security

A. Sivasundari[1*], P. Kumar[2], S. Vinodhkumar[2] and N. Duraimurugan[2]

[1]*Department of Computer Science and Engineering, Misrimal Navajee Munoth Jain Engineering College, Chennai, India*
[2]*Department of Computer Science and Engineering, Rajalakshmi Engineering College, Chennai, India*

Abstract

Cognitive cyber-physical systems (CCPSs) are closed-loop, combined structures that involve both cyber and physical components, each endowed with cognitive features. A crucial problem that must be dealt with in tandem with the quality-of-service (QoS) limitations and related transmission costs is how to safeguard these extremely powerful CCPS. The way to protect these very strong CCPS is an important issue that needs to be addressed in addition to the QoS constraints and associated transmission costs. This chapter introduces a novel approach to secure data handling in artificial intelligence (AI) systems and proactive response networks through the creation of a physical layer–proposed CCPS framework. With the increasing reliance on AI technologies and proactive response networks for various applications, ensuring the security of data transmission and processing has become critical. The proposed framework integrates cognitive capabilities at the physical layer of cyber-physical systems, enabling proactive and adaptive security measures. By leveraging cognitive computing techniques, such as machine learning and pattern recognition, the framework enhances the detection and mitigation of security threats in real-time. This chapter discusses the conceptualization and design of the proposed CCPS framework, highlighting its potential to address

**Corresponding author*: siva.saibabu123@gmail.com

K. Ananthajothi, S. N. Sangeethaa, D. Divya, S. Balamurugan and Shen-Lung Peng (eds.) Securing Cyber-Physical Systems: Fundamentals, Applications and Challenges, (25–44) © 2025 Scrivener Publishing LLC

security challenges in AI systems and proactive response networks effectively. Additionally, the chapter explores the implementation and deployment considerations of the framework, offering insights into its practical application for secure data handling in diverse environments.

Keywords: Cognitive cyber-physical security, secure data handling, artificial intelligence, proactive response network, physical layer defenses, cyber-physical attack

2.1 Introduction

Cyber-physical systems (CPSs) comprise both cyber and physical components. Together, these components form an integrated real-time control system [1], with every one of them are connected by shared communication protocols over communication links like networked computers and the World Wide Web. Cognitive CPSs (CCPSs) have undergone exponential growth [2] that has outpaced advancements in cybersecurity, giving rise to innovative models of threat and safety concerns. Nevertheless, no cohesive framework exists to guarantee safe architecture, virus resistance, and efficient risk reduction. At present, academic and industrial priority is mainly concentrated on consumer-grade Internet of Things (IoT) [3].

Furthermore, security features in industrial control systems (ICS) are thought of either low-priority or an afterthought. This is due to the obsolete and inaccurate perception that the environment of an ICS is still separated from an authorized and air-gapped network [4]. Due to greater access to potentially dangerous networks, there has been a sharp increase in malicious breaches into CCPS, which has resulted in substantial monetary losses and put public safety at risk.

In the past, achieving maximum predictability as well as dependability was the primary objective of ICS design. Therefore, basic cybersecurity procedures like using complex login credentials or imposing strict authenticating specifications were seen as impediments to system accessibility. As a result, those concerned with developers and administrators purposefully averted in taking such actions [5]. In a similar vein, conventional malware prevention programs such as signature-based antivirus solutions were kept out in order to reduce the possibility that false positives may unintentionally quarantine or disable important system functions. The absence of a strict peer review procedure was the reason for this kind of approach [6]. Furthermore, most system vendors had no proper means of providing upgrades or fixes for bugs, so vulnerabilities that were found later on would remain unfixed for the duration of the system. In such instances, network isolation was the only line of defense against attacks and protection. The traditional design tenets were no longer viable as legacy ICS gave way to contemporary CCPS environments. The demands for standard protocols for communication used on the public internet made the historical design considerations impracticable, leading to the broad adoption of wireless networks and the rapid departure from the isolated air-gapped network settings [7].

2.1.1 The Role of AI in Cybersecurity

Artificial intelligence (AI) is the study of using technology, especially computer systems, to simulate human cognitive functions. The processes stated above comprise learning, which is the process of acquiring knowledge and using a set of rules to apply the knowledge so acquired; reasoning, which is the process of applying rules to arrive at conclusions that can be either binding or somewhat approximate; and self-correction. AI has the potential to significantly alter the cybersecurity landscape by offering advanced and automated techniques for detecting, reducing, and managing cyber threats [8]. In the realm of cybersecurity, the use of AI is essential because it simplifies the complex processes involved in locating and addressing cyberattacks and breaches. The key to the whole issue is AI's ability to learn and adapt. Through the scrutiny of large datasets and the knowledge gained from these datasets, AI may identify dangers or malicious activity that cannot be easily identified by humans or take a long time to identify [9].

2.1.2 Usage of CCPS in IoT

CCPS and IoT applications are being used more and more for eHealth and welfare. More recently, CCPS-IoTs have been created that can emulate human cognitive behavior by learning, reasoning, and comprehending the social and physical environments on their own. This type of CCPS-IoT is known as a CCPS-IoT. "The most intelligent applications of the IoT in knowledge-intensive environments will be those that allow human thought processes to become central to the process" [10]. But all of this presents additional challenges: (i) unanticipated spontaneous actions may result from CCPS-IoTs' rising cognitive complexity; (ii) conventional CCPS-IoT risks and flaws novel threats pertaining to its innate cognitive functions will adversely affect CCPS-IoT; (iii) "hacking is possible on 70% of the most popular IoT devices; 80% of these gadgets sparked privacy concerns about the acquisition of private information, such as health-related data"; and (iv) the widespread use of CCPS-IoT will result in a greatly increased attack surface, raising the dangers to public safety for critical infrastructure due to the interfaces that it uses and enhanced adaptability of service and information access [11]. Despite the fact that clinical results are being improved and care delivery is being transformed, which ultimately improves human life, worries regarding the security of health-related data and infrastructure are growing [12]. A new breed of cybersecurity vulnerabilities has emerged due to networking of healthcare gadgets and services. The healthcare industry is the one most exposed to serious security threats [13].

As stated previously, the vulnerability of the CCPS-IoT–empowered healthcare facilities and services to various novel cyber-attacks further aggravates the situation. Eliminating cybersecurity assaults is essential because they have the potential to result in dangers to human life, bodily harm, financial loss, and privacy violations for users. Millions of medical records have been stolen worldwide, according to reports, which also highlight the development in attacks and medical identity theft [14]. AI and cognitive architecture can improve automated intelligent cybersecurity systems for making decisions to expert-level proficiency.

2.2 Challenges and Mechanisms

The following part provides a quick overview of a few of the complex obstacles to developing a cognitive cybersecurity solution, before offering an explanation of creative solutions to these obstacles.

2.2.1 Brief Account of Challenges Faced

The CCPS-IoT uses a cognitive cycle security model, which is defined by the processes of detecting (pay attention to and orienting), planning (plan), execution (decide and act), and acquisition of knowledge (learn). It also includes detection methods and security adaptability. Generally speaking, the goal for any such architecture is to accurately represent the mechanisms underlying human cognition, encompassing the ones that underpin understanding, decision-making processes, control, acquiring knowledge, adaptivity, and actions, at the computer level. Specifically, the issue lies in designing a structural framework that can adjust to the capabilities and restrictions of various CCPS-IoTs while also accounting for the potential dynamic nature of these attributes.

Complex Temporal Feedback Loops: In order to maintain cognitive regulation, some activities need a highly tight feedback loop because they happen at extremely rapid rates. In a slow feedback loop, other actions happen over longer timescales; therefore, cognitive control algorithms may be required to include a larger set of variables. Because of the wide range of temporal loops and associated sharp speed changes, establishing the source and effect of an action can be quite difficult [15].

Complex Interactions: The difficulty lies in capturing and modeling a great number of these interactions more accurately than humans could possibly analyze.

Heterogeneous Intercommunications: Because diverse configurations are a major factor in the remarkable advances in network performance, finding a solution to this is imperative.

Innovative and Intelligent Security Mechanisms: The core issue is in creating privacy and security methods for CCPS-IoT and its crucial elements that are both lightweight and efficient while also including cognitive and distributed analytical and ability to make decisions. It can be difficult to include trust-based cognitive security, which enables a more thorough analysis of attacker behavior and mindset by identifying the attackers' goals. It should be noted that determining the attackers' level of determination and associating their history to the CCPS-IoT system's activities is an uphill climb. Analyzing the behavior of an attacker necessitates the capacity to make assumptions about the motives, attitudes, and behaviors of others [16].

Dynamic Risks and Metrics: Attackers with an adaptive mindset will modify their plans in response to changing security conditions and newly implemented defenses. It is therefore difficult to make the measures themselves adaptable. Furthermore, assessing the quality of systems becomes increasingly difficult as they get more complicated and diverse [17].

Integration of Privacy: The difficulty lies in incorporating the idea of privacy design patterns for adaptation signaling and control into the cognitive model by analyzing the atomic transactions involving personal data that are required for adaptation.

Dynamic Forensics: As the amount of dynamic evidence gathered for every instance grows dramatically, new techniques and tools based on cutting edge technologies such as big data, cloud services, AI/deep learning, CCPS-IoT, and big data are necessary. The difficulty lies in combining these techniques and resources to accurately and efficiently record and track the changing dynamics of the data. Evidence dynamics describes any impact, regardless of purpose, that modifies, moves, hides, or destroys tangible evidence [18].

2.2.2 Innovative Mechanisms

For CCPS-IoT and its vital elements to have privacy and security that is both lightweight and effective, as well as to be able to perform distributed and cognitive decision-making and analysis, cognitive cybersecurity requires smart and creative methods. In order to analyze the behavior of an attacker, the mechanisms must be able to make hypotheses about the intents, character traits, and behaviors of others. These objectives can be achieved by combining game theoretic modeling and analysis, control theory, and AI/deep learning.

The most crucial characteristics of cybersecurity systems for analytics are outline [19] and can be applied to assess the dependability of the systems' operations. The subsequent portion explains how these techniques are implemented with the use of cognitive approaches and AI.

2.3 Using AI to Support Cognitive Cybersecurity

2.3.1 Cognitive Systems

Human cognition includes the real-time understanding of numerous factors, such as circumstances, surroundings, and intention, which influence an individual's problem-solving skills. Thus, the goal of cognitive cybersecurity is to intelligently evoke and reproduce human thought processes and behaviors in order to predict and react to novel and developing risks of security. In order to do this, cognitive cybersecurity uses AI tools that are based on human thought processes in order to identify risks and safeguard cyber networks. These technologies are used by self-learning security systems to perform automated resolutions to issues sans the need for human intervention. These kinds of attacks, often known as cognitive hacking, aim to modify people's behavior to suit the attacker's objectives. In this field, cognitive security efforts encompass both technical solutions that are intended to identify and stop the spread of misleading information and deceptive information as well as non-technical methods that make people less susceptible to manipulation.

2.3.2 AI in IoT

These methods are suitable and are efficient ways to address the various features of communication networks. The following qualities pertain to CCPS-IoT–enabled applications and infrastructures:

- Dynamic: AI methods for uncertain planning make decisions that remain relevant while the domain continues to change.
- Partially Observable: AI systems are proficient in figuring out missing data and extrapolating a scenario to make sense of the circumstances at hand.
- Ambiguous Observations: AI methods are adept at identifying vagueness or low confidence, and they can either acquire additional data to enable discrimination or provide decisions that are suitable for both circumstances.
- Resource Constrained: AI approaches are good at establishing tasks that efficiently manage available resources and scaling solutions according to the platform on which they operate.
- Diverse: Diversity is viewed advantageously by AI approaches because it makes it possible to handle resources in many ways.
- Massive Scale: Incremental planning and learning strategies, along with data mining and machine learning (ML) techniques, have been successful when applied to large datasets.
- Complex Access Policies: Policies can be represented as constraints using knowledge engineering approaches, and constraint reasoning techniques can then be used to swiftly and effectively develop satisfactory alternatives that embrace new information.

2.4 Create a Physical Layer–Proposed CCPS

Creating a physical layer for proposed CCPS involves integrating tangible defenses with cognitive capabilities to fortify data handling and response networks. Protection from cyber-physical dangers is mostly dependent on physical safety regulations, including video surveillance, computer components that are reliable, and access controls. These physical defenses act as the first line of defense, complementing software-based security mechanisms to provide a comprehensive security posture.

The physical layer of CCPS encompasses various elements, including secure data centers, hardened infrastructure, and robust authentication mechanisms. Secure data centers serve as the backbone of AI systems, housing vast amounts of sensitive information and computational resources. Implementing stringent access controls, biometric authentication, and surveillance systems within data centers can mitigate the risk of unauthorized access and physical tampering.

Hardened infrastructure refers to the physical components of AI systems, such as servers, networking equipment, and storage devices, which are fortified against physical attacks and environmental hazards. Techniques such as tamper-evident seals, secure enclosures, and redundant power supplies can enhance the resilience of infrastructure components, ensuring uninterrupted operation and data integrity.

In addition, hardware-driven techniques for encryption along with safe protocols for communications are included in physical layer countermeasures to safeguard data both in motion as well as at ease. Firms can reduce the danger of eavesdropping of information and manipulation by unknown parties by constructing encrypted communication routes and data encryption at the hardware level.

Besides safety precautions, proactive surveillance and reaction skills are included into the physical layer of CCPS to promptly identify and address safety issues. Surveillance systems, intrusion detection sensors, and physical access logs enable organizations to monitor the physical environment for suspicious activities and unauthorized access attempts.

Furthermore, quick events reaction and restoration in the case of a breach of security are made possible by the physical component of CCPS. Business entities might reduce the effect of privacy violations, quickly resume regular operations, and organize prompt reactions to threats via combining AI-driven analytics and automation with physical safety measures.

Collaboration between physical security teams and AI specialists is essential to design and implement an effective physical layer for CCPS. Physical security experts bring expertise in access control, surveillance, and environmental security, whereas AI specialists contribute insights into cognitive computing, anomaly detection, and predictive analytics.

Furthermore, organizations must consider regulatory compliance and privacy requirements when designing the physical layer of CCPS. Compliance with industry standards such as ISO 27001, NIST SP 800-53, and GDPR ensures that physical security measures align with legal and regulatory mandates, thereby reducing the risk of non-compliance penalties and reputational damage.

Continuous evaluation and improvement are integral to maintaining the effectiveness of the physical layer of CCPS. Vulnerabilities in physical safety mechanisms can be effectively addressed by conducting periodic defense examinations, testing for penetration, and scans for vulnerabilities.

In conclusion, the physical layer of CCPS plays a vital role in fortifying data handling and response networks against cyber-physical threats. By integrating physical security measures with cognitive capabilities, organizations can create a robust defense mechanism that safeguards against unauthorized access, tampering, and environmental hazards. Collaboration between physical security teams and AI specialists, regulatory compliance, and continuous improvement are essential for designing and maintaining an effective physical layer for CCPS.

2.4.1 Create a Physical Layer–Proposed CCPS in Healthcare Application

Adaptive collection of data and actuation layer, healthcare stakeholders' infrastructure layer, perception and knowledge layer, and healthcare stakeholders' collaboration layer are the four layers that make up the complete structure of intellectual digital security for CCPS-IoT–supported medical care ecological systems, as shown in Figure 2.1. The creation of an incorporated intellectual structure for thwarting evolving and adapting assaults on the CCPS-IoT–based medicare ecosystems is the aim of this suggested strategy. Consequently, this adds to the worldwide cybersecurity privacy problem. The application of findings from the domains of formal techniques, digital security, reliability, forensic science, AI, and arithmetic along with cognitive computing, maximizing efficiency, and mathematics will need a multidisciplinary plan to achieve this target.

2.4.1.1 Privacy-Aware Collaboration

A fresh viewpoint on progressive and proof-based information risk control is needed in order to assist stakeholders in collaboratively refining hazards and defining mitigation solutions in a privacy-conscious technique. In order to emphasize the profound ambiguities that define complicated medical care ecological systems it is important to consider information and unpredictability in addition to chances. With the use of routine coverage, exchange of data, situational awareness, and visualization, it ought to provide instruments for promoting stakeholder engagement while protecting privacy. Exchange of information is the primary driver of seamless integration, engagement, and collaboration in the healthcare industry. This means that there are new issues and demands to deal with in terms of technological fields, rewards, safety and confidentiality, and administration. An additional viable resolution could be a strategy that is decentralized

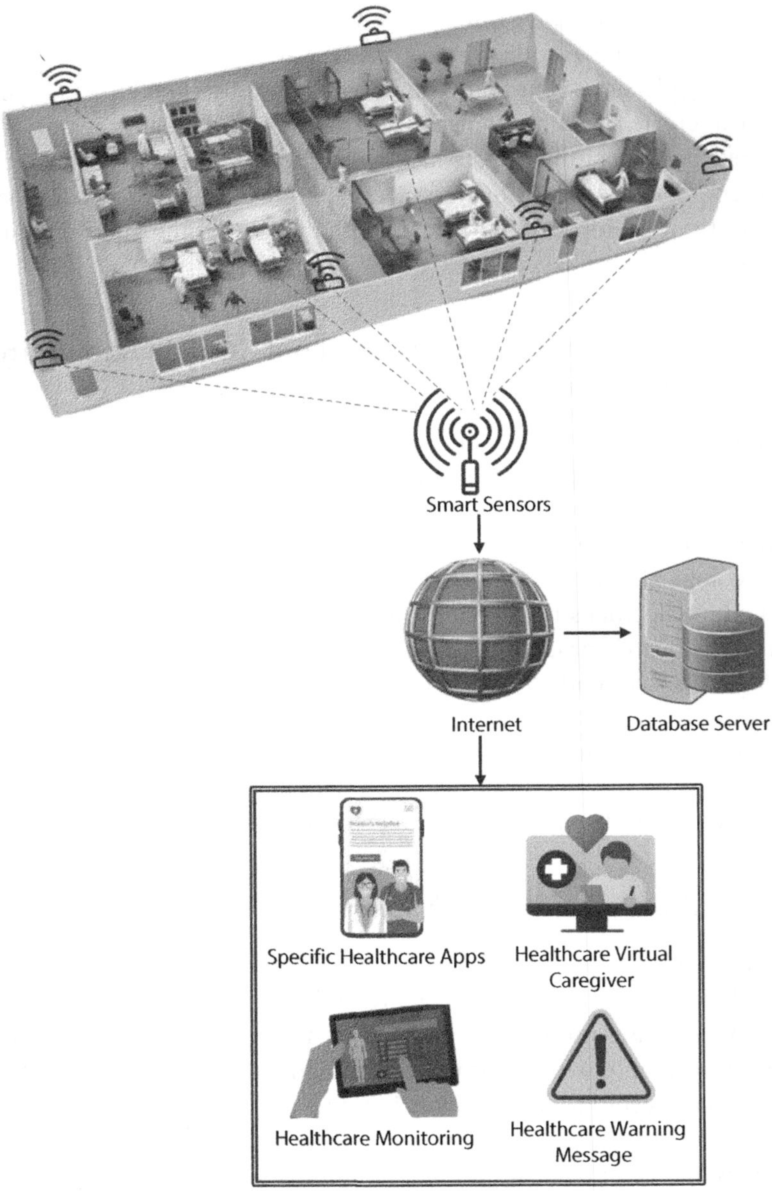

Figure 2.1 Complete structure of intellectual digital security for CCPS-IoT–supported medical care ecological systems.

utilizing blockchain technology to enable this via five processes: identity of patients, information inviolability, gathering of data, liquidity of information, and online accessibility regulations.

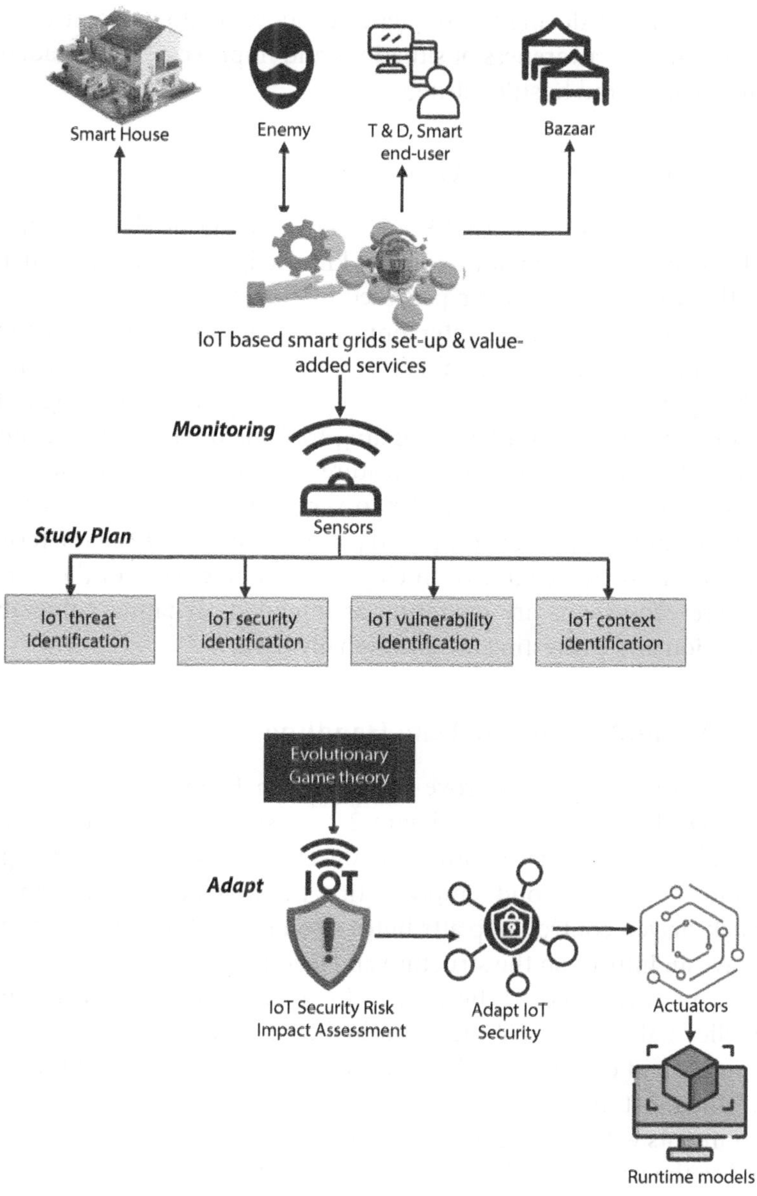

Figure 2.2 Security provide using IoT.

2.4.1.2 Cycle Model of CCPS

The ultimate goal of this framework is to conclude the cognitive cycle by utilizing AI, regulators, negotiations, and creative procedures to proactively perceive CCPS-IoT situations, human conduct, and social settings. It then takes effect and learns from what was done. Comments can be provided at any point during the sequence or loop. By doing so, it becomes easier to establish awareness of situations and improve defensive adaption to shifting goals and hostile settings.

2.4.1.3 Dynamic Security Knowledge Base

A variety of data from its CCPS-IoT scenarios will be dynamically collected and stored in a dynamic security knowledge base of risks and alerts about threats. The perspective provided by this data is quite challenging, given the complexity of the interconnections and growing prevalence of the technology used in medical services ecosystems. Proper articulation and the opportunities they provide for employing ontological logic strategies, ontologies are a highly intriguing tool for organizing and modeling contexts. Making use of these features inside ontologies might assist with the evolving features. In order to verify and track alterations, diffs, novel flaws and dangers, unconfirmed privacy and security characteristics, etc., as proof that the cognitive-intelligence characteristics of the intricate healthcare ecosystems are operating as intended, dynamic vulnerability examination and pentesting are additionally used.

2.4.2 Method for Secure Data Handling

An effort was made to improve the model in Figure 2.1 by adding an intellectual design, as seen in Figure 2.2, to simulate how people might think and act in response to novel and developing concerns regarding privacy and security. Beyond simply stating the loops of control explicitly, feedback-driven control loop attributes also need to be improved because they have an impact on the structure and layout of the entire system.

In recent times, there has been a development of CCPS-IoT, which mimics intellectual behavior of mankind by being capable to acquire knowledge, logic, and comprehend both the social and physical worlds on their own. "The most intelligent applications of the IoT in knowledge-intensive environments will be those that allow human thought processes to become central to the process." All of this presents additional difficulties:

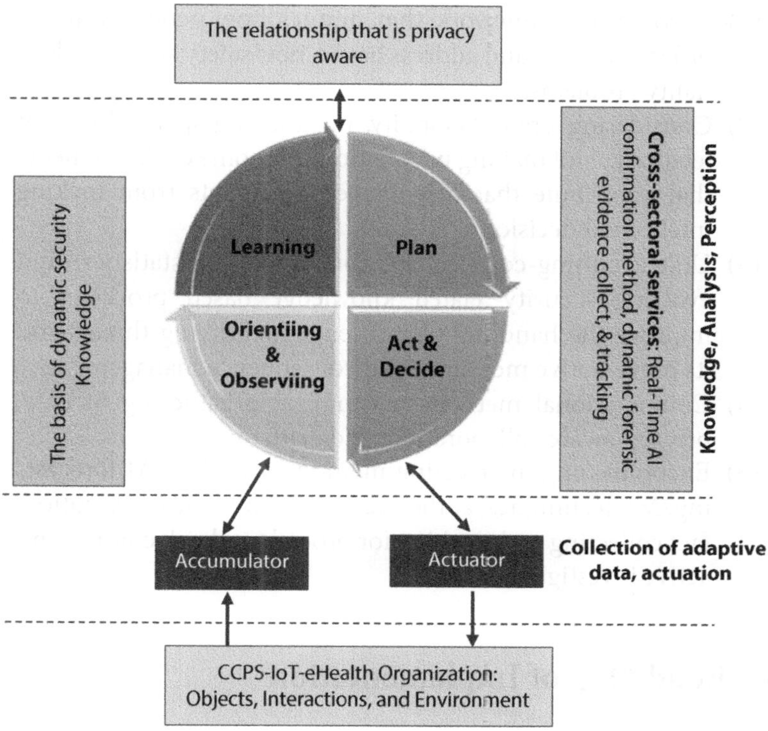

Figure 2.3 Privacy-aware and security provided by CCPS-IoT.

I. CCPS-IoTs' growing cognitive sophistication may cause unforeseen emergent behavior;
II. Conventional CCPS-IoT weaknesses and dangers, as well as new ones relating to their innate cognitive functions, will be the downfalls of cognitive CCPS-IoT;
III. Because of its widespread use, CCPS-IoT will offer a much larger attack surface, increasing the dangers to safety of the general public for critical facilities through its user interfaces and enhanced versatility of accessing data and services.

The primary goal of the strategy and illustrated in Figure 2.3 is to offer a framework for protecting the CCPS-IoT–enabled healthcare ecosystem from evolving and adapting threats. This is going to be accomplished by the following:

(1) A cognitive framework that mimics how people think in order to foresee and address brand-new safety and confidentiality problems;
(2) Considering unpredictability, maximizing spatial loops of feedback, and making negotiations are some of the elements that contribute that help prevent assailants from making intellectual decisions;
(3) Utilize cutting-edge safety, confidentiality, statistics, and evolving security-related knowledge based processes to improve the handling of incidents, identifying threats and its preventative measures, and consequence management;
(4) Computational methods, customizable gathering of data, privacy-aware collaboration, and actuator;
(5) Encompassing intersecting methods including AI forecasting, ML techniques, authentication of the time of execution, fact collecting and tracking for proof-based risk control, and active investigations.

2.5 Road Map of Implementation

Quartet of modules—(i) adaptive intelligent data gathering as well as tracking of security-related data; (ii) using AI-based analytics for prediction (i.e., deep learning algorithms) on the gathered dataset; (iii) the co-operation of stakeholders in risk analysis, threat identification, threat reduction, assessment of vulnerability, and adherence; and (iv) a prototype security-related knowledge base—is being developed.

The efficacy of developing and integrating creative and intelligent techniques for safety, confidentiality, statistics, and the verification of the run time has been shown in a first investigation. These are readily assimilated and improved in this manner for the novel mechanisms. Ultimately, a structure will be designed to simulate cognitive behavior in humans.

2.5.1 AI for CCPS-IoT

These days, AI, ML, and CCPS-IoT are interchangeable because they are both significantly dependent on AI/ML systems. AI has enormous development and creative capacity in CCPS-IoT. The use of AI will be essential in guaranteeing the availability and dependability of these systems, as advancements in both CCPS-IoT rely on the use of wireless technology to sustain efficient operations. AI tools are able to deliver data-analysis and

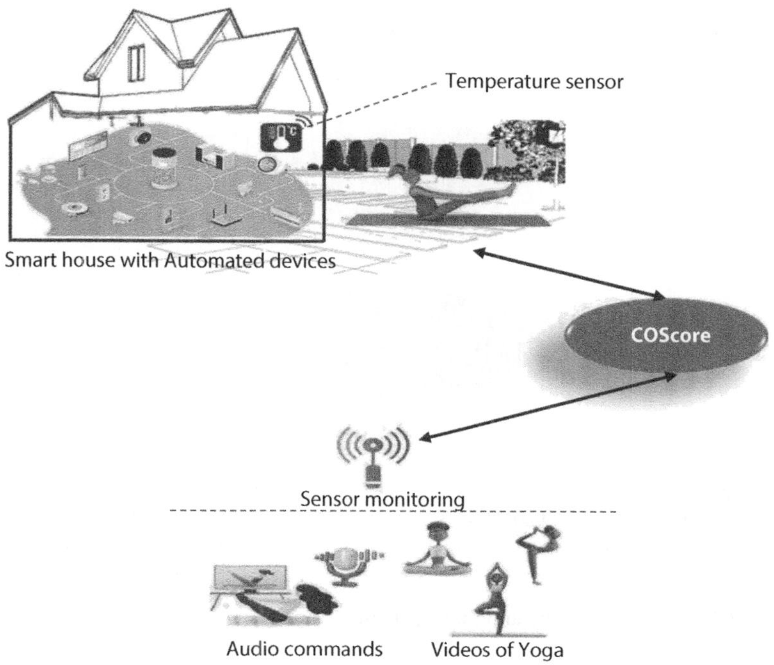

Figure 2.4 Applications of CCPS-IoT using AI.

forecasts with the level of detail and precision required for a smooth and efficient functioning, as both CCPS-IoTs depend on a myriad of detectors and devices. AI will be essential for the combination, evaluation, forecasting, and safety of CCPS-IoT information. Despite the widespread use of Bluetooth networks to connect affordable, efficient, and distributed AI systems, challenges related to data integration, security, and privacy remain significant obstacles. For AI forecast and assessment in CCPS-IoT, numerous novel approaches and methodologies—such as blockchain, edge-learning, and edge-computing—are shown in Figure 2.4. The difficulties of multisensory merging of data and AI security in CCPS-IoT will need to be addressed in subsequent studies.

2.5.2 AI-Enabled Wireless CCPS-IoT to Provide Security

Another significant issue confronting CCPS-IoT is AI security. Having multitudes of digital gadgets linked by internet connections, safety, and protection of customer data are major priorities for the field's study. IoT devices need to be resilient against possible risks given the advancements in adversarial attacks against AI/ML systems. ML and AI systems have to

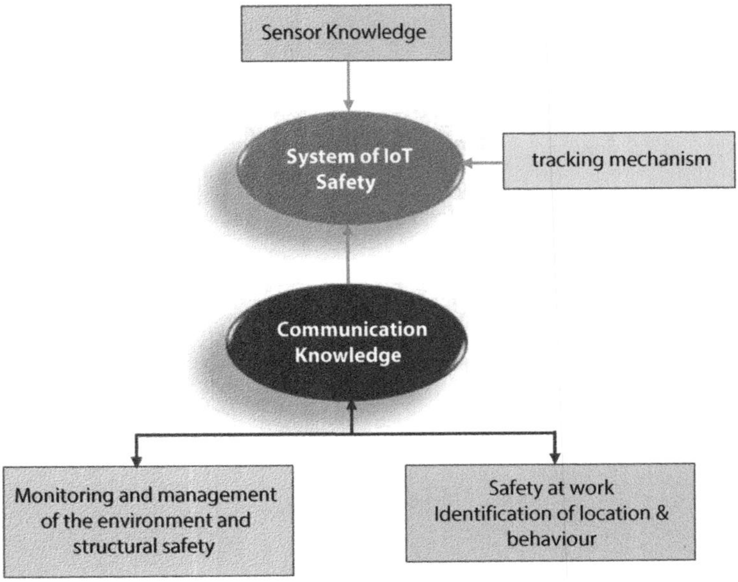

Figure 2.5 Safety monitoring and managements.

become proactive as well as reactive in their protection against adversarial assaults to safeguard consumer data security and privacy because of the wide range of assault surface regions associated with CCPS-IoT shown in Figure 2.5. IoT AI/ML systems will need to be resilient to a variety of hostile threats. It is necessary to identify multiple assaults and take the appropriate precautions to address them.

2.6 Conclusions and Future Enhancement

In conclusion, the development of a physical layer within the proposed CCPS framework represents a significant step forward in fortifying data handling and response networks against cyber-physical threats. By integrating tangible defenses with cognitive capabilities, organizations can create a multi-layered defense mechanism that addresses vulnerabilities at both the physical and digital levels. Strong authentication procedures, hardened infrastructure, and secure data centers are just a few of the components that make up the physical layer of CCPS and add to the general endurance of AI systems. To reduce the possibility of illegal access, manipulation, and security violations, strict access restrictions, monitoring systems, and hardware-based encryption should be put in place. Moreover, enterprises may identify and address safety concerns instantly thanks to proactive surveillance and reaction features incorporated into the physical layer. By leveraging AI-driven analytics and automation, organizations can orchestrate timely responses to security breaches, minimizing the impact on operations and data integrity. Collaboration between physical security teams and AI specialists is essential for designing, implementing, and maintaining an effective physical layer for CCPS. Physical security experts bring expertise in access control, surveillance, and environmental security, whereas AI specialists contribute insights into cognitive computing, anomaly detection, and predictive analytics. Furthermore, confidentiality and adherence to regulations are major factors that influence how the outermost layer of CCPS-IoT is designed and implemented. Compliance with industry standards and regulations ensures that physical security measures align with legal mandates and best practices, reducing the risk of non-compliance penalties and reputational damage.

Continuous evaluation and improvement are necessary to keep the physical layer of CCPS-IoT robust and effective over time. To provide continuous defense against changing cyber-physical threats, regular security assessments, penetration tests, and vulnerability inspections assist in locating gaps in physical safety measures and actively plugging them. In conclusion, the physical layer of CCPS serves as a foundational element in enhancing the security posture of AI-driven systems, providing organizations with the resilience and agility needed to navigate the complex landscape of cyber threats effectively. By integrating physical security measures with cognitive capabilities, organizations can create a robust defense mechanism that safeguards against a wide range of cyber-physical risks, ultimately protecting critical data assets and maintaining stakeholder trust.

Future Directions

Looking ahead, several promising directions emerge for further advancing the physical layer proposed within the CCPS framework:

Integration of Emerging Technologies: Future developments in emerging technologies such as quantum computing, blockchain, and edge computing present opportunities to enhance the capabilities of the physical layer. Integration of these technologies can offer improved security, resilience, and scalability to CCPS implementations.

Enhanced Automation and Orchestration: Increasing automation and orchestration capabilities within the physical layer can streamline security operations and response workflows. AI-driven automation can enable rapid detection, analysis, and mitigation of security threats, thereby reducing the burden on human operators and improving overall response times.

Resilience against Advanced Threats: As cyber threats continue to evolve and grow in sophistication, the physical layer of CCPS must adapt to defend against novel attack vectors and techniques. This includes developing robust defense against insider threats, supply chain attacks, and zero-day vulnerabilities to ensure comprehensive protection of AI-driven systems.

Interoperability and Standardization: Future efforts should focus on promoting interoperability and standardization across different CCPS implementations. This will facilitate seamless integration with existing security frameworks, interoperability between heterogeneous systems, and information sharing among stakeholders, thereby enhancing overall security effectiveness.

Privacy-Preserving Techniques: With increasing concerns about data privacy and regulatory compliance, future developments in privacy-preserving techniques will be crucial for the physical layer of CCPS. Employing strategies like homomorphic cryptography, differential confidentiality, and encrypted multi-party computation can help businesses safeguard sensitive information while still getting insightful insights from AI-driven analytics.

Threat Intelligence and Information Sharing: Collaboration and information sharing among organizations and sectors will be essential for effectively combating cyber threats. Enhancing the physical layer with real-time threat intelligence feeds, sharing of security incident data, and collaboration platforms can help organizations proactively identify and respond to emerging threats more effectively.

Dynamic Adaptation and Resilience: Building dynamic adaptation and resilience capabilities into the physical layer will be critical for mitigating the impact of evolving cyber-physical threats. This includes implementing self-healing mechanisms, adaptive access controls, and resilience to physical infrastructure failures, ensuring continuous protection and availability of AI-driven systems.

Ethical and Societal Implications: As AI-driven systems become increasingly integrated into society, addressing ethical and societal implications becomes paramount. Future developments in the physical layer of CCPS should consider ethical principles such as fairness, transparency, and accountability, ensuring that security measures uphold fundamental human rights and values.

Cross-Domain Collaboration: Encouraging cross-domain collaboration between academia, industry, government, and civil society will be essential for driving innovation and addressing complex security challenges.

Collaborative research efforts, joint initiatives, and public-private partnerships can accelerate the development and adoption of advanced security solutions within the physical layer of CCPS.

Education and Workforce Development: Finally, investing in education and workforce development initiatives will be crucial for building the expertise and skills needed to design, implement, and operate the physical layer of CCPS effectively. This includes training programs, certification courses, and academic research to develop the next generation of cybersecurity professionals and thought leaders.

In summary, future directions for the physical layer of CCPS encompass a wide range of technological, organizational, and societal aspects, requiring collaborative efforts and continuous innovation to address evolving cyber-physical threats effectively. By embracing emerging technologies, promoting interoperability, enhancing resilience, and addressing ethical considerations, organizations can create a robust and adaptive security framework capable of safeguarding AI-driven systems in an increasingly interconnected world.

References

1. Stutz, D., de Assis, J.T., Laghari, A.A., Khan, A.A., Deshpande, A., Kulkarni, D., Grata, E.G., Cyber Threat Detection and Mitigation Using Artificial Intelligence–A Cyber-physical Perspective. *Appl. Artif. Intell. Cybersecur. Anal. Cyber Threat Detect.*, 7, 107–133, 2024.
2. Alvarez-Alvarado, M.S., Apolo-Tinoco, C., Ramirez-Prado, M.J., Alban-Chacón, F.E., Pico, N., Aviles-Cedeno, J., Rengifo, J., Cyber-physical power systems: A comprehensive review about technologies drivers, standards, and future perspectives. *Comput. Electr. Eng.*, *116*, 109149, 2024.
3. Aswale, P.S., Patil, D.P., Vaidya, O.S., Securing Cyber Physical System Using Machine Learning: A Survey on Attack Resistant Algorithms. *Rev. d'Intelligence Artificielle*, *38*, 1, 277–284, 2024.
4. Abdullahi, M., Alhussian, H., Aziz, N., Abdulkadir, S.J., Alwadain, A., Muazu, A.A., Bala, A., Comparison and investigation of AI-based approaches for cyberattack detection in cyber-physical systems. *IEEE Access*, 12, 31988–32004, 2024.
5. Serôdio, C., Mestre, P., Cabral, J., Gomes, M., Branco, F., Software and Architecture Orchestration for Process Control in Industry 4.0 Enabled by Cyber-Physical Systems Technologies. *Appl. Sci.*, *14*, 5, 2160, 2024.
6. Karthikeyan, A., Karthikeyan, K., Swathika, O.G., Cyber-physical security in a stand-alone photovoltaic system for rural electrification. *Next-Generation Cyber-Phys. Microgrid Syst.*, 26, 29–75, 2024.

7. Zhao, C., Du, H., Niyato, D., Kang, J., Xiong, Z., Kim, D., II, Letaief, K.B., Generative AI for Secure Physical Layer Communications: A Survey, 2024, arXiv preprint arXiv:2402.13553.
8. Bindra, S.S. and Aggarwal, A., Security in cyber physical systems: Transformation and challenges. *J. Auton. Intell.*, 7, 4, 1–19, 2024.
9. Tabassum, T., Toker, O., Khalghani, M.R., Cyber–physical anomaly detection for inverter-based microgrid using autoencoder neural network. *Appl. Energy*, 355, 122283, 2024.
10. Parthiban, L., Latchoumi, T.P., Balamurugan, K., Raja, K., Parthiban, R., Cognitive Computing for the Internet of Medical Things, in: *Integrating Blockchain and Artificial Intelligence for Industry 4.0 Innovations*, pp. 85–100, Springer International Publishing, Cham, 2023.
11. Rajamäki, J., Trust Environment for Cyber-Physical Systems: The DYNAMO Approach. *Int. J. Appl. Phys. Eng.*, 3, 1–10, 2024.
12. Balogun, B.F., Tripathi, K., Tiwari, S., JS, S.M., Tyagi, A.K., Original Research Article A blockchain-based deep learning approach for cyber security in next-generation medical cyber-physical systems. *J. Auton. Intell.*, 7, 5, 5522–5532, 2024.
13. Balamurugan, K., Latchoumi, T.P., Satla, S., Machining Studies on AlSi7+ 63% SiC Composite Using Machine Learning Technique, in: *Metal Matrix Composites*, pp. 139–166, CRC Press, Boca Raton, Florida, USA, 2023.
14. Alvarez-Alvarado, M.S., Apolo-Tinoco, C., Ramirez-Prado, M.J., Alban-Chacón, F.E., Pico, N., Aviles-Cedeno, J., Rengifo, J., Cyber-Physical Power Systems: A Comprehensive Review About Drivers, Standards, and Future Perspectives. *Standards Future Perspect.*, 182, 1-21, 2024.
15. Huitzil, C.T., Cognitive Dynamic Systems for Cyber-Physical Engineering, in: *Machine Learning for Complex and Unmanned Systems*, pp. 277–294, CRC Press, Boca Raton, Florida, USA, 2024.
16. Stutz, D., de Assis, J.T., Laghari, A.A., Khan, A.A., Andreopoulos, N., Terziev, A., Grata, E.G., Enhancing Security in Cloud Computing Using Artificial Intelligence (AI). *Applying Artif. Intell. Cybersecur. Anal. Cyber Threat Detect.*, 110, 179–220, 2024.
17. Latchoumi, T.P., Parthiban, L., Balamurugan, K., Raja, K., Vijayaraj, J., Parthiban, R., A Framework for Low Energy Application Devices Using Blockchain-Enabled IoT in WSNs, in: *Integrating Blockchain and Artificial Intelligence for Industry 4.0 Innovations*, pp. 121–132, Cham, Springer International Publishing, 2023.
18. Wang, X., Huang, J., Tian, Y., Sun, C., Yang, L., Lou, S., Wang, F., Parallel Driving with Big Models and Foundation Intelligence in Cyber-Physical-Social Spaces. Research.
19. Saleem, M.U., Usman, M.R., Yaqub, M.A., Liotta, A., Asim, A., Smarter Grid in the 5G Era: Integrating the Internet of Things with a Cyber-Physical System. *IEEE Access*, 12, 34002–34018, 2024.

3

Intelligent Cognitive Cyber-Physical System–Based Intrusion Detection for AI-Enabled Security in Industry 4.0

V. Mahavaishnavi[1]*, R. Saminathan[2] and G. Ramachandran[2]

[1]*Department of Computer Science and Engineering, SRM Institute of Science and Technology, Ramapuram, Chennai, India*
[2]*Department of Computer Science and Engineering, Annamalai University, Annamalainagar, Chidambaram, Tamil Nadu, India*

Abstract

Recently, multidisciplinary academics have become more interested in the cognitive cyber-physical system (CCPS), which combines artificial intelligence (AI) and machine learning (ML) approaches. Brain-inspired computing–based solutions will be essential to commercial information technology in this era of rapidly transforming technological advancements and AI. Industry 4.0's use of CCPS in conjunction with brain-inspired technology will have an enormous impact on how industries develop. Even though CCPSs in the manufacturing sector have many benefits, safety is still a difficult architectural issue. Intelligent technology and computational methods have opened up new opportunities for commercial cyber-physical system (CPS) transformation recently. In the rapidly evolving landscape of Industry 4.0, ensuring robust security measures for CPS is paramount. This chapter proposes an innovative approach leveraging intelligent CCPSs for intrusion detection, with a focus on AI-enabled security. By integrating cognitive computing capabilities into cyber-physical systems, our proposed framework aims to enhance the detection and response mechanisms against intrusions in Industry 4.0 environments. Through the utilization of advanced AI techniques, deep learning, and ML, the system aims to adaptively identify and classify potential security threats in real time. The integration of cognitive capabilities enables the system to learn and evolve, thereby improving its efficacy in detecting novel

**Corresponding author*: vaishu3095@yahoo.com

K. Ananthajothi, S. N. Sangeethaa, D. Divya, S. Balamurugan and Shen-Lung Peng (eds.) Securing Cyber-Physical Systems: Fundamentals, Applications and Challenges, (45–64) © 2025 Scrivener Publishing LLC

and sophisticated cyber threats. This research contributes to the advancement of security measures in Industry 4.0 by presenting a holistic approach that combines intelligent cognitive computing with cyber-physical systems for enhanced intrusion detection and mitigation.

Keywords: Intelligent cognitive cyber-physical systems, AI-enabled security, machine learning, deep learning, cyber-physical systems, anomaly detection, real-time monitoring, adaptive learning

3.1 Introduction

Intelligent cognitive cyber-physical systems (iCCPSs) play a crucial role in enhancing security measures within Industry 4.0 environments. As industrial systems become increasingly interconnected and automated, they become more vulnerable to cyber threats. Intrusion detection system (IDSs) are essential components of cybersecurity (CS) frameworks, tasked with identifying and mitigating potential threats.

3.1.1 Cyber-Physical Systems

The cornerstone of Industry 4.0, as promoted by the Indian government, is the cyber-physical system (CPS) aims to create smart factories and usher in the next phase of industrialization. While a National Science Foundation conference took place in India in 2006, the word "CPS" was initially used. The definition is "a system that is formed by collaborating organizations, endowed with computational capacities and performers of a close relationship that includes the surroundings natural environment, phenomena, utilizing and offering collectively services related to processing and transmission that make information available on the network" [1]. There has been a lot of scientific interest in the CPS. Numerous CPS-based programs, including those for medical care, the energy system, shipping, residences, structures, and towns, have been developed with intelligent manufacturing. CPS has become extremely smart, independent, and complicated. Intelligent public transportation systems, intelligent Industry 4.0 structures, automated healthcare and medical facilities, and smart electricity networks in the electricity business are a few instances of CPS. The relationship between diverse online activity and the physical elements that CPSs provide is extremely complicated [2]. To add to this difficulty, they are subject to significant problems from both planned and unplanned incidents, which makes it extremely challenging to forecast their behaviors (which are classified as "regular" or "poor"). Researchers in business and the academy are becoming increasingly interested in CPS information security as a result of a growth in cyber-attacks and a rise in their sophistication—a phenomenon known as zero-day dangers [3].

3.1.2 Intelligent Cyber-Physical Systems (ISPS)

A new approach, CPS, has been formed by combining individual physical operations with computing. Through the use of artificial intelligence (AI) to get a thorough understanding of the observed surroundings, the CPSs manage the actual operations. As a result, CPSs are built with the intelligence to make exact choices and swiftly take the necessary action. Development potential for intelligent CPS (iCPS) has increased because of the fast-growing links between both the physical and virtual realms and the creation of new smart approaches [4]. Massive, widespread, software-intensive structures, or iCPSs, are capable of managing everyday operations effectively and providing an extensive variety of innovative services and applications. They achieve this by integrating information from multiple sources, including digital and tangible elements, and by implementing cognitive ability methods [5]. The distinction between the real and the digital realms disappears when cognitive processes are integrated into physical things to facilitate cooperation and when these devices are outfitted with connections to the simulated environment. The way information is processed of an activity in a computer simulation may be altered by events that take place in the real world, creating a causal connection that can be used to continually enhance systems. Portable technologies that are smart, mindful of ourselves autonomous, and self-configuring can be developed to enhance the efficiency of processes in a range of applications and aid in addressing several current challenges in society in and decentralized manner while maintaining a high degree of independence [6]. Nevertheless, several obstacles must be removed to implement this extremely diverse paradigm. These difficulties include creating smart physical structures for sensors and interaction, stream of information manufacturing, information analysis, and algorithms for machine learning (ML) to create the self-adapting and context-aware programming that is the backbone of these devices' knowledge [7]. When integrating people as a crucial component of these highly complicated structures, security, interpersonal, and behavioral problems must also be taken into account. Because CPSs maintain robust connections between their human and cyber parts, they are essential to the creation of successful, contemporary intelligent systems across a range of applications that operate in real time. Owing to the intricate interconnection of several elements, CPS presents basic difficulties in several areas, including computer networking, instantaneous information processing, and effective parallel computation, along information perception and gathering [8]. To address the aforementioned issues and satisfy the increasing expectations of linked cars, smart power systems, and home automation, innovations are needed.

3.1.3 Cognitive Cyber-Physical Systems (CCPS)

It is a type of technology that mixes physical elements and computer hardware to provide solutions based on AI have been rapidly evolving in the past few years. To create smart systems, CCPS is utilizing neurobiology to integrate ML or AI. It is essential to corporate computing. Analytical data analysis, online computing, connected gadgets, and AI are used in other programs, such as healthcare systems, intelligent homes, automation, and systems for autonomous vehicles, to automate further procedures [9]. This supporting system is capable of offering decentralized decision-making, connectivity, accessibility of data, and technical support. The steps involved in CCPS identifying an intrusion are shown in Figure 3.1.

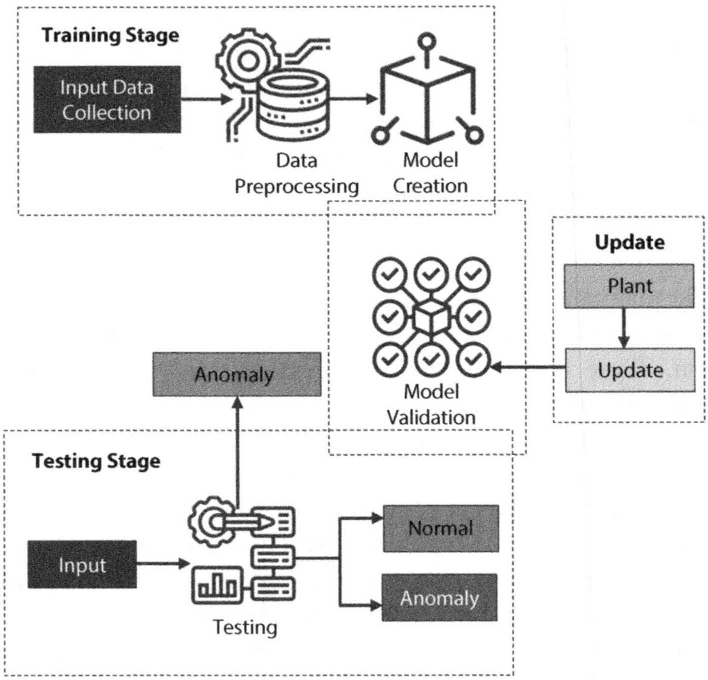

Figure 3.1 Intrusion detection in CCPS.

3.1.4 IDS in Industry 4.0 Using iCCPS

Industry 4.0 is the latest industrial revolution that aims to maximize efficiency and effectiveness while consuming the fewest resources possible. Industry 4.0 technologies have introduced a new production tendency aimed at optimizing resource utilization for maximum output. Information technology production and intelligent production are the cornerstones of Industry 4.0, which consists of enabling the execution of flexible production procedures through the IoT and mass customization [10]. It is reasonable to believe that Industry 4.0 technology will help to increase the organization's sustainability in both society and the economy. By improving resource efficiency, technology associated with Industry 4.0 has a major potential to create environmentally friendly value through the financial, economic, and ecological aspects of durability. IDS works by analyzing information collected from multiple places, such as system activity, records of activity, and network traffic to identify anomalies or patterns that could indicate a hacking attempt [11]. Numerous assaults, such as spyware, scans of ports, and networking probes, can be detected by network based intrusion detection system (NIDS). Host based intrusion detection system (HIDS) is capable of identifying threats from inside in addition to attacks targeted at a particular device or program. IDS come in two varieties: signature-based ones and anomaly-based ones. Techniques that use established characteristics or sequences of known attacks to identify attempts at penetration are known as based on signatures systems for intrusion detection. Conversely, IDSs that use anomalies employ statistical examination and AI methods to identify unusual activity that differs from a system's typical performance [12].

3.1.5 AI in iCCPS-IDS

AI has demonstrated promise in improving CPS intrusion detection efficiency and precision. Conversely, present AI-based detection of intrusion techniques have drawbacks like elevated false positive and false negative rates and constrained scalable. CPS needs an AI-IDS that can get past these limitations and offer reliable protection against assaults [13]. The purpose of the study is to overcome the shortcomings of current methods for intrusion detection by developing an AI-based IDS that can identify and react to attacks in CPS. The AI-enabled network intrusion detection idea aims to maintain accessibility to power while simultaneously enhancing CPS reliability and safety. By learning patterns of normal behavior from historical data, AI-driven iCCPS-IDS can detect deviations in real time and distinguish between benign anomalies and potential cyber-attacks with high accuracy [14].

One of the key merits of integrating AI into iCCPS-IDS is its ability to adapt and evolve. Through continuous learning from new data and experiences, these systems could stay ahead of emerging threats and dynamically adjust their detection algorithms and response strategies. This adaptive approach ensures that iCCPS-IDS remains effective in mitigating evolving cyber threats in the fast-paced and complex environments of Industry 4.0 [15]. Moreover, AI enables iCCPS-IDS to achieve contextual awareness by analyzing data from including sensors, multiple sources, system logs, and network traffic. By understanding the context surrounding security events, these systems can make more informed decisions and reduce false positives, thereby improving operational efficiency and minimizing disruptions to industrial processes. Additionally, AI-driven predictive analytics empower iCCPS-IDS to forecast potential security breaches based on historical patterns, enabling proactive mitigation measures to be taken before attacks occur [16].

Another significant benefit of AI in iCCPS-IDS is its ability to enable autonomous response actions in critical situations [17]. By autonomously triggering response mechanisms such as isolating affected components or reconfiguring system settings, these systems can mitigate security threats in real-time without human intervention, thereby reducing response times and minimizing the effect of cyber-attacks on industrial operations. Overall, the integration of AI in iCCPS-IDS represents a paradigm shift in CS for Industry 4.0, offering proactive threat detection, adaptive defense mechanisms, and improved resilience against evolving cyber threats [18].

3.2 Problem Statement

In Industry 4.0 environments, the increasing integration of AI and CPS technologies has led to heightened vulnerabilities to cyber threats. Existing IDSs often struggle to effectively detect and mitigate these threats due to their incapacity to adapt to the dynamic and complex nature of modern industrial systems. This research aims to address this gap by investigating novel approaches to improve the security posture of Industry 4.0 environments through the design, implementation, and assessment of an iCCPS-based IDS tailored to the unique challenges and requirements of AI-enabled security in Industry 4.0.

3.3 Motivation

Complexity of Industry 4.0 Environments

Industry 4.0 environments are characterized by highly interconnected cyber-physical systems comprising sensors, actuators, controllers, and networks. Therefore, there is a pressing need for advanced intrusion detection mechanisms capable of effectively safeguarding these critical infrastructures.

Rapid Evolution of Cyber Threats

Cyber threats are evolving rapidly, with adversaries constantly developing new techniques and tactics to exploit vulnerabilities in industrial systems. Existing rule-based IDSs often struggle to keep pace with these evolving threats due to their static nature.

Impact of Security Breaches on Operations

Security breaches in Industry 4.0 environments can have severe consequences, including production downtime, equipment damage, and loss of sensitive data. These disruptions not only incur financial losses but also pose risks to employee safety and customer trust. Therefore, there is a strong motivation to deploy robust IDSs that can effectively mitigate security threats and protect industrial operations.

Regulatory Compliance and Risk Management

Tight laws and regulations related to security and safeguarding information apply to businesses functioning in areas including producing goods, power, and transport. Heavy fines and harm to one's character may arise from breaking these restrictions. Implementing AI-enabled IDS demonstrates a proactive approach to CS risk management, helping organizations achieve compliance with regulatory standards and industry best practices.

Opportunities for Innovation and Competitive Advantage

Investing in AI-driven security solutions presents opportunities for innovation and competitive advantage in the rapidly evolving landscape of Industry 4.0. Organizations that embrace cutting-edge technologies to enhance their CS posture are better positioned to differentiate themselves in the market, attract investment, and build trust among stakeholders.

The motivation behind iCCPS-based IDS for AI-enabled security in Industry 4.0 stems from the need to address the complexity of industrial environments, mitigate evolving cyber threats, safeguard operations, ensure regulatory compliance, and capitalize on opportunities for innovation and competitive advantage in the digital era.

3.4 Research Gap

Data Quality and Availability: Industry 4.0 relies heavily on data-driven processes. However, there is often a lack of high-quality, labeled data necessary for training AI models. Research is needed to develop techniques for handling noisy, incomplete, and unstructured data commonly encountered in industrial settings. Additionally, methods for generating data to augment limited datasets could be explored.
Interoperability and Integration: There is a need for research into interoperable AI solutions that can seamlessly integrate with diverse hardware and software platforms. Standardization efforts for AI models, data formats, and communication protocols are crucial to facilitate interoperability.
Explainability and Trustworthiness: AI models used in Industry 4.0 often operate in critical domains where trust, reliability, and safety are paramount. However, many AI techniques, such as deep learning, are often considered black-box models, making it challenging to interpret their decisions. Research is needed to develop explainable AI methods that provide insights into the reasoning behind AI-driven decisions, enhancing transparency and trustworthiness.
Real-Time Adaptation and Learning: Industry 4.0 environments are dynamic and rapidly changing, requiring AI systems to adapt and learn in real-time. Current AI models cannot often continuously learn from streaming data and adapt their behavior accordingly. Research is needed to develop online learning algorithms and reinforcement learning techniques that enable AI systems to adapt to changing environments and evolving requirements.
Privacy and Security: AI-driven systems in Industry 4.0 may process sensitive data, posing privacy and security concerns. There is a need for research into privacy-preserving AI techniques that can analyze data while protecting individuals' privacy rights. Additionally, AI systems themselves are vulnerable to adversarial attacks, highlighting the importance of developing robust and secure AI algorithms resistant to manipulation and exploitation.
Ethical and Societal Implications: The deployment of AI in Industry 4.0 raises ethical and societal concerns regarding job displacement, algorithmic biases, and the concentration of power. Research is needed to address these challenges and develop AI solutions that prioritize fairness,

accountability, transparency, and inclusivity. Additionally, interdisciplinary research involving experts from diverse fields such as ethics, sociology, and law is crucial to ensure responsible AI deployment in Industry 4.0 contexts.

Addressing these research gaps is essential for unlocking the full potential of AI in Industry 4.0 and harnessing its transformative capabilities to drive innovation, efficiency, and sustainability in industrial operations.

3.5 Methodology

By learning patterns of normal behavior from historical data, AI-driven iCCPS-IDS can detect deviations in real-time and distinguish between benign anomalies and potential cyber-attacks with high accuracy. One of the key compensations for integrating AI into iCCPS-IDS is its capability to adapt and evolve. Through continuous learning from new data and experiences, these systems could stay ahead of emerging threats and dynamically adjust their detection algorithms and response strategies. This adaptive approach ensures that iCCPS-IDS remains effective in mitigating evolving cyber threats in the fast-paced and complex environments of Industry 4.0.

Moreover, AI enables iCCPS-IDS to achieve contextual awareness by analyzing data from multiple sources, network traffic, including sensors, and system logs. By understanding the context surrounding security events, these systems can make more informed decisions and reduce false positives, thereby improving operational efficiency and minimizing disruptions to industrial processes. Additionally, AI-driven predictive analytics empower iCCPS-IDS to forecast potential security breaches based on historical patterns, enabling proactive mitigation measures to be taken before attacks occur.

Another significant benefit of AI in iCCPS-IDS is its ability to enable autonomous response actions in critical situations. By autonomously triggering response mechanisms such as isolating affected components or reconfiguring system settings, these systems can mitigate security threats in real-time without human intervention, thereby reducing response times and minimizing the impact of cyber-attacks on industrial operations. Overall, the integration of AI in iCCPS-IDS represents a paradigm shift in CS for Industry 4.0, offering proactive threat detection, adaptive defense mechanisms, and improved resilience against evolving cyber threats.

3.5.1 Training Dataset

The CICIDS2017 dataset serves as the attack detecting the system's input resource. It consists of labeled information, meaning that each piece of information is associated with the right category (things like usual traffic or specific types of assaults). This set of data will be used to train and assess the security breach detection system.

3.5.2 Information for Assessment and Instruction

Two kinds of data are created from the input dataset: both testing and training. Testing information is used to evaluate the detection of intrusions algorithm's effectiveness after it has been developed utilizing training information. Because of this distinction, evaluating the model's generalization performance to new, untested information is made easier.

3.5.3 Model

iCCPS model of the production industry is shown in Figure 3.2. Customized goods are one of the biggest industrial trends. This demands the highest quality, lowest costs, shorter product life cycles, and more customized goods. Production systems must be outfitted with sophisticated features to enable them to adjust to changes in the production process to meet these objectives. Without the need for outside assistance, the smart-cyber-physical management system (CPMS) can react to changes in the working atmosphere promptly and accurately. Consumers use the head-mounted display with automated guidance to choose the product attributes in the digital studio while placing orders at the supervisory levels. Subsequently, the good's data is routed to the processing and design management departments to create the factory's production schedule. During this stage, the most effective management is produced using algorithms based on evolution that draws inspiration from biological sciences, including biological algorithms and ant colony optimization. Using techniques like agent-based dynamic planning and colonic executing manufacturing processes, a plethora of research has tackled organizational optimization issues. The Internet of Services is effectively utilized in Smart-CPMS to share duties, ranging from design to processing management generation. A CPS exhibits smart and independent behavior. AI is used to perform intelligent behaviors like learning and decision-making via reasoning. Machines are equipped with ubiquitous

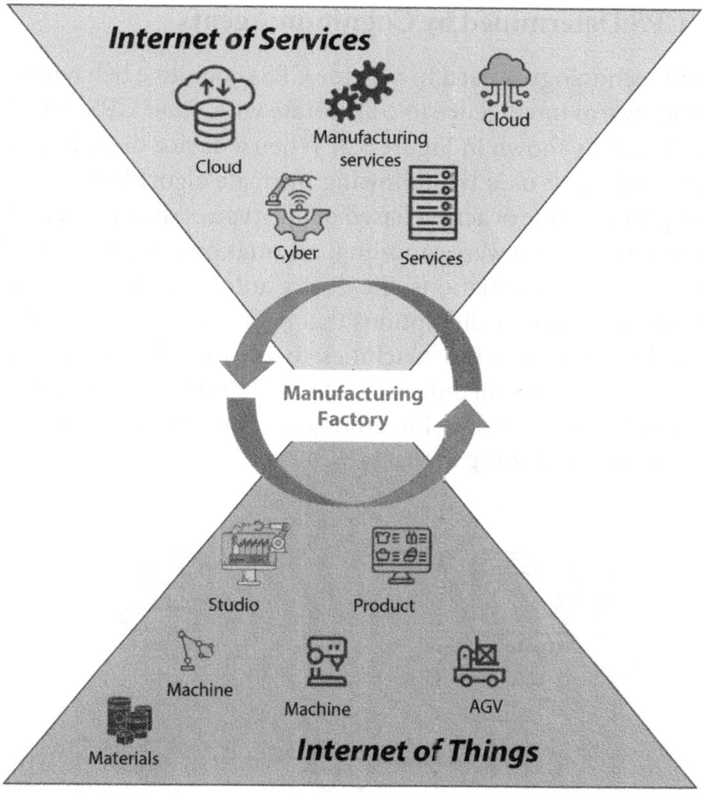

Figure 3.2 iCCPS model for manufacturing factory.

technological advances, which enable real-time monitoring and control. The device is interfaced with workers using a personal digital assistant (PDA) and smartphone, together with human–machine interface (HMI). A computer program with self-characteristics is called an intelligent entity. Figure 3.2 depicts an illustration of a cognitive agent-based CPS with key components including thinking, decision-making, expertise, interaction, and management. The sense modules receive information from monitors about the physical component's condition and use it to diagnose it. The cyberspace component decides based on the state of the delivery. Intelligent technology is used in a knowledge-based thinking system for decision-making. Communicating new ideas, such as the need to collaborate with other CPSs or change the cutting settings for the milling procedure, is the responsibility of the cyber part's management modules. The connectivity modules are responsible for communicating with the PDA, HMI, and additional CPSs.

3.5.4 CPS Determined by Cognition Agents

Intelligent technology is used to provide CPSs cognitive behaviors, such as employing swarm intelligence to collaborate with other CPSs and thinking to make decisions shown in Figure 3.3. When a device disturbance occurs, the associated agent uses the following intricate algorithms to determine the appropriate course of action based on the type of disturbance. The three approaches to recovery were canceling, negotiations, and non-negotiation. When there are no negotiations, the device automatically resolves the disruption; this is useful for disruptions that pass quickly. If not, the machine must collaborate with other machines to identify the right machine to complete its task or reschedule. The use of pheromone values inspired by ant colonies facilitates discussion among CPSs to determine which CPS is most suited for completing the task.

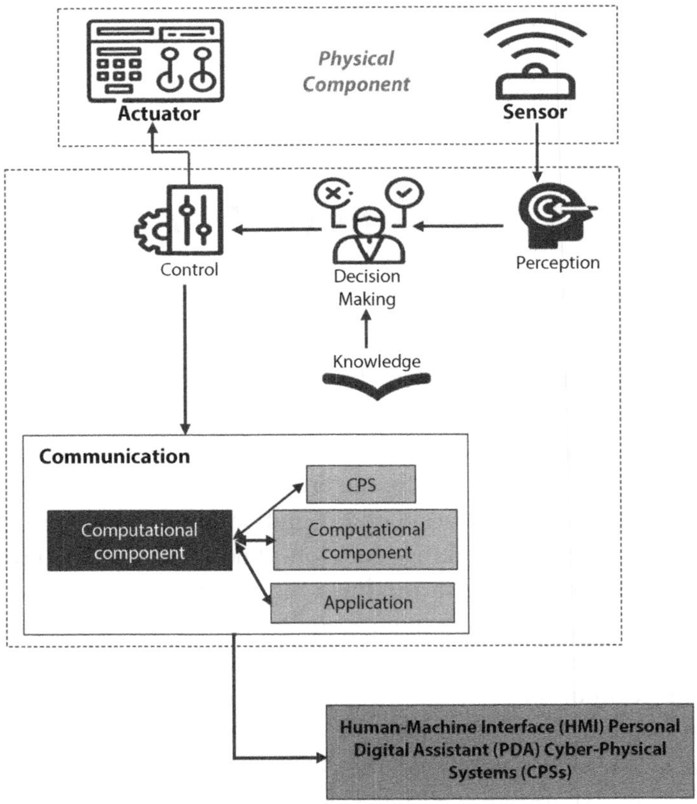

Figure 3.3 Model of iCCPS-IDS.

3.5.5 Useful Implementation of the Actual Device

Throughout the procedure of machining, keeping an eye on the machining state is crucial to controlling the quality of the machined product. To

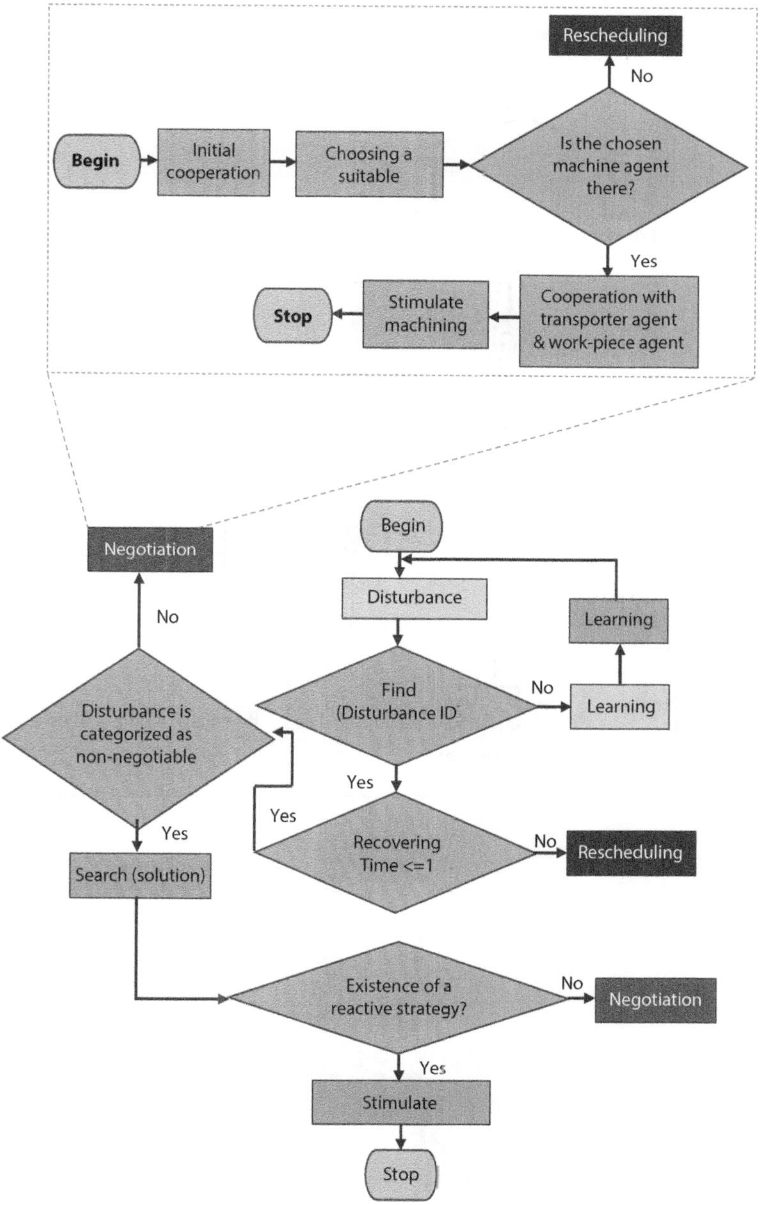

Figure 3.4 Model of iCCPS-IDS using AI.

apply the proposed iCCPS-IDS with AI idea to a specific manufacturing instance, attention was drawn to the self-adapting reducing situation on a fast-speed milling device. The disturbance categorization used to separate the events into internal and external problems is depicted in Figure 3.4.

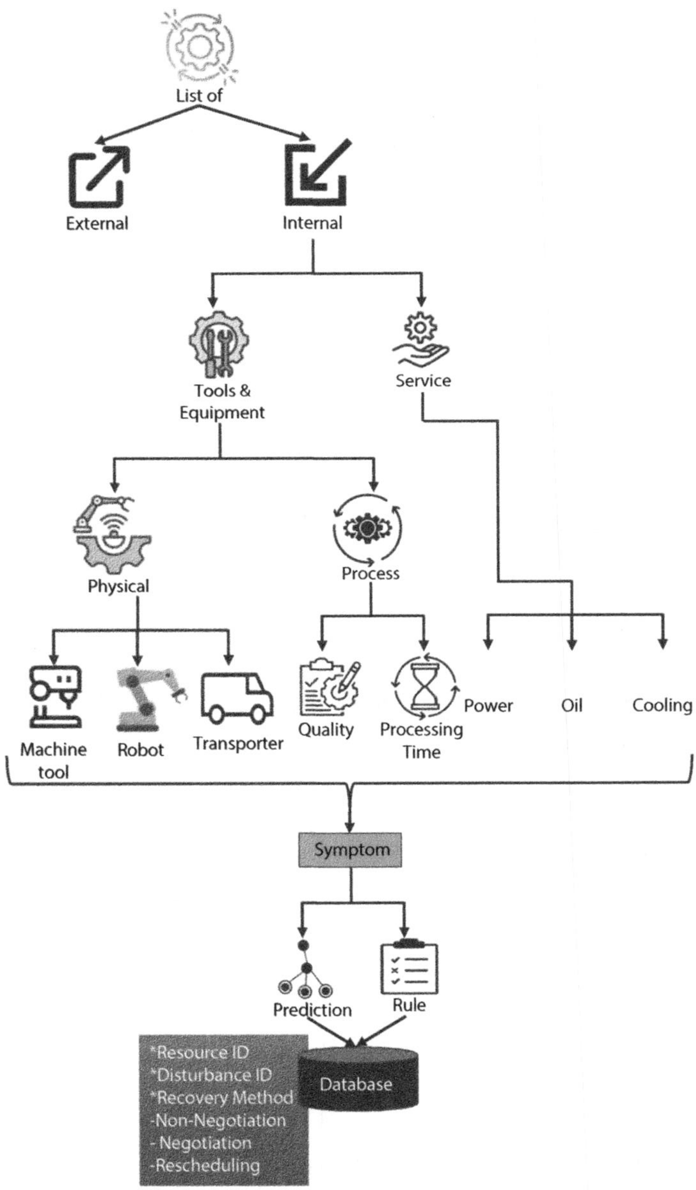

Figure 3.5 Disturbance classification.

External disruptions result from a supplier change or an order modification. Additional disruptions related to physical structures, processes, and services include tool wear and improper procedures. These disturbances were identified by their symptoms, which are then utilized to build the rules or logic to forecast the disturbance that iCCPS-IDS will discover shown in Figure 3.5. The iCCPS-IDS database, which contains details on resources, disturbances, and recovery applications science methods for every disruption, was created on the basis of the categorization of disturbances.

3.6 Importance and Impact of AI-Based Intrusion Detection in iCCPS in Industry 4.0

3.6.1 Need

Nonetheless, current technical advancements are achievable through the use of self-building technology. Opportunity also exists for cognitive structures that exhibit really intelligent human-like effectiveness, which includes "character, inspiration, feelings, etc." (Sun, 2020). The CS threat primarily targets these internet-enabled businesses, making it one of the key issues that has to be addressed. About this I4.0, iCCPS plays a significant role in maintaining the competitiveness of the organization. Given the complexity of the present CPS, issues about ensuring the safety and confidentiality of these programs have greater importance. The potential risks to the cyber, physical, or both dimensions of iCCPS may be interconnected, necessitating the use of sophisticated techniques for risk assessment and identification of vulnerabilities. Anomaly and misuse predictions are the two primary categories into which the IDS approaches are divided. First, characteristics of known assaults are used to forecast abuse. This is considered an incursion because the examined data are connected to the databases. Misuse detectors have very few false positives; however, they are severely constrained. A portion of the prediction techniques rely on clustering techniques. AI techniques have been used extensively in anomaly prediction recently. Previous IDS research takes abuse identification and anomalous predictions into account. The main benefits and drawbacks of anomaly prediction techniques typically lead to their abuse. IDSs from earlier times are used to detect abuse or unusual assaults. To overcome the limitations, concurrent abuse, and anomalous IDS have been implemented.

3.6.2 Challenges

Complexity and Heterogeneity: Industry 4.0 environments are categorized by the integration of sensors, actuators, diverse cyber-physical components, controllers, and communication networks. These components often operate on different protocols and technologies, leading to a complex and heterogeneous infrastructure. Designing AI-based IDS that can effectively monitor and analyze data from such diverse sources while accounting for their inherent complexities is a significant challenge.

Real-time Detection and Response: iCCPS-based IDS must be capable of responding and detecting security threats in real time to prevent disruptions to industrial processes and minimize the impact of cyber-attacks. Balancing the computational requirements of AI with the need for real-time performance poses a considerable challenge.

Anomaly Detection in Dynamic Environments: Industry 4.0 environments are dynamic and constantly evolving, with changes in operational conditions, system configurations, and network traffic patterns occurring frequently. AI-based IDS must be able to adapt to these changes and accurately distinguish between normal and anomalous behavior in real-time. Developing AI algorithms that can effectively detect anomalies in dynamic and complex environments is a significant challenge.

Interpretability and Explainability: While AI techniques such as deep learning have shown remarkable performance in various domains, they often lack interpretability and explainability, making it stimulating to understand the reasoning behind their decisions. In safety-critical applications like intrusion detection, it is essential to have AI-based IDS that can provide explanations for their detections to facilitate human understanding and decision-making. Achieving interpretability and explainability while maintaining high detection accuracy is a challenging research problem.

To tackle these obstacles, multidisciplinary research endeavors are necessary, integrating proficiency in AI, information security, mechanical engineering, and industry-specific understanding of Industry 4.0. By overcoming these challenges, AI-based intrusion detection in iCCPS can play a crucial role in enhancing the security posture of Industry 4.0 environments and safeguarding critical cyber-physical infrastructures.

3.7 Conclusions and Future Directions

AI is outfitted with mental agent technologies that allow the use of human intellectual behaviors to conquer the disruptions inside the manufacturing process. This form of technology is the result of combining cognition and agency technologies. The CPS can exhibit independent traits including control, awareness, and communication thanks to cognition actors. Intelligent technology is applied to cognitive entities to enable them to possess intelligent behaviors, such as using reasoning and understanding to make decisions and learn new things. In conclusion, the integration of AI into IDS within iCCPS offers a promising avenue for bolstering security in Industry 4.0 environments. However, significant challenges must be tackled to fully capitalize on the potential of AI-based IDS in iCCPS. Industry 4.0 environments are inherently complex and heterogeneous, demanding AI algorithms that can effectively navigate and analyze data from diverse cyber-physical components. Furthermore, achieving real-time detection and response necessitates AI solutions capable of processing vast amounts of data swiftly while maintaining high accuracy levels. Adaptability to dynamic environments is another crucial aspect, requiring AI algorithms that can discern anomalies amidst evolving operational conditions and emerging cyber threats. Interpretability and explainability remain paramount, especially in safety-critical applications like intrusion detection, where human comprehension is vital. Additionally, the susceptibility of AI-based IDS to security vulnerabilities, including adversarial attacks, underscores the need for robust algorithms and comprehensive security measures. Despite these challenges, concerted interdisciplinary efforts hold the potential to overcome these hurdles, paving the way for AI-based IDS to fortify the security posture of Industry 4.0 environments and ensure the resilience and reliability of critical cyber-physical infrastructures.

Future Directions

Enhanced Adaptability and Resilience: Future research efforts should focus on developing AI algorithms that exhibit greater adaptability and resilience to dynamic and evolving environments. This includes exploring techniques for continuous learning, self-adaptation, and self-healing to ensure that iCCPS-based IDS can effectively detect and mitigate emerging cyber threats in real-time.

Interpretability and Explainability: Addressing the challenge of interpretability and explainability remains a priority. Future research should seek to develop AI models that not only achieve high detection accuracy but also provide transparent explanations for their decisions. This will enhance human understanding, trust, and acceptance of AI-driven IDSs in safety-critical industrial settings.

Integration of Human Expertise: Human–machine collaboration holds significant potential for improving the effectiveness of AI-based intrusion detection in iCCPS. Future research should explore ways to integrate human expertise, domain knowledge, and intuition into AI-driven decision-making processes, creating synergistic partnerships that leverage the strengths of both humans and machines.

Adversarial Robustness: As adversaries continue to develop sophisticated attacks targeting AI systems, there is a pressing need to enhance the adversarial robustness of iCCPS-based IDS. Future research should investigate techniques for detecting and mitigating adversarial attacks, robust optimization, anomaly detection, and including adversarial training methods specifically tailored to adversarial scenarios.

Privacy-Preserving Techniques: Given the growing concerns around data security and privacy, future research should focus on developing privacy-preserving methods for AI-based intrusion detection in iCCPS. This includes exploring methods for secure and anonymized data sharing, differential privacy mechanisms, and federated learning approaches that enable collaborative model training without compromising sensitive information.

Standardization and Benchmarking: Establishing standardized evaluation frameworks and benchmarks for AI-based IDSs will be essential for comparing performance across different solutions and driving innovation in the field. Future research should prioritize the development of standardized datasets, evaluation metrics, and testing protocols to facilitate rigorous and reproducible evaluation of iCCPS-based IDS.

Human-Centric Design: Finally, future research should prioritize human-centric design principles to ensure that AI-based IDSs are intuitive, user-friendly, and aligned with the needs and preferences of human operators. This includes conducting user studies, incorporating user feedback, and iteratively refining system interfaces to enhance usability, accessibility, and overall user experience.

By following these future directions, practitioners and researchers can accelerate the development and adoption of AI-based IDSs within iCCPS paving the way for more robust, adaptive, and trustworthy security solutions in the era of Industry 4.0.

References

1. Chae, J., Lee, S., Jang, J., Hong, S., Park, K.J., Perspective on Industrial Cyber-Physical Systems (ICPS): From ICPS to AI-Augmented ICPS. *IEEE Trans. Ind. Cyber-Phys. Syst.*, 1, 257–272, 2023.
2. Jeffrey, N., Tan, Q., Villar, J.R., A review of anomaly detection strategies to detect threats to cyber-physical systems. *Electronics, 12*, 15, 3283, 2023.
3. Nair, M.M., Deshmukh, A., Tyagi, A.K., Artificial intelligence for cyber security: Current trends and future challenges. *Autom. Secure Comput. Next-Generation Syst.*, 5, 83–114, 2024.
4. Sarker, I.H., Multi-aspects AI-based modeling and adversarial learning for cybersecurity intelligence and robustness: A comprehensive overview. *Secur. Privacy, 6*, 5, e295, 2023.
5. Haider, U., Nawaal, B., Khan, I.U., El Hajjami, S., AI-Based Secure Wireless Communication Technologies and Cyber Threats for IoT Networks, in: *Cyber Security for Next-Generation Computing Technologies*, pp. 70–83, CRC Press, Boca Raton, Florida, USA, 2024.
6. Jan, Z., Ahamed, F., Mayer, W., Patel, N., Grossmann, G., Stumptner, M., Kuusk, A., Artificial intelligence for industry 4.0: Systematic review of applications, challenges, and opportunities. *Expert Syst. Appl., 216*, 119456, 2023.
7. Tushar, W., Yuen, C., Saha, T.K., Nizami, S., Alam, M.R., Smith, D.B., Poor, H.V., A survey of cyber-physical systems from a game-theoretic perspective. *IEEE Access, 11*, 9799–9834, 2023.
8. Rajagopal, M. and Ramkumar, S., Adopting artificial intelligence in ITIL for information security management—way forward in industry 4.0. In. *Artif. Intell. Cyber Secur. Ind. 4.0*, 3, 113–132, 2023.
9. Silva, M.C., Wearable edge AI towards cyber-physical applications, 2023.
10. Nair, M.M., Deshmukh, A., Tyagi, A.K., Artificial intelligence for cyber security: Current trends and future challenges. *Autom. Secure Comput. Next-Generation Syst.*, 5, 83–114, 2024.
11. Sindiramutty, S.R., Tan, C.E., Tee, W.J., Lau, S.P., Balakrishnan, S., Kaur, S., Aslam, M.F.A., Modern Smart Cities and Open Research Challenges and Issues of Explainable Artificial Intelligence. *Adv. Explainable AI Appl. Smart Cities*, 12, 389–424, 2024.
12. Ullah, I., Adhikari, D., Su, X., Palmieri, F., Wu, C., Choi, C., Integration of data science with the intelligent IoT (IIoT): current challenges and future perspectives. *Digital Commun. Netw.*, 6, 1–19, 2024.
13. Qureshi, K.N. and Newe, T., Artificial Internet of Things. *Artif. Intell. Things (AIoT) New Standards Technol. Commun. Syst.*, 3, 32–49, 2024.
14. Awotunde, J.B., Imoize, A.L., Jimoh, R.G., Adeniyi, E.A., Abdulraheem, M., Oladipo, I.D., Falola, P.B., AIoMT Enabling Real-Time Monitoring of Healthcare Systems: Security and Privacy Considerations, in: *Handbook of*

Security and Privacy of AI-Enabled Healthcare Systems and Internet of Medical Things, pp. 97–133, 2024.

15. Ullah, U., Usama, M., Muhammad, Z., Akbar, A., AI-enabled low-powered wireless area networks for quality air, in: *Low-Power Wide Area Network for Large Scale Internet of Things*, pp. 100–141, CRC Press, Boca Raton, Florida, USA, 2024.
16. Bimpas, A., Violos, J., Leivadeas, A., Varlamis, I., Leveraging pervasive computing for ambient intelligence: A survey on recent advancements, applications and open challenges. *Comput. Netw.*, *239*, 110156, 2024.
17. Hazra, A., Adhikari, M., Awasthi, L.K., 6G and Distributed Computing for IoT: A Survey, in: *WSN and IoT*, pp. 264–290, CRC Press, Boca Raton, Florida, USA, 2024.
18. Yadav, S.P., Yadav, S., Raj, P., de Albuquerque, V.H.C. (Eds.), *Advances in Fuzzy-Based Internet of Medical Things (IoMT)*, John Wiley & Sons, Hoboken, New Jersey, USA, 2024.

4

Resilient Cognitive Cyber-Physical Systems: Conceptual Frameworks, Models, and Implementation Strategies

R. Manivannan[1]* and M.P. Vaishnnave[2]

[1]Department of CSE, Vel Tech Rangarajan Dr.Sagunthala R&D Institute of Science and Technology, Avadi, Chennai, India
[2]Department of CSE, Sathyabama Institute of Science and Technology (Deemed to be University), Chennai, India

Abstract

Cognitive cyber-physical systems (CCPSs) are closed-loop applications connected systems that combine mechanical and cyberspace parts with cognitive capabilities. A key problem that must be handled in tandem with the quality-of-service limitations and related transmission expenses is ensuring the safety of these extremely powerful CCPS. This section covers the characteristics of CCPS, discusses possible threats to safety, and offers well-known physical layer security alternatives. An examination of robust cognitive cyber-physical networks is presented in this chapter, with an emphasis on simulations, conceptual structures, and execution techniques. As cyber-physical structures become more intricate and linked, it is crucial to make sure they are resilient to a range of risks and difficulties. The integration of mental capacities to improve resilience and adaptation is highlighted in the section's examination of the theoretical structures, supporting resilient organizations. It also explores concepts that make resiliency in cyber-physical structures easier to comprehend and analyze, including topics like response adaptation, tolerance for errors, and healing itself. The section also covers methods of implementation that are needed to realize robust CCPS. These approaches cover topics such as networked sensors, making choice methods, and system architectural planning. The goal of this investigation is to shed light on the creation and implementation of robust cognitive cyber-physical structures across a range of settings and uses.

**Corresponding author*: manichandran1692@gmail.com

K. Ananthajothi, S. N. Sangeethaa, D. Divya, S. Balamurugan and Shen-Lung Peng (eds.) Securing Cyber-Physical Systems: Fundamentals, Applications and Challenges, (65–86) © 2025 Scrivener Publishing LLC

Keywords: Cognitive cyber-physical systems, integrated closed-loop solutions, security, quality of service, physical layer security, implementation strategies, adaptive responses, system architecture design

4.1 Introduction

The final objective of employing cyber facilities, which includes both software and hardware for monitoring, computation, and interaction, is to proactively track and control the physical surroundings from the cyber to the physical and vice versa. The cyber-physical system (CPS) is an arrangement that tightly connects cyberspace and physical objects [1]. It is now one of the most significant and well-liked software for computers. Electronic and computer technology is going to be present in and essential to a wide range of physical objects and constructions. Cognitive CPSs (CCPSs) have the potential to alter how we engage with the natural world surrounding us, and the Internet has transformed interpersonal communication and made it easier for us to communicate and transact with other humans [2]. The combination of significant developments in network technological advances, programs, and equipment forms the foundation for the Internet's deployment. Similarly, CCPSs may be understood as the combination of management structures, sensors, and embedded technologies. A multitude of technology developments are creating opportunities for CCPS enhancement. As sensors grow smaller and smaller, their cost is dropping. In addition, wireless connectivity has advanced, Internet bandwidth has increased, and new sources of energy are continually becoming more abundant [3]. Computer components are getting fewer shapes and higher capacities at less energy usage. Therefore, in the industries of aerospace, defense, power systems, medical, and travel, the CCPS is also growing to be increasingly challenging. A CCPS may be conceptualized as the application of a computer's rational and quantitative characteristics to monitor and manage the constant and changing features of real-world processes. It is extremely difficult to effectively manage precise mathematical calculations [4]. One challenge that has to be managed is the unpredictability and delay from a discrete-time systems electronic management system to an actual time physical environment. Mistakes and security concerns need to be managed and handled quickly. Other challenges that need to be addressed for the CCPS area to advance are synchronization within an organization and over-complication [5].

To implement precise relationships between cyber and real things, a CCPS frequently uses actuators and sense devices, sometimes referred to as characters or managers in certain situations [6]. Actuators and processors may modify the physical variables, whereas sensors (cyber items) can be employed for tracking the physical surroundings. To illustrate the many ways in which devices such as sensors and controllers might communicate, we will utilize an instance of a windy energy system (Figure 4.1), wherein three different forms of conversations are known to occur [7]. For example, to determine whether to charge or empty the storage device and the

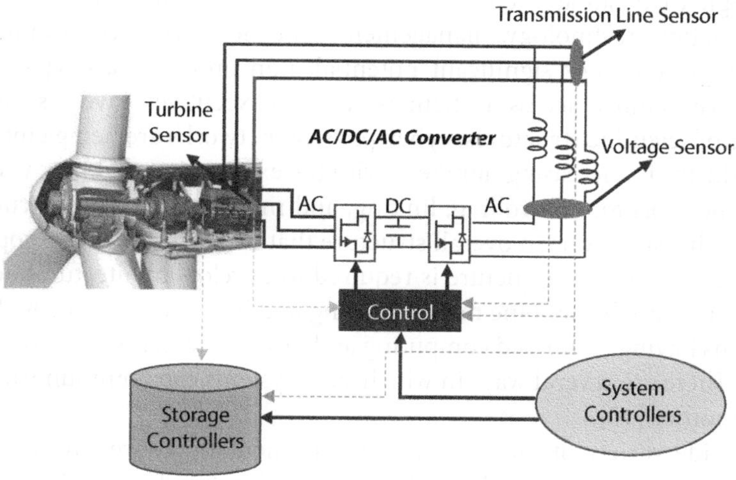

Figure 4.1 CCPS used sensors.

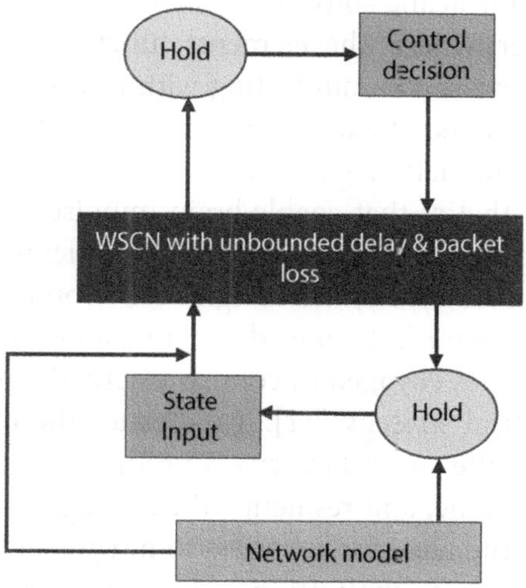

Figure 4.2 CCPS state transition.

amount of energy demand that it should manage, an energy storage controller must collaborate with different controllers shown in Figure 4.2.

A connected control framework with inputs (sensor information) and exports (the control group instructions) may be used to illustrate the interaction between the sensor's information and controllers [8]. Effectively overseeing a firm in the exceptionally competitive and dynamic marketplace of the 21st century requires being able to leverage the most cutting-edge methods and tools accessible while attaining the greatest effectiveness through their suitable combination with more traditional ways. While Information Technology, management, and methods of communication might present very significant potential, non-professionals typically do not have as much access to them as business executives have. As the next phase of scientific structures, cyber-physical networks are being embraced by industry in increasing numbers, with the expectation that they will provide the tools for controlling, linking, and modeling disparate structures [9]. In this situation, an overall structure that can be extended to sophisticated company infrastructure is required to develop architectural designs that can strongly combine manufacturing and business systems. A class of systems having combined computing and physical features is referred to as CPS. There are several ways in which such systems can communicate with one another [10].

A wide variety of multifaceted, environmentally aware, and interconnected machines are produced by the linked networks, which are modified. This type of system has sophisticated elements, such as physical activation, transmission of information, collection of information, and sensors. The mechanical and software elements of cyber-physical networks are intricately intertwined. The elements function at various temporal and geographical levels, communicating with one another in a variety of context-related manners. The development and creation of future aircraft and spacecraft, combination gas-electric cars, fully autonomous urban traveling, and prosthetics that enable brain impulses to regulate material objects are some of the possibilities for study problems. The fourth industrial century, or Industry 4.0, has a significant connection to the CCPS paradigm. Superior manufacturing adaptability and simple, greater participation from all parties engaged in company activities are two advantages of this new industrial strategy [11]. To advance the industrial plan and achieve the goal of the smart factory—a production environment that is flexible, flexible, holonic, and resilient—the strategic requirements in this respect reaffirmed the need for suppliers to integrate expanded capability into the core of business applications. These features might be used for controlling and overseeing modifications and alterations. Toward person conversations with company executives made it abundantly evident that collaborative efforts with suppliers of technology were necessary to guarantee the gradual improvement of operations toward the goal of a smart factory, which would ultimately lead to superior production and durability. Every part of real buildings as well as digital gadgets needs a certain amount of security protection. To guarantee its resilience, a decentralized coordinating layer that is extensible is essential [12]. With Industry 4.0, the CCPS may encompass billions of devices; therefore, a highly scalable interaction between devices is required. By performing trustworthy linkage inferences on a created object-alarm graph, the study in this sector proposed numerous approaches to extract relevant details from a vast quantity of inconsistent information. The following CCPS-related areas of study are crucial to accelerating the evaluation of this novel idea: resilience buildings, architectural components for redundant optimization, and optimization of the sensor network organization. The discipline of intelligent technology study has applications in those areas. The real study focuses on constructing and assessing a large-scale collection of collaboration structures, namely CCPSs, using a method called formal concept analysis [13]. In industrial facilities including power stations, refineries for oil, and manufacturing facilities, decentralized network–based systems are growing more and more common. This kind of technology is made up of a variety of different devices with varying capacities for resources that are networked together via communication infrastructures. CCPS are an innovative model that resulted from the transition of such structures into a cyberspace realm, linking the cyber world of communication and computation with the world of reality [14]. To observe and regulate physical operations, CCPSs integrate communication infrastructure, technological advances in computers, and external systems.

Here, we demonstrate CCPS architecture with yet another civilian case. Figure 4.3 depicts an intelligent water supply infrastructure. Physical elements include storage tanks, standards, and pipelines. This technology allows scientists to monitor water consumption. Additionally, they can forecast where the greatest amount of water will be utilized. Its structure is multi-layered. The real circulation of water, such as in a sink's storage tank, makes up a single layer. This section contains cyberspace things or sensors that relay information about how much and when the liquid will be utilized to upper-level cyber items, including computer systems. This enables the machines to distribute water to the appropriate locations at the appropriate times. It also makes it possible to keep an eye on the water flow's management side. It does this by keeping an eye on how much water is consumed at each home and how much is delivered to that area.

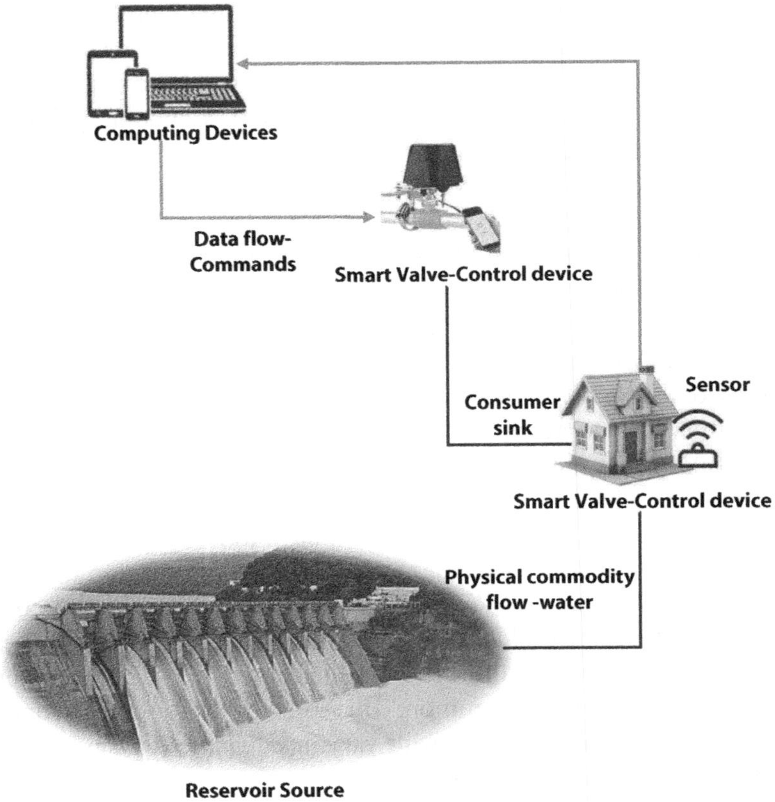

Figure 4.3 CCPS example: water distribution system.

Fewer are going to be transmitted to that portion than what is being utilized if there is a leakage, allowing them to identify the fault or leakage [15].

4.1.1 Problem Statement

Within the field of CCPS, combining cyber and physical elements with cognitive skills offers a viable path toward further advances in technology. Meanwhile, quality-of-service (QoS) limitations and related transmission expenses are taken into account, and the safety of these extremely powerful CCPS becomes a crucial problem. The complex problem of securing CCPS while upholding cost-effectiveness and effectiveness criteria is covered in this section. It draws attention to the characteristics of CCPS and outlines possible dangers to safety while highlighting the necessity of teamwork in overcoming these obstacles. Additionally, this section explores the idea of physical layer security (PLS) solutions as a well-known strategy to increase CCPS's resistance to safety hazards. It is now essential to provide resiliency due to the increasing number and interconnection of physical and cyber systems. To improve flexibility and durability, the section emphasizes the significance of philosophical structures in supporting resilient organizations. Specifically, it focuses on integrating intellectual capacities. Moreover, models that support the comprehension and examination of resiliency in CCPS are covered; these include adaptive reactions, acceptance of faults, and healing processes. The chapter also examines ways to implement for achieving robust CCPS, including topics like making choice computations, networks of sensors, and system architectural planning.

4.1.2 Motivation

The following are the reasons for investigating robust CCPS, listed in key highlights:

Transformative Opportunities: Production, medical care, transportation, and architecture are just a few industries that may undergo innovation if cognitive abilities were integrated into CCPS.
Efficiency and Autonomy: CCPSs are critical for maintaining vital services and infrastructure because they provide previously unheard-of effectiveness, versatility, and independence.
Safety Problems: Cyberattacks, manual alteration, and information breaches are just a few of the many dangers to safety that CCPS are vulnerable to as they get more intricate and networked.
Implications of Compromises: The necessity for robust safeguards is highlighted by the possibility of operational interruption, protection compromising, and violations of confidentiality security compromises in CCPS.
Complexity of Cognitive Capabilities: Adding cognitive capabilities to CCPS adds further levels of complexity and calls for creative solutions to protect against known and unknown dangers.
Improving Flexibility and Resiliency: CCPSs that exhibit resilience have self-healing mechanisms, greater flexibility, and tolerance for errors, enabling them to operate efficiently under challenging circumstances including cyberattacks.
Interdisciplinary Collaboration: To create comprehensive strategies for protecting CCPS while maximizing efficiency and affordability, scholars, professionals, policymakers, and business partners must collaborate across the boundaries of disciplines.

Socio-Economic Progress: By guaranteeing the safety, dependability, and durability of CCPS, everyone may open up new avenues for advancement and creativity in several fields, which will eventually raise living standards and promote economic development.

4.2 Materials and Methods

Redundancy is the capacity of suppliers to have many options; it is the replication of essential parts or operations of an organization. A reliable framework needs redundant parts (physical redundancy) or several configurations for the parts of operating systems (functioning redundancies). Redundancy was originally meant to increase the reliability of systems; however, it can potentially manifest as computational flaws. The scientific literature provides a variety of approaches for handling redundant optimization issues. A heuristic criterion that considers a corresponding rise in dependability against a decrease in effectiveness is presented to determine the point at which redundancies are to be incorporated. Two debugging techniques are proposed as a structure for gathering information and debugging formal requirements for CCPS. The first one looks for incorrect or missing temporal logic specifications without taking the framework into account, whereas the second one may be utilized to analyze responsive needs about system assessment traces. The customer research confirms that numerous subtle mistakes made by specification modelers may be fixed by the debugger structure and that requirements mistakes are a regular occurrence. Redundancy analysis can also help avoid hardware breakdown that is not taken into account during the development process. Redundancy might therefore need to be included in actual systems. Understanding the domain and its implementation contexts can facilitate the unification of data representation and allow for the reusing of components, hence reducing redundant data when agents understand semantics. An ontology for the system's domain is defined to minimize redundant knowledge within the model and streamline the process of interpreting data. Although the redundancy issue has been examined from a variety of angles, our method concentrates on the fundamental proof that is derived from the formal information that is collected through information grouping. To evaluate and intelligently manage the amount of data, navigate through unpredictable settings, and ultimately achieve optimized results, it is now more important than ever to construct mental representations of the systems.

The majority of work on resilience studies the consequences of disturbances using some facet of the theory of networks. Assuming homogeneous nodes is not feasible due to the study of several networks. Structures that operate under this premise are unable to examine certain kinds of systems. Certain research studies have looked at nodes that have the same role but differing capabilities, and they were able to provide a roadmap of CCPS technology enablers for three distinct kinds of networks. These networks are designed to provide robust service selections and to control capabilities including power for processing, preservation, and connectivity.

The durability of multilayer systems has gained interest recently as a means of characterizing heterogeneous networks. There are two techniques to model networks as multiple layers. Several physical layers may make up the network's infrastructure, or it may need assistance from other levels. The idea of independent network evaluations has been presented by the findings of research in this area to emphasize the features that distinguish these connections. By using this research on CCPSs, system planners may examine how a failure in a particular network can affect another and how a tiny percentage of nodes removed from an interdependent network might cause it to fail spectacularly. At crucial nodes, these findings can then direct the distribution of resources. Reliability for decentralized systems may be enhanced by using agent-based approaches, quality of information measurements, and modeling of system subsystems. A self-contained, decentralized, and resistant surveillance apparatus that can adjust and reorganize itself according to the situation is put forth. In this study, monitors are linked to a quality of information measurement, and readings from the sensors are used to estimate variables related to the process.

In the case of a truly global heterogeneity of the system, it might be challenging to represent each system component in addition to the quality of information measures as required by this structure. An agent-based architecture serves as the foundation for a combined diagnostic and management technique that is proposed to guarantee resiliency in terms of effectiveness and reliability. In this study, a conceptual structure with a structure consisting of three layers is proposed, and its features, hardware autonomy, and cognition are also covered. Meanwhile, it could be challenging to apply the proposed clever strategies on wireless nodes or other diverse networked devices. Numerous studies have also examined the issue of resiliency augmentation in wireless sensor networks (WSNs). A WSN system with an effective resistant management structure is proposed. By using a smart and resistant management method to maintain operating normality in the context of wireless interfering situations like frequency jamming or signal blockage, it focuses on the effectiveness of control. Nevertheless, this method ignores the other parts of a CCPS and only considers the WSN portion.

4.3 CCPS Design Challenges

Three characteristics (3S) are included in a robust CCPS layout: (1) stability: the management method must constantly ultimately arrive at a stable decision outcome, regardless of how the surroundings produce noisy and unclear elements; (2) systematizes: the cyber and actual parts must be smoothly combined into a systematic structure; and (3) safety: the framework ought to have the capacity to identify and preventative measures the cyber-physical interactions assaults.

The following four issues need to be resolved to create a CCPS with this level of resilience:

(1) Dependability: A crucial component of any CCPS is reliability. For instance, the intelligent physical world architecture aids in incorporating adaptive behaviors into the CCPS. Greater reliability is a result of flexibility. Here, information derived from raw physical processes is gathered, and a smart computing environment governs the framework. Three domain features apply to A_p when viewed as a black box system: computation, transparency, and programming. Three crucial reliability categories—quality of service, tolerance for errors, and timeliness—can be met using these attributes. The QoS gauges how effectively the system's capabilities are distributed based on the user's current application. The impact of a failure on an organization is measured by fault tolerance. To ensure reliability in the event of failure, certain requirements must be satisfied.

(2) Consistency: To assist with this, the AcmeStudio framework is employed. It produces surroundings for the design of buildings. The structure of the process used to verify consistency is depicted in Figure 4.4. In AcmeStudio, the B_A and network view are contrasted for consistency. The graph morphism plug-in verifies that the system view is consistent. Examine the component-connector graph of the B_A.

(3) Reliability: Program performance and physical needs are, sometimes, at odds. Programs are virtually 100% reliable because they execute the same set of instructions in the same order every single time they are performed. But time is just as important to mechanical structures as operation, and software for computers can have timing errors. This mismatch puts CCPSs at risk by creating a great deal of

ambiguity and unpredictability. Uncertainties in machines may be addressed in two main ways: either employ techniques to rectify mistakes brought about by faulty dependability in the electrical systems or minimize unpredictability of every part to the point where dependability is extremely near to 100%. To explain the dynamics of the CCPS time advancement, researchers might, for instance, use a hidden Markov model or a regression analysis framework. As a result, using the historical state developments, researchers can forecast the structure's state for the next phase.

(4) Cyber-Physical Mismatch: In contrast, these dynamics are better described as a succession of events without time meaning in the cyber world. The challenge may be analyzed using two main methods: cyberizing physical systems (C_tP), which involve imposing cyber features and interactions on an actual system, and physicalizing the cyber (P_tC), which involves representing the program and cyber elements interactively in real time. Cyber-physical coupling security (CPS): A CCPS must withstand both intentional and accidental failures. In particular, we are going to address how we may construct a robust CCPS by utilizing a suitable management model and matching safety approaches. From the standpoint of control and surveillance safety, physical structures in CCPS are vulnerable to cyber security flaws (Figure 4.4). Here are a few instances of CCPS assaults: In 2008, a senior CIA analyst reported that cyber intrusions had compromised certain critical infrastructure systems, underscoring the vulnerability of these systems to potential attacks. Strengthening cybersecurity protocols, monitoring network activities, and enhancing encryption methods are essential steps to mitigate such risks.

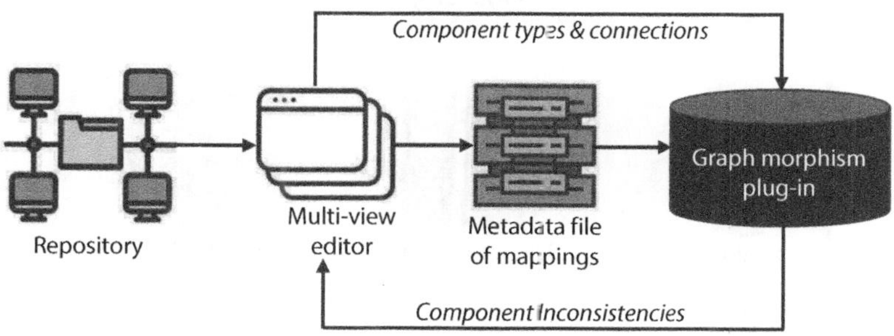

Figure 4.4 Flow of design checking using consistency.

To provide complete CCPS protection, people might not be able to employ standard, all-purpose internet safety techniques. This is because the majority of CCPS safety measures require tight integration with the actual manufacturing control elements that underpin them. For instance, an implantable medical device (IMD), a type of CCPS, can be placed in the body to perform both cyber-to-physical organ regulation and physical-to-cyber clinical monitoring. Pacemakers, insulin pumps, neuron stimulators, and other devices are examples of common IMDs. A wireless energy charging assault on an IMD is a serious problem because it can lead to the IMD overheating if the perpetrator knows the coil resonant frequencies. Because transfers of energy differ greatly from information transport, it makes no sense to secure the electrical charging waves using

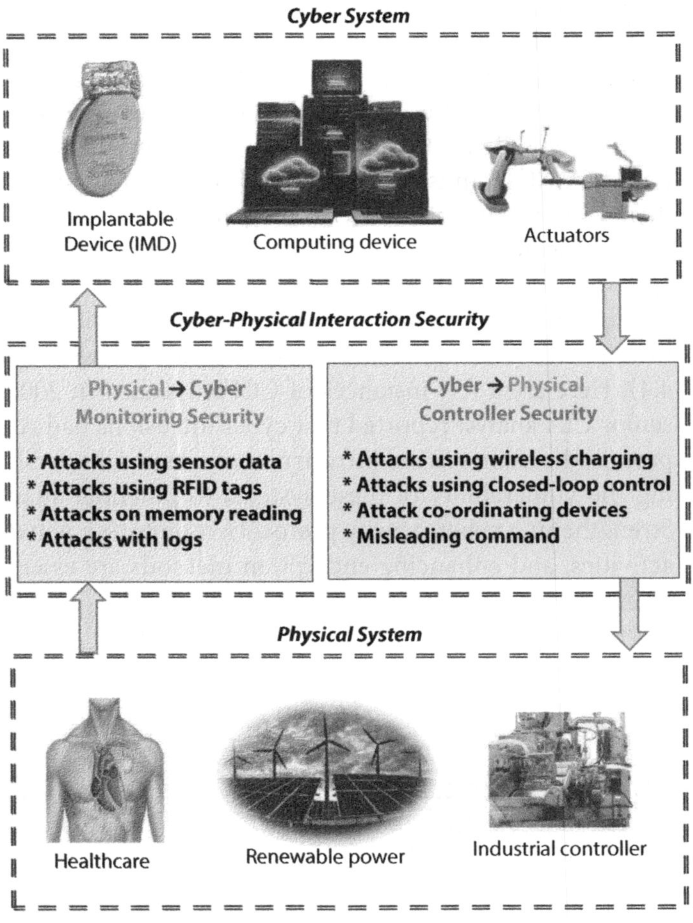

Figure 4.5 CCPS security perspective.

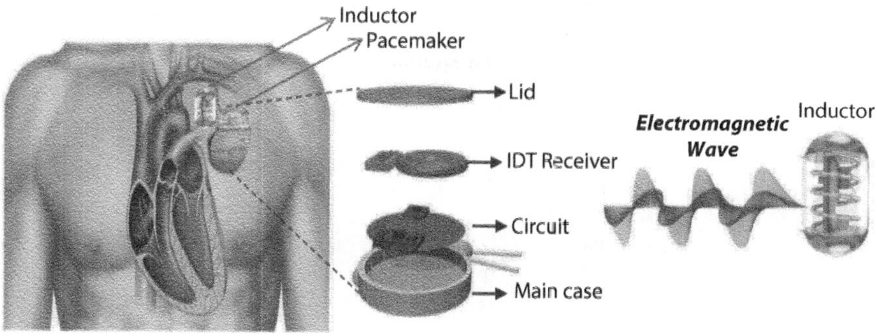

Figure 4.6 Wireless IMD power charge.

traditional cryptographies (Figure 4.5). To address the aforementioned problem, researchers might employ a CCPS-oriented safety approach (Figure 4.6): controlling the physical item (circuit capacitors) using a cyber-strategy (chaotic maps) prevents an adversary from figuring out the energy charging resonance speed that subtly changes quantities.

4.4 Cyber-Physical Systems Principles and Paradigms

Computational and mechanical operations are integrated into CPSs. Such systems aim to integrate real-world physical items with ubiquitous computer and communication infrastructures. CCPS completes the current study to understand the systems independently by focusing on the real relationship that exists between human beings and electronic components. Industry 4.0 is an additional significant emerging framework that specifically considers the following: creative machines and robots, such as surrounding understanding, adaptable oversight, and human–robot communication; massive information; the network quality of service; energy conservation and decentralization; virtual industrial development, concerning the idea of "virtual plants and goods"; value networking, which seeks to achieve electronic integration along the entire supply chain and through various production procedures; and virtual the industrial revolution. Within this framework, physical procedure management within embedded systems might be considered a subset of the broader concept of CCPS.

An organization is defined as an intricate framework consisting of several interconnected constituent structures with which everyone contributes human effort that is in a state of reasonably stable equilibrium. The

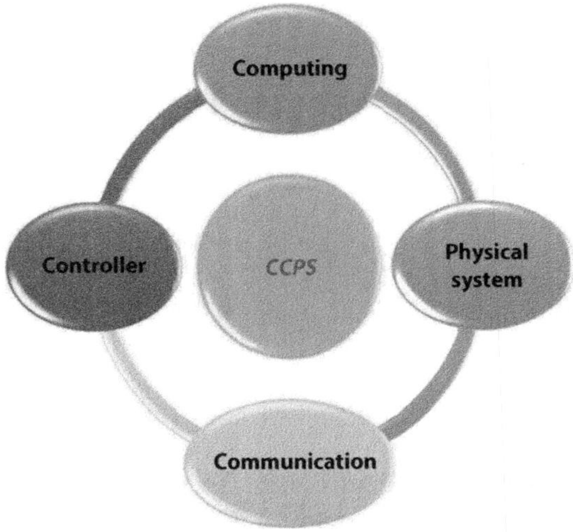

Figure 4.7 CCPS as a multidisciplinary view.

Smart Cyber Enterprise can stand for the future wave of businesses in this setting. The following version of sophisticated interconnected devices, known as intelligent CPSs (ICPSs), displays dispersed cognition. Complex cyber-physical networks can be developed by the integration of various feedback loops between the Internet of Things (IoT) and the Internet of Services. Figure 4.7 illustrates how CCPS develops from intricate relationships between embedded technologies (e.g., smart intersections in particular, networks of communications, and controllers on board cars), which are built on connectivity and collaboration and incorporate human–technology engagement in application procedures. Another crucial aspect that must be considered is the interaction among the system's components. A real-time network of communications that can ensure system performance latencies and speeds is necessary for cyber-physical organizations. Various management goals can be accomplished simultaneously by forming various loops of control inside the framework and architecture of the communication system. Two key problems brought on by the distributed character of CCPS are the locations of the components and the temporal separation between individuals engaged in the management loops.

From a technological perspective, the following are some commonly known features of CCPS:

Network Complexity: Because there are so many dispersed nodes in a typical CCPS, the network is frequently enormous. Capacity limitations: Embedded electronics have limitations regarding energy consumption, connectivity, speed through, productivity, etc.

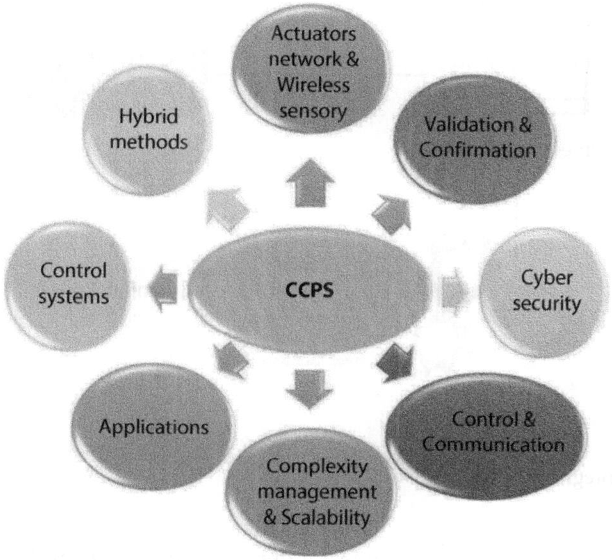

Figure 4.8 CCPS main components.

- Hybrid Transport and Huge Information: A lot of information is produced because there are many sensors and networks;
- Uncertainty: In CCPS, a variety of variables can lead to unpredictability, including mistakes in sensor evaluations, computer modeling programs, wireless connectivity dependability, and network architecture modifications;
- The difficulties in structure and behavior make it more difficult to analyze, evaluate create, verify, and apply CCPS.

Composition structures and more automatic or organized methods for demonstrating connectedness must be the foundation for subsequent technologies. The intricacy and diversity of CCPS need the use of specialized techniques and instruments to confirm and validate the accuracy of the overall system architecture. Figure 4.8 provides an overview of all the elements related to this new paradigm.

4.4.1 CCPS Conceptual Framework

Adopting concepts from successful corporate structures serves as a foundation for the concept framework's creation. To address inherent disintegration and variability and enable an innovative method for promoting

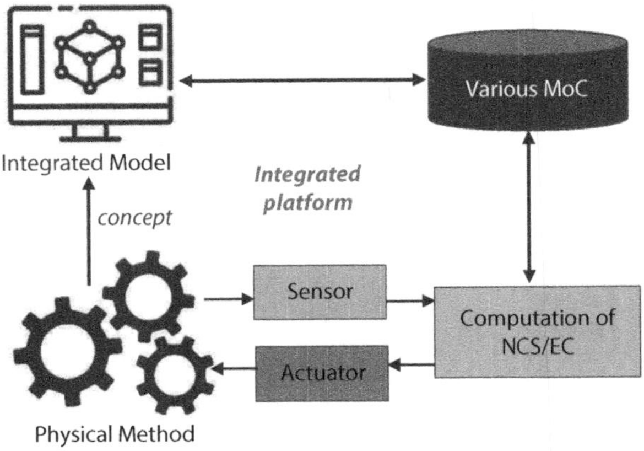

Figure 4.9 Integration of all levels.

numerous uses, the authors suggest a generic clever comprehensive structure founded on the IoT idea. The proposed platform offers the consumer a digital, adaptable environment filled with features corresponding to gadgets, integrated systems, connected control networks, and intelligent objects. To achieve its objectives, the system in question must take into account the primary factors of variability, interoperability, and structure across several conceptualization levels of difficulty, including structures, software structures, and control levels. Multi-domain modeling that has been evaluated at different levels of topologies and conceptualization, in addition to multi-scale controllers incorporated into connected control networks, should all be merged at the degree of abstraction. To accomplish the functionality needed by the company strategy envisioned at the level of abstraction, intelligent items and systems are going to be connected at the level of functionality (Figure 4.9).

The combination of these layers using the programming languages, methods, and techniques that will enable the platform's capabilities to facilitate application creation, performance evaluation, and validation will be the most challenging part. The platform's framework is going to include an architectural design space and platform-wide assets in the library describing parts, structure regulations, conceptualization regulations, improvement regulations, and interactions that determine legal relationships because it will need to take variation into account, which includes various mathematical representations, both software and hardware, analog and electronic, the internet and physiological, and incorporating various intelligent objects. The interconnections and methods of communication will turn out to be essential assets from this perspective. Classification, combination searching, and focused concentration are examples of generalized operations that will intelligently handle the system's diverse elements' complexities and variety. It will mostly operate at the level of abstraction, outlining several stages of improvement from the first specification to the last execution. Modeling conversations, features, and execution needs will be made possible in this fashion, maintaining consistency across model elements and avoiding model element misconnection. In addition to managing the system's needs, the platform will be able to enhance the quality and flexibility of model assessment by taking complexity and duration into account. Co-designing mechanical structures and control devices, coordinating connected computational power with physical systems while taking time into account, and parallelism in interconnected, dispersed cognitive and physical networks are additional challenges that need to be resolved.

4.4.2 CCPS Modeling

Speed and efficiency are two non-functional characteristics of CCPS design that must be taken into consideration in addition to functionality considerations like behavior and accuracy. A theory of timed actors is introduced; it stands in contrast to the traditional behavioral and operational enhancements that rely on limiting behavior sets. Improvement of this framework enables time-deterministic abstract concepts, which lowers complications and increases performance. It demonstrates how this approach might be applied to improve CCPSs' duration and effectiveness. In creating these expansive and complicated structures, abstractions and composition are two essential elements. The interface concept is one of those theories that emphasize simultaneous and dynamic behavior. Process networks along with information circulation, two player-oriented theories of computing, serve as inspiration for the interactions, which are referred to as player interactions. On their result ports, players produce tokens, and, on their communication ports, they consume currencies. The relationships between the inputs and the outcomes sequencing of separate occurrences that take place along a certain time axis are known as activities. The fact that this approach permits deterministic representations of non-deterministic processes makes it intriguing. It is costly or hard to simulate correctly for a variety of causes, including significant implementation variation, communications latency, variable planning, and other factors. Conversely, time-deterministic systems are better suited for establishing analytic limits and incur less from information exploding issues.

4.4.3 Other Modeling Issues in CCPS

We cannot accurately anticipate the potential future condition of a program using present popular techniques for programming based on the original code, the application's beginning state, and the length of time that has passed. The design of the CCPS becomes challenging when such a program is included in anatomical structures that have mechanical characteristics. Moreover, discrepancies between the management program and the real plant's dynamics might result in several mistakes that could have disastrous effects on the overall system. Modern cyber techniques like CPU education planning, machine memory structures, storage garbage disposal, multi-thread manufacturing, social media, and recyclable element libraries—which refrain from displaying historical characteristics on their interfaces—introduce massive chronological variation, even though CPUs are now sufficiently fast to regulate numerous physical things. Whereas physical operations must be performed at the appropriate moment, CCPS does not rely on rapid computing. It is difficult to integrate physical and digital operations. Hybrid system concepts have emerged as a result of this difficulty. Nevertheless, the mixing of automatons in comparatively fundamental structures with conventional differential equations has hindered the advancement of hybrid systems concepts.

The theory of control serves as the foundation for the homogeneous concept of time in these frameworks. In such structures, time (t) is simultaneously accessible to every system component. By integrating control theories with general concepts, various dynamical structures—such as interconnected oscillators and mobile or combinatory sensors—can be characterized. However, many of these dynamical structures lack a uniform time model that governs the motion of objects.

A Cyber-Physical Control System (CCPS) is created by combining mechanical and mathematical operations. Computational processes utilize computer and networking technologies to monitor and regulate physical procedures, relying on feedback control loops to achieve this goal. The mathematical aspect of the process is governed by signals received from these feedback loops. Consequently, based on calculations and feedback messages, the control device dynamically adjusts the system, and this process repeats continuously.

Therefore, an architect must have a deep understanding of the evolving dynamics of computer systems, software, and the physical processes requiring management. A hybrid framework emerges when the actual operations of a CCPS are represented as continuous-time models of dynamical behaviors and computational processes. Various programs are available for modeling evolving systems.

An advanced version of Model-Driven Development (MDD) is Model-Integrated Computing (MIC). It is a methodology and toolset designed for the structured organization, evaluation, modification, and representation of different aspects of software development throughout its lifecycle. MIC employs metaprogramming, domain-specific modeling (DSM), and model transformations.

4.5 Conclusions and Future Enhancements

To sum up, the design of CCPSs is a complex process that involves combining cyber-physical components, mental processes, and rigorous safety standards. As this investigation progresses, it becomes clear that CCPS development will not be effective until several critical issues are resolved. It becomes clear that interdisciplinary cooperation is essential, requiring the combination of knowledge from several domains, such as science and technology, engineering, neurology, and psychology. Crafting unified cognition structures, methods, and interactions that smoothly integrate cyber and physical elements requires teamwork. Furthermore, establishing robust safety precautions to defend against a variety of dangers, including physical invasions, online assaults, and information breaches, is crucial to the design of CCPS. The intricacy of CCPS is further highlighted by real-time reactivity and flexibility, which need flexible methods and structures able to quickly adjust to changing situations and growing scales. A human-centric strategy is also necessary, putting customer service, accessibility, and trust first to guarantee CCPS's broad acceptance and efficacy across a variety of fields. Going forward, overcoming these obstacles and realizing the revolutionary potential of CCPS to better enhance society and people's quality of life will need ongoing study, creativity, and cooperation.

4.5.1 Future Enhancements

Several approaches to improving CCPS are presented, motivated by the necessity to tackle persistent issues and seize new chances. The following are some possible areas to improve in the future:

Higher-Order Cognitive Architectures: Create more complex mental frameworks that simulate learning, thinking, and making decisions seen in humans. Utilize developments related to cognitive research, neural networks, and computational intelligence to build CCPS that are more intelligent, adaptive, and autonomous. Modern safety measures and resiliency tactics should be incorporated into CCPS design to guard against emerging cyber threats and maintain system stability. This is known as safe and resilient development. To improve safety and resistance to both physical and electronic digital assaults, incorporate self-healing processes, systems for detecting intrusions, and sophisticated methods of encryption. Real-time Adaptive Technologies: These systems improve CCPS by allowing quick responses to dynamic system motion, interactions between users, and changing environmental conditions. Provide continuously adjustable methods and structures that maximize energy savings, utilization of resources, and efficiency in unpredictable and changing contexts.

Approaches that are Scalable and Interoperability: Create CCPS architecture that is both expandable and interoperability so they can be easily integrated with the current cyber-physical network and expanded upon in the future. Provide standardized communications structures, procedures, and connectors to promote cooperation and compatibility among various CCPS systems and domains. Human-Centric Design: To improve accessibility, customer satisfaction, and trust in CCPS, pay attention to human-centric design concepts. Design user-friendly panels, clear processes for making decisions, and intuitive interfaces that encourage customer adoption and embrace by incorporating user input, evaluation of usability, and psychological assessment. Ethical and Regulatory Considerations: To guarantee the responsible and ethical use of cognitive technologies, address ethical and regulatory concerns in the design, implementation, and operation of CCPS. Establish policies, benchmarks, and oversight structures that advance equity, responsibility, and openness in the creation and application of CCPS.

Interdisciplinarity in Cooperation: To drive innovation and development in CCPS, encourage information exchange and cross-disciplinary cooperation among researchers, industry practitioners, policymakers, and stakeholders. Promote cooperation across many fields, such as psychology, policy, computer science, and engineering and ethics to tackle intricate problems and investigate novel prospects in the creation and implementation of computer-aided perception systems.

Fully realize the potential of CCPS to transform several industries, including healthcare, infrastructure, transportation, and manufacturing, and to raise people's quality of life on a global scale. This can be achieved by pursuing these future improvements.

References

1. Alvarez-Alvarado, M.S., Apolo-Tinoco, C., Ramirez-Prado, M.J., Alban-Chacón, F.E., Pico, N., Aviles-Cedeno, J., Rengifo, J., Cyber-physical power systems: A comprehensive review about technologies drivers, standards, and future perspectives. *Comput. Electr. Eng.*, *116*, 109149, 2024.
2. Damm, W., Hess, D., Schweda, M., Sztipanovits, J., Bengler, K., Biebl, B., Veith, E., A Reference Architecture of Human Cyber-Physical Systems–Part I: Fundamental Concepts. *ACM Trans. Cyber-Phys. Syst.*, *8*, 1, 1–32, 2024.
3. Parthiban, L., Latchoumi, T.P., Balamurugan, K., Raja, K., Parthiban, R., Cognitive Computing for the Internet of Medical Things, in: *Integrating Blockchain and Artificial Intelligence for Industry 4.0 Innovations*, pp. 85–100, Springer International Publishing, Cham, 2023.
4. Liang, Q., Zhao, S., Zhang, J., Deng, H., Damm, W., Hess, D., Forrest, L., Cyber-physical systems. *ACM Trans.*, *8*, 1, 2024.
5. Kamran, Q. and Becker, M., The Design of the Cyberphysical Navigator Model as a Sustainable Framework Enhancing Organisational Resilience, in: *Building the Future with Human Resource Management*, pp. 95–125, Springer International Publishing, Cham, 2024.
6. Banerjee, S., Jesubalan, N.G., Kulkarni, A., Agarwal, A., Rathore, A.S., Developing cyber-physical system and digital twin for smart manufacturing: Methodology and case study of continuous clarification. *J. Ind. Inf. Integr.*, *38*, 100577, 2024.
7. Latchoumi, T.P., Parthiban, L., Balamurugan, K., Raja, K., Vijayaraj, J., Parthiban, R., A Framework for Low Energy Application Devices Using Blockchain-Enabled IoT in WSNs, in: *Integrating Blockchain and Artificial Intelligence for Industry 4.0 Innovations*, pp. 121–132, Springer International Publishing, Cham, 2023.
8. Qi, W., Chen, C.H., Niu, T., Lyu, S., Sun, S., A multisensory Interaction Framework for Human-Cyber–Physical System based on Graph Convolutional Networks. *Adv. Eng. Inf.*, *61*, 102482, 2024.
9. Yuan, H., Yuan, Y., Zhong, Y., Xia, Y., Incomplete Information-Based Resilient Strategy Design for Cyber-Physical Systems Under Stochastic Communication Protocol. *IEEE Trans. Ind. Electron.*, 2024.
10. Halder, S., Afsari, K., Akanmu, A., A Robotic Cyber-Physical System for Automated Reality Capture and Visualization in Construction Progress Monitoring, 2024, arXiv preprint arXiv:2402.07034.
11. García, S.N.M., Sánchez-Cabrera, A., Schiavone, E., Skarmeta, A., Integrating the manufacturer usage description standard in the modelling of cyber–physical systems. *Comput. Stand. Interfaces*, *87*, 103777, 2024.
12. Balamurugan, K., Latchoumi, T.P., Satla, S., Machining Studies on AlSi7+ 63% SiC Composite Using Machine Learning Technique. In. *Met. Matrix Compos.*, 139–166, 2023.

13. Sood, V.M., Singh, Y., Bhargava, B., Narang, S.K. (Eds.), *Intelligent Security Solutions for Cyber-Physical Systems*, Chapman and Hall/CRC, an imprint of CRC Press, Boca Raton, FL, USA, 2024.
14. Piardi, L., Leitão, P., Queiroz, J., Pontes, J., Role of digital technologies to enhance the human integration in industrial cyber–physical systems. *Annu. Rev. Control*, *57*, 100934, 2024.
15. Balogun, B.F., Tripathi, K., Tiwari, S., JS, S.M., Tyagi, A.K., Original Research Article A blockchain-based deep learning approach for cyber security in next-generation medical cyber-physical systems. *J. Auton. Intell.*, *7*, 5, 2024.

5

Cognitive Cyber-Physical Security Challenges, Issues, and Recent Trends Over IoT

Chinnaraj Govindasamy

Department of Computer Science and Engineering, Saveetha School of Engineering, Saveetha Institute of Medical and Technical Sciences, Chennai, Tamil Nadu, India

Abstract

The main goal of current Internet of Things (IoT) research is to determine how to make common devices capable of autonomously seeing, hearing, and smelling their surroundings. These objects may be linked in order to share their observations. With the ability to adjust to changes more quickly than artificial intelligence (AI), human intelligence is regarded as superior to AI. AI systems are in high demand in the modern era due to a mounting quantity of data that is becoming difficult for mankind to analyze. These AI systems still are not capable of managing multiple tasks, mindfulness, social abilities, or quicker adaptation. The problems, concerns, and current developments in cognitive cyber-physical security over IoT networks are examined further in the upcoming chapter. As more and more devices become connected, it is imperative to take strong security precautions. The particular security issues raised by IoT environments—such as data privacy, scalability, resilience, and interoperability to cyberattacks—are examined in this chapter. Additionally, it looks into the newest advances in cognitive computing methods including the processing of natural languages, machine learning, and deep learning and how they might be used to improve cybersecurity in IoT-enabled cyber-physical systems. Through the examination of current obstacles and the application of new developments in cognitive computing, this study seeks to offer guidance for the creation of secure solutions for IoT networks.

Email: cgovindcs@gmail.com

K. Ananthajothi, S. N. Sangeethaa, D. Divya, S. Balamurugan and Shen-Lung Peng (eds.) Securing Cyber-Physical Systems: Fundamentals, Applications and Challenges, (87–108) © 2025 Scrivener Publishing LLC

***Keywords*:** Cognitive computing, cyber-physical systems, IoT, complexity management, real-time threat detection, data security, scalability, heterogeneity

5.1 Introduction

Dynamic technological advancements in several domains, such as nanotechnology and wireless sensors, are essential to the growth of the Internet of Things (IoT). Global efforts have been made over the past 10 years to assist in advancing such revolutionary developments from concepts to specific outcomes or applications by the research community, suppliers of services, operators of networks, standard development companies, and others. In a technical sense, the majority of emphasis has been directed toward areas like networking, computing, and communication, among other things, all of that are highly significant subjects [1]. Contend that in the absence of broad cognitive capability, IoT feels similar to an ungainly stegosaurus—all muscle, with no intellect. IoT must be equipped with high-level intelligence and cognitive capabilities to unlock its full potential and effectively address persistent challenges.

Furthermore, a study on current market research shows that the number of machine devices deployed globally is expected to reach 75.4 billion by 2025, demonstrating the increasing maturity, dependability, and widespread adoption of these technologies. The production procedure will be entirely automated in Industry 4.0, with no manual involvement required. This means that response time, network latency, and dependability are very important needs. In order to make decisions that are as precise and timely as feasible, technology for data transmission and decision-making must be optimized [2].

IoT, which allows for the interconnection of anything, anywhere, at any time, has recently become a very serious research field. Unexpected amounts of gadgets for user applications—such as mobile gadgets, household items, and transportation—have been connected through the use of IoT. A few examples of consumer apps that can provide users with comfort, productivity, and information that will assist consumers manage their time and assets more efficiently are smart homes, smart cities, smart grids, and smart transportation [3]. Industry 4.0, which extends technology, aims to apply IoT to production. This has the ability to greatly increase industrial factories' and plants' intelligence, performance, effectiveness, and security [4].

The functioning, linkages, and knowledge of industrial systems are made possible by the control, networking, and computing infrastructures that comprise cyber systems. Production and automation systems that use machinery to carry out specific generation and automation activities are known as physical systems [5]. Control mechanisms are essential to IoT because they manage a vast array of machinery, including detectors, actuators, and tools. For a variety of distributed operations in industrial systems, networking technologies provide for the prompt transfer of data and control signals. Computing systems offer the statistical framework required to facilitate the rapid acquisition, storing, data analyzation, and data process in a versatile, extremely dependable, and effective way. It should be noted that machine learning can be used to every connected device. At last, the automation and production processes make up the physical components [6].

The number of systems that combine digital (cyber) systems with the real environment has significantly increased due to advancements in digital electronics; these systems are referred to as cyber-physical systems (CPSs) [7]. Consideration of special difficulties and intricate functional, reliability, and performance criteria necessitates a great deal of thinking in the design of CPS. The essential issue formulations, system-level needs, and emerging challenges in CPS design have all been covered in a number of chapters. The CPS concept is introduced, and research directions for CPS design are outlined. In particular, this chapter highlights the shortcomings of conventional separation sections, the requirement for consistent timing actions, and the absence of spatial concepts in current programming language models for the construction of CPS. CPS systemic elements from the perspectives of science and the impact on society are discussed. In order to integrate cyber systems with physical systems, two methods are proposed: cyberizing the physical and physicalizing the cyber [8].

Furthermore, as illustrated in Figure 5.1, Industrial Internet of Things (I-IoT) might be conceptualized as a triple-layered architecture. The material layer, program layer, and transmission layer comprise the three tier structure as seen from the perspective of industrial systems [9]. Smart supply chains, smart factories, smart plants, and other applications in industry make up the application layer. These smart industrial applications make use of a wide range of actuators and sensors to provide precise control, prompt surveillance, and effective administration.

The amalgamation of many networks for communications, including 5G, machine-to-machine (M2M), software-defined networking (SDN), wireless sensor and actuator networks, and others, is known as the communication layer. In order to facilitate the integration of a significant number of sensors as well as actuators in smart industrial applications, a range of network approaches will be required. Ultimately, the material layer is made

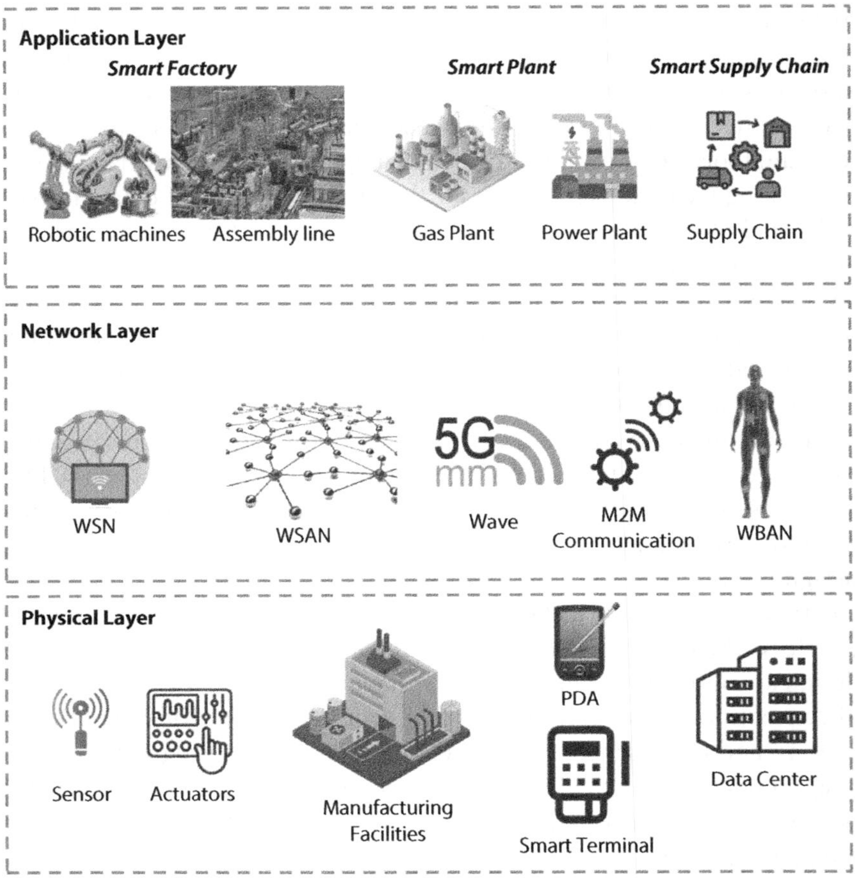

Figure 5.1 IoT system architecture.

up of various commonly used physical components, including industrial production and automation-related items like actuators, sensors, production machinery, facility utilities, and other items [10].

I-IoT is followed by the different industrial applications in the physical system (left), including predictive analytics (PA) and fault analysis (FA). A substantial quantity of info will be produced from various gadgets and instruments at every stage of the production lifecycle. Systems for computing, networking, and control are crucial to the integration and interconnection of parts and physical systems. They also carry out control and monitoring tasks that ensure the smooth operation of physical systems [11].

The flow of cyber-physical systems (CCPS) with Industrial Internet of Things (I-IoT) involves the integration of physical devices, sensors,

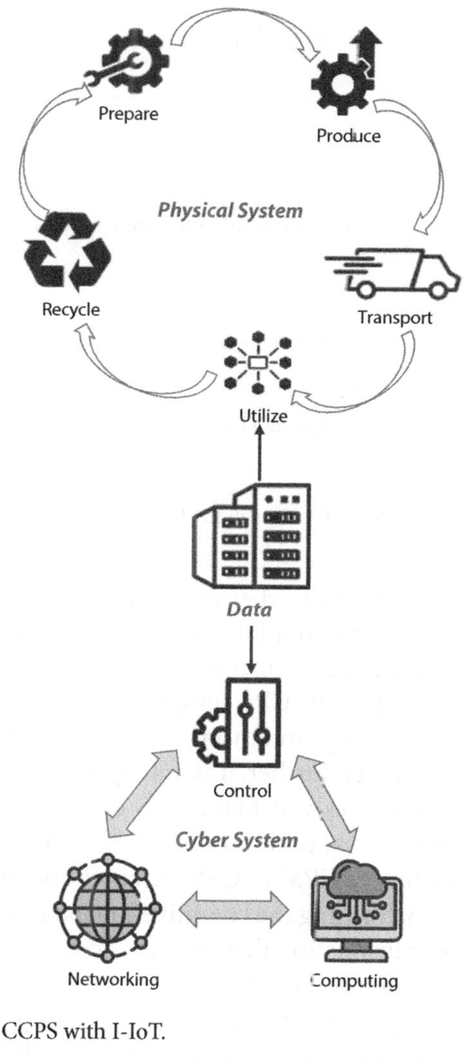

Figure 5.2 Flow of CCPS with I-IoT.

and computational elements to optimize industrial processes (Figure 5.2). It starts with sensors collecting real-time data from the physical system, which is then communicated via networks for further analysis. Edge computing may pre-process the data to reduce latency. The data is stored in cloud systems where advanced analytics, including predictive analytics (PA) and fault analysis (FA), are applied. This leads to automated decision-making and control actions, enhancing efficiency, performance, and predictive maintenance. Continuous feedback loops ensure system optimization and adaptation.

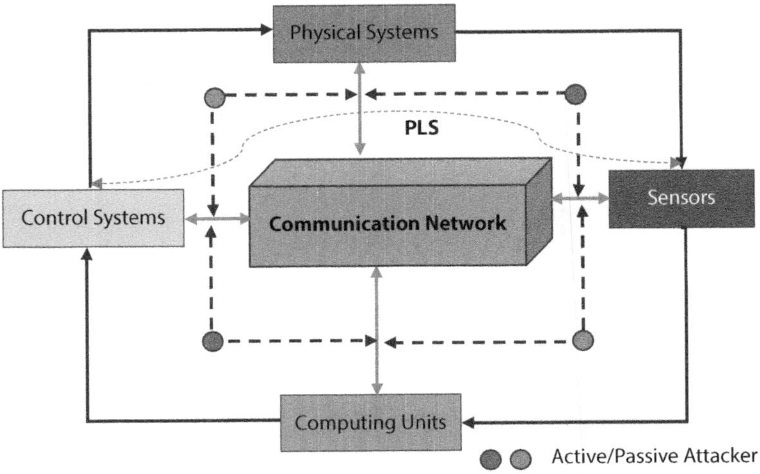

Figure 5.3 Layered architecture of CCPS using IoT.

A closed-loop integration of cyber and physical components results in a CPS offers comprehensive solutions for a range of applications shown in Figure 5.3. There are unique functional needs and limitations for each CPS application. Consequently, CPS components and apps become available and flexible for evolving circumstances at any moment regardless of the location. Going one step further, it is anticipated that the introduction of 6G's cognitive capabilities will make CPS even more responsive. The primary purpose of these skills is to establish concepts for resource allocation. The term "cognitive CPS" (CCPS) refers to the integration of cognitive radios with CPS, forming the cognitive capabilities to gather data on frequency supply or transmission demands to increase the efficiency [12].

Due to its open structure, wireless communication environments are vulnerable to wide-ranging cyberattacks that originate in the CCPS's physical layer. Given the diversity of cognitive qualities, such breaches have the ability to gather or manipulate sensed data that might lead to the termination of network-enabled mechanical heart pacing or a nuclear power plant disaster. Consequently, in order to ensure CCPS resilience, physical layer security is a prerequisite [13].

Because there is an association among the quality of service (QoS) and security, they ought to be assessed jointly for total consumer happiness. QoS and CPS security needs are not concurrently considered in many research in the literature. A utility model built around safety and standard of service is put out by [14]. A model that trades off privacy and performance and suggests a flexible strategy for varying privacy needs was examined.

Conventional safety precautions are discussed along with any potential costs to the system architecture. Despite the fact that these projects link the safety and standard of service paradigms, they do not cover all of the characteristics that make up CCPS. In particular, the cognitive capacity of CCPS can potentially impart environmental awareness concerning the perceived degree of security risk [15].

5.1.1 From IoT to CCPS-IoT

Unfortunately, a large number of IoT applications currently in use still heavily rely on cognitive processing by humans. One of the main purposes of this study is to establish the concept of the "cognitive IoT," in which common things operate as agents and communicate with the social networks or/and physical world with the least amount of human interaction.

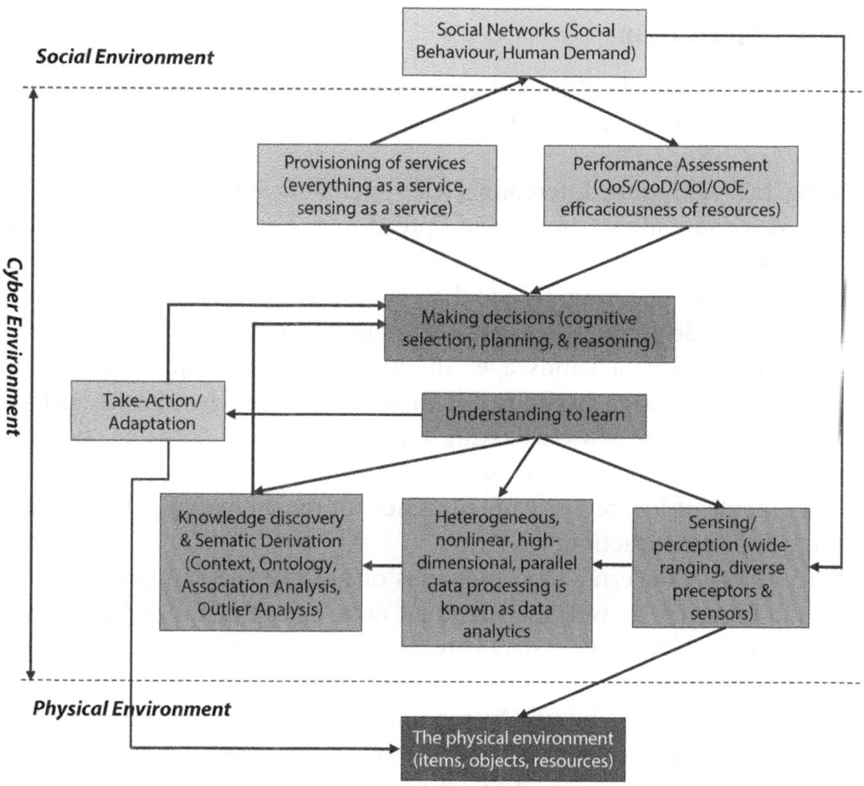

Figure 5.4 Framework of iCCPS–I-IoT.

5.1.2 Fundamental Cognitive Tasks

The Cognitive Internet of Things (CIoT) concept is shown in Figure 5.4. In general, CIoT functions as a direct link between the social and physical worlds, bringing together social behavior, human demand, and other elements to produce.

- The perceptors in the detecting control layer process incoming stimuli to detect their surroundings and relay their findings to the higher layer. Actuators then use the surroundings to operate the perceptors. The detection control layer is directly interfaced with the physical world.
- The sensing data is efficiently analyzed by the data-semantic-knowledge layer to produce relevant semantic and knowledge.

5.2 Motivation and Challenges

5.2.1 Motivation

Investigating the difficulties, concerns, and current developments in CCPS related to the IoT is motivated by a number of important aspects.

Rising IoT Adoption: Interconnected systems have multiplied exponentially as a consequence of the widespread use of IoT gadgets throughout a variety of industries, which involves producing, transporting, medical care, and urban planning. Due to their widespread use, these intricate ecosystems provide privacy problems that require a better comprehension.
Cybersecurity Threat Landscape: The increasing interconnectedness and ubiquity of IoT devices expose them to increased cyberattacks surface. Cybercriminals are always looking for ways to break into IoT systems, steal confidential information, or interfere with vital functions. Protecting deployments of IoT requires an awareness of these changing dangers and taking appropriate action.
Data Privacy Concerns: Large volumes of sensitive data, including operational, financial, as well as individual data, are gathered and processed by IoT devices. Improving data privacy safeguards and reducing the likelihood of privacy violations can both benefit from cognitive techniques.
Complexity and Scalability: Overcoming the intricacy and expandability of IoT networks presents formidable obstacles. Implementing efficient safety measures gets more difficult with a variety of devices, protocols,

and communication networks. Scalability issues can be resolved by using cognitive approaches, which have the ability to automate security duties, evaluate massive amounts of data in real time, and adapt to changing IoT settings.

Regulatory Compliance: IoT-operating firms have to abide by strict regulations, including general data protection regulation (GDPR), health insurance portability and accountability act (HIPAA), and industry-specific guidelines. Adherence to these requirements demands strong security protocols in order to safeguard confidential information and guarantee responsibility. Firms are able to accomplish and sustain legal compliance with the help of CCPS systems.

Innovation and Advancement: Using cognitive technology in cyber-physical security creates opportunities for growth and creativity. Firms may create proactive safety protocols, foresee emerging dangers, and improve incident response capabilities by utilizing machine learning, artificial intelligence (AI), and predictive analytics. This encourages the IoT security framework resiliency and ongoing advancement.

The primary drivers for investigating CCPS issues related to the IoT are to protect networked systems, maintain confidentiality of data, guarantee regulatory compliance, and promote innovation in order to efficiently handle increasing cybersecurity risks.

5.2.2 Challenges

In the backdrop of the IoT, these are undoubtedly a few of the major difficulties concerning CCPS shown in Figure 5.5.

Heterogeneity of Devices and Protocols: IoT ecosystems are made up of a wide variety of gadgets with different functionalities, designs, and protocols for connectivity. Considering this variety, connecting cognitive security mechanisms presents compatibility and standards problems.

Data Volume and Velocity: IoT gadgets produce enormous volumes of information quickly. Advances in cognitive computing techniques and scalable infrastructure are needed to handle and evaluate this data in real time to identify irregularities and safety concerns.

Resource Constraints: A lot of IoT gadgets have constrained computing resources, like memory, processing speed, and energy. It is quite difficult to set up cognitive security algorithms on machines with limited resources and still retain efficiency and effectiveness.

Privacy Preservation: Conclusions for cognitive security can examine private information gathered by IoT devices, which raises privacy and confidentiality issues. Maintaining user trust and regulatory compliance requires striking a balance between the necessity for efficient safety precautions and maintaining privacy obligations.
Threats and Vulnerabilities in Security: Programming errors, incorrect setups, and unsecured channels of interaction are just a few of the safety flaws that can affect IoT devices. IoT devices are also more open to attacks because of their interconnectedness, which increases the likelihood of falling victim to ransomware, malware, and denial-of-service (DoS) attacks, among other cyber threats.
Adversarial Attacks and Threat Intelligence: The methods used by "bad actors" to exploit vulnerabilities in IoT systems are constantly evolving. Proactive defense tactics and strong threat intelligence methods are necessary for identifying and thwarting adversarial assaults, such as insider dangers and zero-day breaches.
Complexity and Scalability: Numerous dynamic, complicated settings with a vast number of networked gadgets and services are common to IoT implementations. One major problem is scaling cognitive security solutions to fit the size and complexity of IoT environments while maintaining manageability and seamless integration.
Regulatory Compliance: Firms implementing IoT solutions must adhere to industry standards and data protection laws, such as GDPR, HIPAA, and ISO/IEC 27001. IoT security projects become more challenging when it comes to ensuring that cognitive security measures maintain efficacy and efficiency while adhering to regulatory constraints.
Human Factors and Trust: The success of cognitive security solutions is heavily dependent on human variables, such as user conduct, understanding, and trustworthiness. Important components of IoT security include user education regarding security best practices, building trust in automated security mechanisms, and resolving usability issues.

A comprehensive strategy that incorporates technical approaches, structures for regulatory compliance, user education, and cooperation among IoT ecosystem players is needed to deal with these issues.

5.3 Security

Although research on the security-QoS trade-off for encryption-based CPS networks exists, there is currently a lack of application of physical

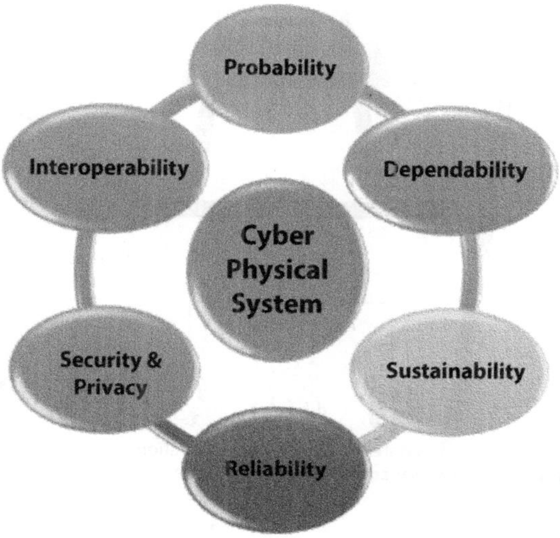

Figure 5.5 Cyber-physical system challenges.

layer security (PLS) rules to manage use-case-specific costs and QoS requirements. According to control center awareness, CCPS chooses a PLS policy from the system's attainable distribution principles in this paradigm shown in Figure 5.5. The network might contain spoofers, jammers, or eavesdroppers, among other non-legitimate nodes. The control center's three primary components are the managers for configuration, adaption, and context. These devices gather data from detectors, risk estimation, and communication channels regarding atmospheric dangers and transformations in the environment. According to customer preferences, they further set up the physical layer settings of the complete system. The control center subsequently updates broadcast specifications by providing information to sensors and actuators. Our objectives for this chapter are as follows:

- To suggest the application of a utility, an adaptable standard quality metric that can be utilized when selecting a transmission plan.
- To suggest a versatile control design that permits the application of various PLS policy permutations.
- To show, with simulation outcomes as evidence, the adaptability and suitability of the approach in a test setting intended for a range of use-cases.

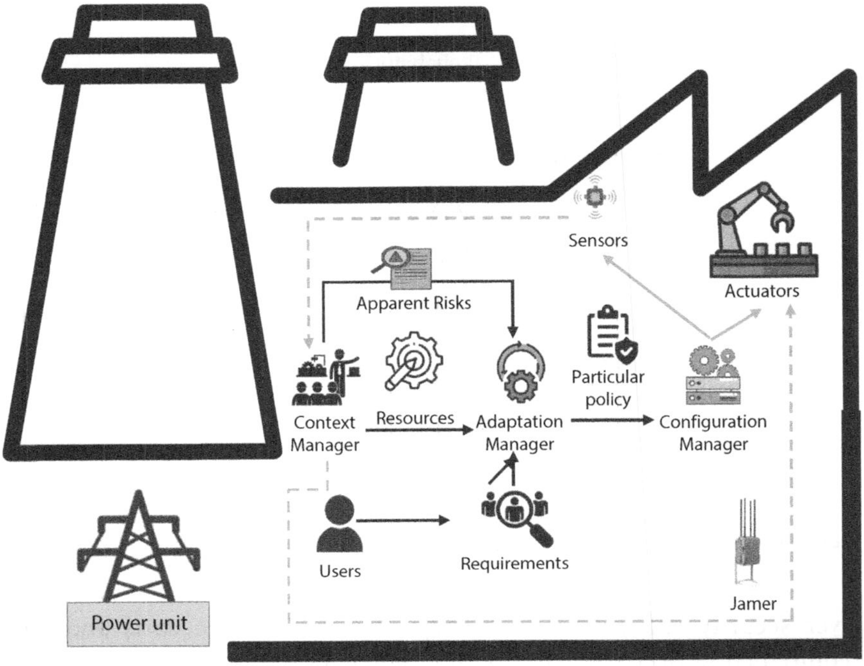

Figure 5.6 Application used proposed system.

With a specially adapted utility feature chosen in accordance with the requirements of the relevant CCPS application, this approach seeks to meet the QoS limitations and safety measures shown in Figure 5.6. 5G technologies offer pervasive connection, which can be leveraged to integrate cognitive functions in CCPS applications. This increased system awareness is a result of this cognition, which goes beyond just estimating the instantaneous resource utilization. By flexibly opting for the best transmission policy while optimizing their functionality, CCPS systems can respond to the challenging operational needs, available resources, and environmental risks. This is done by taking user preferences and contextual data into account.

5.3.1 Physical Layer Attacks

The most well-known indirect assault is eavesdropping. The assailant may pose an imminent CCPS as they covertly attempt to intercept continuous data transfer. In CCPS applications, sensitive healthcare, location, and consumption info may be transmitted. A skilled eavesdropper could get confidential and classified data throughout this process. Attacks referred to as "jamming" are aggressive and produce strong signals that mimic noise and obstruct normal communication. Spectrum monitoring, which looks for unusual variations in power levels, can be used to identify jamming assaults. Modifying the broadcast wavelength in response to jamming signal detection is the primary countermeasure.

Another ongoing threat is spoofing, which resembles functioning like a genuine transmitter following the verification procedure. Modified, falsified, or erased data can be used by the spoofer to interact with the authorized recipient. A physical layer spoofing attack may yield fake sensor data. Our CCPS system is greatly affected by the assault because of mistakes made on a feedback loop and the resulting effects on the policy selection process. Replaying involves transmitting outdated data that is obtained from a valid broadcaster in a manner similar to spoofing and targeting CCPS safety. Once a jamming assault has been fruitful, relaying and spoofing can be produced to evade the CCPS applications tracking procedure.

The category of violent assaults includes man-in-the-middle assaults. By creating fictitious data, the attacker prevents direct connection between nodes while remaining anonymous. In strong assault circumstances, the assault can be succeeded by an eavesdropper assault. One type of vigorous attack that disables the recipient's accessibility is the path-based DoS attack. To carry out this attack, a lot of flooding packets are produced. This can lead to the receiver node's battery running out, particularly in sensor-based networks as those used in medical CPS applications. One preventative measures is to alter the transmission frequency. This assault primarily affects our CCPS algorithm's cost component as opposed to its security component.

Attacks against the legitimacy of the system fall into two categories: false node attacks and node capture/outage. The CCPS function could be jeopardized if the encryption keys are exposed by a node capture assault. The network can be gradually shrunk in size since the node outage attack focuses on the system's operation. The development of formerly mentioned assaults, such as spoofing, jamming, and eavesdropping, may be caused by implanted bogus nodes.

5.3.2 Physical Layer Security

PLS policies are mentioned in books on wireless safety as a way to supplement existing strategies and offer an extra line of security, especially against eavesdroppers. Performance indicators for current PLS technologies can be assessed using secrecy capacity and secrecy pressure. In order to reduce the eavesdropper's wiretap bandwidth, artificial noise (AN) policies aim to produce noise-like sound signals in all possible directions other than the direction of the authorized recipient. This generates an extra signal for safety the higher usage of electricity results in high expenditures. This strategy may not increase QoS, but it can only be implemented for safety reasons with numerous antennas for transmission under budgetary limits. Another method for supplying security is the subcarrier–based AN methodology. Using this technique, the transmitting device superposes the message's information and the AN at some subcarriers while sending pilot AN signals at other subcarriers. Assuming flawless channel estimation, the eavesdropper cannot cancel out the noise term, but the recipient can do so by using pilot noise signals.

Safety precaution called AI causes the receiving node to produce signal modulation that makes no sense. It shares characteristics with the AN policy, but it solely affects the safety and cost aspects, which come with higher power usage. In order for the receiver node to produce AI signals, it needs to be equipped with many radio frequency chains. A signal processing technique called beam creation generates receiver-oriented beams to improve data throughput and reduce transmission errors. It can lessen the signal's interstellar propagation, enhancing defense versus listening in on conversations. Beam forming is intended to reduce interference and improve QoS independent of security and economic implications. Several antennas are required at the transmitter node due to the unique beam forming policy layout. This method can be used in conjunction with AI- and AN-based security solutions.

5.3.3 Main Constituents

- **User** supplies the specifications. Additionally, it allocates weights based on the significance of each security, QoS, and cost component to be employed in the utility computation. Every transmission's weights can be updated by the user. Essentially, the user chooses which dimensions are more significant.
- **Requirements**, which the consumer may modify, provide the necessary operational areas that maintain the intended QoS throughout the operations. Multidimensional phrases called requirements denote the limits of several framework needs, including coverage, latency, bandwidth consumption, and data rate. It is assumed that there is no connection between nodes under the specified required thresholds.

- **Risks** stands for the crucial value that must be reached in order to have a secure communication. Secure transmission is rendered impossible if the level of security offered over the framework is lower than this one. Remember that the multidimensional security strategy requires you to provide risk levels for every security dimension. In this case, numerous metrics could be established while accounting for different aspects of security.
- **Available policies:** Useful PLS policies for maintaining system security are taken into consideration in this chapter. Techniques including beam forming, physical layer key generation, AI, AN, and forward error correcting code assistance are used in PLS literature. The network's resources directly influence the rules that are available. For instance,

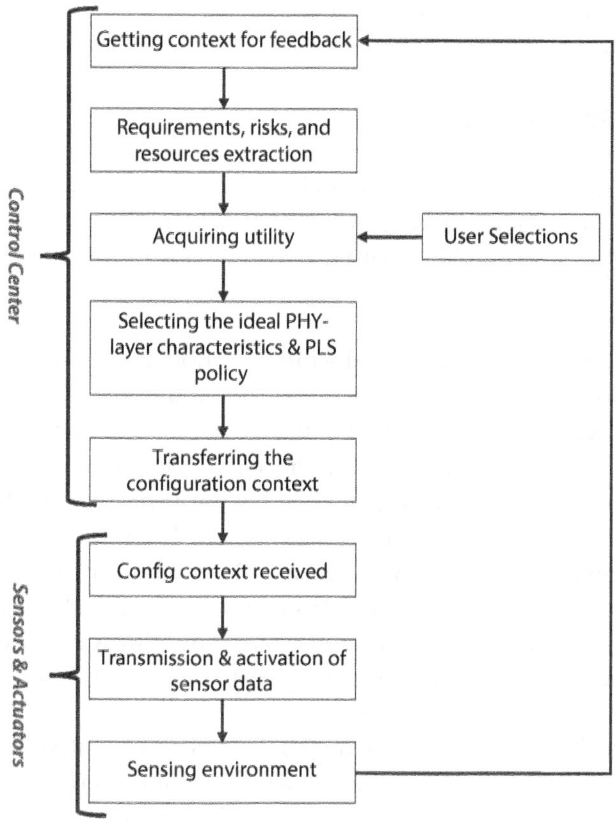

Figure 5.7 Functions carried out by the CCPS components.

beam formation related policy is not attainable if every node receives a single antenna.

- **Context** is referred to as any information pertaining to user-system interactions. Two classes—feedback context and configuration context—can be used to classify the context. The actuator and sensor nodes provide the feedback settings to the control hub. The details of the system's physical transmission characteristics and the chosen PLS policy are contained in the configuration context.

Figure 5.7 shows the framework flowchart illustrating the functions carried out by the CCPS components. The actuators and sensors give the system its cognitive structure by detecting ambient threats and the surrounding environment, whereas the control center determines the optimal PLS strategy. The utility in the policy-making process is the weighted average of several multidimensional performance indicators. It serves as the primary performance metric for a PLS policy.

5.4 Research Gap

Finding areas where current research is inadequate or where additional studies are necessary is a key component of identifying research gaps in the field of CCPS via IoT. Potential research gaps in this area include the following:

Scalable Cognitive Security Solutions: Although cognitive techniques have the potential to improve IoT security, additional study is required to provide scalable solutions that can quickly process and evaluate massive amounts of real-time IoT data. This entails investigating cutting-edge architectures, optimization strategies, and algorithms to meet the resource limitations of IoT devices while preserving scalability and efficacy.

Privacy-Preserving Cognitive Security: Research on privacy-preserving cognitive security methods for IoT systems is lacking. Building confidence in cognitive security solutions requires looking into ways to do security analysis and threat detection without jeopardizing user privacy or letting unauthorized parties access important data.

Adversarial Machine Learning in IoT Security: Cognitive security systems face major problems from adversarial machine learning approaches, especially in the context of the IoT. To maintain the accuracy and integrity of security analysis, research is required to provide strong defenses against adversarial attacks, such as evasion and poisoning attacks, that target cognitive security algorithms.

Human-Centric Cognitive Security: It is not well-known how human factors and user-centric design approaches can be included into IoT cognitive security systems. Investigation is required to build cognitive interfaces that improve user awareness, trust, and engagement with security measures as well as to investigate user views, actions, and processes for making decisions relevant to IoT security.

Interoperability and Standardization: Interoperable cognitive security solutions in heterogeneous IoT contexts are lacking in standardized structures and conventions. In order to allow cognitive security systems to be seamlessly integrated into a variety of IoT platforms, devices, and applications, research is required to build open standards and interoperability rules.

Real-World Deployment and Evaluation: Empirical studies assessing the efficacy, ease of use, and feasibility of cognitive security solutions in actual IoT installations are scarce, despite advancements in the field. To evaluate how cognitive security technologies affect IoT security posture and resilience, field experiments, case studies, and longitudinal evaluations must be conducted.

Regulatory and Ethical Considerations: Deploying cognitive security solutions in IoT networks raises ethical and legal issues that require further research. In order to gather, process, and share IoT data securely while preserving peoples' rights and liberties, this entails looking into legal frameworks, compliance specifications, and ethical standards. Identifying and addressing these research gaps can significantly advance the state-of-the-art in CCPS over IoT, leading to more robust, scalable, and privacy-preserving security solutions for interconnected systems.

5.5 An Automatic Security Manager for CCPS Using IoT

5.5.1 Combatting Erroneous Estimations

A crucial component of the framework's cognitive activities is the impact of estimating errors. In the event of an inaccurate estimation, the control center can select the inappropriate policy, which could result in system performance issues or security breaches. An incorrect judgment made at the control center could result in additional feedback link security breaches. Sensing data may be manipulated, fabricated, or jammed as a result of potential assaults on these networks. In some cases, Eve can use game-theoretic strategies to exploit these attacks, or PLS techniques like beamforming can neutralize them.

5.5.2 Detection and Classification

Detection of the abnormality is necessary to improve CCPS robustness. Numerous explanations, such as sensor malfunctions, environmental changes, and active hackers, can be further examined and categorized in relation to this aberration. Depending on the type of assault or the assailant's proximity to surrounding genuine nodes, the effects of active attacks will vary.

5.6 Conclusions and Future Enhancement

It is anticipated that the CCPS will have a significant influence on how to interact with the physical environment and offer a viable paradigm for the design of present and future designed systems. The concept of CPS emphasizes the integrated system design over the separate attention to the physical or cyber systems provided this study on relevant literature that covered practical applications and popular research topics in an effort to throw some light on the history, vocabulary, conceptually linked ideas, and current issues in CPS. CPSs include a wide range of applications at various scales because CPS is an extremely broad research topic. To sum up, the field of CCPS in the context of the IoT offers a complicated terrain full of problems that need to be resolved in order to protect the confidentiality, integrity, and robustness of networked systems. The complexity of these issues, which range from security flaws in IoT devices to worries about data privacy, calls for an all-encompassing strategy that includes industry cooperation, user education, technology innovation, and regulatory compliance. Even with the inherent complexity, there are ways to progress and get better at handling these problems. Organizations can successfully mitigate cyber threats by developing proactive security measures, improving threat detection capabilities, and automating response mechanisms by utilizing cognitive computing techniques like machine learning and AI.

Furthermore, enhancing understanding of users, optimizing resource-constrained devices, and standardizing interoperability can all help to create more reliable and secure IoT ecosystems. While preserving individual rights and liberties, regulatory compliance frameworks and ethical concerns are essential in directing the creation and application of cognitive security solutions. Ultimately, cooperation among stakeholders—researchers, legislators, business executives, and end users—is needed to address the problems and obstacles in CCPS across the IoT. It can create a safer and more resilient IoT ecosystem that maximizes the promise of networked systems while guarding against cybersecurity risks by cooperating to develop, educate, and adapt to changing threats.

Future Enhancement

Advanced Threat Detection Techniques: Future studies can investigate more sophisticated methods of detecting threats, such as deep learning- and machine learning–based anomaly detection, behavior analysis, and predictive analytics. By proactively identifying and mitigating cyber threats in real time, these strategies help improve the security posture of IoT ecosystems.

Privacy-Preserving Security Solutions: Creating cognitive security solutions that protect privacy will be crucial to addressing the growing concerns about data confidentiality and privacy. Future improvements might include performing security analysis and threat detection while protecting sensitive data by federated learning, differential privacy, and cryptography techniques.

Edge Computing and AI Integration: AI capabilities combined with edge computing will allow dispersed cognitive security systems to function closer to IoT gadgets, resulting in lower latency and bandwidth needs. In the future, localized threat identification and response could be achieved by implementing lightweight AI models and algorithms on edge devices.

Quantum-Safe Security: Future developments in CCPS via the IoT will need to take into account the possible threat that quantum computers offer to current encryption methods as they develop. The long-term security of IoT ecosystems will depend on research into quantum-safe security measures including post-quantum cryptography and quantum-resistant algorithms.

Blockchain-Based Security Solutions: IoT data and transaction security and integrity could be improved with the use of blockchain technology. Subsequent improvements might potentially involve utilizing blockchain-based solutions, like smart contracts and distributed ledgers, to create immutability, trust, and transparency in IoT ecosystems. This would help to reduce security issues related to data entry and manipulation.

Collaborative Threat Intelligence Sharing: IoT stakeholders, such as equipment makers, suppliers of services, and security professionals, can improve situational awareness and respond quickly to new cyber threats by forming cooperative threat intelligence sharing networks. The creation of standardized platforms and standards for safe and private exchange of threat intelligence sharing may be one of the next improvements.

User-Centric Security Design: User-centric security design principles—which emphasize usability, accessibility, and transparency—will be given priority in future improvements to CCPS via the IoT. To enable people to make knowledgeable security options, upgrades could include creating user-friendly user interfaces, offering practical security advice, and promoting user education and awareness.

Organizations can develop trust and confidence in the dependability and integrity of interconnected systems, boost the security posture of IoT ecosystems, and reduce emerging cyber threats by adopting these future enhancements. To foster innovation and meet the changing difficulties in CCPS via IoT, collaboration between researchers, industry stakeholders, and policymakers will be crucial.

References

1. Liang, Q., Zhao, S., Zhang, J., Deng, H., Damm, W., Hess, D., Forrest, L., Cyber-physical systems. *ACM Trans.*, *8*, 1, 1–23, 2024.
2. Alvarez-Alvarado, M.S., Apolo-Tinoco, C., Ramirez-Prado, M.J., Alban-Chacón, F.E., Pico, N., Aviles-Cedeno, J., Rengifo, J., Cyber-physical power systems: A comprehensive review about technologies drivers, standards, and future perspectives. *Comput. Electr. Eng.*, *116*, 109149, 2024.
3. Mercorelli, P., Nemati, H., Zhu, Q., Industry 4.0 more than a challenge in modeling, identification, and control for cyber-physical systems, in: *Modeling, Identification, and Control for Cyber-Physical Systems Towards Industry 4.0*, pp. 1–14, Academic Press, San Diego, California, USA, 2024.
4. Serôdio, C., Mestre, P., Cabral, J., Gomes, M., Branco, F., Software and Architecture Orchestration for Process Control in Industry 4.0 Enabled by Cyber-Physical Systems Technologies. *Appl. Sci.*, *14*, 5, 2160, 2024.
5. Karthikeyan, A., Karthikeyan, K., Swathika, O.G., Cyber-physical security in a stand-alone photovoltaic system for rural electrification. *Next-Gener. Cyber-Phys. Microgrid Syst.*, 29–75, 2024.
6. Sood, V.M., Singh, Y., Bhargava, B., Narang, S.K. (Eds.), *Intelligent Security Solutions for Cyber-Physical Systems*, CRC Press, Boca Raton, FL, USA, 2024.
7. Noor, M.M., Selamat, A., Husain, N.A., Krejcar, O., Security and Safety in Cyber-Physical System (CPS): An Inclusive Threat Model. *J. Adv. Res. Appl. Sci. Eng. Technol.*, *40*, 2, 176–202, 2024.

8. Piardi, L., Leitão, P., Queiroz, J., Pontes, J., Role of digital technologies to enhance the human integration in industrial cyber–physical systems. *Annu. Rev. Control*, *57*, 100934, 2024.
9. Bindra, S.S. and Aggarwal, A., Security in cyber physical systems: Transformation and challenges. *J. Auton. Intell.*, *7*, 4, 19–36, 2024.
10. Laraib, A., Sial, A., Ujjan, R.M.A., Addresses the Security Issues and Safety in Cyber-Physical Systems of Drones, in: *Cybersecurity Issues and Challenges in the Drone Industry*, pp. 381–404, IGI Global, Hershey, PA, USA, 2024.
11. Stutz, D., de Assis, J.T., Laghari, A.A., Khan, A.A., Deshpande, A., Kulkarni, D., ... & Grata, E.G., Cyber Threat Detection and Mitigation Using Artificial Intelligence–A Cyber-physical Perspective. *Appl. Artif. Intell. Cybersecur. Anal. Cyber Threat Detect.*, 107–133, 2024.
12. Wen, L., Design automation system synchronization for cyber physical system with dynamic voltage and frequency scaling in industry 5.0. *Meas.: Sens.*, *31*, 100981, 2024.
13. Karthikeyan, S. and Nagamani, G.M., An Architecture of Cyber-Physical System for Industry 4.0, in: *Digital Transformation: Industry 4.0 to Society 5.0*, pp. 259–283, Springer Nature Singapore, Singapore, 2024.
14. Ali, J.A.H., Gaffinet, B., Panetto, H., Naudet, Y., Cognitive systems and interoperability in the enterprise: A systematic literature review. *Annu. Rev. Control*, *57*, 100954, 2024.
15. Saleem, M.U., Usman, M.R., Yaqub, M.A., Liotta, A., Asim, A., Smarter Grid in the 5G Era: Integrating the Internet of Things with a Cyber-Physical System. *IEEE Access*, 12, 34002–34018, 2024.

6

Cognitive Cyber-Physical Security With IoT: A Solution to Smart Healthcare System

P. Shanmugam[1*], Mohamed Iqbal M.[2] and M. Amanullah[3]

[1]*Department of Computer Science and Engineering, Rajalakshmi Engineering College, Chennai, India*
[2]*Department of Information Technology, Sri Sivasubramaniya Nadar College of Engineering, Chennai, India*
[3]*Department of Computer Science and Engineering, Saveetha School of Engineering, Saveetha Institute of Medical and Technical Sciences, Chennai, India*

Abstract

Academic and business involvement in healthcare has increased due to the quick advancement in medical and computing technology. Nevertheless, most healthcare systems cannot offer specialized consumers a personalized capacity service and do not consider clients. Using cognitive technology in combination with the Internet of Things (IoT), the current section suggests a unique way to improve cyber-physical safety inside intelligent medical facilities. As more and more IoT devices find their way into medical facilities, it is critical to make sure that safety protocols are strong. The approach makes use of cognitive computing features like machine learning and the processing of natural languages to identify and eliminate safety concerns instantly. The framework gathers and analyses data from multiple locations inside the healthcare system using IoT monitors and components, allowing for the preemptive detection of possible compromises to security. By using this method, the new approach improves the innovative healthcare networks' general safety postures while guaranteeing the accessibility, security, and reliability of private client data and medical equipment.

**Corresponding author*: shanmugam.p@rajalakshmi.edu.in

K. Ananthajothi, S. N. Sangeethaa, D. Divya, S. Balamurugan and Shen-Lung Peng (eds.) Securing Cyber-Physical Systems: Fundamentals, Applications and Challenges, (109–132) © 2025 Scrivener Publishing LLC

Keywords: Cognitive cyber-physical security, Internet of Things, smart healthcare system, threat detection, data privacy, machine learning, adaptive security measures

6.1 Introduction

The eHealth and well-being industry has witnessed a notable surge in the use of diverse cyber-physical system (CPS)–Internet of Things (IoT) applications [1]. Over the last few years, cognitive CPS (CCPS)–IoT has developed cognitive capacities including instruction, reasoning, and self-aware comprehension of its interpersonal and physical surroundings. But with greater complexity comes new dangers related to cybersecurity with CCPS-IoT. The danger of attacks on cybersecurity involving information and healthcare equipment has increased due to the increasing interdependence of healthcare systems [2]. The healthcare ecosystem's CCPS-IoT is vulnerable to a range of newly developed cyber-attacks. Poor safety may lead to damage to property, monetary losses, invasions of user confidentiality, and even dangers to human life. Unfortunately, the amount of detail, dynamism, and significant degree of connection of CCPS-IoT–enabled medical facilities have proven too much for the safety solutions now in use to handle [3]. Thus, establishing cognitive cybersecurity inside the CCPS-IoT–supported medical environment requires a novel strategy. The purpose of this study is to introduce the concept and technique of cognitive cybersecurity that allows for the modeling of attacker behavior, determination of their intents, and prediction of future assaults. This approach anticipates and resolves new hazards to privacy and security by using a cognitive framework that can mimic human thinking tendencies [4]. Our objective is to strengthen defenses against attacks in the CCPS-IoT–enabled healthcare environment by introducing creative components like safety, confidentiality, and adaptive safety measurements. We also plan to address collaborative mindful confidentiality, methods for computationally flexible collecting information, and the incorporation of cross-sectoral approaches like artificial intelligence (AI) forecasting and real-time testing in this section [5]. This strategy is anticipated to lower attack danger; improve cybersecurity in CCPS-IoT in the healthcare industry; and safeguard the confidentiality, honesty, and confidentiality of private medical information. This study will advance knowledge of cognitive cybersecurity for CCPS-IoT within the framework of the medical environment by emphasizing the pressing need for practical safety measures. Aggressive steps are anticipated to be attained in safeguarding customers' safety and confidentiality in this developing period and defending important systems through collaborated efforts among investigators, healthcare providers, and specialists in cybersecurity [6].

CPS-IoT applications are being used more and more for eHealth and well-being. These kinds of applications include self-driven person surveillance, provider-driven supervised surveillance, and social information gathering and advertising. Cisco projects that the IoT and cloud computing will enable over 50 billion items to be connected to society by 2020. Recently, additional CCPS-IoTs have been created that can mimic individual cognitive behaviors by learning, reasoning, and comprehending their physical and social surroundings on their own. This type of CCPS-IoT is known as a CCPS-IoT. "The most intelligent applications of the IoT in areas that require knowledge are going to be those that allow human cognitive processes to become central to the process" [7].

Facilities and products related to healthcare are more advanced, vital, and linked than previously. Issues regarding the safety of healthcare information and equipment are growing even as advancements in medical results and treatment delivery improve the lives of people. A new type of cybersecurity weakness has been introduced into medical services and products by increased interconnection. Because of this, the medical sector is the one most exposed to serious safety risks. As previously said, the vulnerability of the CCPS-IoT–enabled healthcare facilities and facilities to various developing cyber-attacks exacerbates the problem [8]. Because of their features of disintegration, interconnectivity, variability, and cross-organizational nature—which provide an increased threat surface—CPS-IoT technologies have been designated as secure and safety highly susceptible to attacks. Preventing cybersecurity assaults is essential because they have the potential to result in danger to people's lives, bodily harm, financial loss, and violations of privacy for consumers [9]. According to news accounts, many thousands of health information have been taken worldwide, highlighting the development in assaults and the rise in theft of medical information. The increase in cyber-physical threats demonstrates that the difficulty, unpredictability, dynamic nature, and high connection of CCPS-IoT–enabled medical facilities and critical infrastructures are challenges that cannot be met by the safety solutions available today. Intelligent algorithms and cognitive frameworks can improve autonomous smart safety systems for making decisions to expert-level proficiency [10].

The attackers will also modify their plans in response to newly implemented safeguards and changes in the safety environment. Therefore, novel approaches to constructing intellectual cybersecurity are desperately needed for CCPS-IoT–enabled medical environments. To more effectively avoid resulting assaults, this article suggests and provides intelligent safety along with concepts that allow for the investigation of attackers' behaviors by gathering their goals, forecasting and assessing their resolve, and connecting these with the operation of CCPS-IoT and sensitive infrastructure networks [11].

6.1.1 Motivation

The following are the main reasons for investigating cognitive cyber-physical security using IoT as a remedy for smart healthcare systems:

Improved Medical Attention: It is possible to give patients more individualized and effective healthcare by incorporating IoT devices into medical facilities. These gadgets can manage compliance with medications, keep an eye on vital signs, and provide medical professionals access to real-time medical information.

Productivity and Savings in Costs: Intelligent healthcare systems can reduce human labor, optimize the allocation of resources, and simplify operations. Both individuals and medical professionals may save money as a result of this.

Data-Driven Decision Making: Medical professionals can make better judgments thanks to the wealth of data produced by IoT devices. Improvements in evaluation, therapy strategies, and preventive measures may result from the analysis of this information.

Better Patient Results: Effective healthcare systems can help avoid medical catastrophes, lower the rate of hospital readmission, and eventually enhance outcomes for patients through continuous surveillance and prompt identification of medical concerns.

Security Issues: IoT integration of devices does, nevertheless, also bring with it dangers to cybersecurity, such as device manipulating others, unauthorized access, and information compromises. Protecting confidential medical information and guaranteeing the accessibility and reliability of medical facilities are the driving forces behind the investigation of cognitive cyber-physical safety.

Regulatory Compliance: Adopting strong safety procedures is essential to upholding compliance and averting legal consequences.

Patients need to have faith that sensitive data about their medical condition will be kept private and safe. Putting in place strong safety safeguards and open handling of information procedures is necessary to fostering confidence in smart healthcare organizations.

Innovations and Technology Progress: Adopting cognitive cyber and physical safety offers healthcare providers a chance to innovate and progress technologically. Scientists and providers may fully utilize IoT technology in the delivery of healthcare by tackling safety concerns.

The overall goal for integrating physical and cybersecurity with IoT in intelligent medical facilities is to maximize the advantages of connected technology while reducing the security threats they provide to improve healthcare shipment excellence, availability, and protection.

6.1.2 Need and Contribution

6.1.2.1 Need

Numerous crucial needs lead to the necessity for intelligent cyber-physical safety with IoT in intelligent medical systems:

Safeguarding Private Health Information: Large volumes of confidential information about patients, such as health information, test findings, and medical histories, are handled by healthcare organizations. Maintaining the safety of patients and adhering to information security laws require ensuring the security, reliability, and accessibility of this information.

Security Connected Technologies: By collecting health indicators, enabling remote monitoring of patients, and promoting patient-provider contact, IoT devices are essential to smart healthcare organizations. Nevertheless, these gadgets are vulnerable to a range of online dangers, including virus infestations, compromised data, and unapproved entry. Strong safeguards are required to protect IoT devices and keep them from serving as gateways for cyber-attacks.

Preventing Health Services Disruption: Cyber-attacks directed at healthcare organizations can have serious repercussions, such as impairing the security of patients, incurring monetary losses, and interrupting medical services. Providing uninterrupted medical care and protecting the health of patients require sophisticated medical facilities to be resilient against cyber-attacks.

Reducing Operational Risks: Safety incidents in intelligent medical facilities have the potential to impair workflow, reduce output, and damage public confidence in the sector. The use of proactive risk; Mitigation techniques, including computerized intrusion detection, safety evaluations, and emergency response processes, must be implemented to effectively reduce operational hazards and ensure the uninterrupted provision of medical care. Handling Regulation Conformity: Health Insurance Portability and Accountability Act (HIPAA) in the US and general data protection pegulation (GDPR) in the EU are two examples of the strict regulations that medical organizations must abide by when it comes to data safety and security. To secure client knowledge and prove compliance with regulatory requirements, compliance with these rules requires the deployment of comprehensive safety precautions, encrypted information methods, access restrictions, and records of audits.

Establishing Confidence and Satisfaction: To take full advantage of smart systems of healthcare, consumers and medical professionals need to have faith in their reliability and safety. Establishing trust among stakeholders regarding the confidentiality and authenticity of their information and medical facilities necessitates honest and forthcoming discussion about safety protocols, aggressive risk reduction techniques, and prompt reaction to security problems.

In conclusion, protecting responsive medical information, securing gadgets that are connected, preventing problems with medical procedures, mitigating operational hazards, assuring compliance with laws and regulations, and fostering stakeholder confidence and dependability are the main reasons why mental cyber-physical security with IoT is necessary for intelligent medical facilities. Healthcare organizations may use the ground-breaking potential of IoT technology while protecting the safety and confidentiality of patients by attending to these demands.

6.1.2.2 Contribution

In smart medical facilities, cognition cyber-physical safety with IoT makes a significant and varied contribution across multiple significant domains:

Improved Safety Posture: Healthcare organizations may strengthen their safety measures against changing digital dangers by using cognitive technology, AI methods, and advanced analysis. To reduce risks and protect critical medical information, intelligent cyber-physical safety measures include proactive danger identification, continuous surveillance, and adaptive response methods [12].

Enhanced Protection of Patients and Security of Information: Sturdy security procedures safeguard patient data accessibility, security, and honesty, guaranteeing that private medical records are shielded from malevolent intrusions, compromises of information, and illegal access. In the end, this improves client security and confidentiality in smart medical settings by fostering confidence among individuals, medical professionals, and other partners.

Effective Risk Management: Healthcare businesses may detect, evaluate, and reduce safety risks with the use of mental cyber-physical safety measures. Organizations may minimize their effect on the treatment of patients and the healthcare industry by proactively identifying variations, mitigating problems, and preventing safety incidents from beginning to develop through the use of ongoing surveillance, and behavioral assessment, including statistical analysis [13].

Regulatory Compliance Assurance: To stay out of trouble with the law and keep patients' confidence, medical facilities must ensure compliance with stringent privacy laws like GDPR and HIPAA. By putting comprehensive access oversight, encrypted methods, audit records, and knowledge management processes in place to safeguard patient knowledge and prove compliance with laws and regulations, cognitive cyber-physical safety measures make it easier to comply with legal obligations.

Optimized Healthcare Deliveries: Effective healthcare networks that are safe and dependable let medical professionals give high-quality treatment more quickly and effectively. Cognitive cyber-physical safety measures help to optimize healthcare delivery, expedite procedures, and enhance outcomes for patients by guaranteeing the accessibility and authenticity of medical information, reducing cybersecurity threats, and preserving continued operations.

Development and Technology Development: In the healthcare sector, creativity and advancements in technology are fostered by the combination of cognitive cyber-physical safety with IoT. Medical organizations can unlock new possibilities for telemedicine, personalized medical care, remote surveillance of patients, and data-driven knowledge by solving safety issues and leveraging the transformative power of the IoT. This will lead to creativity and ongoing enhancement in medical care delivery representations.

Global Health Resilience: Cyber-attacks on medical systems offer serious dangers to the sustainability of worldwide health in an increasingly digitalized and networked society. Healthcare organizations can contribute to worldwide medical safety and resilience by improving defense against cyber-attacks, safeguarding vital medical facilities, and ensuring consistency of treatment through the implementation of cognitive cyber-physical safety measures in innovative healthcare systems across the globe.

In conclusion, improved safety standing position, better safety for patients and privacy, efficient risk control, confidence of compliance with laws and regulations, optimized delivery of care, inventiveness, advances in technology, and global health endurance are all benefits of integrating intellectual cyber-physical safety with IoT in intelligent medical facilities. Cognition cyber-physical safety measures are essential for securing medical facilities, preserving the health of patients, and driving healthcare forward by tackling these important areas.

6.2 Medical CCPS with IoT

Every medical cyber-physical systems (MCPS) has separate network infrastructures and integrated control devices [14]. As seen in Figure 6.1,

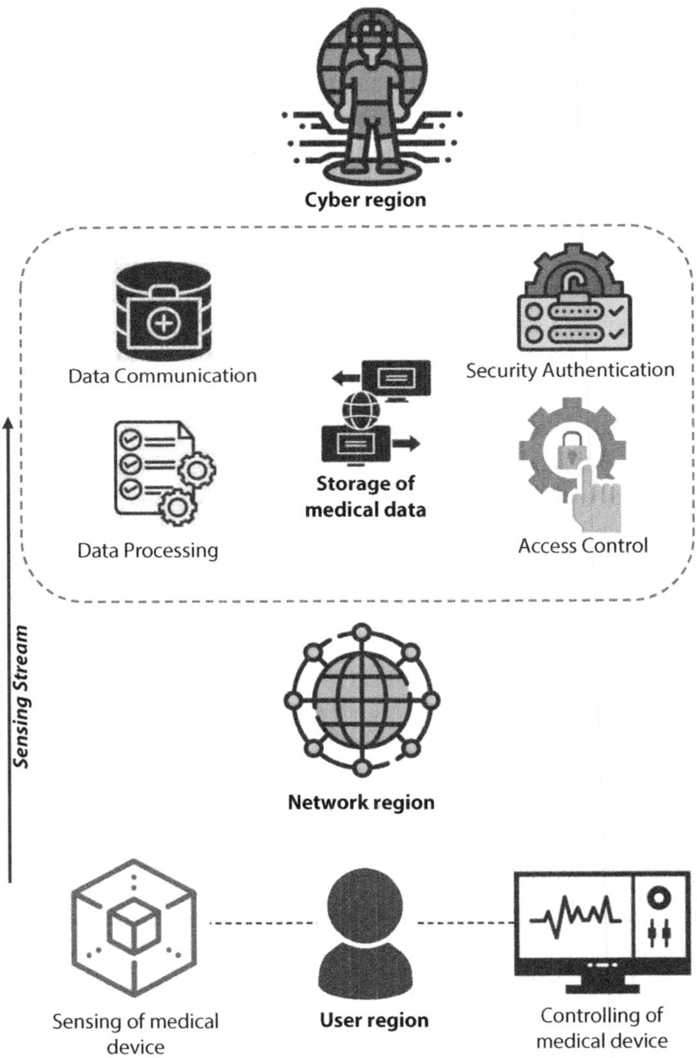

Figure 6.1 Framework of MCPS.

cyberspace (which includes the network's environment) and the physical environment (containing the user environment) comprise the fundamental basis of MCPS. The real-world basis of MCPS is its surroundings. It comprises various types of hard actual-time healthcare sensor components, medical evaluation components, and an individual's space made up of various users. It also collects information about control from the internet to operate physical equipment and sends sensing data to cyberspace through devices that sense. The central hub of MCPS is cyberspace, which handles customer and medical data processing, storing, and accessibility security oversight. The cyberspace functions as the neural center of MCPS. It gathers sensing data from the real world via network communication structures, recognizes, archives, processes, and analyzes it.

CPS-IoT places more emphasis on the creation and study of virtual applications that operate within real-world settings [15]. It builds a system of closed-loop enabling systems centered on state monitoring, immediate evaluation, technological making choices, and precise communication between online environments and real-world space. A key component in the conventional MCPS structure is information feedback and tracking of patients.

The layer of applications was used for analysis or display of images. It can accomplish this by using the constantly changing information of the network of sensors and tracking structure to transfer computation and tracking from the self-sufficient structure to a distant monitoring center. The features of MCPS include dynamic reorganization, high robotics, excellent reliability and safety for CCPS, cross-domain delivery, multidomain communication, complicated space area, and restricted physical assets. Data on healthcare for patients, electronic medical record (EMR), national wellness, procedures and treatments, and other topics are all included in the medical area. A growing number of them are highly secure, robust real-time systems that are managed by computer networks that consist of both hardware and software elements. In the areas of control and fusing structures, sensing and wireless networks, safety, stability, and dependability, embedded devices and abstraction calculating, building models, safety authorization, and information accountability, further study and improvement on MCPS are required [16]. The assessment of bio-modalities, such as classic fingerprint, iris, and face verification, for user identification and authorization has significantly expanded in the last several years. Before being sent to the cloud in the above network, information gathered from the gathering layer that sensors have gathered is kept in the cloudlet devices that are closest to them. In the purchasing layer, the cloud serves as an information system and intermediary to transmit choices from the physician's office

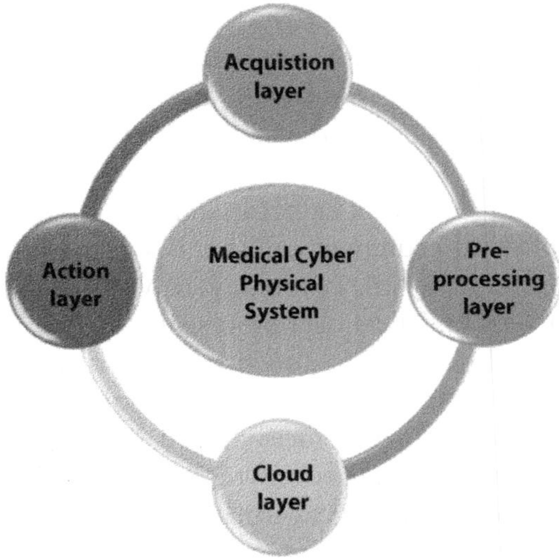

Figure 6.2 MCPS layers.

to the patient. The majority of these networks think about sending their computing resources to a cloud setting. On-device AI nodes are new in several recent research to lessen the load on the cloud shown in Figure 6.2. Therefore, there are two main obstacles that bio-modal identification in an MCPS may encounter. These are as follows:

- First, because the MCPS's centralized design depends on cloud computing, there may be a noticeable lag in the network when recognition judgments are made remotely.
- Second, attaining superior quality of detection is frequently associated with highly computational machine learning (ML) models, which necessitate an enormous quantity of data examples. Currently, it is challenging to design lightweight detection techniques with outstanding precision for tiny devices with limited resources that are close to acquiring layer sensors. In actuality, the problem is still not thoroughly studied, and the methods now in use do not specifically address MCPS.

6.2.1 IoT Device for AI Solution

As an important alternative to depending only on the cloud for learning and identification activities on the medical device side, device AI solutions were emphasized. They provide important benefits including quick reaction times, improved dependability, heightened secrecy, and effective network capacity utilization. In addition to these benefits, it can enable ML algorithms to operate on handheld electronics for picture security and identification [17].

6.2.2 Traditional Bio-Modality Spoofing Detection

In the past, techniques for detecting face spoofing involved modeling user behavior, depending on additional devices, requiring user participation, and primarily using data-driven characterization approaches. In-printing artifacts and micro-texture patterns added into fictitious fingerprint samples throughout the collection process were detected using local binary patterns. The partial least square (PLS) classification was utilized in conjunction with an analysis of the color, appearance, and form of the facial area to distinguish a phony biometric sample from an authentic one. Image-based assaults have been studied, and a method called frequency entropy evaluation was new for identifying instances of spoofing. Visual rhythm evaluation was used to collect temporal data on face spoofing attempts using videos. It was new to apply the fast Fourier transformation in the range of frequency domain to identify iris faking and validate the high-frequency spectral magnitude. The best features are chosen using a sequentially floating selection of features before being fed to a quadratic discriminant classification.

To detect fingerprint vitality, a set of characteristics including ridge power and orientation, ridge consistency and information, and the stability of the ridge-valley architecture were new. Prominently colored patterns like the hills and valleys of the fingerprinting modalities were assessed using the Weber local image descriptor. Binarized statistical image features were investigated; in-depth research is done on filter learning using natural picture data, hard-coded characteristics, and generic texturing patterns for fingerprint spoofing identification.

6.2.3 MCPS Using AI Device

The detectors attached to the user are located in the data collection phase. The body's sensors keep an eye on bodily functions and transmit sensory data to the corresponding cloudlet. Typically, information collected by a healthcare cyber-physical network has been routed to the cloud, where it might be used to make centralized selections. The cloud can cause a considerable delay in the user's decision reaction, despite its tremendous

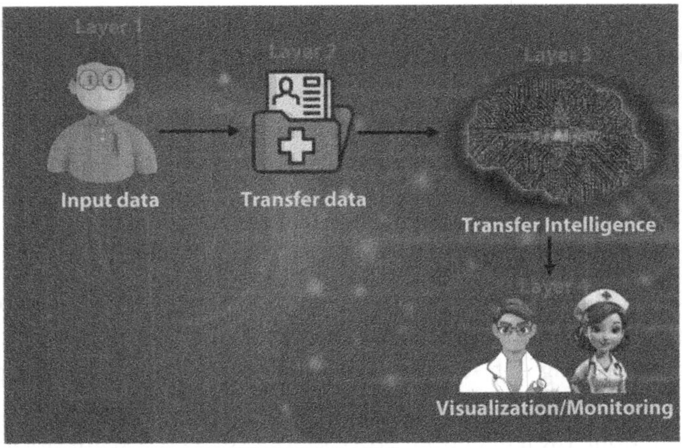

Figure 6.3 MCPS using AI device.

computing efficiency. Furthermore, an individual may not be able to connect to the cloud service if an uplink network is down. In this scenario, a single point of failure brought on by the cloud's centralized making decisions structure has the potential to bring down the entire system. Nevertheless, an independent layer-2 AI cloudlet node on the device itself may serve as a stand-in for the consumer's authorization, enabling the machine to connect to the internet without requiring the backend server.

The conventional information route is depicted by the dotted lines. Nevertheless, the information may only alternately go up to the layer-2 proximal devices in our new structure. Over a predetermined length of time, layer-2 devices are further linked to the internet to transmit logs and health information. The operations level, where the carers live, is then connected to the cloud via the Internet. Healthcare facilities and physicians gather data that is transmitted to the cloud from layer 2 to carry out particular tasks by application-specific requirements. As a result, the knowledge production that is typically accessible at the next level is regularly transmitted to the second-level on-device AI nodes, which are likewise rich in the processing and storage of information in its raw form shown in Figure 6.3.

6.3 Functional and Behavioral Perspectives

- Realizing the collection, delivery, assessment, storage, use, and access to customers' health information is a major responsibility in the field of medical clinical informatics. It may be split into the following two categories of structure based on various duties and purposes.

- The transmission Construction: This area of study concentrates on how to make sure health information can be sent effectively across communication methods, such as IPv6-based community medical IoT and edge computing-based smart health systems. The levels of the IPv6-based communal health IoT are depicted in Figure 6.4.

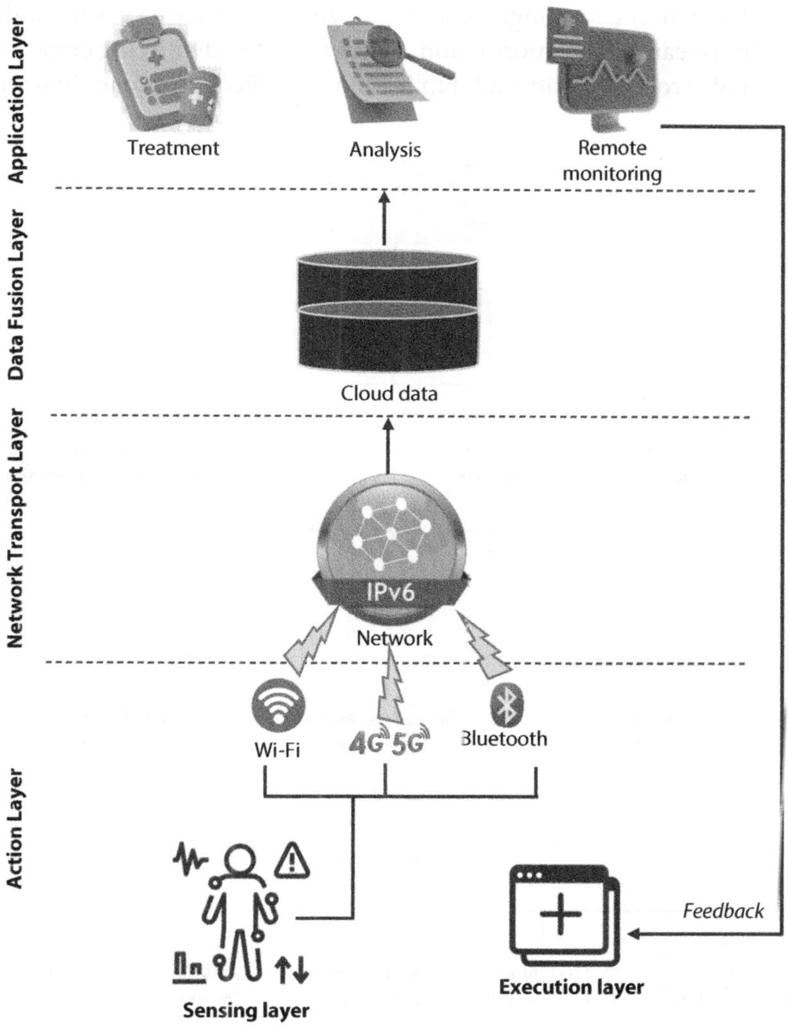

Figure 6.4 Layers of MCPS-IoT.

- Data Analysis and Understanding Construction: This area of study focuses on the evaluation and processing of healthcare information, particularly on how to effectively aggregate, change, filter, and mine large amounts of information related to medical thinking to offer a foundation for decision-making.

The primary components of the information treatment system for MCPS massive information treatment include information the application, data evaluation, information storage, preliminary processing of data, and information collecting. As seen in Figure 6.5, pre-processing of data, including cleaning the information, which includes identifying errors, correction of errors, integrity and duplication identification, comes first when

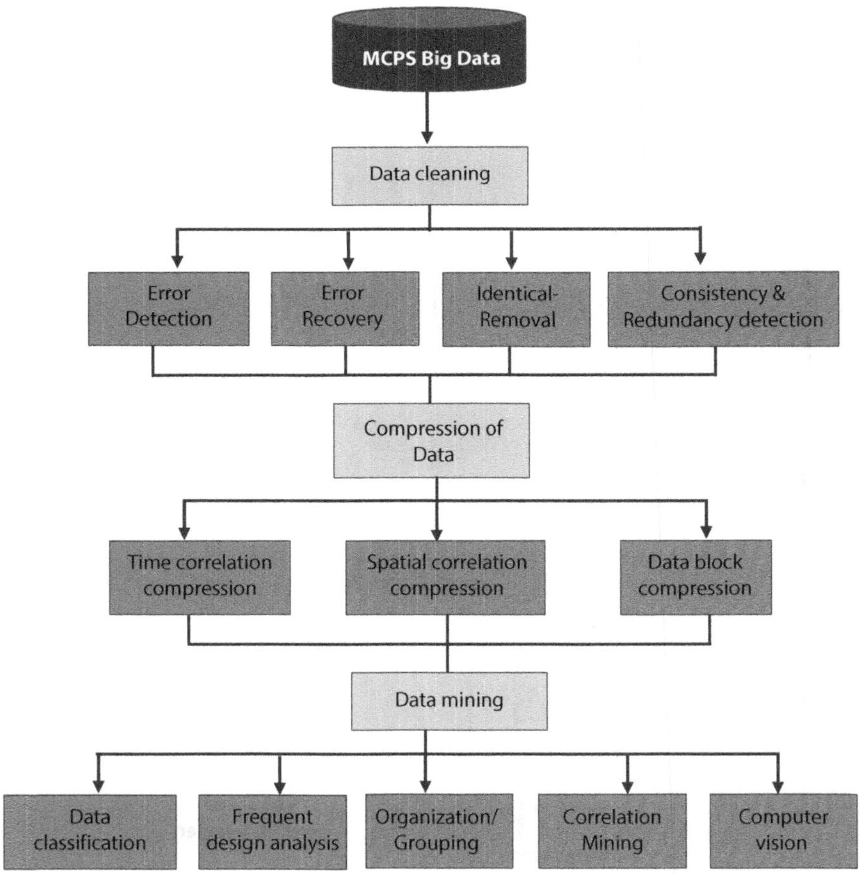

Figure 6.5 Big data processing of MCPS.

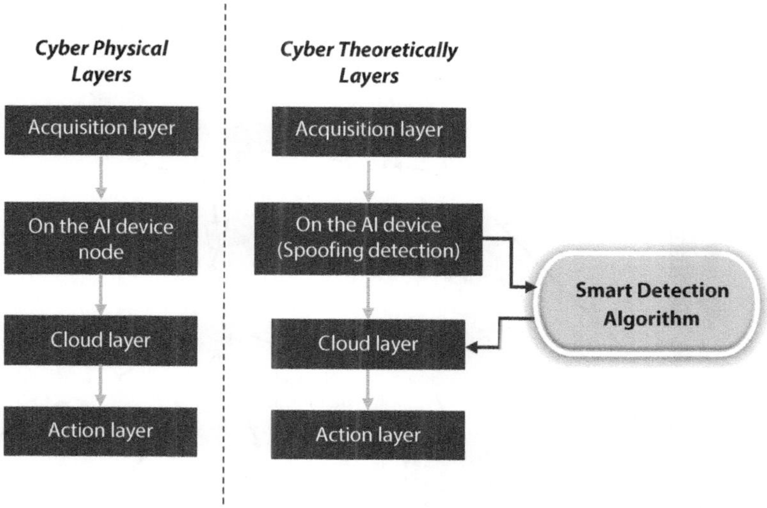

Figure 6.6 MCPS using AI device based on practical and theoretical representation.

the vast amounts of information of MCPS are gathered. The dataset is then reduced in size using compression techniques, completing the data storage process. Analyzing and mining data are the final steps in implementing technologies like data visualization. Information characterization, periodicity pattern evaluation, categorization, accumulation, association mineral extraction, and other processes are all included in data mining techniques.

AI allows the node to make decisions quickly and forms a decentralized collaboration AI system that protects confidentiality by employing the cloudlet. Therefore, as seen in Figure 6.6, the cloud might update the mental recognition model on the on-device AI-based component to maintain efficiency.

6.4 Modeling and Verification Methods of MCPS

A growing number of significant medical events, including chemotherapy, medication distribution, rehabilitation following surgery, and evaluation, include the usage of MCPS. As Figure 6.7 illustrates, it involves some jobs and technologies that are directly tied to life for humans, such as the Da Vinci surgical robot, whose actions might have an impact on patients' wellness at every opportunity. Therefore, to comply with security standards, the system needs to be thoroughly tested before being used. Security is defined by ISO 60601, an international norm for medical equipment, as

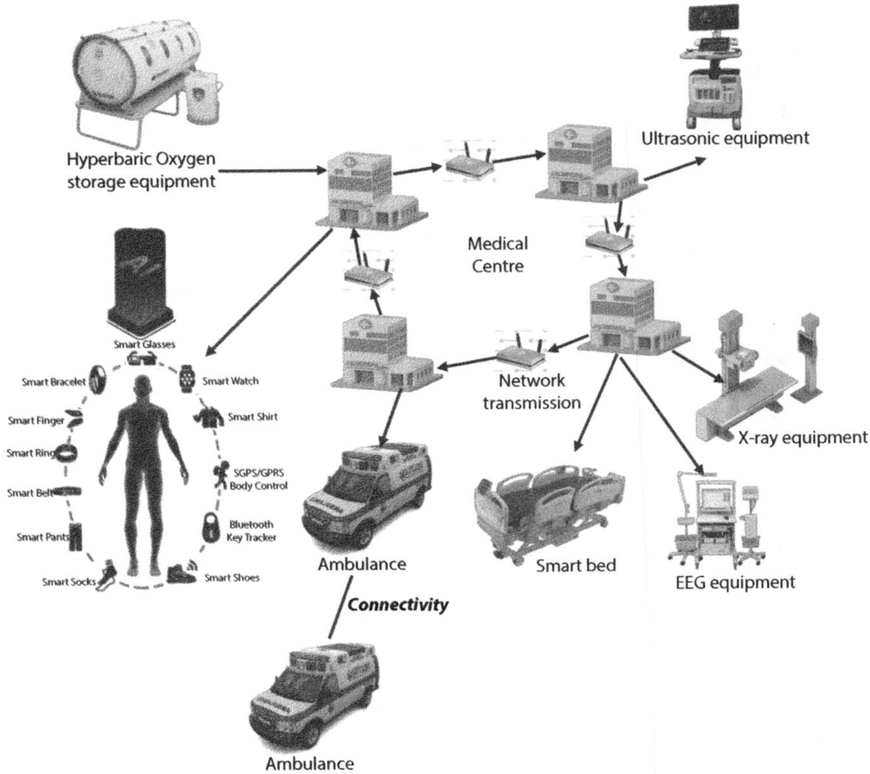

Figure 6.7 CCPS –AI in smart healthcare system.

preventing healthcare operations from posing an intolerable danger to the surrounding environment or individuals. Preventing damage to patients is the fundamental objective of all security protocols.

6.4.1 MCPS Modeling Based on ICE

The prerequisites for the secure incorporation of medical devices and other technology in healthcare facilities are established by the integrated clinical environment (ICE), a conceptual operational architecture, and standards in MCPS. To aid in system creation and improve anterior capabilities, experts construct a medical system approach according to this conceptual framework. As a high-level framework for MCPS explanation, ICE may be thought of. Using input and output analysis, the model is employed in this approach for testing and evaluating the healthcare device's functionality. This technology can be applied, for instance, to ventilation systems that are linked to artificial lung models. It took distinct forms at various levels of abstraction and examined components validation of the healthcare system at several levels of generalization. It provides a generic, expandable, and useful approach for hierarchy attribute validation in complicated MCPS.

6.4.2 MCPS Modeling Based on Component

A novel approach to system construction is component technologies. The complicated system is split up into multiple components based on its function and structure. The components are connected by a single, uniform connection standard, and every one of them may have an organizational hierarchy. Customers just need to understand the functionality of every component and the supplied connecting standards; with this information, they can rapidly design the model and carry out simulations and testing of the model. They do not need to be familiar with the specifics of every component's functional execution. The term "MCPS component" refers to the element used in the MCPS domain. The term "MCPS component" describes the fundamental parts of the MCPS framework, which include autonomous behavior, compositional framework, and characteristics. The connection to the computer, which is utilized for transmitting information and receiving, is the component's connection. Through ports, components are interconnected and cooperate. The component can be categorized into several levels when used with the concept of CCPS hierarchy modeling. As a result, two categories of parts exist: atomic elements and composite parts. The term "atomic component" describes the lowest element, which possesses the most fundamental characteristics and functions and is incapable of holding other components. At the apex of the component hierarchy is a combination element, which has a somewhat sophisticated design and function and can comprise several atomic parts or other composite elements.

6.5 Artificial Intelligence for Cognitive Cybersecurity

Autonomous educational systems called cognitive structures are meant to mimic how the human brain works. The goal of cognitive cybersecurity is to imitate human thought and behavior to predict and address threats to safety. AI technological advances, which make use of methods like neural networks, natural language processing, and sentiment assessment, are vital in this area. Security resolving issues may be automated by cognitive safety mechanisms, which are capable of self-learning. Furthermore, cognitive safety can aid in thwarting cyberattacks like cognitive security breaches, which alter how people think shown in Figure 6.8. The cognitive safety plan incorporates both technological and non-technical solutions, such as techniques to lessen people's susceptibility to exploitation and technological techniques to identify and stop the dissemination of false information. AI technology is important when it comes to cognition security. A few relevant AI techniques are knowledge technology, AI, networked AI, time management and scheduling, and systems with multiple agents. To capture complicated information for safety issue solutions, knowledge mining is applied. Through sophisticated statistical analysis, AI enables neural networks to continuously derive insights and acquire information. Complex attack patterns can be identified thanks to deep learning. Safety duties are organized and coordinated via the use of organizational and time management approaches. Multi-agent systems and dispersed AI aim to find global methods while addressing the peculiarities of varied, dynamic, and decentralized contexts. The network communication features of CCPS-IoT, such as its dynamic nature, partial observability, ambiguous assessments,

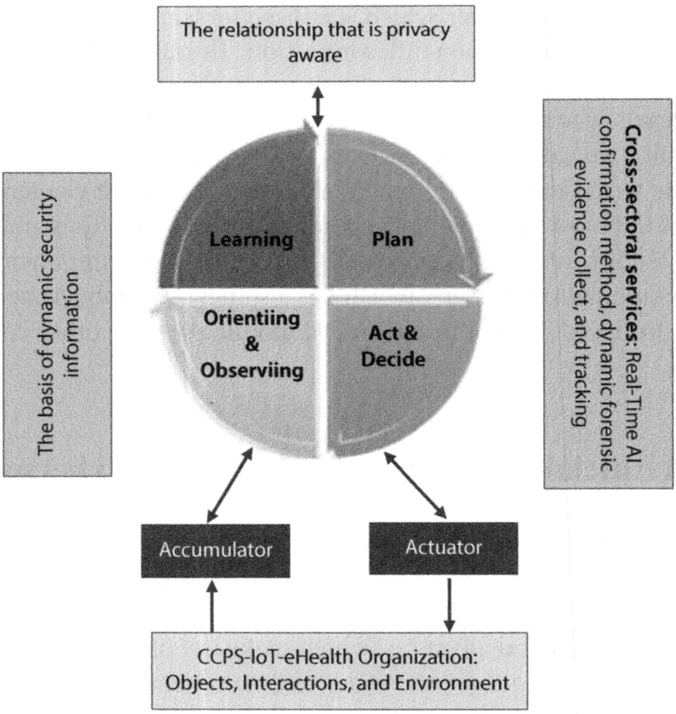

Figure 6.8 The CCPS using IoT in healthcare.

resource restrictions, variation, enormous magnitude, and complicated accessibility regulations, are also pertinent to the discussion of these AI methodologies. Cybersecurity solutions that leverage AI and ML can improve real-time reactions to incidents and accelerate threat identification. Large amounts of organized and unorganized information might be managed by these technologies, allowing for the identification of linkages and patterns that may be beyond the scope of human comprehension.

6.5.1 Privacy-Aware Collaboration

To mitigate risks and successfully handle threats in the complex healthcare environment, dynamic, based on evidence risk control must be put into place. This calls for a privacy-aware strategy that prioritizes stakeholder cooperation via safe information sharing, reporting, and visualization. Interchangeability, communication, and working together are the keystones of sharing information in the medical sector. However, they also bring with them additional security, privacy, technological, motivation, and regulatory challenges. Using blockchain technology in a decentralized manner is one viable remedy. Through features like digital access controls, collection of data, information availability, client identity management, and information permanence, this technology may make cooperation easier. Blockchain technology allows for decentralized sharing of information while maintaining anonymity through well-defined access controls. To support intellectual privacy and security safeguards, this promotes efficient and fruitful collaboration in cybercrime and data across the many tiers of the complex medical environment.

6.5.2 Cognitive Security Cycle Model

The goal of the CCPS-IoT cognitive safety cycle model is to close the cognitive loop by defending against threats and gaining knowledge from the actions made. This approach makes use of controls, creative processes, AI, and trade-offs. In addition, the model takes into account human behavior, the larger social environment, and the changing nature of CCPS-IoT. It then makes use of this comprehension to implement suitable actions and extract important insights from the procedure. The cycle of this paradigm has four steps: learn, observe and orient, decide and act, and plan. Adaptive collection methods are used in the observe and orient stage to track and comprehend stimuli including arrangements, customer behaviors, dangers, weaknesses, and connections to the physical setting. The model gains knowledge in the learning stage through views, findings, choices, and actions. The methodology creates plans in the plan stage by determining the objectives wanted and taking scheduling into account. The model chooses the best safety approach and puts it into practice in the decide and act stage by making physical changes to CCPS-IoT equipment or by implementing it. Capturing human cognitive processes, responding fast to hackers, and taking into account the variety and change of the CCPS-IoT environment are some of the issues this model faces. This paradigm uses methods including AI, enormous amounts of information in processing, and precise decision-making. To preserve anonymity and security during customer interactions, the cognitive framework is also utilized to comprehend consumers in a variety of scenarios.

6.6 Conclusions and Future Direction

6.6.1 Conclusions

To simulate human cognitive reactions to changing privacy and safety risks inside the CCPS-IoT healthcare environment, this section presents a cognitive cybersecurity framework. To provide cross-sectoral offerings, this framework seamlessly incorporates ML, cognition approaches, forensics, and cutting-edge safety technologies. This building construction, which consists of four main layers—collaborative, vision and understanding, collecting information and mobility, and infrastructure—builds on ideas from numerous study initiatives. Future stages of this study will go into the minute details of every architectural element and validate them using a sequence of simulations and useful system demonstrations in actual use cases. Human cognitive viewpoints in our future research endeavors, covering both cognitive benefits and possible biases. To sum up, cognitive cyber and physical safety in conjunction with IoT represents a critical advancement in the development of intelligent medical facilities, tackling the intricate relationship between the internet, safety, and the treatment of patients. Healthcare companies may strengthen their defenses against changing cyber threats and seize new possibilities for productivity and creativity by integrating cognitive technology, AI, and sophisticated data analytics. The identification of five essential needs—safeguarding private health information, protecting gadgets that are connected, avoiding service interruptions, guaranteeing compliance with regulations, and cultivating stakeholders' trust—is what propels the development of secure intelligent healthcare systems. To reduce risks and improve accessibility and confidentiality, cognitive cyber-physical safety devices provide proactive danger identification, continuous surveillance, and flexible reaction capabilities. Healthcare organizations may enhance the satisfaction of patients, optimize the provision of healthcare, and simplify operations while managing the intricate world of technology and compliance with laws and regulations by adopting intelligent cyber-physical safety.

6.6.2 Future Directions

Advanced Threat Intelligence: To foresee and proactively address new cyber risks in intelligent medical surroundings, subsequent attempts will concentrate on exploiting sophisticated threat identification capabilities, such as threat modeling, threat hunting, and analytical forecasting.

Autonomous Safety Operations: Healthcare providers will be able to streamline safety measures, improve incident reaction times, and adaptably defend against changing cyber threats thanks to the creation of autonomous safety operations driven by AI and ML.

Blockchain Technologies: By enabling safe and verifiable operations while guaranteeing patient confidentiality and information independence, the incorporation of the technology known as blockchain offers promise for improving the safety, honesty, and openness of medical information transmission.

Edge Computing Safety: To reduce safety issues and guarantee privacy and honesty, there will be an increasing emphasis on safeguarding devices on the edge, networks, and information processing at the network periphery as edge computing becomes more widely used for medical IoT installations.

Zero Trust Architecture: To stop lateral threat movements and safeguard vital healthcare resources, the concepts of zero trust architecture—which emphasize continual confirmation, and restricted access, including micro-segmentation—will be used more widely.

The establishment of safe healthcare IoT standards and protocols is vital to guarantee connectivity, and resiliency, including in intelligent healthcare environments. This will promote a uniform security strategy across heterogeneous medical environments.

Privacy-Preserving Methods: Healthcare organizations will be able to derive useful information from confidential medical information while maintaining patient privacy and confidentiality thanks to developments in privacy-preserving technology like federated training, homomorphic cryptography, and differentiating privacy.

Human-Centric Security: To reduce threats from insiders, fraudulent transactions assaults, and human mistakes that represent serious dangers to medical information safety, a focus on human-centric safety precautions will give priority to consumer understanding, behavior data analysis, and retraining.

Global advancements in medical records security, confidentiality, and compliance with regulations will be fueled by ongoing changes to legislation and requirements, as well as by aggressive industry cooperation and knowledge exchange.

Ethical Considerations: To ensure that moral standards and societal ideals are aligned with the responsible creation and installation of cognitive cyber-physical safety measures in smart medical facilities, more importance will be placed on moral issues such as computational equity, openness, and responsibility.

These prospects will impact the environment for cognitive cyber-physical safety with IoT as healthcare organizations keep developing and embracing digitization. This will enable healthcare organizations to navigate novel obstacles, take advantage of novel possibilities, and protect the next phase of healthcare shipment. Assuring the safety, confidentiality, and dependability of medical information and facilities while realizing the complete potential of smart healthcare systems may be achieved via interdisciplinary cooperation, creativity, and a shared dedication to patient-focused treatment.

References

1. Huitzil, C.T., Cognitive Dynamic Systems for Cyber-Physical Engineering, in: *Machine Learning for Complex and Unmanned Systems*, pp. 277–294, CRC Press, Boca Raton, Florida, USA, 2024.
2. Liang, Q., Zhao, S., Zhang, J., Deng, H., Damm, W., Hess, D., Forrest, L., Cyber-physical systems. *ACM Trans.*, 8, 1, 10–32, 2024.
3. Bharathi, V., Vulnerability Detection in Cyber-Physical System Using Machine Learning. *Scalable Comput. Pract. Exper.*, *25*, 1, 577–591, 2024.
4. Sood, V.M., Singh, Y., Bhargava, B., Narang, S.K. (Eds.), *Intelligent Security Solutions for Cyber-Physical Systems*, CRC Press, Boca Raton, Florida, USA, 2024.
5. Rathore, S., and Park, J. H., A blockchain-based deep learning approach for cyber security in next generation industrial cyber-physical systems. *IEEE Transactions on Industrial Informatics*, 17, 8, 5522–5532, 2020.
6. Latchoumi, T.P., Parthiban, L., Balamurugan, K., Raja, K., Vijayaraj, J., Parthiban, R., A Framework for Low Energy Application Devices Using Blockchain-Enabled IoT in WSNs, in: *Integrating Blockchain and Artificial Intelligence for Industry 4.0 Innovations*, pp. 121–132, Springer International Publishing, Cham, 2023.

7. Wu, J., Jin, J., Wu, C., Challenges and Countermeasures of Federated Learning Data Poisoning Attack Situation Prediction. *Mathematics*, *12*, 6, 901, 2024.
8. Retzlaff, C.O., Das, S., Wayllace, C., Mousavi, P., Afshari, M., Yang, T., Holzinger, A., Human-in-the-Loop Reinforcement Learning: A Survey and Position on Requirements, Challenges, and Opportunities. *J. Artif. Intell. Res.*, *79*, 359–415, 2024.
9. Balamurugan, K., Latchoumi, T.P., Satla, S., Machining Studies on AlSi7+ 63% SiC Composite Using Machine Learning Technique, in: *Metal Matrix Composites*, pp. 139–166, CRC Press, Boca Raton, Florida, USA, 2023.
10. Karthikeyan, A., Karthikeyan, K., Swathika, O.G., Cyber-physical security in a stand-alone photovoltaic system for rural electrification. *Next-Generation Cyber-Phys. Microgrid Syst.*, 2, 29–75, 2024.
11. Serôdio, C., Mestre, P., Cabral, J., Gomes, M., Branco, F., Software and Architecture Orchestration for Process Control in Industry 4.0 Enabled by Cyber-Physical Systems Technologies. *Appl. Sci.*, *14*, 5, 2160, 2024.
12. Ali, J.A.H., Gaffinet, B., Panetto, H., Naudet, Y., Cognitive systems and interoperability in the enterprise: A systematic literature review. *Annu. Rev. Control*, *57*, 100954, 2024.
13. Parthiban, L., Latchoumi, T.P., Balamurugan, K., Raja, K., Parthiban, R., Cognitive Computing for the Internet of Medical Things, in: *Integrating Blockchain and Artificial Intelligence for Industry 4.0 Innovations*, pp. 85–100, Springer International Publishing, Cham, 2023.
14. Karthikeyan, S. and Nagamani, G.M., An Architecture of Cyber-Physical System for Industry 4.0, in: *Digital Transformation: Industry 4.0 to Society 5.0*, pp. 259–283, Springer Nature Singapore, Singapore, 2024.
15. Stutz, D., de Assis, J.T., Laghari, A.A., Khan, A.A., Deshpande, A., Kulkarni, D., Grata, E.G., Cyber Threat Detection and Mitigation Using Artificial Intelligence–A Cyber-physical Perspective. *Appl. Artif. Intell. Cybersecur. Anal. Cyber Threat Detect.*, 7, 107–133, 2024.
16. Banerjee, S., Jesubalan, N.G., Kulkarni, A., Agarwal, A., Rathore, A.S., Developing cyber-physical system and digital twin for smart manufacturing: Methodology and case study of continuous clarification. *J. Ind. Inf. Integr.*, *38*, 100577, 2024.
17. Ravindra Krishna Chandar, V., Baskaran, P., Mohanraj, G., Karthikeyan, D., Deep iterative fuzzy pooling in unmanned robotics and autonomous systems for Cyber-Physical systems. *J. Intell. Fuzzy Syst.*, 36, 1, 1–19, 2024. (Preprint).

7

Cognitive Cyber-Physical Security with IoT and ML: Role of Cybersecurity, Threats, and Benefits to Modern Economies and Industries

P. Anbalagan*, A. Kanthimathinathan and S. Saravanan

Department of Computer Science and Engineering, Annamalai University, Annamalai Nagar, Chidambaram, India

Abstract

The application of artificial intelligence (AI) in cyber-physical systems has both present and future obstacles that are reviewed in this literature survey. The used technique bore similarities to a taxonomy analysis and literature evaluation of intricately linked and coupled cyber-physical systems inside the Internet of Things (IoT). IoT concepts, infrastructures, and frameworks are receiving more attention in academic and technical publications. With the proliferation of IoT devices and the integration of machine learning (ML) algorithms, there is a growing need to address security challenges in cyber-physical systems. This paper explores the potential threats posed by cyber-attacks and the benefits derived from leveraging ML for enhanced security measures. By analyzing the intersection of cybersecurity, ML, and IoT technologies, this research aims to provide insights into mitigating threats and maximizing the benefits of cognitive cyber-physical security in various sectors, ultimately contributing to the advancement of modern economies and industries.

Keywords: Cognitive cyber-physical security, Internet of Things, cybersecurity, security measures, risk assessment, predictive maintenance, intrusion detection, adaptive security systems

**Corresponding author*: anbalagansamy@gmail.com

K. Ananthajothi, S. N. Sangeethaa, D. Divya, S. Balamurugan and Shen-Lung Peng (eds.) Securing Cyber-Physical Systems: Fundamentals, Applications and Challenges, (133–156) © 2025 Scrivener Publishing LLC

7.1 Introduction

When artificial intelligence (AI) was first introduced to our society, many people raised concerns about the potential threats that it may pose [1], upcoming. Technology has the capacity to build itself, even in today's technologically advanced society [2]. It is a popular belief that "Borg–eye and the We–I" monsters might emerge from wearing technology devices that are connected to one another. Regarding the implications of AI decision-making on the economy and society, it is important to consider its potential benefits and challenges.

An excellent illustration of how AI and Internet of Things (IoT) may coexist is the Tesla vehicle. Autonomous cars can now evaluate road conditions, determine the best speed to drive at, and anticipate traffic patterns and pedestrian movements to AI [3]. Intelligent building development is another example of COVID-19. AI integrated with smart sensors can open doors, switch on lights, and determine the best time to heat or cool a space. This will include biological and health monitoring systems and the integration of robots and intelligent edge devices [4].

AI enables more than just decision-making; it also facilitates the movement and operation of various items. This study found a relationship between AI and the cognitive cyber-physical security (CCPS) showing how they rely on one another to control physical processes. The IoT is a significant advancement in AI research and has emerged as a subclass of CCPS lately. An IoT technology allows computer equipment to operate without direct human or computer contact [5].

A brief review of earlier industrial revolutions shows how they came before the present situation [6]. The idea that water and steam may be used for automation emerged during the first industrial revolution and mapping of five C's with CCPS levels is shown in Figure 7.1. A century later, with the start of the Second Industrial Revolution, electric power was used for mass manufacturing for the first time. The Third Industrial Revolution brought about the introduction of the notion of automation in the 1970s [7]. This subject may seem contentious and wide to some because it is a relatively new idea. This study aims to verify the veracity of the myth that Industry 4.0 can only be implemented by large businesses due to its significant financial resource requirements [8].

In the rapidly evolving landscape of cybersecurity, CCPS emerges as a promising paradigm, integrating cutting-edge technologies such as IoT and machine learning (ML) to fortify the defense mechanisms of cyber-physical systems. This interdisciplinary approach harnesses the power of cognitive computing to augment the security posture of interconnected systems,

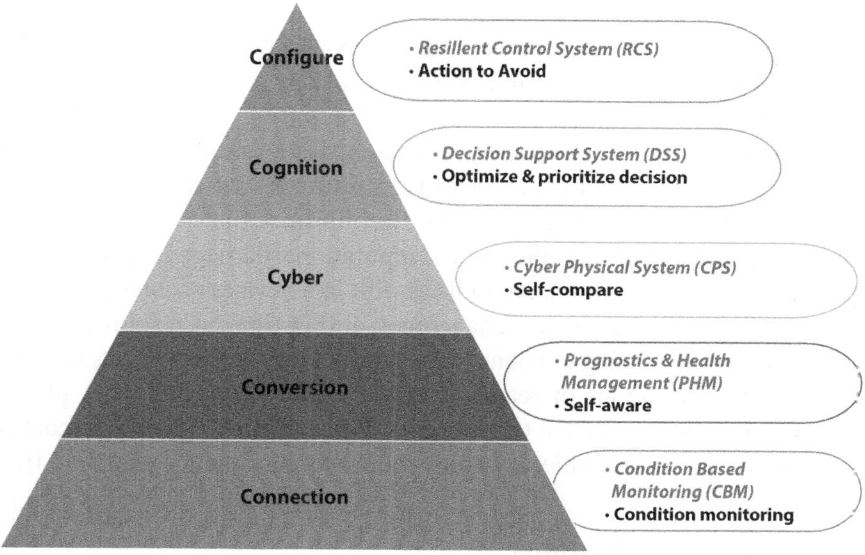

Figure 7.1 Mapping five-C architecture with CCPS levels.

which encompass both digital and physical elements. As industries increasingly rely on IoT devices to monitor, control, and optimize physical processes, the need for robust security measures becomes paramount. In this context, the fusion of cognitive capabilities with IoT and ML presents novel solutions to mitigate cyber threats and safeguard critical infrastructure [9].

The role of cybersecurity within the realm of CCPS with IoT and ML is multifaceted, encompassing various aspects ranging from threat detection to incident response. Traditional cybersecurity approaches often struggle to cope with the scale and complexity of IoT ecosystems, where a multitude of devices continuously generate data streams [10]. By leveraging ML algorithms, CCPS frameworks can analyze this deluge of data in real time, enabling proactive threat detection and rapid response to security incidents. Furthermore, cognitive systems have the capacity to learn from past incidents and adapt to evolving threats, thereby enhancing the resilience of cyber-physical systems against emerging risks [11].

However, along with its transformative potential, CCPS with IoT and ML also introduces new challenges and vulnerabilities. The interconnected nature of IoT ecosystems amplifies the attack surface, providing adversaries with multiple entry points to infiltrate networks and compromise sensitive data. Moreover, ML models themselves are susceptible to adversarial attacks, where adversaries exploit vulnerabilities in the learning algorithms to manipulate system behavior. Privacy concerns also loom large, as the proliferation of IoT devices raises questions about data ownership, consent, and protection of personal information [12].

Despite these challenges, the benefits of adopting CCPS with IoT and ML extend beyond cybersecurity to encompass economic and industrial advantages. By fortifying the security posture of critical infrastructure and industrial systems, organizations can minimize the risk of costly data breaches, operational disruptions, and reputational damage [13]. Moreover, the integration of cognitive capabilities with IoT devices enables predictive maintenance, dynamic risk management, and optimized resource allocation, thereby enhancing efficiency and productivity across various sectors. As modern economies increasingly rely on interconnected cyber-physical systems, the imperative to embrace CCPS with IoT and ML becomes imperative to ensure resilience, innovation, and sustainable growth [14].

7.1.1 Key Contributions

CCPS with IoT and ML involves the integration of cognitive computing, IoT devices, and ML algorithms to enhance the security of cyber-physical systems. Here are some key contributions, roles of cybersecurity, threats, and benefits to modern economies and industries:

Enhanced Threat Detection and Response: ML algorithms can analyze vast amounts of data generated by IoT devices to identify patterns indicative of cyber threats or anomalous behavior. Cognitive capabilities enable systems to learn from past incidents and continuously adapt to evolving threats, enhancing threat detection and response capabilities.

Predictive Maintenance: IoT sensors embedded in physical infrastructure can collect real-time data on equipment performance. ML algorithms can analyze this data to predict when maintenance is required, helping to prevent costly downtime and ensuring optimal operation of critical infrastructure.

Improved Access Control and Authentication: Cognitive systems can utilize ML algorithms to analyze user behavior patterns and detect suspicious activities, enhancing access control and authentication mechanisms. This helps mitigate the risk of unauthorized access to sensitive systems and data.

Dynamic Risk Management: ML algorithms can analyze data from various sources, including IoT devices, to assess cybersecurity risks in real time. Cognitive systems can dynamically adjust security measures based on the current threat landscape, ensuring proactive risk management.

Automated Incident Response: ML-powered systems can automate incident response processes by quickly identifying and containing security breaches. Cognitive capabilities enable systems to analyze the context of security incidents and take appropriate actions to mitigate their impact.
Threat Intelligence and Information Sharing: ML algorithms can analyze vast amounts of cybersecurity data to extract valuable threat intelligence. Cognitive systems facilitate the sharing of this intelligence across industries and organizations, enabling proactive defense against emerging threats.
Challenges and Threats: Despite its benefits, CCPS with IoT and ML also presents challenges and threats. These include the potential for ML models to be manipulated by adversaries, privacy concerns associated with the collection of IoT data, and the risk of IoT devices being compromised and used as entry points for cyber-attacks.
Economic and Industrial Benefits: The adoption of CCPS with IoT and ML offers significant economic and industrial benefits. By enhancing cybersecurity measures, organizations can reduce the risk of costly data breaches and operational disruptions. Additionally, improved efficiency and reliability of critical infrastructure contribute to economic growth and competitiveness.

In summary, CCPS with IoT and ML plays a crucial role in enhancing the security of modern economies and industries by leveraging cognitive computing, IoT devices, and ML algorithms to detect and respond to cyber threats effectively. However, it also presents challenges and threats that must be addressed to realize its full potential.

7.1.2 Problem Statement

The intersection of cybersecurity, ML, and the evolving landscape of digital technologies presents a multifaceted challenge to modern economies and industries. Cybersecurity has become paramount as organizations contend with an increasingly sophisticated array of threats, including data breaches, malware attacks, and ransomware. These threats not only jeopardize sensitive information but also undermine consumer trust and financial stability. Amidst this backdrop, ML has emerged as a promising approach to bolster cyber defenses. Leveraging algorithms for anomaly detection, pattern recognition, and predictive analysis, ML offers potential solutions to identify and mitigate risks in real time. However, the effectiveness of ML in cybersecurity hinges on various factors, including access to high-quality training data, algorithmic complexity, and adaptability to dynamic threat landscapes. As modern economies and industries navigate this complex terrain, understanding the interplay between cybersecurity, ML, and the broader digital ecosystem is imperative for both mitigating risks and harnessing the transformative benefits of these technologies.

7.1.3 Motivation

Increasing Interconnectivity: The widespread adoption of IoT devices has led to a highly interconnected digital ecosystem where devices communicate and exchange data seamlessly. This interconnectedness presents both opportunities for efficiency and convenience and vulnerabilities that can be exploited by malicious actors.
Cybersecurity Challenges: The integration of IoT devices introduces numerous cybersecurity challenges, including vulnerabilities in device firmware, inadequate authentication mechanisms, and susceptibility to distributed denial-of-service attacks. It is of utmost importance to address the challenges that arise in guaranteeing the security, privacy, and accessibility of IoT systems and the information they process.
ML for Threat Detection: ML algorithms offer a powerful approach to enhance cybersecurity in IoT environments. By analyzing vast amounts of data generated by IoT devices, ML models can detect patterns indicative of malicious activities, identify anomalies in device behavior, and predict potential security threats before they escalate.
Dynamic Threat Landscape: The evolving nature of cyber threats requires adaptive and proactive security measures. ML enables IoT systems to continuously learn from new data and adapt their defense mechanisms accordingly. This dynamic threat response is essential for mitigating emerging threats and staying ahead of cyber attackers.
Benefits to Modern Economies and Industries: Effective cybersecurity in IoT ecosystems is essential for maintaining consumer trust, protecting sensitive data, and ensuring the reliability of critical infrastructure. By leveraging ML for threat detection and response, industries can enhance their resilience to cyber-attacks, minimize operational disruptions, and safeguard their bottom line.
Integration of Cognitive Capabilities: The integration of cognitive capabilities into cyber-physical systems enables autonomous decision-making and adaptive responses to security incidents. Cognitive systems can analyze complex data streams from IoT devices, identify potential security risks, and take proactive measures to mitigate threats, thereby enhancing overall system security and resilience.

7.2 CCPS Associated with IoT

Generating value requires the capacity to assess and forecast events in real time, both past and present. AI is needed as data is always evolving and generating new information. In the production process, intelligent manufacturing technology infrastructure may result in considerable time and cost savings. Autonomous AI will be used in social and economic decision-making. With the hyper-connected economy's huge economic potential, this shift has already started. The advantages of digital economy networking for future economic development have already been shown by studies [15].

AI progress in cyber-physical systems the urge to produce value is what motivates privacy. In today's world, the importance of social and economic ideas cannot be overstated. Any organization's objectives are determined by its guiding ideals [16]. A novel approach to integration and a thorough comprehension of CPS and the cognitive architecture of Industrial Internet of Things (IIoT) may be necessary for physical and cyber subsystems [17]. It could be required to integrate IIoT notions on physical system control with human-CPS interaction in order to get this information. This digital transformation is supported by various technologies such as AI, automation, robotic swarm operations, autonomous cognitive and digital twin systems, and CCPS networks [18].

This method has been frequently employed to generate quick prototypes before mass production because it was an affordable way to produce high-quality goods in small numbers [19]. Advanced manufacturing technologies and real-world situations both include computer-generated data [20]. It is possible to create visuals from this data that blend in with the viewer's surroundings. In a dynamic workplace, augmented reality helps employees in real-time with challenging tasks. AI technologies facilitate the execution of tasks by machines and computers that are similar to those carried out by persons in industrial processes [21].

Robotic manufacturing processes are becoming more and more capable of optimizing logistics networks, task administration, and smart production planning in unison with industrial automation devices [22]. Robotic production systems and digital twins that rely on data analysis can significantly reduce production time and enhance output quality. Huge robotic arms can lift a great deal of weight. However, there are still many applications where human aid with robots is necessary. Co-bots are robots that can work alongside people without posing a health risk. Robots that operate in teams are adaptable and have the capacity to pick up new skills [23].

Humanoid robots provide a different approach. Autonomous robots are used in large-scale manufacturing as tools to increase output quality, increase productivity, and reduce labor costs [24]. But industrial robots are too costly, particularly for small and medium-sized businesses.

Small and medium-sized enterprises (SMEs) have more access to co-bots that are lightweight and easy to develop [25]. To guarantee the interconnectedness of commodities, materials, and equipment, effective business communication necessitates the assimilation of data in both horizontal and vertical systems. The digitalization of vertical integration enables product life cycle management, real-time manufacturing logistics based on the IoT, and automated production processes. Horizontal digitization is the process of integrating data with important suppliers, customers, and partners. A digital environment in which data flow facilitates proper functioning is generated by combining vertical and horizontal digitalization [26].

Businesses that leverage data must incorporate Industry 4.0 technologies in order to surpass their competitors. Autonomous production systems that use mobile robotics, fault diagnosis, object identification algorithms, and vision and navigation tools, are critical components of this. Implementing Industry 4.0 requires a shift not only in production but in all activities and services throughout the entire value chain.

7.2.1 Reasons in Favor of Cognitive Analytics

Due to the constant changes in the cyber risk environment, it is hard to distinguish between the two. Determining the precise amount of money that will be lost as a result of cybercrime is difficult. It is difficult to calculate the whole amount of potential harm brought on by cyber risk without a technique of impact assessment quantities of probability data. Real-time monitoring and risk distribution across several technological platforms are required to build such a system. This necessitates regularly assessing the network's susceptibility. Cognitive analytics are required to address some of the latest challenges, including the possession of digital data and the way certain topics are covered by the media.

Complexity Management: When it comes to handling the complexity of contemporary data settings, cognitive analytics shines. The abundance of large data and a variety of data sources may make it difficult for standard analytics techniques to glean insightful information. With the help of ML and natural language processing, cognitive analytics is able to evaluate massive amounts of data, spot trends, and extract useful information even from unstructured sources.

Real-time Insights: Real-time data stream analysis is made possible by cognitive analytics, giving businesses quick insights into shifting patterns, irregularities, and possible threats. This skill is very beneficial in dynamic contexts where rapid choices may have a big impact on the result, such as supply chains, cybersecurity, and financial markets.
Adaptive Learning: The capacity of cognitive analytics to continually learn and adapt is one of its main advantages. When faced with novel data, ML algorithms employed in cognitive analytics may iteratively improve their models, increasing the precision and applicability of insights. Organizations may remain sensitive to shifting consumer preferences and changing business situations thanks to this adaptive learning process.
Contextual Understanding: Beyond standard data analysis, cognitive analytics takes into account contextual information and understands the nuances of human language. Cognitive analytics systems can analyze unstructured data, like as emails, social media posts, and customer feedback, by using natural language processing techniques. This allows the systems to provide more insights into the attitudes, preferences, and behaviors of its users.
Predictive Capabilities: Cognitive analytics has the ability to more accurately identify future trends, dangers, and opportunities by using sophisticated predictive modeling approaches. By using ML algorithms to find patterns and connections in past data, predictive analytics may foresee future events and facilitate proactive risk reduction and decision-making.
Automation and Efficiency: Numerous parts of data analysis are automated by cognitive analytics, which streamlines decision-making procedures and lessens the need for human involvement. Cognitive analytics increases efficiency and production by automating repetitive operations like pattern recognition, anomaly detection, and data preparation. This frees up human resources to concentrate on more important activities.
Competitive Advantage: By using data-driven insights to spur innovation, enhance consumer experiences, and streamline business procedures, companies that use cognitive analytics may achieve a competitive advantage. Organizations may remain ahead of the competition and make better choices by using cognitive analytics to find hidden patterns, spot new trends, and predict client demands.

7.2.2 Analyses of Current Cyber Risk Data

In the digital economy, synchronization and component failure present difficulties that must be addressed by building essential infrastructures using rigorous CPS methods. I4.0's general adoption has been hampered by a lack of standards. It is crucial to take into account the network as a whole in addition to the unique security threats that a single firm may be facing while doing I4.0 and IIoT cyber risk assessments.

In order to comprehend the changing threat environment and put appropriate cybersecurity measures in place, it is essential that current cyber risk data be analyzed. The following are a few significant evaluations of recent cyber risk data:

Trend Identification: Organizations may spot new trends and patterns in cyberattacks by analyzing data on cyber risk. Through the monitoring of threat actors' methods, complexity, and frequency, companies may predict prospective attacks and modify their cybersecurity strategy appropriately.

Vulnerability Assessment: Organizations may find vulnerabilities in their systems and networks with the use of cyber risk data analysis. Organizations are able to prioritize remediation efforts and dedicate resources to solve the most significant security holes by reviewing data on exploit activity, patching progress, and known vulnerabilities.

Threat Intelligence Integration: By merging cyber risk data with outside threat intelligence sources, companies may get important insights into threat actors' tactics, methods, and procedures. Organizations may improve their threat detection capabilities and more accurately identify indications of compromise by matching internal data with external threat feeds.

Risk Quantification: Organizations may measure their cybersecurity risk exposure and rank their risk mitigation initiatives by analyzing cyber risk data. Organizations may decide how best to allocate resources and implement risk management techniques by evaluating variables including the possibility of cyberattacks, the possible impact on company operations, and the efficacy of current safeguards.

Behavioral Analytics: By examining user activity and network traffic data, companies may identify irregularities and dubious actions that may point to a cyberattack. Organizations may detect departures from typical patterns of behavior and take preemptive measures to neutralize any hazards before they become more serious by using behavioral analytics approaches and ML algorithms.

Incident Response Optimization: By revealing the efficiency of current reaction protocols and the underlying reasons for security events, the analysis of cyber risk data helps enhance incident response procedures. Organizations may improve incident response skills and lessen the effect of future security breaches by carrying out post-event studies and pinpointing areas for improvement.

Compliance Monitoring: Organizations may prove compliance with industry standards and legal obligations by using cyber risk data analysis. Organizations may make sure they comply with legal and regulatory requirements pertaining to cybersecurity by tracking important security metrics, regularly evaluating risks, recording security controls, and mitigating actions.

In general, firms must analyze current cyber risk data to stay ahead of developing threats, safeguard their resources and sensitive information, and keep their cybersecurity posture resilient.

7.3 Materials and Methods

7.3.1 Role of Cybersecurity in CCPS with IoT and ML

Threat detection and risk management: Cybersecurity is essential to detecting and reducing hazards related to cognitive cyber-physical systems. Through the implementation of comprehensive risk assessments and strong security measures, enterprises may detect any weaknesses in ML algorithms, IoT devices, and associated networks. Cybersecurity systems also minimize the possibility of security breaches and system compromises by enabling proactive threat detection and response methods to identify and neutralize cyberattacks instantly.

Data Privacy and Confidentiality: It is critical to protect data privacy and confidentiality because of the massive volume of data produced by ML algorithms and IoT devices. Cybersecurity tools including data anonymization, access restrictions, and encryption help safeguard private data from illegal access and guarantee adherence to privacy laws like the California Consumer Privacy Act and the General Data Protection Regulation. Organizations may increase stakeholder confidence and reduce the risk of data breaches and legal repercussions by protecting data privacy.
Integrity and Resilience of Systems: The integrity and durability of cognitive cyber-physical systems depend on cybersecurity measures. Organizations may reduce the risk of malware attacks, unauthorized modifications to IoT devices, and illegal changes to ML models by using methods like code signing and secure boot and by putting safe development procedures into place and regularly performing security audits. Cybersecurity solutions also help businesses create redundancy and robust architectures to reduce the effect of cyberattacks and system failures on vital activities.

Threat Intelligence and Incident Response: Organizations may get useful threat information and insights into new attack pathways and cyber threats by using cybersecurity solutions. Through the usage of threat intelligence streams, enterprises may remain up to date on the most recent malware strains, security flaws, and hacking strategies used by threat actors. Furthermore, by establishing incident response rules and processes, businesses may efficiently react to security problems and lessen their impact on cognitive cyber-physical systems. This is made possible by cybersecurity solutions.
Regulatory Compliance and Governance: For regulatory compliance and governance in cognitive cyber-physical ecosystems, cybersecurity is essential. Organizations may show their dedication to security and reduce the legal and reputational penalties associated with non-compliance by following industry-specific legislation and standards like the NIST Cybersecurity Framework, ISO 27001, and IEC 62443. Cybersecurity solutions also make it easier to put best practices and security controls into place to comply with legal requirements and guarantee the reliability and integrity of cognitive cyber-physical systems.

For cognitive cyber-physical systems integrating IoT and ML to be secure, private, and resilient, cybersecurity is essential. Organizations may reduce cyber threats, safeguard sensitive data, and preserve the availability and integrity of vital infrastructure and operations by putting strong security measures in place.

7.3.2 ML in Cognitive Cyber-Physical Security with IoT

The adaptive cyber-physical-human (CPH) system's success criteria and metrics are linked to the extent, pace, and thoroughness of the cyber-physical and human–element adaptation. The degree of predictability, trust, and shared awareness within the adaptive CPH system are also important parameters that are difficult to quantify but have "proxies." The online ML influenced by user behavior, sensor data, and actuator operations can help the human and cyber-physical components adapt to each other more effectively shown in Figure 7.2.

7.3.3 Threats to Modern Economies and Industries

The stability, prosperity, and competitiveness of modern economies and sectors may be significantly impacted by a wide variety of old and emergent challenges. These are a few of the main threats:

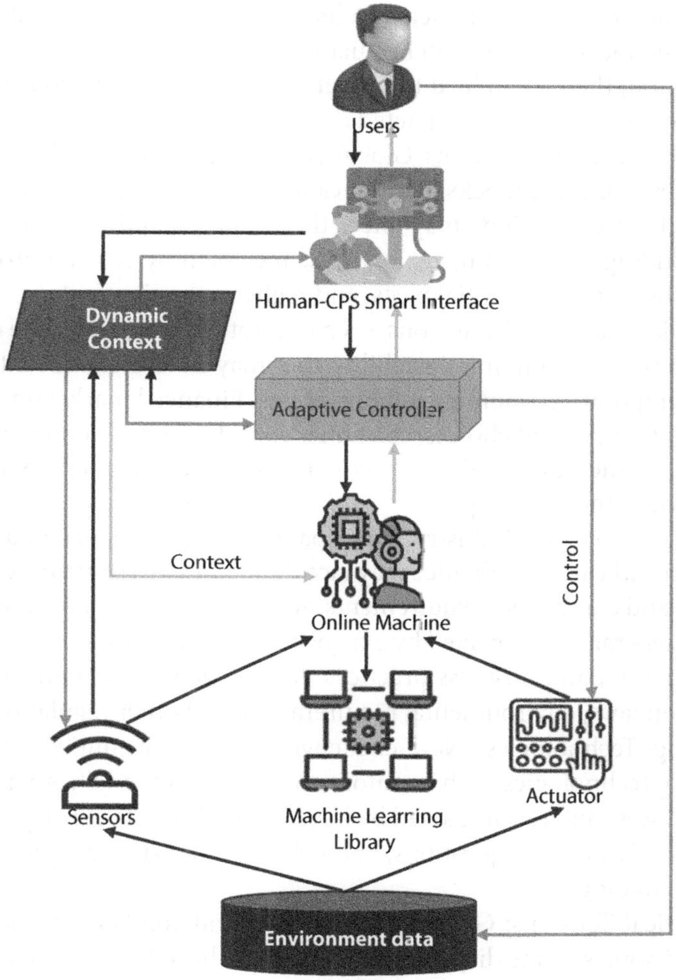

Figure 7.2 Functional architecture of adaptive CPH systems.

Cyber Attacks: One of the biggest risks to contemporary economies and companies is cyberattacks. Malware infections, ransomware, data breaches, phishing, and denial-of-service assaults are just a few of the many ways that these attacks might manifest themselves. Cyberattacks have the potential to destroy customer confidence, compromise sensitive data, and interfere with vital infrastructure, all of which may result in monetary losses and harm to one's reputation.

Data Breaches: For companies in various sectors, including banking, healthcare, retail, and government, data breaches can be extremely hazardous.

If unauthorized access or theft results in the exposure of sensitive data, such as financial records, intellectual property, or personally identifiable information, then it can lead to monetary losses, legal consequences, and reputational harm for the impacted organization.

Supply Chain Disruptions Global supply networks may be disrupted by pandemics, cyberattacks, natural catastrophes, and geopolitical events. Supply chain disruptions may affect the resilience and efficiency of sectors including manufacturing, logistics, and retail by causing production delays, shortages of essential parts, and higher operating costs.

Economic Instability: Recessions, exchange rate swings, and trade disputes are examples of economic instability that may have a significant impact on contemporary economies and businesses. Financial market uncertainty may affect investment choices, consumer confidence, and company growth strategies, which can result in lower consumer spending, job losses, and a downturn in the economy.

Regulatory Changes: Industry participants in highly regulated areas like energy, healthcare, and finance may face difficulties as a result of regulatory changes and compliance requirements. A company's profitability and competitiveness may be impacted by expensive modifications to its operations, infrastructure, and business practices due to changes in trade laws, data protection laws, environmental requirements, and other regulations.

Emerging Technologies: New challenges and opportunities arise from emerging technologies such as automation, AI, and the IoT. A wide range of businesses might be impacted by issues including data privacy, algorithmic prejudice, ethical questions, and cybersecurity risks related to developing technology.

Geopolitical Tensions: Geopolitical tensions and conflicts, including territorial disputes, trade disputes, and sanctions, have the potential to cause anxiety for firms operating in impacted countries, disrupt global supply chains, and impair international trade flows. For businesses with international operations, geopolitical instability may result in heightened geopolitical risks, market volatility, and currency changes.

Natural Disasters and Climate Change: Storms, earthquakes, floods, wildfires, and other natural catastrophes pose serious hazards to businesses situated in areas vulnerable to disasters. The impact of climate change includes rising sea levels, severe weather conditions, and a shortage of resources. These effects may lead to disruptions in business operations, damage to infrastructure, and increased operating costs. Various sectors, such as insurance, tourism, and agriculture, could be affected by the consequences of climate change.

A diverse strategy is needed to counter these challenges, including strong risk management plans, cybersecurity investments, supply chain diversity, regulatory change adaption, and proactive actions to lessen the effects of geopolitical unrest and climate change. In a world that is increasingly unpredictable and interconnected, modern economies and businesses can enhance their resilience, sustainability, and long-term competitiveness by identifying and addressing potential risks and threats.

7.3.4 Benefits to Modern Economies and Industries

Numerous innovations and circumstances may assist modern economies and enterprises in different ways. The following are some main advantages:

Increased Efficiency: Efficiency gains are a result of automation, process optimization, and technological advancements in many different sectors. Simplified processes, lower expenses, and more productivity help modern economies prosper economically by increasing production.
Innovation and Competitiveness: Innovation creates new goods, services, and business models, which, in turn, propels economic development. Research and development, technology adoption, and talent development are industries that invest in these areas because they acquire a competitive advantage that boosts salaries, creates jobs, and raises living standards.
Global Connectivity and Trade: Global commerce and connectivity, which promote cross-border exchanges of products, services, and ideas, are advantageous to modern economies. Businesses may increase their client base, explore new income streams, and get access to global resources and talent by entering foreign markets.
Infrastructure Development: Infrastructure improvements, such as those in the energy, communication, and transportation sectors, promote long-term development and increase economic activity. Increasing trade and investment result from modern economies' increasing interconnectedness, lower transportation costs, and easier access to markets.
Human Capital Development: For contemporary economies to prosper, education, skill development, and talent retention are essential. Putting money into education and training programs guarantees a workforce with the necessary skills to keep up with technology, spur innovation, and boost the economy.
Sustainable Development: Sustainability and environmental stewardship are becoming more and more important in modern economies as a means of addressing global issues including pollution, resource depletion, and climate change. Sustainable practices support long-term environmental

health and economic resilience. Examples of these activities include the use of renewable energy, trash reduction, and circular economy efforts.
Diversification and Resilience: Economic resilience is improved by industry and income stream diversification, which lessens reliance on a particular market or sector. Diversified economies are advantageous to modern economies because they can endure shocks from the outside world, adjust to shifting market circumstances, and seize new possibilities.
Access to Information and Technology: The digital revolution has made information and technology more accessible to everyone, enabling people and companies to compete globally, develop, and work together. Increased connection, information accessibility, and the democratization of entrepreneurship are all beneficial to modern economies because they promote social mobility and economic inclusion.
Quality of Life Improvements: Prosperity in the economy leads to enhancements in the standard of living, including greater social services, infrastructure, healthcare, and education. Contemporary economies place a high priority on human well-being and work to achieve inclusive development that benefits all societal groups.
Resilience to Shocks and Crises: Diverse, flexible, and resilient modern economies are better able to weather shocks and crises like pandemics, natural catastrophes, and downturns in the economy. Proactive risk management techniques, strong social safety nets, and emergency response systems all aid in reducing the effects of crises and promoting recovery.

All things considered, innovation, infrastructure expansion, human capital investment, sustainability practices, technology breakthroughs, and resilience-building initiatives all contribute to the prosperity of contemporary economies and companies. Economies may raise living standards, accomplish sustainable development, and provide chances for prosperity and well-being for everyone by using these advantages.

7.4 Outcomes

The following scientific techniques were used to process the secondary data (Figure 7.3):

(i) The analytical method that divides a challenging research problem into smaller, easier-to-manage pieces. The study that was provided looked into the information found in both local and international literature in the mapped research region utilizing the following techniques:

(ii) The synthesis method, which synthesizes and processes knowledge;

(iii) The comparison method, which finds a relationship between the researched knowledge, objects, or phenomena, enabling the acquisition of new knowledge about the researched issue;

(iv) The exploration method helps comprehend the current situation better;

(v) The explanation method seeks to derive theoretical conclusions from the examined knowledge, which is arranged into causal dependencies and logical contexts, serving as the foundation for the formulation of theoretical conclusions regarding the research problem. This approach was used in this study to interpret the results of the analyses that were conducted.

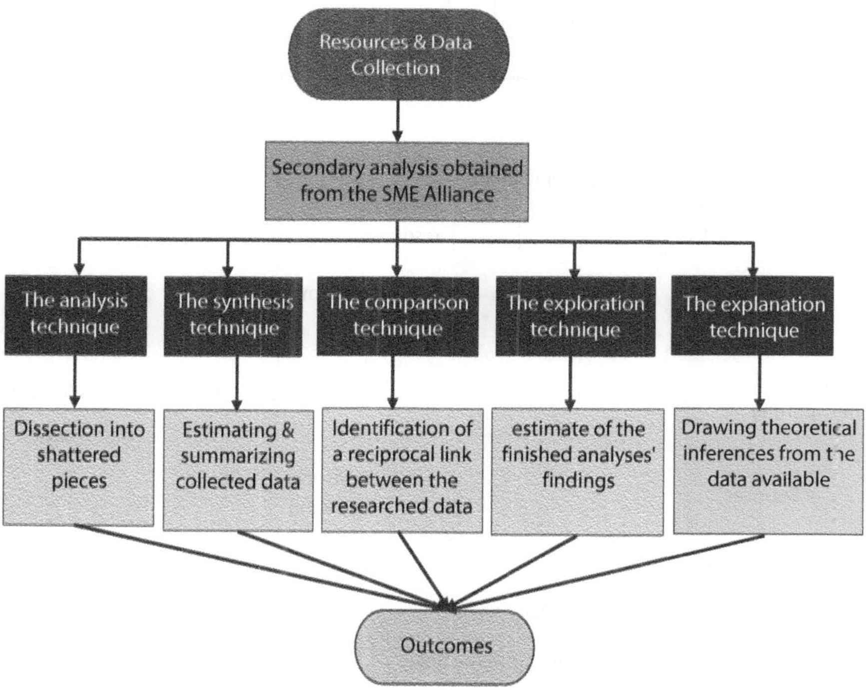

Figure 7.3 Methodology analysis.

Analyses of comparisons were also included in the research. A study of 268 organizations revealed that 56.5% of German enterprises do not fully comply with Industry 4.0 implementation requirements. Twenty percent of those surveyed said that they were just marginally ready for the novice level-1 implementation approach. Of the requirements in Table 7.1, just 0.3% were considered extraordinary, achieving level-5 implementation.

Figure 7.4 demonstrates significant disparities in the adoption of digital technologies by SMEs in various domains based on country-average percentages of firms using the technology between 2015 and 2023.

Table 7.1 Levels of implementation.

Level	Designation
0	Outsider
1	Trainee
2	Intermediate
3	Experienced
4	Expert
5	Top Professional

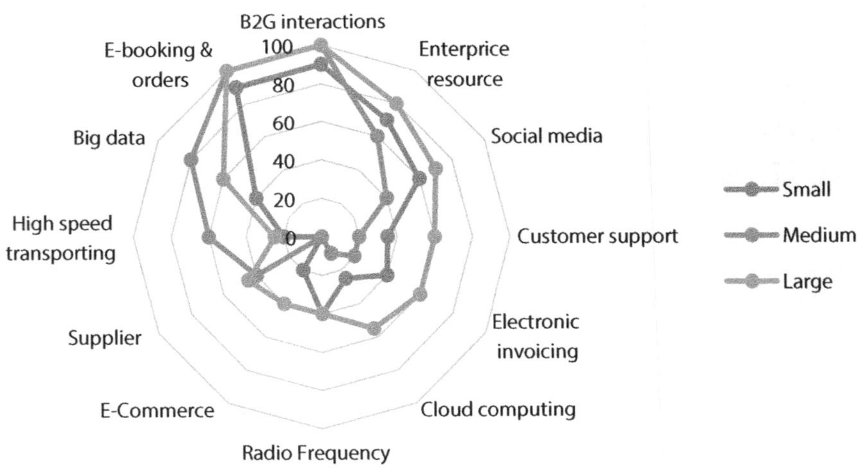

Figure 7.4 Adoption of SME gaps in many areas.

7.4.1 AI-Enabled Management Technology and Approach Taxonomy

In order to comply with the taxonomy outlined in the literature review, the design of was altered. The CPS architecture consists of five tiers. A summary may be used to monitor the creation of a new CPS design. We will start by discussing the existing 5C design, which is shown in Figure 7.1 of this study and will serve as a basis for evaluating the findings of our inquiry. The aim of the latest research is to enhance our understanding of CPS architecture by categorizing newly released information.

7.4.2 Essential Self-Adapting System Technologies

Each level of the CPS design must include a cyber-component, in addition to its individual components. People, processes, and data will become more interconnected as CPS develops. For all parties concerned, this will raise the value of networked interactions and transactions. The literature often looks at different technologies for feedback handling. Combining financial, informational, and physical assets with cutting-edge methods of process control are some examples of these technologies. The feedback loop is another technology that is often studied. Industry digitalization offers a chance to gain a competitive advantage. After a thorough analysis of relevant literature, it was found that the following platforms, processes, domains, and cultures most need cognitive feedback: All facets of business, including product development, production, and logistics, need advances in CPS.

7.4.3 Attack Malware Classifier

A concise overview of the AI used by CCPS was provided. The relationship between CCPS and these elements is established through grounded theory, and some of the connections are highlighted below. Ideas from CCPS that have the potential to be used include "cognitive societies" and "cognitive communities," among other similar concepts. One may simulate self-awareness in CCPS by using the categories and connections. Concepts with more connections are positioned lower in the table, whereas ideas with fewer connections are positioned higher. One may see this by examining the summary. Several social systems and platforms were developed as a consequence of the categorization of the data gathered from the examination of relevant literature. The conceptual framework and understanding of related ideas presented in this study are supported by research data, which reinforces the taxonomy approach to these concepts. The taxonomic categories in an effort to enhance the CPS's existing structure, which was in need of refinement, were created. The "cyber" layer is not included in our taxonomy as it was not a fundamental component of the idea when it was initially proposed. It was started with the assumption that the cyber component would be a part of every level of the CPS design.

7.5 Conclusions and Future Direction

In conclusion, the interplay of IoT, ML, and cognitive cyber-physical systems with cybersecurity highlights how crucial preventative measures are to defending contemporary businesses and economies. Organizations must prioritize cybersecurity in order to successfully counter emerging risks as technology continues to transform our linked environment. Organizations may enhance their cybersecurity protocols and guarantee the integrity of networked systems by incorporating cognitive capabilities and using ML algorithms for proactive threat identification. Furthermore, there are advantages and disadvantages to integrating IoT devices into cyber-physical systems. To guard against malicious exploitation and unauthorized access, strong encryption and secure-by-design principles are essential. Enacting laws that support cybersecurity best practices, encourage investment in cyber defense technology, and encourage cross-sector information exchange requires cooperation between stakeholders and regulatory agencies. In the end, contemporary economies and sectors can confidently traverse the cyber environment, assuring sustained growth and prosperity in an increasingly digital world, by investing in skills development, embracing innovation, and being watchful in the face of rising dangers.

Future Directions

Future developments in cybersecurity, ML, and cognitive cyber-physical systems integrating IoT seem to be well-positioned for growth and innovation. The future terrain will be shaped by many important areas:

Enhanced Threat Intelligence: More advanced threat intelligence capabilities will result from future developments in AI and ML. Organizations will be able to proactively anticipate and mitigate cyber risks and keep ahead of emerging attack vectors with the help of predictive analytics and automated threat detection systems.

Augmented Cyber Defense: AI-driven decision-making skills will be progressively integrated into cognitive cyber-physical systems, allowing for autonomous real-time responses to cyber threats. These technologies will improve overall cyber defense posture and supplement human security teams by dynamically adapting to changing settings and threats.

Secure IoT Ecosystems: Security will be a top priority in the design of future IoT devices, which will have strong authentication, encryption, and access control features. By guaranteeing the integrity of data and communications, edge computing and blockchain technologies can further improve the security and privacy of IoT ecosystems.

Quantum-Safe Cryptography: Future cybersecurity solutions will concentrate on creating encryption algorithms that are resistant to quantum computing in order to defend against new cryptographic threats. In a post-quantum world, protecting sensitive information and communications will need quantum-safe encryption.

Privacy-Preserving Technologies: Future cybersecurity solutions will give priority to privacy-preserving technologies like homomorphic encryption, differential privacy, and secure multi-party computing as data privacy standards continue to change. Thanks to these technologies, enterprises will be able to evaluate sensitive data while upholding individual privacy rights and adhering to legal obligations.

Interdisciplinary Research: Future investigations into cognitive cyber-physical systems, ML, and cybersecurity will progressively center on interdisciplinary methods that include knowledge from other disciplines, including computer science, engineering, psychology, and ethics. Working together will spur innovation and solve difficult problems where technology and society converge.

Ethical AI and Bias Mitigation: For ML applications to be successful in the future, it will be critical to address ethical issues and reduce algorithmic prejudice. In AI-driven decision-making processes, organizations will place a high priority on justice, accountability, and transparency. This will guarantee that cybersecurity solutions respect moral principles and guard against unforeseen repercussions.

Global Collaboration and Governance: Addressing the global cybersecurity concerns will need international collaboration and regulatory frameworks. The establishment of cyberspace rules of conduct, the encouragement of information exchange and cooperation among stakeholders, and the improvement of cyber resilience globally will be the main objectives of future initiatives.

In summary, innovation, cooperation, and a focus on resolving new risks and social issues will define the future of cybersecurity, ML, and cognitive cyber-physical systems with IoT. Organizations may create sustainable growth and prosperity in the digital era by adopting these trends and allocating resources toward research and development, therefore constructing robust and secure digital ecosystems.

References

1. Huitzil, C.T., Cognitive Dynamic Systems for Cyber-Physical Engineering, in: *Machine Learning for Complex and Unmanned Systems*, pp. 277–294, CRC Press, Boca Raton, Florida, USA, 2024.
2. Liang, Q., Zhao, S., Zhang, J., Deng, H., Damm, W., Hess, D., Forrest, L., Cyber-physical systems. *ACM Trans.*, *8*, 1, 10–32, 2024.
3. Bharathi, V., Vulnerability Detection in Cyber-Physical System Using Machine Learning. *Scalable Comput. Pract. Exp.*, *25*, 1, 577–591, 2024.
4. Sood, V.M., Singh, Y., Bhargava, B., Narang, S.K. (Eds.), *Intelligent Security Solutions for Cyber-Physical Systems*, CRC Press, Boca Raton, Florida, USA, 2024.
5. Balogun, B.F., Tripathi, K., Tiwari, S., JS, S.M., Tyagi, A.K., Original Research Article A blockchain-based deep learning approach for cyber security in next-generation medical cyber-physical systems. *J. Auton. Intell.*, *7*, 5, 5522–5532, 2024.
6. Latchoumi, T.P., Parthiban, L., Balamurugan, K., Raja, K., Vijayaraj, J., Parthiban, R., A Framework for Low Energy Application Devices Using Blockchain-Enabled IoT in WSNs, in: *Integrating Blockchain and Artificial Intelligence for Industry 4.0 Innovations*, pp. 121–132, Springer International Publishing, Cham, 2023.
7. Wu, J., Jin, J., Wu, C., Challenges and Countermeasures of Federated Learning Data Poisoning Attack Situation Prediction. *Mathematics*, *12*, 6, 901, 2024.
8. Retzlaff, C.O., Das, S., Wayllace, C., Mousavi, P., Afshari, M., Yang, T., Holzinger, A., Human-in-the-Loop Reinforcement Learning: A Survey and Position on Requirements, Challenges, and Opportunities. *J. Artif. Intell. Res.*, *79*, 359–415, 2024.
9. Balamurugan, K., Latchoumi, T.P., Satla, S., Machining Studies on AlSi7+ 63% SiC Composite Using Machine Learning Technique, in: *Metal Matrix Composites*, pp. 139–166, CRC Press, Boca Raton, Florida, USA, 2023.
10. Karthikeyan, A., Karthikeyan, K., Swathika, O.G., Cyber-physical security in a stand-alone photovoltaic system for rural electrification. *Next-Generation Cyber-Phys. Microgrid Syst.*, 16, 29–75, 2024.

11. Serôdio, C., Mestre, P., Cabral, J., Gomes, M., Branco, F., Software and Architecture Orchestration for Process Control in Industry 4.0 Enabled by Cyber-Physical Systems Technologies. *Appl. Sci.*, *14*, 5, 2160, 2024.
12. Ananthajothi, K., Rajasekar, P., Amanullah, M., Enhanced U-Net-based segmentation and heuristically improved deep neural network for pulmonary emphysema diagnosis. *Sādhanā*, 48, 33, 2023. https://doi.org/10.1007/s12046-023-02092-5.
13. Parthiban, L., Latchoumi, T.P., Balamurugan, K., Raja, K., Parthiban, R., Cognitive Computing for the Internet of Medical Things, in: *Integrating Blockchain and Artificial Intelligence for Industry 4.0 Innovations*, pp. 85–100, Springer International Publishing, Cham, 2023.
14. Karthikeyan, S. and Nagamani, G.M., An Architecture of Cyber-Physical System for Industry 4.0, in: *Digital Transformation: Industry 4.0 to Society 5.0*, pp. 259–283, Springer Nature Singapore, Singapore, 2024.
15. Stutz, D., de Assis, J.T., Laghari, A.A., Khan, A.A., Deshpande, A., Kulkarni, D., Grata, E.G., Cyber Threat Detection and Mitigation Using Artificial Intelligence–A Cyber-physical Perspective. *Appl. Artif. Intell. Cybersecur. Anal. Cyber Threat Detect.*, 7, 107–133, 2024.
16. Banerjee, S., Jesubalan, N.G., Kulkarni, A., Agarwal, A., Rathore, A.S., Developing cyber-physical system and digital twin for smart manufacturing: Methodology and case study of continuous clarification. *J. Ind. Inf. Integr.*, *33*, 100577, 2024.
17. Ravindra Krishna Chandar, V., Baskaran, P., Mohanraj, G., Karthikeyan, D., Deep iterative fuzzy pooling in unmanned robotics and autonomous systems for Cyber-Physical systems. *J. Intell. Fuzzy Syst.*, 46, 1–19, 2024. (Preprint).
18. Javaid, M., Haleem, A., Singh, R.P., Suman, R., An integrated outlook of Cyber–Physical Systems for Industry 4.0: Topical practices, architecture, and applications. *Green Technol. Sustain.*, 1, 1, 100001, 2023.
19. El-Kady, A.H., Halim, S., El-Halwagi, M.M., Khan, F., Analysis of safety and security challenges and opportunities related to cyber-physical systems. *Process Saf. Environ. Prot.*, 173, 384–413, 2023.
20. Ghansah, F.A. and Lu, W., Cyber-physical systems and digital twins for "cognitive building" in the construction industry. *Constr. Innov.*, 30, 23–46, 2023.
21. Ananthajothi, K., Karthikayani, K., Prabha, R., Explicit and implicit oriented Aspect-Based Sentiment Analysis with optimal feature selection and deep learning for demonetization in India. *Data Knowl. Eng.*, 142, 102092, 2022. ISSN 0169-023X, https://doi.org/10.1016/j.datak.2022.102092.
22. Kumar, P.S., Karthiga, M., Balamurugan, E., Cyber ML-Based Cyberattack Prediction Framework in Healthcare Cyber-Physical Systems, in: *Computational Intelligence in Robotics and Automation*, pp. 141–159, CRC Press, Boca Raton, Florida, USA, 2023.
23. Baheti, R., Gill, H., Cyber-physical systems. *The Impact of Control Technology*, 12, 1, 161–166, 2011.a

24. Jeffrey, N., Tan, Q., Villar, J.R., A review of anomaly detection strategies to detect threats to cyber-physical systems. *Electronics*, 12, 15, 3283, 2023.
25. Demertzi, V., Demertzis, S., Demertzis, K., An overview of cyber threats, attacks and countermeasures on the primary domains of smart cities. *Appl. Sci.*, 13, 2, 790, 2023.
26. Ashokkumar, K., Parthasarathy, S., Nandhini, S., Ananthajothi, K., Prediction of grape leaf through digital image using FRCNN. *Meas.: Sens.*, 24, 100447, 2022. ISSN 2665-9174, https://doi.org/10.1016/j.measen.2022.100447.

8

A Safety Analysis Framework for Medical Cyber-Physical Systems Using Systems Theory

K. Ananthajothi[1]*, K. Balamurugan[2], D. Divya[3] and T.P. Latchoumi[4]

[1]*Department of Computer Science and Engineering, Rajalakshmi Engineering College, Chennai, India*
[2]*Faculty of Mechanical Engineering, SRM Madurai College of Engineering and Technology, Pottapalayam, Tamil Nadu, India*
[3]*Department of Computer Science and Engineering, Jerusalem College of Engineering, Chennai, India*
[4]*Department of Computer Science and Engineering, SRM Institute of Science and Technology, Ramapuram Campus, Chennai, India*

Abstract

In present years, cyber-physical systems (CPSs) have gained a lot of interest and are regarded as emergent technologies. It integrates information and computing with the real world. Applications for CPS include biosystems, power, production, airplanes, automobiles, chemical procedures, building infrastructure, medical care, and transport. To improve the treatment and care of patient results, medical cyber-physical systems (MCPSs) integrate computer networks, software, and healthcare equipment. Moreover, because these structures are linked and have an opportunity to break down catastrophically, guaranteeing their reliability and security is a difficult task. In this research, we suggest an assessment of the safety method for MCPS based on systems theory. Our method provides a comprehensive framework for finding, evaluating, and reducing safety concerns throughout the system's lifespan. It draws from the ideas of systems theory and CPS. A formal modeling language to describe the behaviors, conversations, and structure of the entire system was established. This will make it possible to systematically identify the hazardous elements and possible breakdown modes. Our solution streamlines

**Corresponding author*: kanandjothime@gmail.com

K. Ananthajothi, S. N. Sangeethaa, D. Divya, S. Balamurugan and Shen-Lung Peng (eds.) Securing Cyber-Physical Systems: Fundamentals, Applications and Challenges, (157–176) © 2025 Scrivener Publishing LLC

earlier danger detection, dynamic risk evaluation, and proactively security oversight in MCPS by combining methods from system security engineering and CPS. Through investigations and simulated tests, researchers showcase the efficacy of our strategy and its potential to improve medical CPS security and resilience in practical problems in medical facilities.

Keywords: Medical cyber-physical systems, safety analysis, systems theory, cyber-physical systems, hazard identification, risk assessment, safety engineering, formal modeling

8.1 Introduction

Cyber-physical systems (CPSs) have garnered interest from the academic, commercial, and governmental sectors because of their noteworthy impacts on the environment, economics, and society [1]. Interest in CPSs has increased recently because of the area's ability to benefit the community, business, the environment, and individual residents. In addition, the fast improvements in laptop, interaction, and storage technologies have led to domination and creativity in data transfer networks. The forthcoming generation of combined interactions, computer, and administration systems is referred to as virtual and physical systems; however, a precise term is lacking [2]. When it comes to biological data, these systems aim for reliability, efficacy, and power. Concurrently, studies conducted to achieve these objectives mostly focus on achieving safety in the CPS. According to the system-theoretic accident and processes (STAMP) accident cause model, insufficient control or enforcement related to security restrictions on the system's layout, growth, and administration leads to accidents instead of failures of components [3]. The integrated approach is used to create danger logs, identify dangers, and set up system management framework modeling. As a result, this thesis effectively proposes an optimization technique—the integrated strategy—to offset the drawbacks of modeling using the STAMP. This method describes the social and cyber-organizational defects using a set of hierarchy structures for control. Because cyber-physical devices are deeply integrated across multiple important infrastructures, any security breaches in these computer networks might have severe implications [4]. For example, if the cars' interface systems malfunction and erroneous distance information is sent, then a collision may result. Consumers increasingly rely on all available automotive alternatives, which have made the situation even worse with the introduction of self-driving cars [5].

Along with safety considerations, confidentiality of CPSs is a major problem. Large geographic distances and copious volumes of data are frequently produced by CPS, which are essential for data interpretation and decision-making [6]. The system may employ complex algorithms to acquire data and make informed judgments [7]. Furthermore, data theft may occur at any stage of the infrastructure, including the collection, processing, streaming, and storing of data [8]. Once more, many of the CPS design techniques employed today do not consider data security, so putting any information obtained at risk [9]. A great deal of study has been done on the challenges and impediments involved in creating a CPS, providing a wide spectrum of systems and multidisciplinary studies. The electrical infrastructure, environmental preservation, interactions, and monitoring systems are some of these difficulties [10]. A portion of these challenges are associated with the CPS itself, platforms and structural growth, both hardware and software architecture, programs, and human interactions (e.g., limitations, abstract concepts, and quality-of-service requirements).

A condition that poses a danger of harm to individuals or the environment is referred to as a hazard. A hazard is a condition or state that, with the correct environmental circumstances or set of actions, might result in an accident. Taking into account potential dangers might help prevent accidents [11]. It is necessary to do a thorough study of the software about system dangers while building safe systems. Special precautions must be made, and the causing software must be created so that these possible dangers can be reduced or eliminated, as well as the risks that come with them. Early system safety evaluations, carried out while defining the function of the software in the system specifications phase, start to identify possible health risks related to certain designs and operations [12]. These pilot investigations, together with subsequent program and security assessment research, identify situations in which application programs either contribute to or will help control a danger. A program security study will be conducted on this program, which is categorized as health-critical. The first step in determining the software security standards required to support the expansion of the software specifications definition is to conduct program safety research [13]. The program will get these specifications so they may be improved upon and included in the requirements for software specification. Limits (such as red lines and boundary values), sequence of events, time limitations, voting logic, hazardous hardware failure detection, failure tolerance, caution, dangerous instructions, warn interactions, etc., are a few instances of computer program security specifications [14]. System safety evaluations are carried out continuously throughout the project. To ensure that adjustments and discoveries made at the system level are implemented into the software as needed, the program security evaluation procedure must keep reviewing the outcomes of the systems studies [15].

Furthermore, the system safety assessments receive input from the software safety analyses. The safety assessment investigations are not carried out in a vacuum; rather, they are a specific component of the system-wide security study [16]. The following are the goals of systems and program danger evaluation:

- Identifying the critical program and system segments—that is the ones that are most important for security.
- Permitting the use of more thorough methods and controls to program areas that are crucial to the system's security.
- Finding and examining safety concerns connected to the software to either eliminate them or assist in the reduction of related risks
- Determining the types of failure that may result in a dangerous condition of the system and offering suggestions for modifications.
- Determining the order in which the inputs might cause the program to produce an unsafe state of system operation and making suggestions for modifications.

8.2 Background

8.2.1 Cyber-Physical Systems

Several studies have been conducted on the viability of using private information encryption to address issues with CPSs [17]. It has drawn interest from experts and scholars in a wide range of fields and produced several potent methods. Duplicate network information has been reported. Furthermore, the location of network information was scratched globally for the first time using the tangled sequencing encrypting technique [18]. By swiftly adding the information and using it to replace the intended pixel, a fake pixel was created in this region. Based on the required computing, the incorporated data might be quickly extracted from ciphertext, according to [19]. All of the targeting pixels are retrieved when the person receiving them decrypts the information, revealing the verification tokens that were shielded by two layers of security. These results were confirmed and showed that the methods provided a great deal of rapid and useful input [20]. However, the approach had issues including inadequate recovery of information and excessive latency while querying information because certain shared information was overlooked. A digital information encryption technique for networking confidentiality built around common critical symbolic frequencies identifying was introduced to solve the problem of low-level anti-deciphering capabilities [21].

8.2.2 Quality-of-Service Issues in CPS

The purpose of presenting the results of simulations was to evaluate the performance of various prediction techniques. Initially, the unified integration of information, uncertainty and control (UIUC) research lab researchers tackled the main issues related to merging sensors, PCs, and network systems with separate information centers, clusters, connections, and the World Wide Web [22]. The building was divided into four sections: the administrative, medical, hospitality, and residence connections. Investigation of CPS information focused on event identification, reliable data, space-time examination, secrecy, and the security of cyber-physical information systems. They incorporated different information networks for health instruments, sleep monitoring, and assessing height as important elements. A novel technique for safe color picture encryption was presented utilizing a chaotic system that could be easily deciphered in a single cycle of processing. The cryptographic key that will be used in the consternation and release stages is initially generated via a function called a hash. The results of the field study demonstrated that this strategy was more secure than earlier strategies and impervious to a range of dangers, such as blockage and unequal assaults. The risks that CPSs confront and the machine learning (ML)–based security methods implemented to address them were documented. The equipment, system, and software elements of a CPS were delineated along with their corresponding responsibilities. The cyber-physical assaults were categorized according to their taxonomies, with an emphasis on those that take advantage of the physics of the target system. This included the state of online safety for water supply systems at the time, the difficulties that still need to be solved, and the quantity of materials in this area.

8.2.3 Medical Cyber-Physical Systems

A two-layer system structure was described, wherein medical data are stored off-chain but are nevertheless shareable on the blockchain. Using the proposed multi-trapdoor hashing operation, a certificate-less aggregated signature approach was presented for block chain technology MCPS. This approach maintained computational and storage effectiveness while meeting the strict safety standards needed for MCPSs. The researchers hypothesized that combining the multiple duties for physical and cyber safety may strengthen operational and technological cyber and physical safety resilience, increase operational cyber safety expertise in coast infrastructure, and additionally enhance communication between stakeholders.

8.3 The Systems-Based Safety Analysis Observation for MCPS

Upon examination of software-related mishaps, the following significant findings on security evaluation in medical electronic and physical systems may be drawn. These insights apply to all CPS in general. They are as follows: Both the hardware and the program levels are used for danger assessment. It is fundamental to the creation of safe infrastructure. Hazards at the system level are conditions that might cause an accident. Software hazard assessment finds the mechanisms of failure that can cause a condition to become dangerous. The majority of mistakes found in functional applications may be traced back to insufficient or flawed specifications. If the requirement has all the information required to prevent ambiguity and does not require any further explanation to allow for correct development and confirmation, then it is considered finished.

Constructing secure structures involves several tasks, one of which is determining, defining, and validating security standards and safety-critical criteria. Methods of Design for Medical Cyber: To create stronger structures, physical systems must not only exhibit the required operational performance but also meet safety standards and limitations. Durability and variety are among the most often used techniques in hardware structures to lower risks. Systems like fail-safe concepts self-examination, handling of exceptions, operator or user alerts, and modifications are examples of component identification and control systems. The development of software for MCPS must impose security limitations. The related security programming criteria must be met by the architectural specifications. The security criteria derived from system implementation and danger assessment are monitored throughout the assessment to ensure that the system meets these standards as designed.

8.3.1 Identification of Critical Requirements in MCPS

When designing the specifications for a MCPS, security demands, security limitations, and security-critical criteria are all crucial because an increasing number of devices are becoming safety-critical. Healthcare

CPS standards are often successful, information, or interface requirements that must be appropriately implemented if hazards and the injuries they are connected with are to be eliminated or mitigated. In contrast, security requirements are a sort of high-quality requirement. The functions mentioned above are derived from those found in the NATO Standardization Agreement. The most popular approach to addressing security specifications during technological advances is to concentrate on identifying needs that are vital for security. Typical examples of safety restrictions include stringent interlocks and physical guards surrounding moving parts, security measures when working with power and managing hazardous materials, and required indication placement. When a non-software system is put through security evaluations, it is generally assumed that failures are what start most accident sequences.

As a result, these systems are evaluated in scenarios that replicate or create outside factors that might lead to disappointments, including extremely high or low temperatures or high vibration. Unsafe software system actions, however, do not usually come from malfunctions. When there are uncertainties or omissions in the specifications, unsafe behaviors may result. It is also feasible that the rules pose a risk but are not acknowledged. As a result, depending only on testing that includes putting the system through harsh circumstances is probably not going to work as well for software-intensive systems as it may for non-software systems. This implies that general software testing techniques, such as limits assessment, could not be useful for identifying risky activity. Rather, knowing the risks and the dangerous circumstances that might lead to a hazard's existence is usually necessary to test a software system for unsafe behaviors.

8.3.2 A Systems Theory–Based Method for Safety Analysis in Medical Cyber-Physical Systems

Figure 8.1 illustrates the process of combining hazard detection along with the security assessment technique. To put this evaluation into practice, there are many processes involved. The following is a description of the precise procedures for carrying out security assessment and hazard identification on MCPS using a combined method:

a) The risks can be determined on the basis of the functionality and MCPS system needs. The specialist identifies the framework of governance and control actions for MCPS and describes the high-level risks that might cause system accidents as well as safety criteria and limits.

b) Various levels of hierarchy, interactions among these levels, and control feedback loops are included in the MCPS the system's security hierarchy management concepts. A human or a machine that is part of a healthcare cyber-physical network is represented by every link in a graph. With excellent describing capabilities, Petri-Nets or the Architecture Analysis and Design Language (AADL) may be used to develop control frameworks. Moreover, AADL can be thought of as the graphical network definition and designing structural perspective of MCPS.
c) Evaluating the likelihood of inadequate control measures for MCPS that result in risky states with the specified guidance conditions based on fundamental dangers and security restrictions on the system level.
d) Utilizing the regulatory architecture and fault tree analysis (FTA). Determine the causative elements. Determine the achievable condition when the control action ends. Use the types of hierarchical control structure models to pinpoint the probable reasons for risky controlling activities.
e) For additional risk assessment and safety-guided architecture, develop a hazard journal by system-theoretic process analysis (STPA). The system factor that corresponds to every high-level danger is provided together with the corresponding function or aim stage. The causes indicated in the hazard log serve as a guide to the control weaknesses found in the STPA risk assessment. Data on the degree of danger and, if requested, the classification of the ensuing loss are included in the magnitude of the consequence.
f) Define system element requirements which provide each functional component or subsystem at the level of intent definition with requirements, design limitations, and security constraints. Make design choices to put the restrictions and needs into practice. Make a formal model of the design of the control system.
g) Create safety-guided design (SGD) utilizing new security requirements and restrictions and with the assistance of STPA. The STPA procedure and the system design process are even more intertwined in SGD.

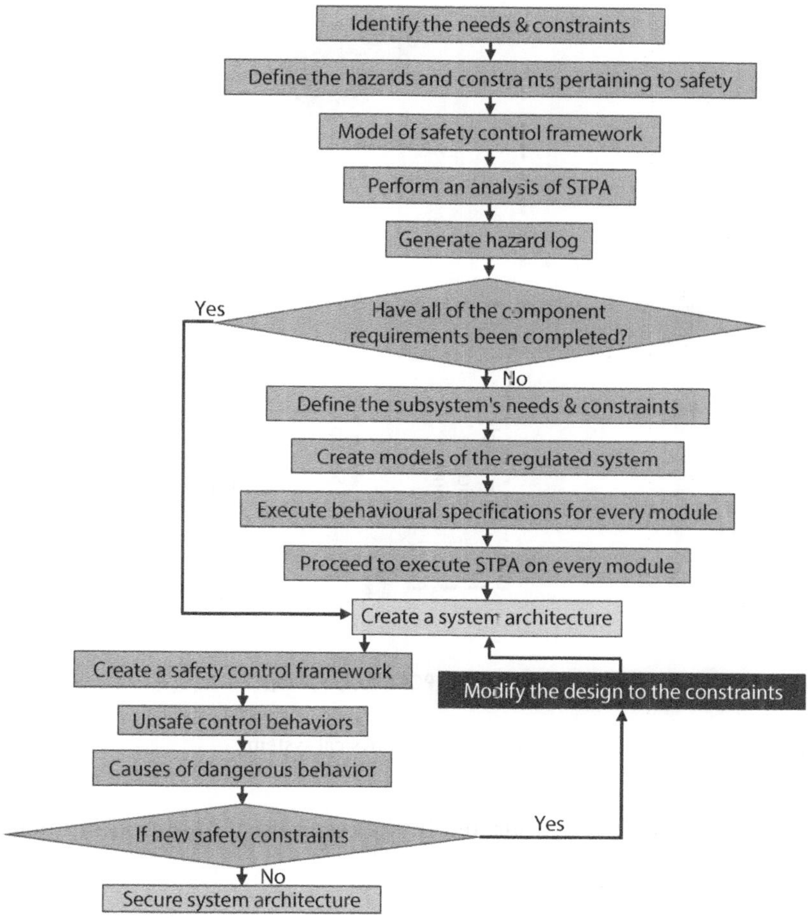

Figure 8.1 Flowchart of system-theoretic method to safety analysis in MCPS for safe system.

8.3.3 MCPS in Patient-Controlled Analgesia

The system links a pulse oximeter, an administrator, and a patient controlled analgesia (PCA) pump to constantly track an individual's blood oxygen saturation (SpO2), a measure of how well the individual is responding to analgesic medication. Regretfully, PCA-MCPS is still insufficient to keep patients safe. For instance, serious overdoses might result from drug abuse and improper training. Nonetheless, these human mistakes cannot be identified or prevented by the current PCA-MCPS. Some individuals may have a significant delay in the onset of respiratory responses after medication administration. Therefore, the whole dose given to the individual's

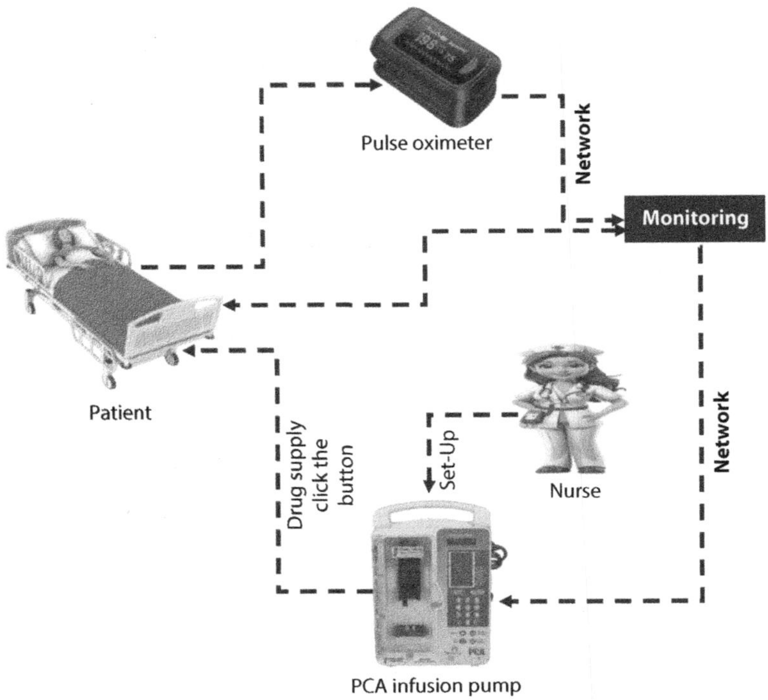

Figure 8.2 Closed-loop PCA–medical cyber-physical system.

body cannot be directly reflected in the respiratory condition of the individual shown in Figure 8.2.

8.4 Improved Wireless Medical Cyber-Physical System (IWMCPS)

The data collection straight, the stage of pre-processing data, the cloud computing straight, and the execution levels are the four common elements of MCPS designs. This part contains the operating and security requirements for each class.

8.4.1 Level: Data Acquisition

Consumers have easier access to health information thanks to body area networks (BANs), which collect and transmit information to a nearby computerized gadget, like the cloudlet. Battery-powered sense devices in

BANs employ Bluetooth or ZigBee methods, whereas passive arrays of sensors driven by RFID do not need batteries.

8.4.2 Layer: Data Aggregating

The low power of the BAN detector necessitates the usage of clouds or concentrations for an intermediate technology. Sensors send data collected over Bluetooth to an intermediary the server, which acts as a concentrator. By concentrating the data from every device and sending aggregated to the clouds, an element in the most important IoT-based structural construction element makes individually poor devices have usually powerful characteristics. Information is gathered by a cloudlet from more powerful devices, such as smartphones. A cloudlet is often built on a different machine and has dedicated connections to the internet. Cloud-based architectural blocks of information, in general, allow fewer powerful gadgets to function on par with higher-powered ones by combining information from all of the instruments and sending it to the cloud for analysis.

8.4.3 Level: Storing

A lot of cloud services use business association agreements to store medical information. Healthcare organizations use the cloud for calculating, which is a second important reason, for managing apps in their cloud computing environments or information centers. Therefore, only highly developed cryptography systems can ensure secrecy on a cloud platform. These methods have gained popularity recently as potential applications for remote health monitoring devices. The proposed IWMCPS structure for the model is depicted in Figure 8.3. The purchasing, preliminary processing, online, and levels of activity are its four tiers. The acquisition layer

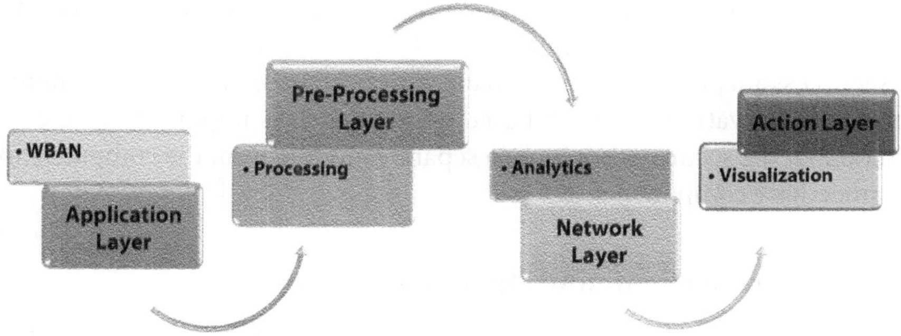

Figure 8.3 The proposed IWMCPS model architecture.

is used to first gather the information from the sensors, which is subsequently transformed into the next layer. The information that has been processed is stored and examined by the cloud layer. The information is visualized by the action layer to aid in making better judgments regarding the patient's medical problems.

8.4.4 Level: Action

Either "dynamic" or "silent" action levels are possible. Proactive action makes use of an actuator—a mechanical system, for example—to act by applying the results of computations running on the cloud. Surgical procedures aided by robots are one instance of this kind of activity. Passive tasks include no physical actions. The study of results from healthcare applications is supported by the authorities. Within 10 to 20 minutes, clinicians may see the monitoring results for 25–30 persons using an easy procedure like long-term (24-hour) monitoring of an ECG. The collection layer collects information gathered by the sensors initially, and the subsequent layer pre-processes it. The data has finally been processed and is examined and saved in the cloud. The actions layer provides an animated illustration of the information, as seen in Figure 8.1, which helps in the analysis of the health issues of the patients.

8.4.5 IWMCPS Architectural Research

The IWMCPS's logical framework breaks down larger components—such as the machine's core, detectors, and communication—into smaller ones. The data gathered is either utilized to detect human behavior in medical services or to provide data regarding the health of the community. The sensors and the buildings in the person's surroundings are connected. Video technology uses cameras to record the environment to identify moving objects and deduce movements like sprinting, running, bending, and strolling. This is an example of a video-focused approach. Both safety and user access adaptability can be enhanced by permission that utilizes photos and an observation approach based on actions. It is important to understand that the security core is not a separate module from the compute and connectivity components.

8.4.6 Core of Communications and Sensors

Data networking and embedded devices are the result of technologies that combine computing and practical connections. As previously indicated,

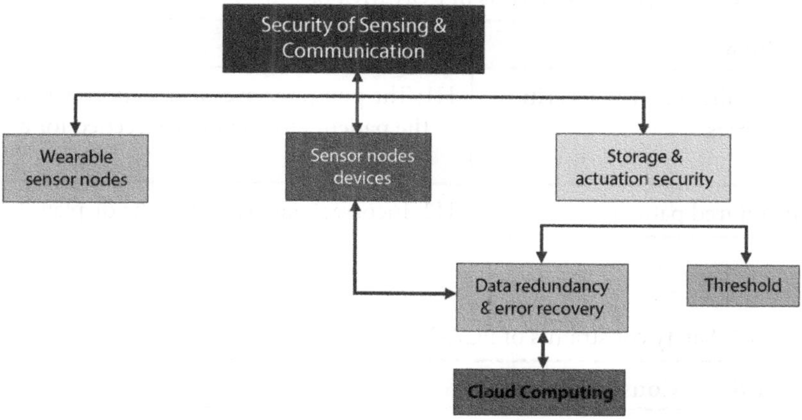

Figure 8.4 IWMCPS workflow model.

compared to its normal ad hoc wireless counterparts, wireless networking functions at a higher level, on a wider scale, with fewer devices, and has tighter ties to the physical environment. Therefore, to sustain wireless sensor networks for an extended period, it is imperative to facilitate a restricted-energy supply. Given the critical nature of CPS systems, a variety of computation and interaction tasks must be finished within time constraints to prevent uncomfortable or even catastrophic outcomes. Providing strong support in the major electromagnetic sensor node networks is a big and difficult area of study. Based on activities surveillance and image-based registration can improve accessibility safety and adaptability. The security core functions as a single platform for every interaction and computation module rather than having its module. It shows how information moves from sensed information to gateway information, which is stored for further examination across multiple database systems. Preparing, path, setting, targeted moderate accessibility, etc., are some of the major issues facing research. Through the reconfiguration of translations and computation mechanisms, hierarchical telecommunications can divide the network into many tasks shown in Figure 8.4. This guarantees that the connectivity core may be used to enhance MCPS patient monitoring in a versatile and timely manner.

8.5 Hazard Analysis on PCA-MCPS

The following system-level risks are pertinent to this description of a mistake shown in Table 8.1.

Table 8.1 Accidents and hazards in PCA-MCPS.

Accidents	Hazards
Patient dies or sustains critical injuries.	H1: The pump receives instructions when the patient's tolerance is exceeded for a dosage.
The injured patient	H2: Incorrect data is sent to the display.

Table 8.2 Safety constraints of PCA-MCPS.

Hazards	Constraints
H1	If an excess infusion is indicated by the patient's vital signs, then the controller has to order the pump to stop.
H2	The patient's vital signs must be updated on the display by the controller.

8.5.1 System Safety Constraint

Following the definition of system dangers, the associated security constraints—restrictions on how the organization can accomplish its goals—should be communicated shown in Table 8.2.

8.5.2 System Safety Control Structure

Following the definition of the dangers and associated safety restrictions, a typical socio-technical organizational framework with security management processes—referred to as a hierarchical security management design—should be specified. Figure 8.5 illustrates this framework. Creating the system's security monitoring framework is the next stage. Finding security violations of constraints that could be brought on by other associated loops of control is the primary goal of control loop analysis.

8.5.3 Identify Unsafe Control Actions

Every high-level danger is analyzed using the STPA approach. The two parts of the STPA are recognizing the system's risky management and figuring out how these control actions may take place. A systematic approach for hazard assessment is the STPA. Rather than focusing just on component

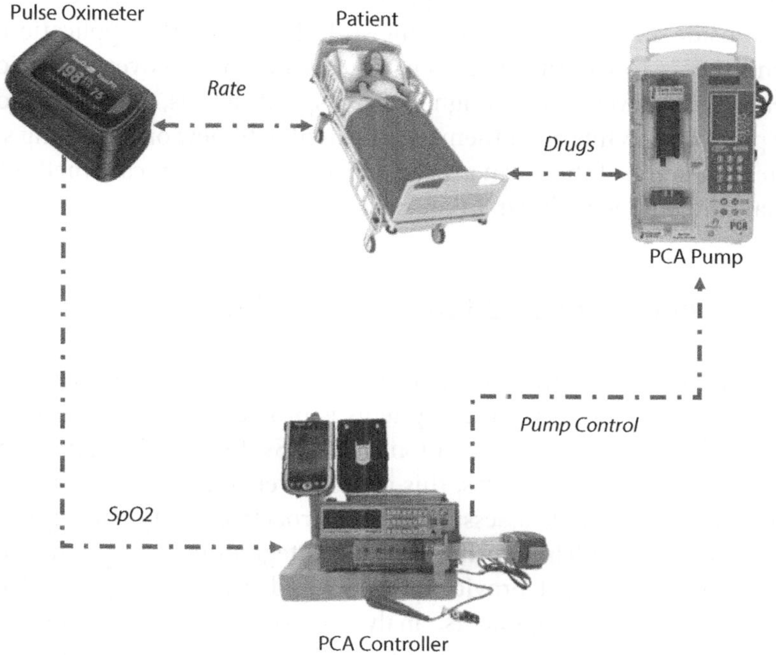

Figure 8.5 Control structure of PCA-MCPS.

breakdowns or breakdown occurrences, this model takes into account dangers and reasons on a global scale.

8.5.4 Specifying Causes

The next stage after identifying risks is to determine causative variables, which are crucial in determining qualities that may be used as mitigation measures against the danger. The causative causes may be considered from the perspective of control faults because risks arise from insufficient control and enforcement of safety limits. This categorization of control defects is used to assess the security control architecture diagram. The following situations might result in insufficient enforcement of security restrictions for incorrect or absent instruction input: The health of the individual is misrepresented by the numbers obtained from the physiological monitors; the system fails, and the pump continues to operate regularly, regardless of the condition of the patient.

In addition to component breakdowns, conclusions derived from a systems-theoretic method of security assessment additionally involve failures in the interactions between components or between parts and human beings inside an organizational framework. Following the application of systems theory to security analysis in MCPSs and the discovery of various novel dangers, several new design choices, specifications, and suggestions were produced. While all of them may be used with new or upcoming system testers, some of them can also be added to the present case method to alleviate difficulties as shown in the particular incident.

8.6 Conclusions and Future Directions

To sum up, a thorough framework for resolving the intricate security problems present in these networked systems is provided by the systems-theoretic method for security evaluation in MCPSs. By leveraging principles from systems theory and CPSs, this approach enables early hazard identification, dynamic risk assessment, and proactive safety management. Through formal modeling techniques and integration with system safety engineering practices, it provides a structured methodology for identifying safety-critical components, analyzing potential failure modes, and implementing appropriate risk mitigation measures. The demonstrated effectiveness of this approach in real-world case studies underscores its potential to enhance patient safety and improve the reliability of MCPSs. Moving forward, further research and development efforts should focus on refining and validating this approach, as well as exploring its application in diverse healthcare settings to ensure the continued advancement of safety in MCPS.

Future Directions

Future directions for research and development in the realm of safety analysis in MCPSs encompass several key areas:

1. **Advanced Modeling Techniques:** Explore the use of advanced modeling techniques, such as formal methods and simulation-based approaches, to enhance the accuracy and comprehensiveness of safety analysis in MCPS. This could involve the development of modeling languages, tools, and methodologies tailored specifically for MCPS safety analysis.
2. **Integration of Artificial Intelligence:** AI/ML algorithms could analyze vast amounts of data from MCPS components

to detect anomalies, predict potential safety hazards, and recommend appropriate mitigation strategies.

3. **Quantitative Risk Assessment:** Develop methodologies for quantitative risk assessment in MCPS, including probabilistic modeling techniques and quantitative metrics for evaluating safety risks. Quantitative risk assessment frameworks could provide a more objective and quantitative understanding of safety risks in MCPS, facilitating informed decision-making and resource allocation.
4. **Cybersecurity Considerations:** Expand the scope of safety analysis in MCPS to include cybersecurity considerations, such as threat modeling, vulnerability assessment, and intrusion detection. Given the increasing prevalence of cyber threats targeting healthcare systems, integrating cybersecurity analysis into MCPS safety frameworks is essential for ensuring comprehensive protection against both physical and cyber threats.
5. **Human Factors and Usability:** Incorporate human factors and usability considerations into MCPS safety analysis, including the impact of user interfaces, workflow design, and human–machine interaction on patient safety. Understanding how human factors influence the safety and effectiveness of MCPS can help design systems that are intuitive, error-resistant, and supportive of clinician decision-making.
6. **Regulatory Compliance and Standards:** Address regulatory compliance and standards requirements specific to MCPS safety, ensuring alignment with regulatory frameworks such as the FDA's guidance on medical device cybersecurity. Developing standardized approaches for MCPS safety analysis can facilitate regulatory compliance and interoperability across different healthcare systems.
7. **Long-Term Safety Monitoring:** Establish mechanisms for long-term safety monitoring and surveillance of MCPS deployed in real-world healthcare environments. Continuous monitoring of MCPS performance, safety incidents, and adverse events can provide valuable insights for refining safety analysis methodologies and improving system resilience over time.

Scientists and clinicians may push the boundaries of security evaluation for MCPSs and improve the security of patients and medical service dependability by concentrating on these prospects.

References

1. El-Kady, A.H., Halim, S., El-Halwagi, M.M., Khan, F., Analysis of safety and security challenges and opportunities related to cyber-physical systems. *Process Saf. Environ. Protection*, 173, 384–413, 2023.
2. Alshalalfah, A.L., System-Level Analysis and Design of Safety-Critical Cyber Physical Systems, 2023, (Doctoral dissertation, Concordia University).
3. Cassottana, B., Roomi, M.M., Mashima, D., Sansavini, G., Resilience analysis of cyber-physical systems: A review of models and methods. *Risk Anal.*, *43*, 11, 2359–2379, 2023.
4. Liang, Q., Zhao, S., Zhang, J., Deng, H., Damm, W., Hess, D., Forrest, L., Cyber-physical systems. *ACM Trans.*, *8*, 1, 244, 2024.
5. Anto, K., Swain, A., Roop, P., A novel framework for the design of resilient cyber-physical systems using control theory and formal methods. *IEEE Access*, 11, 73556–73567, 2023.
6. Al Maruf, A., Niu, L., Clark, A., Mertoguno, J.S., Poovendran, R., A timing-based framework for designing resilient cyber-physical systems under safety constraint. *ACM Trans. Cyber-Phys. Syst.*, *7*, 3, 1–25, 2023.
7. Johnphill, O., Sadiq, A.S., Al-Obeidat, F., Al-Khateeb, H., Taheir, M.A., Kaiwartya, O., Ali, M., Self-healing in cyber–physical systems using machine learning: A critical analysis of theories and tools. *Future Internet*, *15*, 7, 244, 2023.
8. Ananthajothi, K., Karthikayani, K., Prabha, R., Explicit and implicit oriented Aspect-Based Sentiment Analysis with optimal feature selection and deep learning for demonetization in India. *Data Knowl. Eng.*, 142, 102092, 2022. ISSN 0169-023X, https://doi.org/10.1016/j.datak.2022.102092.
9. van-Lopik, K., Hayward, S., Grant, R., McGirr, L., Goodall, P., Jin, Y., Conway, P.P., A review of design frameworks for human-cyber-physical systems moving from industry 4 to 5. *IET Cyber-Phys. Syst.: Theor. Appl.*, 18, 169–183, 2023.
10. Hamzah, M., Islam, M.M., Hassan, S., Akhtar, M.N., Ferdous, M.J., Jasser, M.B., Mohamed, A.W., Distributed Control of Cyber Physical System on Various Domains: A Critical Review. *Systems*, *11*, 4, 208, 2023.
11. Latchoumi, T.P., Parthiban, L., Balamurugan, K., Raja, K., Vijayaraj, J., Parthiban, R., A Framework for Low Energy Application Devices Using Blockchain-Enabled IoT in WSNs, in: *Integrating Blockchain and Artificial Intelligence for Industry 4.0 Innovations*, pp. 121–132, Springer International Publishing, Cham, 2023.

12. Gürcan, O., Yakymets, N., Tucci-Piergiovanni, S., Radermacher, A., Multi-agent optimization for safety analysis of cyber-physical systems: Position paper, 2024, arXiv preprint arXiv:2403.16904.
13. Ashokkumar, K., Parthasarathy, S., Nandhini, S., Ananthajothi, K., Prediction of grape leaf through digital image using FRCNN. *Meas.: Sens.*, 24, 100447, 2022. ISSN 2665-9174, https://doi.org/10.1016/j.measen.2022.100447.
14. Annaswamy, A. M., Khargonekar, P. P., Spurgeon, S. K. (Eds.), Cyber-physical-human systems: fundamentals and applications. John Wiley & Sons, New Jercy, USA, 2023.
15. Poursoltan, M., Methodological and operational framework for the validation and improvement of Cyber-Physical and Human Systems based on modelling and simulation, 2023, (Doctoral dissertation, Université de Bordeaux).
16. Parthiban, L., Latchoumi, T.P., Balamurugan, K., Raja, K., Parthiban, R., Cognitive Computing for the Internet of Medical Things, in: *Integrating Blockchain and Artificial Intelligence for Industry 4.0 Innovations*, pp. 85–100, Springer International Publishing, Cham, 2023.
17. Awotunde, J.B., Oguns, Y.J., Amuda, K.A., Nigar, N., Adeleke, T.A., Olagunju, K.M., Ajagbe, S.A., Cyber-Physical Systems Security: Analysis, Opportunities, Challenges, and Future Prospects. *Blockchain Cybersecur. Cyber-Phys. Syst.*, 21–46, 2023.
18. Balamurugan, K., Latchoumi, T.P., Satla, S., Machining Studies on AlSi7+63% SiC Composite Using Machine Learning Technique, in: *Metal Matrix Composites*, pp. 139–166, CRC Press, Boca Raton, Florida, USA, 2023.
19. Kaloudi, N. and Li, J., AST-SafeSec: Adaptive Stress Testing for Safety and Security Co-analysis of Cyber-Physical Systems. *IEEE Trans. Inf. Forensics Secur.*, 102, 1234–1237, 2023.
20. Tushar, W., Yuen, C., Saha, T.K., Nizami, S., Alam, M.R., Smith, D.B., Poor, H.V., A survey of cyber-physical systems from a game-theoretic perspective. *IEEE Access, 11*, 9799–9834, 2023.
21. Simeone, A., Grant, R., Ye, W., Caggiano, A., A human-cyber-physical system for Operator 5.0 smart risk assessment. *Int. J. Adv. Manuf. Technol., 129*, 5, 2763–2782, 2023.
22. Jamal, A.A., Majid, A.A.M., Konev, A., Kosachenko, T., Shelupanov, A., A review on security analysis of cyber physical systems using Machine learning. *Mater. Today Proc., 80*, 2302–2306, 2023.

9

Cognitive Cybersecurity and Reinforcement Learning: Enhancing Security in CPS-IoT Enabled Healthcare

A. Arokiaraj Jovith[1]*, M. Sangeetha[2], D. Saveetha[1] and S. Antelin Vijila[3]

[1]Department of Networking and Communications, College of Engineering and Technology, SRM Institute of Science and Technology, Kattankulathur, Chennai, Tamil Nadu, India
[2]Computer Engineering Department, University of Technology and Applied Sciences, Nizwa, Sultanate of Oman
[3]Dept. of CSE, Manonmaniam Sundaranar University, Abhishekapatti, Tirunelveli, India

Abstract

Comprehensive safety precautions are essential for protecting confidential patient information and upholding system reliability in the context of Cyber-Physical Systems (CPS) and the Internet of Things (IoT) in medical care. When combined with Reinforcement Learning (RL), Cognitive Cybersecurity becomes a powerful tool for improving protection in CPS-IoT-enabled healthcare settings. This study investigates how to strengthen the safety position of healthcare systems by integrating RL approaches with cognitive cybersecurity concepts. This strategy makes use of cognitive capabilities like machine learning, artificial intelligence, and advanced data analysis, along with reinforcement learning's capacity to adjust and gain knowledge from evolving circumstances. This allows for proactive threat identification, quick reaction to incidents involving security, and responsive security solution implementation. This study demonstrates the effectiveness of cognitive cybersecurity and reinforcement learning (RL) in reducing safety hazards and maintaining the robustness of CPS-IoT-enabled healthcare ecosystems through an in-depth examination of case studies and demonstrations. The results highlight the significance of adopting cutting-edge cybersecurity strategies to handle

**Corresponding author*: arokiara@srmist.edu.in

K. Ananthajothi, S. N. Sangeethaa, D. Divya, S. Balamurugan and Shen-Lung Peng (eds.) Securing Cyber-Physical Systems: Fundamentals, Applications and Challenges, (177–198) © 2025 Scrivener Publishing LLC

changing safety concerns in the healthcare industry and open the door for greater safe and dependable healthcare systems.

***Keywords*:** Cognitive cybersecurity, healthcare ecosystems, machine learning, artificial intelligence, threat detection, healthcare data protection, resilient security, reinforcement learning

9.1 Introduction

The utilization of several CPS-IoT applications in the field of eHealth and well-being has significantly increased [1]. Over the past few years, CPS-IoT has developed cognitive capacities like reasoning, learning, and self-aware comprehension of its social and physical surroundings. Nevertheless, cognitive CPS-IoT also poses additional problems with security due to its more complicated nature. The likelihood of security breaches involving information and healthcare supplies has increased due to the healthcare infrastructure's increasing interconnectedness [2]. The healthcare ecosystem's CPS-IoT is vulnerable to a range of newly developed cyberattacks. Inadequate cybersecurity can lead to threats against people's lives, monetary loss, physical harm, and privacy violations for users.

Nevertheless, the complexity, dynamics, and high degree of connectedness of CPS-IoT-enabled healthcare services have proven too much for the security solutions existing in use [3]. As a result, establishing cognitive cybersecurity within the CPS-IoT-supported healthcare ecosystem requires a novel strategy. The purpose of this study is to introduce an idea and technique of cognitive cybersecurity that allows for the modeling of attacker behavior, determination of their intents, and prediction of future attacks. This approach anticipates and resolves new privacy and security issues by using a cognitive framework that can mimic human behavioral traits. Our objective is to strengthen defenses against attacks in the CPS-IoT-enabled healthcare environment by introducing creative components like security, privacy, and dynamic security knowledge metrics [4].

We will also investigate collaborative awareness of privacy, computational methods, flexible data gathering, and the incorporation of cross-sectoral approaches such AI predicted results and runtime checking in this study [5]. This strategy is anticipated to lower assault danger, improve cybersecurity in CPS-IoT in the healthcare industry, and safeguard the protection, credibility, and confidentiality of private health information. This study will advance knowledge of cognitive cybersecurity for CPS-IoT within the framework of the healthcare environment by emphasizing the dire requirement for practical safety measures. Proactive steps are anticipated to be taken to safeguard vital infrastructure and guarantee consumer safety and confidentiality in this changing time via cooperative efforts among cybersecurity specialists, healthcare professionals, and research scholars [6].

Figure 9.1 illustrates the four-layer design of the conventional Medical Cyber-Physical System. Before being sent to the cloud in this network, information from the data capture layer that the detectors obtained is saved in the cloudlet devices. To communicate decisions made by the doctor to the patient taking part in the purchasing layer, the cloud serves as an IT infrastructure and middleman [7]. Nearly all of those networks think about sending the computational effort to a cloud setting. On-device AI nodes are proposed in certain new studies to lessen the load on the public cloud [8].

Therefore, there are two main obstacles that bio-modal authorization in an MCPS may encounter. Primarily, because the MCPS's centralized architecture depends on cloud computing, there may be a noticeable delay in the network when detection judgments are made remotely. The procedure for making decisions is slowed down by cloud-based detection solutions, and the confidentiality of the information gathered from the acquisition layer is compromised because the information must be transferred to the cloud for processing [9].

Secondly, deep learning models possessing high computational power, which necessitates a great deal of information instances, are frequently

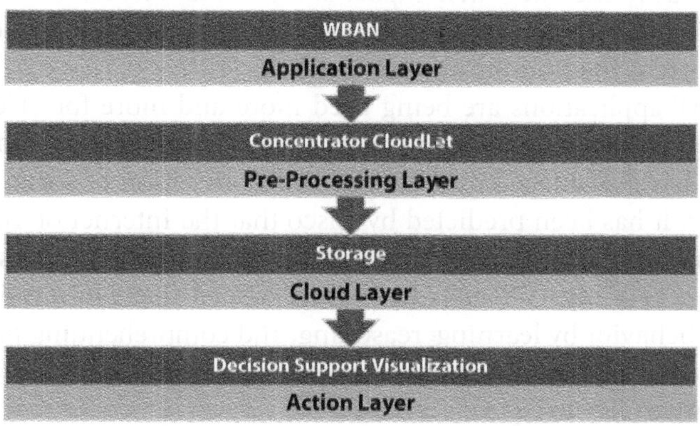

Figure 9.1 Medical cyber-physical system.

associated with excellent detection rates. In addition, the more characteristics there are, the more intricate the algorithms get. In the field of computing goals, every pixel value in an image is regarded as a separate characteristic, and the quantity of characteristics grows as the number of pixels in the image decreases [10]. Some traits, meanwhile, can be duplicated or so insignificant, not to matter sufficiently to be included in the identification. It is challenging to design the lightest detection algorithms with outstanding precision for devices that are smaller with limited resources that are close to acquisition layer sensors. In actuality, the problem has not yet received enough attention, and MCPS is not the main focus of the existing approaches [11].

In light of the aforementioned conditions, we utilized cloudlet nodes in our research to offer an effective on-device AI method for performing decentralized computing close to the MCPS acquisition layer. Furthermore, we have put forth a lightweight intelligent detection approach designed to identify bio-modality counterfeiting in cloudlet nodes [12]. Thus, at a reasonable efficiency, the local computing price of the cloudlet nodes can be lowered and the delay caused by the network can be kept to a minimum.

Issue of an MCPS centralized computing engine for the bio-modality spoofing detection technique. Consequently, find that the centralized design introduces concerns with latency and confidentiality because information must pass across the gathering layer, the cloudlet, and finally the cloud [13]. Determine how to choose between using a lightweight detection mechanism and preserving the high precision required for a proximal cloudlet node. A probabilistic forest model is trained using characteristics plus significant statistical parameters that are retrieved through choosing features. Due to the integrated impact of the random forest model, picking features, and augmentation mechanisms, the proposed technique considerably shortens the training and testing times [14].

CPS-IoT applications are being used more and more for eHealth and well-being and such applications include self-driven human monitoring, provider-driven managed monitoring, and aggregation of social data and marketing. It has been predicted by Cisco that the Internet of Things and cloud computing will enable over 50 billion items to be linked to society by 2020. More recently, CPS-IoTs have been created that can mimic human cognitive behavior by learning, reasoning, and comprehending their physical and social surroundings on their own. This type of CPS-IoT is known as a cognitive CPS-IoT [15].

The most intelligent applications of the Internet of Things in knowledge-intensive environments will be those that allow human thought processes to become central to the process [16]. (i) When CPS-IoTs' cognitive complexity increases, unanticipated emergent behavior may result; (ii) cognitive CPS-IoTs will face both new dangers relating to their innate cognitive functions and classic CPS-IoT weaknesses and dangers; (iii) It is possible to hack 70% of the most widely used IoT devices; 80% of these devices sparked confidentiality concerns about the acquisition of highly classified data, such as health-related data; and (iv) the widespread use of CPS-IoT will result in a much larger attack surface, raising the risks to critical infrastructure's public safety due to its interfaces and increased flexibility in accessing services and information [17].

Even though patient outcomes are being improved and the provision of care is being transformed, which ultimately improves the lives of people, worries regarding the safety of medical data and equipment are growing. A new breed of cybersecurity vulnerabilities has been introduced into medical devices and services by increased interconnection [18]. The healthcare industry is the one finest exposed to serious security threats. The vulnerability of the CPS-IoT-equipped healthcare facilities and amenities to various developing cyber assaults exacerbates the existing scenario. These features of disintegration interconnectivity, heterogeneity, and cross-organizational nature—thus creating an increased assault surface—CPS-IoT systems are categorized as secure and privacy-sensitive systems. It is crucial to avoid cybersecurity assaults because they can cause dangers to people's lives, bodily harm, monetary loss, and breaches of privacy for consumers. Millions of medical records have been taken worldwide, according to reports, which also emphasize the development in assaults and medical identity theft [19]. The increase in cyber-physical threats demonstrates that the complexity, unpredictability, dynamic nature, and the increased connection between healthcare services that are CPS-IoT enabled and the critical infrastructures are challenges that cannot be met by the level of protection measures available today. Automated intelligent cybersecurity decision-making systems can be enhanced to expert-level proficiency through the use of AI and cognitive design [20].

The primary goal of the proposed strategy is to offer a framework for protecting the CPS-IoT-enabled healthcare environment from dynamic and adaptive threats. This will be accomplished by (1) a cognitive architecture that mimics how people think to predict and react to unprecedented and developing privacy and security risks, (2) trade-offs along with other relevant elements to anticipate attackers' cognitive decision-making cycle, consider instabilities, and maximize temporal feedback loops, (3) combining cutting-edge safety, confidentiality, statistics, and dynamic security knowledge base processes will improve risk avoidance, identifying threats, handling incidents, and impact mitigation, (4) cooperative efforts that respect privacy, computational methods, flexible data gathering, and actuation, and (5) combining cross-cutting methods for risk management which are evidence-based, including dynamic forensics, run-time verification, AI predictive analytics, evidence collecting, and tracing.

9.2 Methodology

9.2.1 Device AI Solutions

Instead of depending solely on the cloud, device AI solutions were emphasized as a significant instrument for learning and identification activities on the device's side. Offer important benefits like quick reaction times, improved dependability, heightened privacy, and effective network capacity utilization. In addition to these benefits, it can enable machine learning algorithms to operate on handheld devices for image confidentiality and identification. Next-generation networks like MCPS, which identify bio-modalities in real-time through spoofing, might profit from the advantages of on-device AI as well.

9.2.2 Detect the Spoofing of Bio-Modality

Local Binary Patterns (LBP) were employed to detect printing artifacts and micro-texture features that were added to fictitious biometric data during the whole collection procedure. To distinguish a phony biometric specimen from an authentic the texture, color shade, and facial area shape forms have been investigated and a Partial Least Square (PLS) classifier has been used. Gabor wavelets were investigated for face spoofing assaults that are mask-based. These featured Gabor graphs with a similarity metric based on Gabor phase and local Gabor binary pattern histogram sequences.

Fast Fourier Transform to identify iris faking and confirm the high-frequency spectrum intensity. Detection of Iris liveness techniques varies approaches that are based on hardware that based on software that uses texture analysis to identify an intruder wearing contact lenses imprinted on another person's pattern. In-depth research is done on filter learning using natural image data, hard-coded characteristics, and common texture patterns for biometric counterfeiting identification.

9.2.3 Detect the Spoofing of Bio-Modality Using Machine Learning

The challenge of spoofing detection is still unresolved despite all these methods. Machine learning-based detection techniques have performed admirably in recent years. As a result, several machine learning-based spoofing techniques for biomodality spoofing detection have been put out previously. Several publicly available databases were used to verify the outcomes utilizing the face, iris, and fingerprint modality. Recurring and convolutional neural network techniques were combined to produce a context-aware deep structure to identify high-level characteristics in an image. These systems' fundamental issue is that they need complex, heavy-weight algorithms that cannot execute quickly enough without the usage of GPUs adding a layer of computational expense. An Adaboost improved using k-means clustering was proposed to maximize image detection precision. The latter two algorithms' performance in the spoofing detection problem of bio-modality is unknown. MCPS design uses this as an authentication verification technique; the proposed strategy seeks to utilize a strong random forest algorithm in conjunction with a novel feature-leveraging method to produce enhanced characteristics in addition to the random forest-based choice of features for the detection of multi-factor deception problems.

9.3 Challenges and Mechanisms

The evolving, complicated, unpredictable, and highly connected nature of CPS-IoT-empowered healthcare services and critical infrastructures must be addressed by cognitive cybersecurity to combat the ever-changing threats that are dynamic and adaptive. The subsequent part provides a quick overview of a handful of the complex obstacles to developing a cognitive cybersecurity solution, followed by an explanation of creative solutions to these obstacles.

9.3.1 Challenges

The aim is to represent every cognitive activity in humans, including the fundamental ones such as perception, decision-making, control, learning, adaptivity, and action, at the computational level. Specifically, the issue lies in designing an architecture that can adjust to the capabilities and restrictions of various CPSIoTs, while also accounting for the potential dynamic nature of these attributes which are capabilities and constraints.

Feedback loops that are Complex temporal: To maintain cognitive regulation, some activities need a highly tight feedback loop since they happen at very high rates. In a slow feedback loop, other actions happen over longer timescales, therefore cognitive control algorithms might need to include a larger set of variables. Because of the wide range of temporal loops and their sharp speed changes, determining the source and effect of an action can be quite difficult.

Complex interactions: The difficulty lies in capturing and modeling a great number of these interactions more accurately than humans could analyze.

Heterogeneous intercommunications: Since diverse configurations constitute a major factor in the remarkable advances in network performance, finding a solution is imperative.

Trade-offs and influencing elements: Prevent adaptive assaults by undermining attackers' ability to make cognitive decisions by accounting for uncertainty. Figuring out and understanding more limitations and other important control aspects that influence the attacker's and defender's cognitive processes constitutes a separate endeavor.

Security mechanisms: It can be difficult to include trust-based cognitive security, which enables enhanced and thorough analysis of attacker behavior by identifying the attackers' goals. It should be noted that determining the attackers' level of determination and tying their past involvement to the CPS-IoT system's activities is an exhausting endeavor. Analyzing the behavior of an attacker necessitates the capacity to make assumptions about the motives, attitudes, and behaviors of others.

Dynamic risks and metrics: Attackers with an adaptive mindset will modify their plans in response to changing security conditions and newly implemented defenses. It is therefore difficult to make the measures themselves adaptable. Assessing the quality of systems becomes ever more challenging as they get more complicated.

Dynamic forensics: As the amount of dynamic evidence gathered for each case grows profoundly, new techniques and tools based on cutting-edge technologies such as big data, cloud services, artificial intelligence/deep learning, CPS-IoT, and big data are required. The difficulty lies in combining these techniques and resources to accurately and efficiently record and track the dynamics of the evidence. Evidence dynamics describes any impact, regardless of purpose, that modifies, moves, hides, or destroys tangible evidence.

9.3.2 Innovative Mechanisms

Perform distributed and cognitive analysis and decision-making, cognitive cybersecurity requires intelligent and imaginative methods. These need to incorporate trust-based cognitive security, which enables an in-depth examination of the behavior of the attacker by proceeding to identify the attackers' intents, whereby projecting and estimating their level of determination, and connecting their past behavior with the CPS-IoT system's activity. To analyze the behavior of an attacker, the mechanisms must be able to make assumptions about the intents, character traits, and behaviors of others.

The capacity to gauge and react to attackers so adaptive — who, in turn, alter their strategies in reaction to newly put-in-place countermeasures and shifting security conditions —must be made possible by adaptive metrics. These objectives can be achieved by suitably combining game theoretic modeling and analysis, control theory, and AI/deep learning. Control theory can be used to generate assault plant seeds. The best defensive tactics can be found using (a) adversarial risk analysis, (b) game theory, and (c) minimax analysis. Privacy should be incorporated into the systems from the beginning via the following methods: privacy impact analysis, design pattern formulation (constructive approach), the creation of models (data kinds), transaction identification, and assessment via the construction of artifacts.

9.4 Cognitive Cyber-Physical Systems and Reinforcement Learning

The Hash value should begin with and possess an extensive number of zeros. The nonce is used for the generation of a cryptographic hash when the chain's first block, also known as the genesis block, is first formed. The data is permanently linked to a hash and a nonce until it is mined, and it is regarded as signed until this stage shown in Figure 9.2. Each block present in the ledger is given a distinct hash and nonce, which also has a reference to the hash of the preceding block in that ledger. This makes mining a difficult task, particularly when the chains are longer. Miners typically employ sophisticated and advanced software to solve the challenging challenge of utilizing the nonce to determine an adequate hash value.

Blockchain is built, and changes made to one block will have an impact on all following blocks. This feature makes it almost impossible to modify blockchain since this requires a lot to be computed and processing capacity

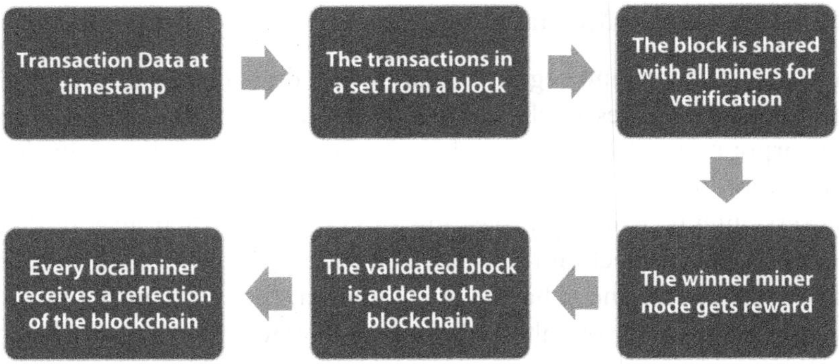

Figure 9.2 The blockchain technology flow.

to identify gold nonces. Each of the nodes in the network acknowledges the block when it has been successfully mined, and so the winning miner node is rewarded financially. The most important task when integrating the blockchain architecture is to have an ethical group of miners who can protect from threats. The reason is that, in the real world of mining, it is difficult to find miners who are 100% sincere. Earlier, it was thought that the most profitable mining technique, according to conventional wisdom, was genuine mining, which was embedded into the blockchain protocol.

Selective, evaluative, and delayed feedback are all used simultaneously by RL to address and deal with the sequential decision-making problem. For medical applications, this makes the RL-based sequential decision-making approach a special and excellent choice shown in Figure 9.3. By appropriately utilizing reward systems designed to reward good behavior and punishment systems designed to punish bad behavior, an agent trained with reinforcement learning becomes capable of acting intelligently in an environment unfamiliar. This strategy assigns a negative value whenever unwanted behaviors occur and a positive value for favorable acts conducted by the agent. To arrive at an optimal solution, it programs agents in a way that the rewards are maximized overall over the long run. These long-term objectives encourage the agent to keep going after bigger targets and not vice versa. Agents eventually acquire the ability to downplay the negative and focus on the positive. Based on the agent's behavior of action taken in state S, it is assumed that the agent acquires from the environment and as a reward for state R_{t+1}, will reach state S_{t+1}. RL is adaptable enough to consider treatment side effects and doesn't need a lot of contextual information to produce reasonably well-informed conclusions.

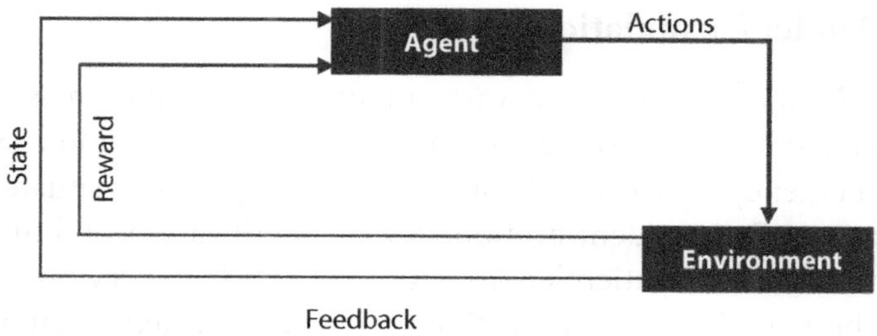

Figure 9.3 A typical reinforcement learning model.

One important aspect of the RL learning framework is its capacity to converge to an optimal approach without delving much into the nuances of the blockchain architecture. Figure 9.4 illustrates how distributed learning works by sending data to the client model, or local model. The global model updates and combines the trained weights. Eventually, the global model can be taught to make predictions using fresh data. With the help of distributed learning, several users can create potent shared machine learning models without disclosing any personal information, tackling crucial concerns like data security and privacy.

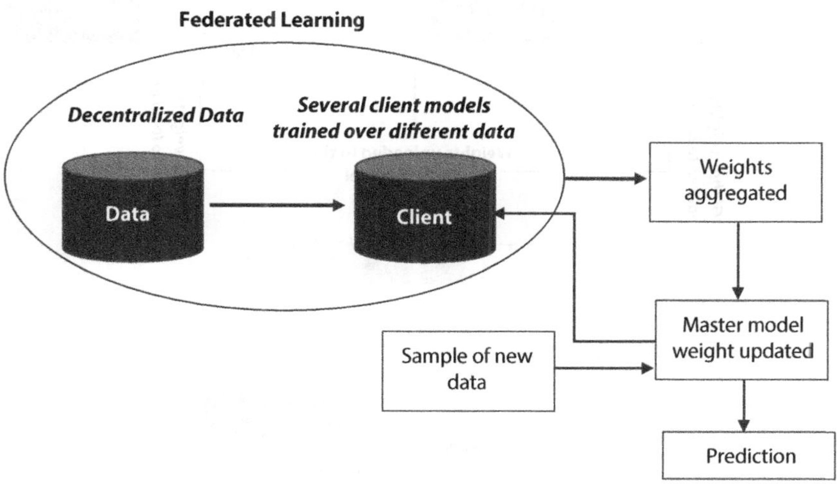

Figure 9.4 Distributed learning workflow model.

9.4.1 Model Formulation

Utilizing MCPS equipment, a vast amount of information is obtained for each patient. This info includes data collected from remote surgeries, linked emergency vehicles, and patient monitoring devices situated in various locations. Patient identification, device identification, and timestamp, an assortment of the patient's data is also collected at every point in time and can be regarded as a transaction. A block is created when a specific amount of transactions combine to form a Merkle tree and every block

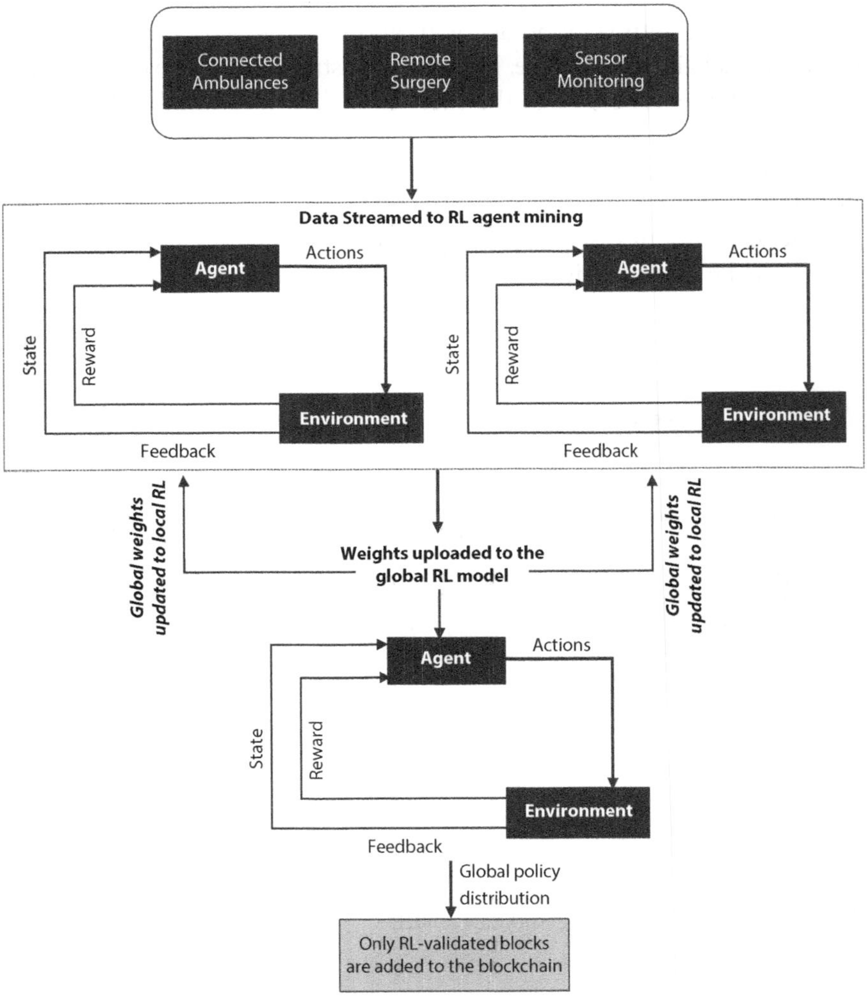

Figure 9.5 Workflow diagram of the proposed model.

has a nonce value inserted into it, which is linked in a chain with the block that comes before it. This block content is gathered as feed value by a small number of locally distributed RL agents functioning as miner nodes, and they decide whether or not to add it to the chain. That specific RL dealer will be given an adverse reward if any insecure transactions are added to the existing chain as a result of their actions. A storage memory base containing a probability distribution for every action on every state observed, with the greatest chance for the most lucrative reaction to be selected on a particular state, is updated for each local RL agent after a predetermined amount of time. The global RL model receives these memory weights and creates an aggregated memory base, which is then updated for all local models. Until the models accurately detect the attacks, this refinement process continues. Figure 9.5 is a visual representation of our proposed model's whole workflow.

The objective is to identify fraudulent transactions and prevent them from being appended to the blockchain. The process may differ depending on how the sensor condition evolves. The SGD complexity can be expressed as $(k \times n^2)$, where k represents the number of sensors and n represents the data sample that is taken into consideration for every iteration. The strategy calls for iteratively going over every sensor's data collection, using a vectorized version of the k data sample each time to train the model. (n^2) might be thought of as the worst-case level of detail. For our Fed RL model, this means that the final time complexity is $(m\times (n^2))$.

9.4.2 AI in CCPS

The proposed approach aims to provide an integrated cognitive framework in the CPS-IoT-enabled healthcare ecosystem that can handle evolving and adapting risks in a resilient manner. The goal of this structure is to address global cybersecurity issues in the field of healthcare. A multidisciplinary strategy combining knowledge from formal techniques, mathematics, forensics, cybersecurity, artificial intelligence, and trust is required to achieve this goal. The entire cybersecurity architecture concerning the healthcare ecosystem that is CPS-IoT enabled is shown in Figure 9.6. The following paragraphs offer succinct descriptions of the main purposes of the important building components in every single layer.

Our proposed on-device AI-based MCPS architecture is depicted in Figure 9.7. The conventional data path is depicted by the dotted lines. Nevertheless, this information can only alternatively flow up to the proximal device's layer 2 in our proposed architecture. Over a predetermined length of time, Layer 2 devices are further hooked up to the cloud

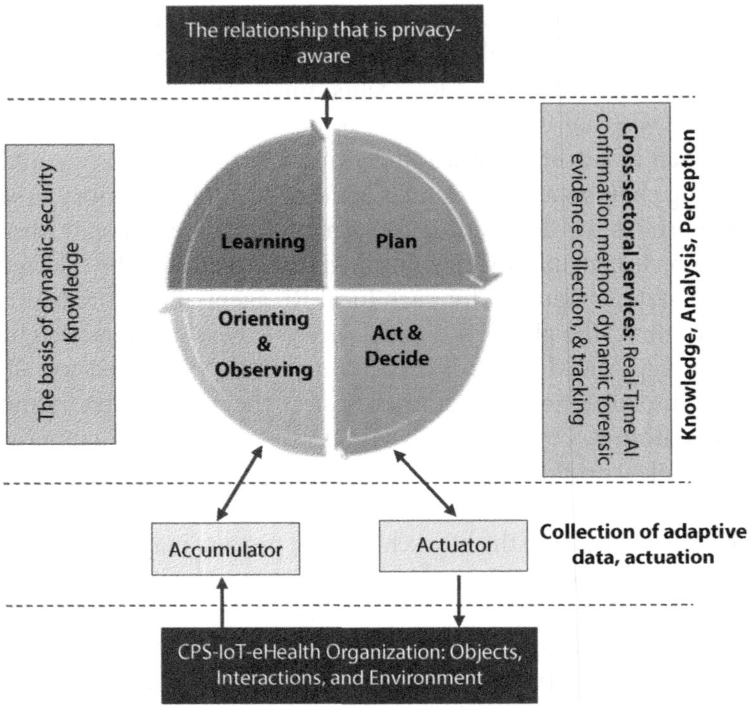

Figure 9.6 The proposed approach.

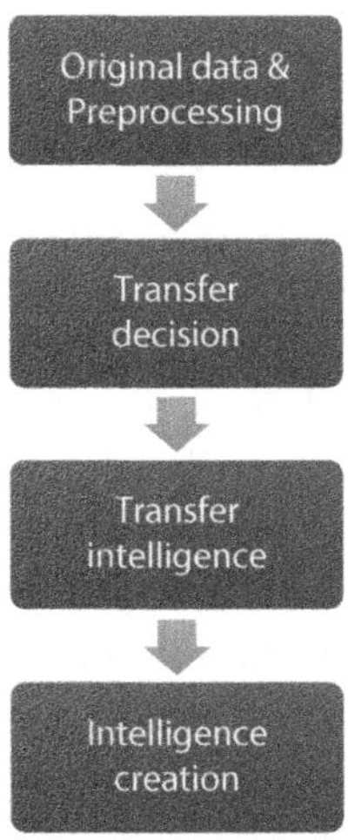

Figure 9.7 MCPS based AI.

to transmit reports and health information. The action layer, where the caregivers exist, is then connected to the cloud via the Internet shown in Figure 9.8. Hospitals and physicians, who are caretakers, gather data that is transmitted to the cloud from Layer 2 to carry out specific tasks by application-specific requirements shown in Figure 9.9.

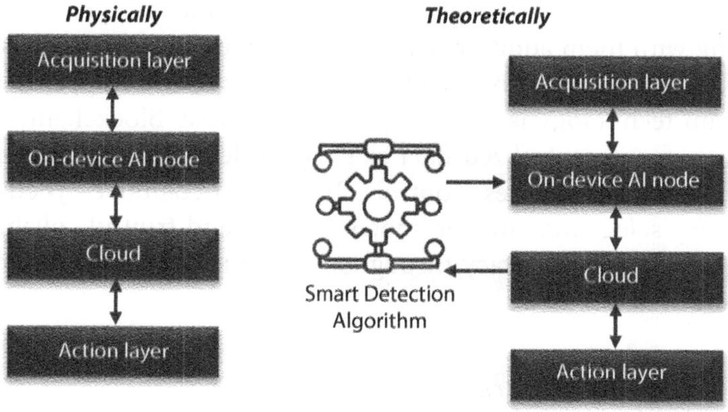

Figure 9.8 MCPS based on the physical and theoretical representation of AI.

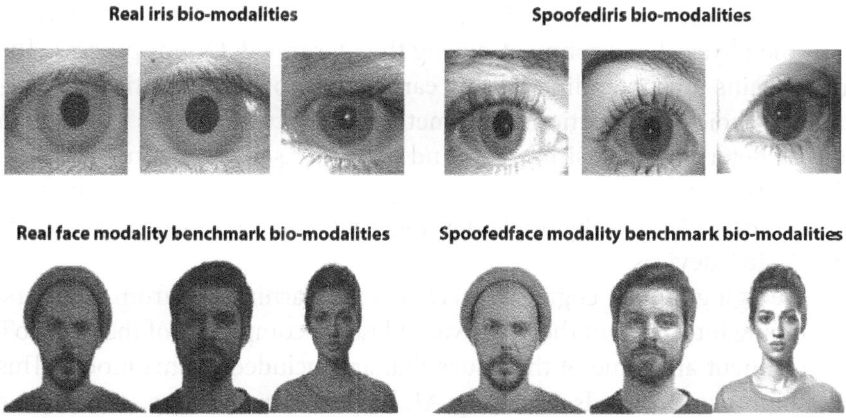

Figure 9.9 Security levels.

9.4.2.1 Privacy-Aware Collaboration

To mitigate vulnerabilities and successfully handle challenges in the complex healthcare ecosystem, evolving, and evidence-based risk administration must be put into place. This calls for a privacy-aware strategy that prioritizes stakeholder collaboration via the safe exchange of data, reporting, and visualization. Interoperability, interaction, and collaboration are the keystones of data sharing in the healthcare industry. However, they also bring with them additional safety, confidentiality, technological, promotion, and administrative challenges. A decentralized approach using blockchain technology is one intriguing alternative. Blockchain technology allows for decentralized data sharing while maintaining anonymity through well-defined access controls. To support cognitive cybersecurity and privacy safeguards, this promotes efficient and fruitful collaboration in cybersecurity and privacy throughout the many levels of the intricate healthcare system.

9.4.2.2 Cognitive Security Cycle Model

The goal of the CPS-IoT cognitive security cycle model is to close the cognitive loop by defending against assaults and gaining knowledge from the actions made. Trade-offs, AI controllers, and creative methods are all used in this type of approach. In addition, the framework takes into account the actions of people, the larger social setting, and the dynamics of CPS-IoT. It then makes use of this comprehension to implement suitable actions and extract important insights from the procedure. The cycle of this paradigm has four steps: Observe & Orient, Learn, Plan, and Decide Act. Adaptive data collectors are used to monitor and comprehend stimuli including configurations, user behaviors, threats, vulnerabilities, and interactions with the physical environment during the Observe & Orient process. The model gains understanding in the Learn step through perceptions, observations, choices, and actions. The methodology creates plans in the Plan step by determining desired goals and by taking scheduling into account. The model chooses the best security approach and puts it into practice in the Decide & Act step by implementing it via making physical alterations to CPS-IoT devices.

Leveraging human cognitive mechanisms, learning fast from attackers, and taking into account the many variables and complexity of the CPS-IoT environment are some of the issues that are included in this model. This paradigm uses methods including AI, huge data processing, and precise decision-making, and this is done to preserve confidentiality and privacy during user interactions, the cognitive model is also utilized to comprehend consumers in a variety of scenarios.

9.4.2.3 Need

Ontologies have proven to be crucial tools for formally and effectively modeling and managing settings within the complex healthcare ecosystem. Through the use of ontologies, reasoning techniques can be applied to efficiently support context management and dynamic modeling. Furthermore, the amalgamation of dynamic vulnerability scanning and penetration testing provides a mechanism for the regular evaluation and monitoring of modifications in vulnerabilities, threats, security protocols, privacy protections, and other relevant characteristics. This constant watchfulness guarantees that cognitive intelligence in the intricate healthcare ecosystem operates as it should.

9.4.2.4 Cross-Sectoral Techniques

AI tools are essential to predictive analysis and the integration of cognitive approaches such as reasoning, machine learning, and contextual analysis in the cognitive security cycle model. When it comes to early detection of incidents related to cybersecurity, these methods have shown a greater degree of efficiency. This integrated solution guarantees strict adherence to cybersecurity requirements by enabling continuous verification throughout system operation. In particular, threat situations and monitoring requirements are ever-changing, and Dynamic Context Monitoring is used to keep an eye on such developments. This feature enables quick adjustments to changing contexts and makes runtime validation compliant with relevant monitoring standards easier. The analysis and identification of the roots of crimes or incidents is done by continuous ongoing evidence gathering and tracing. To help with crime reconstruction, establish evidence-based risk management approaches, and enhance the effectiveness and dependability of recording and tracking the fluctuating nature of evidence, this method includes the dynamic collection, tracking, and mapping of evidence in addition to the utilization of AI techniques and deep learning in the field of forensics-related investigation. Thus, to ensure effective security and risk management in complex healthcare ecosystems, the employment of AI approaches, runtime verification, dynamic context monitoring, and continuous evidence collecting and tracing are essential.

9.4.2.5 Actuation and Data Collection

Objectives are to guarantee accurate data gathering, keep the volume of data gathered to a minimum, and mechanize the process by dynamically changing to various scenarios and settings. For both real-time and historical security analysis, the data-collecting infrastructure needs to be brought up to be very scalable and fast as when it comes to critical healthcare infrastructure and services, intelligence, resiliency, timeliness, and reliability are required for collecting and evaluating security data. It additionally needs to adhere to communication rules and regulations to recognize possible threats effectively. For adaptable and efficient analysis processes, predictive/regression algorithms including logistic regression, KNN regression, support vector regression (SVR), and linear regression are suitable options. Furthermore, the application of deep learning processes will be critical in identifying complex patterns of attack and potential hazards.

9.5 Conclusions and Future Directions

In conclusion, a viable strategy to improve security in CPS-IoT-enabled healthcare ecosystems is the merging of Cognitive Cybersecurity and Reinforcement Learning (RL) which presents a rather promising approach. This technique facilitates proactive threat identification, swift reaction to incidents of security, and adaptive security measures by utilizing cognitive skills like machine learning, artificial intelligence, and sophisticated analytics in conjunction with reinforcement learning's flexibility and learning mechanisms. By examination of case research and experiments has allowed us to show how effective this strategy is at reducing security risks and guaranteeing the stability of healthcare systems. Nevertheless, it is crucial to recognize that privacy, ethics, and regulatory compliance must all be carefully considered when deploying cognitive cybersecurity and RL in healthcare domains. To build more secure and resilient healthcare ecosystems, future research should concentrate more on resolving the foregoing problems and improving the integration of cognitive cybersecurity and RL. All things considered, by adopting cutting-edge cybersecurity techniques, we can strengthen the security of connected devices and systems, more effectively safeguard sensitive patient data, and guarantee the availability and integrity of healthcare services in a world growing more digitally dependent.

9.6 Future Directions

1. **Privacy-Preserving Techniques:** Create and put into practice privacy-preserving strategies to guarantee the confidentiality of patient data while utilizing RL and cognitive cybersecurity to improve security.
2. **Ethical Considerations:** Address the ethical issues such as data privacy, justice, accountability, and openness when using RL and cognitive cybersecurity in the healthcare industry.
3. **Regulatory Compliance:** When implementing cognitive cybersecurity and RL solutions in healthcare environments, make sure that they comply with healthcare standards and regulations, such as the FDA (Food and Drug Administration) guidelines, GDPR (General Data Protection Regulation), and HIPAA (Health Insurance Portability and Accountability Act).
4. **Interdisciplinary Research:** To create comprehensive strategies for cybersecurity in healthcare, and encourage interdisciplinary cooperation between cybersecurity specialists, medical professionals, data scientists, and legislators.
5. **Deployments in Real-World:** Perform case studies and real-world deployments to verify the efficacy of RL and cognitive cybersecurity solutions in various healthcare scenarios and contexts.
6. **Adaptation through Continuous Learning:** Allow systems to learn continuously and adapt to changing cybersecurity risks and healthcare issues by implementing feedback loops, continuous monitoring, and reinforcement learning techniques.
7. **Efficiency of Resource and Scalability:** Provide RL and cognitive cybersecurity algorithms that are scalable and resource-efficient so they can be implemented in resource-constrained CPS-IoT systems, which frequently appear in healthcare settings.
8. **Design for Human-Centric:** Using a human-centric design approach, create cognitive cybersecurity and reinforcement learning solutions that take patients' and healthcare providers' usability, accessibility, and user experience into account.
9. **Collaborative Defense Strategies:** To jointly protect against cyber threats and vulnerabilities in healthcare ecosystems,

and encourage cooperation and information exchange between government agencies, cybersecurity researchers, and healthcare organizations.

10. **Education and Training:** To improve their capacity to protect healthcare systems, offer cybersecurity practitioners and healthcare professionals education and training programs on the concepts and applications of RL and cognitive cybersecurity.

The exploration of these prospective paths and the pushing of cybersecurity boundaries for CPS-IoT-enabled healthcare ecosystems even further could guarantee the privacy, security, and resilience of healthcare services in an increasingly digitally and globally interconnected world.

References

1. Prawiyogi, A.G. and Meria, L., For a CPS-IoT Enabled Healthcare Ecosystem Consider Cognitive Cybersecurity. *Int. Trans. Artif. Intell.*, *2*, 1, 24–32, 2023.
2. Wankhade, M., Evolution of machine learning in cyber physical system. *Online J. Distance Educ. e-Learning*, *11*, 1, 1–19, 2023.
3. Javaid, M., Haleem, A., Singh, R.P., Suman, R., An integrated outlook of Cyber-Physical Systems for Industry 4.0: Topical practices, architecture, and applications. *Green Technol. Sustain.*, *1*, 1, 100001, 2023.
4. Bindra, S.S. and Aggarwal, A., Security in cyber-physical systems: Transformation and challenges. *J. Auton. Intell.*, 7, 4, 2024.
5. Jeffrey, N., Tan, Q., Villar, J.R., A review of anomaly detection strategies to detect threats to cyber-physical systems. *Electronics*, *12*, 15, 3283, 2023.
6. Dharmasiri, N.T.D., Nanayakkara, N. W. A. G. N., Abeyasinghe, U., Wisidagama, N.S., Karunarthne, M.L., Ranasinghe, D.M.M., Artificial Cognition based Medical Diagnosis and Treatment Recommendation System: A Review, 2023.
7. Kato, T., Fukumoto, N., Sasaki, C., Tagami, A., Nakao, A., Challenges of CPS/IoT Network Architecture in the 6G Era. *IEEE Access*, 12, 62804–62817, 2024.
8. Daniel, S.A., Victor, S.S., Emerging Trends in Cybersecurity for Critical Infrastructure Protection: A Comprehensive Review. *Comput. Sci. IT Res. J.*, 5, 3, 576–593, 2024.
9. Soni, T., Kaur, R., Gupta, D., Sharma, A., Gupta, G., The Cybersecurity Ecosystem: Challenges, Risk and Emerging Technologies, in: *2023 7th International Conference on Trends in Electronics and Informatics (ICOEI)*, IEEE, pp. 699–703, 2023, April.

10. Chauhdary, S.H., Alkatheiri, M.S., Alqarni, M.A., Saleem, S., An efficient evolutionary deep learning-based attack prediction in supply chain management systems. *Comput. Electr. Eng.*, *109*, 108768, 2023.
11. Abdalzaher, M.S., Fouda, M.M., Elsayed, H.A., Salim, M.M., Toward secured IoT-based smart systems using machine learning. *IEEE Access*, *11*, 20827–20841, 2023.
12. Wang, S., Ko, R.K., Bai, G., Dong, N., Choi, T., Zhang, Y., Evasion Attack and Defense On Machine Learning Models in Cyber-Physical Systems: A Survey. *IEEE Commun. Surv. Tutor.*, 26, 930–966, 2023.
13. De Azambuja, A.J.G., Plesker, C., Schützer, K., Anderl, R., Schleich, B., Almeida, V.R., Artificial intelligence-based cyber security in the context of industry 4.0—a survey. *Electronics*, *12*, 8, 1920, 2023.
14. Kumar, Y. and Kumar, V., Security in IoT systems using natural language processing: Future challenges and directions. *Internet Technol. Lett.*, *6*, 4, e411, 2023.
15. Javaid, M., Haleem, A., Singh, R.P., Suman, R., Towards insight cybersecurity for healthcare domains: A comprehensive review of recent practices and trends. *Cyber Secur. Appl.*, 100016, 1–13, 2023.
16. El-Hajj, M., Itäpelto, T., Gebremariam, T. Systematic literature review: Digital twins' role in enhancing security for Industry 4.0 applications. *Secur. Privacy*, 7, e396, 2024.
17. Saeed, S., Altamimi, S.A., Alkayyal, N.A., Alshehri, E., Alabbad, D.A., Digital transformation and cybersecurity challenges for businesses resilience: Issues and recommendations. *Sensors*, *23*, 15, 6666, 2023.
18. Epiphaniou, G., Hammoudeh, M., Yuan, H., Maple, C., Ani, U., Digital twins in cyber effects modeling of IoT/CPS points of low resilience. *Simul. Modell. Pract. Theory*, *125*, 102744, 2023.
19. Sobb, T., Turnbull, B., Moustafa, N., A Holistic Review of Cyber-Physical–Social Systems: New Directions and Opportunities. *Sensors*, *23*, 17, 7391, 2023.
20. Podder, A. and Paul, S., Recent Trends of Artificial Intelligence in the Internet of Things, 2023.

10

Navigating the Digital Landscape: Understanding, Detecting, and Mitigating Cyber Threats in an Evolving Technological Era

Manikandan J.[1*], Hemalatha P.[2], Jayashree K.[3] and Rajeswari P.[4]

[1]*Department of Information Technology, St. Joseph's College of Engineering, OMR, Chennai, Tamil Nadu, India*
[2]*Department of Computer Science and Engineering, Vel Tech Rangarajan Dr. Sagunthala R&D Institute of Science and Technology, Chennai, India*
[3]*Panimalar Engineering College, Department of Artificial Intelligence and Data Science, Chennai, Tamil Nadu, India*
[4]*Department of Computer Science and Engineering, SRM Institute of Science and Technology, Ramapuram, Chennai, India*

Abstract

The shift to online activities, accelerated by the COVID-19 pandemic, has increased internet usage and led to a rise in online criminal activity. The adoption of technologies like cloud computing, IoT, social media, wireless communication, and cryptocurrency has driven this change. However, these technologies' interdependence has introduced new online safety concerns and vulnerabilities to cyberattacks. One significant trend is "cyber assaults as a service," where cybercriminals offer automated attack services to third parties, broadening their illegal activities' reach and impact. This approach allows cybercriminals to scale their operations and become more formidable. Examples of cyber assaults include malware, DDoS, phishing, man-in-the-middle, password attacks, remote attacks, and privilege escalation. Traditional security measures such as firewalls, intrusion detection systems, antivirus software, and access control lists are no longer sufficient to counter these advanced threats. Thus, exploring new defense strategies

**Corresponding author*: jmanekandan@gmail.com

K. Ananthajothi, S. N. Sangeethaa, D. Divya, S. Balamurugan and Shen-Lung Peng (eds.) Securing Cyber-Physical Systems: Fundamentals, Applications and Challenges, (199–224) © 2025 Scrivener Publishing LLC

against cyber assaults is crucial. Advanced technologies like blockchain, big data, cloud platforms, deep learning, and machine learning offer potential solutions to detect and combat cyber threats. However, these solutions may still be susceptible to evasion strategies, underscoring the need for thorough examination to develop effective defenses against sophisticated cyber-attacks.

Keywords: Malware, distributed denial of service (DDOS), blockchain, big data, cloud platforms, deep learning, machine learning

10.1 The Digital Transformation: Shaping Modern Business Dynamics

A paradigm shift has occurred in the way that organization's function and connect with their customers as a result of the rapid progress of digital technologies in recent years. This transition, which is frequently referred to as the digital transformation, covers the incorporation of digital technologies into all parts of corporate operations, ranging from marketing and sales to customer service and supply chain management. The widespread adoption of digital tools and platforms to facilitate the streamlining of processes, the improvement of efficiency, and the acceleration of innovation is the driving force behind the digital transformation [1]. The ever-increasing desire for improved connectivity and accessibility is one of the primary forces that is driving the digital transformation. As a result of the rise of internet-connected devices such as smartphones, tablets, and other technologies, consumers today anticipate having digital experiences that are consistent across a variety of channels. Companies who are unable to incorporate this new reality into their operations run the risk of falling behind their competitors and losing market share [2]. Additionally, the digital transformation has resulted in a blurring of the barriers between physical and digital places, which has opened up new potential for businesses to interact with their customers in novel ways.

The digital transformation has not only resulted in an increase in operational efficiency and consumer engagement, but it has also resulted in the opening of new revenue streams and business models. A few examples of how businesses are utilizing digital technology to create value and earn revenue include online platforms, digital marketplaces, and subscription-based services. These are just a few examples. The digital revolution, on the other hand, poses a number of problems and hazards for enterprises. Cybersecurity threats, worries about data privacy, and the requirement for digital upskilling are just some of the difficulties that organizations have to deal with in this day and age given the prevalence of digital technology [3]. In addition, because of the quick pace of technological change, firms are required to continuously adapt and develop in order to maintain a competitive advantage over their rivals.

10.2 Impact of COVID-19: Accelerating the Digital Shift

There has been a quick shift towards remote work and virtual collaboration, which is one of the most apparent effects that COVID-19 has had. Organizations quickly embraced digital platforms such as video conferencing, cloud-based collaboration tools, and project management software in order to support remote work arrangements. This was done in response to the closure of physical offices and the implementation of travel restrictions. The implementation of this change not only made it possible for corporate activities to go without interruption, but it also brought to light the possibility that working remotely will become an established norm in the era following the epidemic [4].

In a similar vein, the education industry went through a considerable transformation as a result of the transition that schools and universities made to online learning modalities. E-learning platforms, digital textbooks, and virtual classrooms have become indispensable tools for delivering educational content to students who are located in remote locations and engaging them in the learning process. In spite of the fact that it was initially motivated by necessity, the adoption of online education has resulted in discussions regarding its long-term viability and the possibility that it could improve learning outcomes beyond the epidemic. Consumers attempted to minimize in-person encounters and adhere to social distancing standards, which led to an acceleration in the adoption of e-commerce and digital payment solutions. In addition, the pandemic expedited the adoption of these solutions. Retailers swiftly shifted their focus to online platforms in order to communicate with customers, while contactless payment methods acquired universal adoption as a more secure alternative to cash transactions. Telemedicine emerged as a crucial instrument for the delivery of distant healthcare services and consultations as a result of the pandemic, which also resulted in the healthcare industry experiencing a digital revolution. A revaluation of traditional forms of healthcare delivery was prompted as a result of patients' acceptance of virtual appointments for routine checkups, prescription refills, and mental health support. As

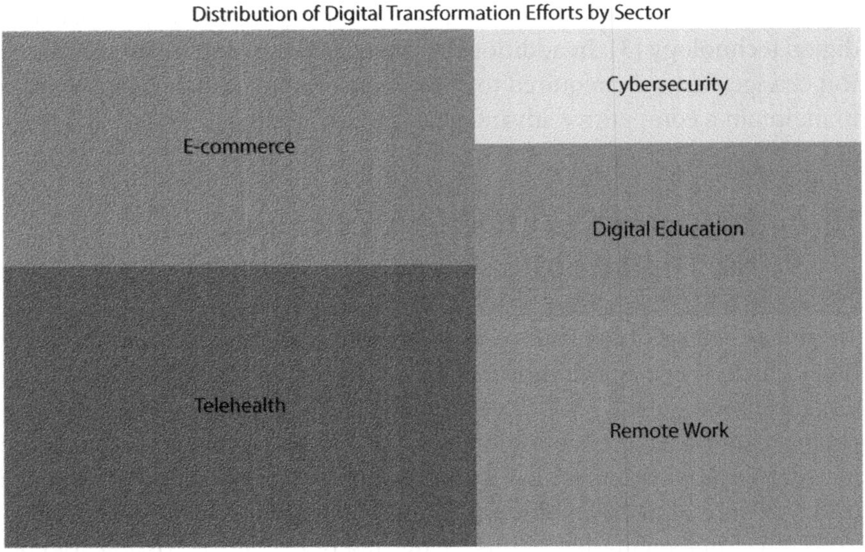

Figure 10.1 Impact of COVID-19: Digital transformation efforts by sector.

society adjusts to the new normal, it is anticipated that the trends towards remote employment, online education, e-commerce, telemedicine, and digital connectivity will continue [5]. This will usher in a digital-first period that is characterized by an increased reliance on technology to negotiate the intricacies of a world that has been affected by a pandemic.

Figure 10.1, which is the TreeMap visualization, illustrates the distribution of digital transformation efforts across different sectors, showcasing the sectors that have experienced the most significant impact in accelerating the digital shift due to the COVID-19 pandemic. Sectors such as Telehealth and E-commerce appear to have higher levels of digitalization efforts compared to others, highlighting their importance in adapting to the challenges posed by the pandemic and leveraging digital technologies for continued operations and service delivery.

10.3 Online Safety Concerns: Navigating the Digital Landscape

In today's world, digital safety is more essential as anyone can imagine. The internet is an incredibly dangerous place where a multitude of people and businesses must carry out numerous operations. The problems range from data breaches to identity theft and consumers getting attacked.

People must understand their digital environment to address this new age properly and be conscious of potential threats. Some of the online safety concerns include [6].

- **Data Breaches and privacy worries:** Concerning the world's ever-increasing amount of online personal and sensitive information, data breaches are a nearly prevalent danger. Cybercriminals, for instance, hack databases, networks, and other ere systems to steal access to personal information, banking details, financial records, and proprietary business information.
- **Privacy issues and risks:** So, cybersecurity should be cautious about any possible risks associated with a data breach and the need for appropriate measures to enhance security and privacy.
- **Identity theft and fraudulent transactions:** Identity theft is another significant issue for many cybercriminals and is perpetrated utilizing people's stolen personal information. For hackers, obtaining access to the list can be used to open fraudulent accounts, make advance payments, or other unauthorized purposes. One means of using educational measures to teach people the necessity of safeguarding their personal information and equipment and implementing Identity verification measures.
- **Cyberattacks and malicious attacks:** Individual users, companies, and even critical infrastructure are all exposed to a higher threat of cyber-attack and malware, phishing, ransomware, and DDoS. Malicious threats can specifically target software loopholes, critic networks and operation, human care, and device threats representative of compromise. Therefore, firewalls and employee's preparation are just some of the methods to protect the business from hackers.
- **Social engineering and online crimes:** More notably, social engineering approach includes phishing emails, social media scams, and fraudulent websites often manipulate people into providing them with sensitive info online social networks. Recognize the signs and feeling secure when interacting on the internet to avoid becoming a victim of online networking scams and criminal activity.
- **Exclusive threats and hazards:** as innovation continues to develop, new vulnerabilities, threaten cybersecurity

specialists and some businesses. Therefore, regular risk monitoring and proactive actions are required to address the evolving danger.

10.4 Interplay of Digital Technologies: Vulnerabilities and Threats

To begin, the contemporary digital landscape is characterized by the interplay of diverse digital technologies, which expose various vulnerabilities and threats that organizations face. This subtopic will examine the complex interactions between diverse digital technologies and their vulnerabilities, and the threats to cybersecurity.

10.4.1 Introduction to Digital Technologies

Elucidate how each digital technology benefits organizations, such as increased efficiency and connectivity and product and process innovation.

- **Vulnerabilities from digital technologies:** Secondly, discuss the vulnerability posed by each digital technology. For example, cloud computing is vulnerable to data breaches, access breaches, and credential theft due to shared infrastructure. IoT is vulnerable to security breaches and cyber-attacks due to inadequate IoT security by design and configuration and with inadequate security measures and testing. AI systems are vulnerable to adversarial attacks and data poisoning, which can cause bias or induction vulnerability [7].
- **Threat landscape in the digital era:** Likewise, explore the emerging threat landscape fueled by digital technologies. Cyber threats such as DDoS attacks, ransomware, phishing, and malware continue to threaten businesses. Furthermore, the increasingly sophisticated cyber-attacks target key infrastructure through the exploitation of digital technologies' vulnerabilities.
- **Emerging threat vectors:** Additionally, assess the existing and emerging threat vectors that result from digital technologies' interplay. For example, supply chain attacks targeting interconnected suppliers and partners. Attacks involve AI that targets vulnerabilities in AI based on machine learning.

Attacks targeting the decentralized model, enabled by blockchain [8].

- **Impact on cybersecurity posture:** Finally, this section should assess the impact of digital technologies on cybersecurity. Digital technologies have contributed to cumulative interconnectedness, which has increased cyber risks and made traditional security measures ineffective. Therefore, we need to be proactive in securing all digital touchpoints and predict emerging threats. Therefore, organizations should adopt a competent cybersecurity strategy that proactively identifies and patches vulnerabilities and implement sophisticated security measures to combat emerging threats [9].
- **Mitigation strategies and best practices:** Offer recommendations on how to mitigate cyber threats resulting from the combination of these digital technologies. Precisely this process would involve comprehensive frameworks, regular risk assessments, and robust security measures. Regular risk assessment provides organizations with the up-to-date analysis of existing threats. Insights from the analysis enable the organization to make strategic decisions on the cybersecurity measures that should be considered immediately [10].

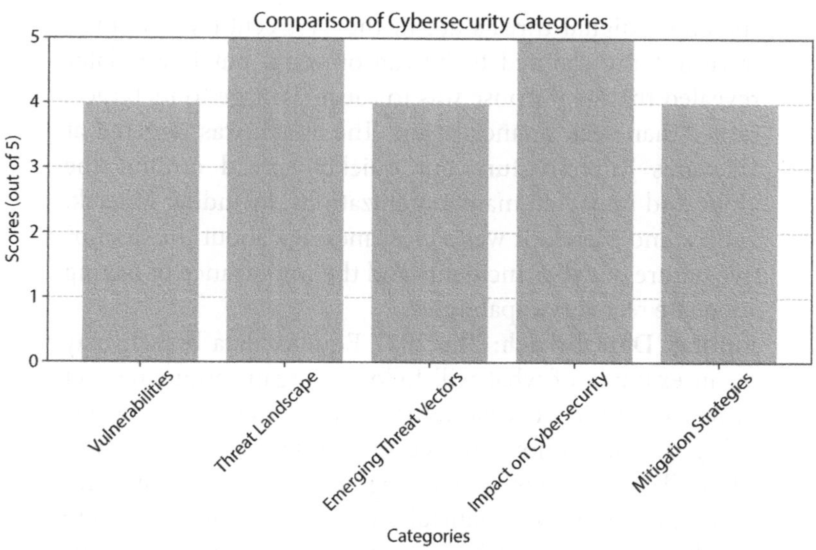

Figure 10.2 Comparison of different categories on cybersecurity.

Figure 10.2, clearly explores clear comparison of various categories of cybersecurity.

10.4.2 Case Studies and Examples

This section should further elaborate on the key insights using case studies and examples. These include elaboration on the key cybersecurity challenges faced and solutions used to mitigate the threats.

- **Target Data Breach:** In this case, cybercriminals obtained access to the company's systems after exploiting the vulnerability in the network of the retailer's HVAC vendor. Millions of customers' personal and financial data were compromised as a result. The incident demonstrated the importance of understanding supply chain risks and establishing a sufficient level of monitoring over third-party vendors' cybersecurity practices.
- **WannaCry Ransomware Attack:** It is a compelling example of how digital technologies have become engines of threats that had global implications. The ransomware used a vulnerability in Microsoft's Windows operating system to infect targeted networks and encrypt data.
- **NotPetya Cyberattack:** The 2017 NotPetya cyberattack is a vivid demonstration of how widespread and rapidly spreading digital threats are in the 21st century. The malware initially claimed to be ransomware, but it was later revealed that its purpose was to cause damage to its targets rather than seek financial gain. The attack was targeted at Ukraine's infrastructure but quickly spread around the globe and impacted many organizations, including Maersk, FedEx, and Merck. It was a clear message about the disruptive nature of cyber incidents and the importance of having adequate recovery capabilities.
- **Equifax Data Breach:** The 2017 Equifax data breach may be an example of what will follow if organizations neglect cybersecurity in data handling. In this attack, cybercriminals gained unauthorized access to the sensitive data of over 147 million people when hacking Equifax's website application. The company's financial and reputational losses were significant, and it soon faced the serious consequences of the

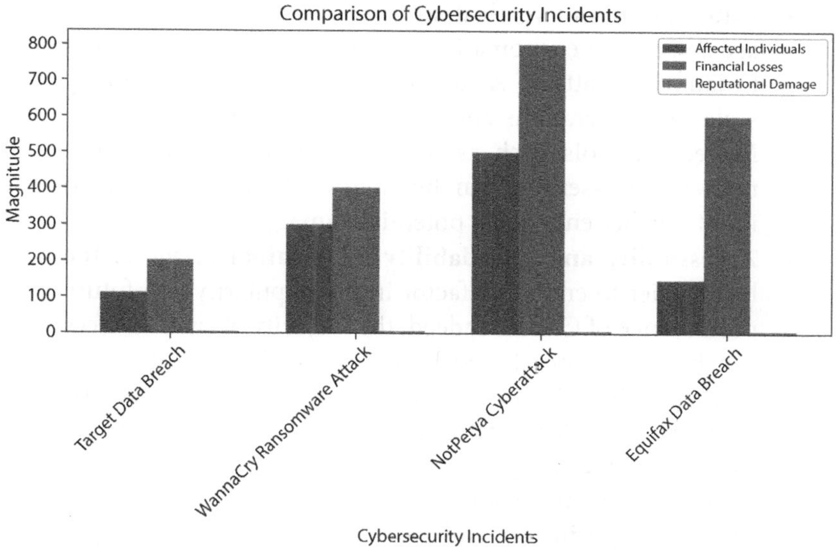

Figure 10.3 Comparison of various cybersecurity attacks.

incident due to the loss of consumer trust [11]. Also, comparison of various cybersecurity attacks is given in Figure 10.3.

10.5 Rise of Cyber Assaults as a Service: Automating Criminal Activities

Over the past years, a distinctive pattern has emerged in the cybercrime field where criminal activities have become commoditized and automated, leading to the development of Cyber Assaults as a Service. The following section will discuss the origin and potential for such developments for cybersecurity in the digital age. The notion of CAaaS is key to this discussion. In short, CAaaS represents the provision of cyberattack automation to other criminal entities, enabling them to conduct high-quality attacks without requiring advanced technical expertise. Such services are typically advertised on the darknet or various forums, where criminals offer their services, including distributed denial-of-service, malware distribution, phishing, and ransomware-as-a-service [12].

- **Automation and vertical scaling:** CAaaS platforms leverage considerable automation to remove most steps required to launch an attack. As a result, threat actors can rapidly scale their operations and hit a greater number of targets. Moreover, tools such as botnets, exploitation kits, and malware-as-a-service can be used with minimal human input, further enhancing potential damage.
- **Accessibility and affordability of criminal services:** the low barrier to entry is a factor in the popularity and future prominence of CAaaS. Indeed, the majority of such services can be readily purchased by anyone with access to illicit markets, which includes unskillful potential threat actors. As a result, the democratization of cybercrime has occurred as more people and groups used the acquired tools to profit from or impact the world.
- **Erosion of perimeter and store defense:** CAaaS is largely an entry point around regular security processes. Given the broad commoditization of such attacks, criminals no longer need to develop their tools and techniques. As a result, the usual dimensions of defense, such as perimeter measures or modern AI systems, become generally ineffective.
- **Cause and Impact on Cybersecurity Landscape:** CAaaS has influenced the cybersecurity landscape leading to new threats and challenges targeting organizations and individuals. As the dark web continues to actively host automated and commodified cybercrimes, cybersecurity professionals must enact a proactive approach to detect, mitigate and prevent CAaaS-targeted attacks.
- **The Multi-Faceted Approach:** For organizations to address the increasing CAaaS threat, a multi-faceted approach that entails robust threat intelligence, proactive monitoring, and response capabilities is critical. Through the deployment of advanced algorithms, machine learning, and threat hunting, security teams can easily identify and stop CAaaS targeted attacks, minimizing the damages suffered.
- **Collaborative Efforts between Stakes:** Moreover, a collective approach to combatting CAaaS should be promoted to enhance existing cooperation and information sharing among stakeholders. The engagement and collaboration

between government bodies, law enforcement, private sectors, and cybersecurity researchers will facilitate the sharing of learnings and threat-derived awareness to intercept, detect, and prosecute criminals leveraging CAaaS platforms.

- **Regulatory, and Legal Factors:** In addition, policymakers, and regulators must enforce laws that prevent cybercriminal activities and hold criminals accountable for the crime committed. Legal authorities should develop a legal framework that mirrors the emerging threats ensuring law enforcement agencies have the required authority and tools to investigate and prosecute CAaaS operators.
- **User Awareness and Education:** Lastly, user awareness and education are essential for building a cyber-resilient society. Identifying and detecting CAaaS threats and best practices to mitigate them, must be communicated to organizations and individuals to empower them [13]. Figure 10.4 displays the rise of cyber assaults as a service.

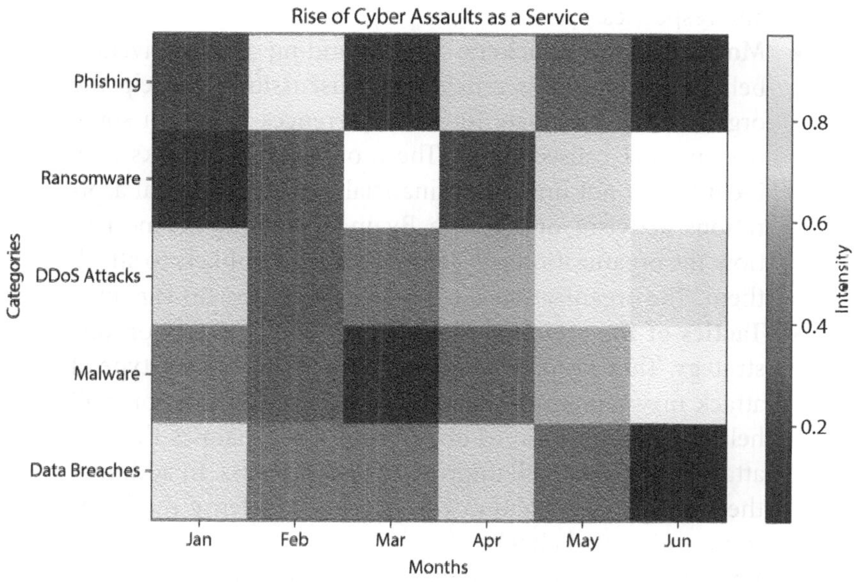

Figure 10.4 Rise of cyber assaults as a service.

10.6 Evolving Threat Landscape: Understanding Modern Cyber Attacks

Given the rapidly changing digital landscape, organizations need to appreciate the nature and strategies of modern cyber-attacks to effectively protect themselves. Therefore, this subtopic aims at discussing the various dynamic aspects of cyber threats; included is the well-structured understanding of the types of attacks, the attacker's motivations, and tactics they employ. Figure 10.5 clearly gives the comparison of various types of cyberattack.

- **Types of cyber-attacks:** This section will thoroughly explain the various dynamic types of cyber-attacks that exist. Including, traditional types such as malware, phishing, and ransomware will be tackled. Also, there are other new types of cyber-attacks including supply chain attacks, zero-day strikes, among others. This section will shed light upon the kind of attacks that exist, and the organization will understand what each attack is about. It is necessary to understand what one faces before formulating measures of prevention and responses.
- **Motivation of attackers:** understanding the motivation behind the attacks is crucial. The discussion will help the organization anticipate future occurrences based on some reasons that caused them. The motivation to attacks may include, but not limited to financial benefits, political aspirations, activism, or sabotage. By understanding the motivation, the organization will get who likely or unlikely to attack them. The organization can, by doing that, remain vigilant.
- **Tactics of the attacker:** The attacker does not rely on one strategy. They keep on changing the pattern, but the type of attack may remain the same. This part of the subtopic will help the organization to understand the dynamics that the attack employs. It will improve their awareness. In addition, the strategic organization can develop a defense mode for some anticipated attacks.
- **Emerging trends in attacks:** Given the advancement in technology, cyber attackers are also improving in their ways. It discusses the new ways attackers have developed. Such ways may include a variety of ways of phishing, ransomware

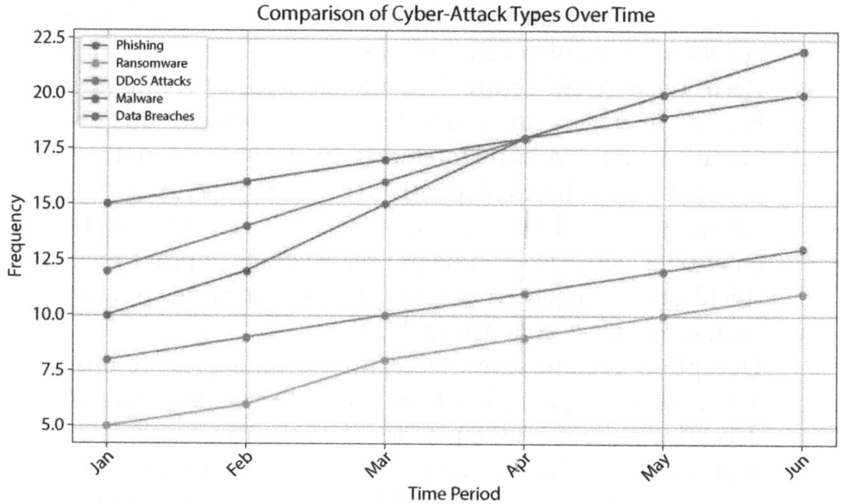

Figure 10.5 Comparison of various types of cyberattack.

service provision, and other established cyber and other new ways. First, to remain aware, the organization can also develop new ways of combating attacks [6].

10.7 Beyond Conventional Security Measures: The Need for Advanced Defense

Traditional cybersecurity approaches are insufficient in protecting organizations against cyber threats in the modern quickly changing technology-driven world. This section discusses the critical need for cutting-edge defense mechanisms that are different from normal traditional security activities to help organizations significantly reduce cyber risks.

- **Rise of Advanced Persistent:** Threats Advanced Persistent Threats are a notable threat to organizations because they are devious, directed, constant, and substantial in their criticality. APTs differ significantly because they are mostly orchestrated by well-armed and financially endowed threat actors with a motive like industrial espionage and nation sabotage. APTs use advanced invasion methods since they try to recover capacity, a trait that demands organizations to put in place advanced protection methods like threat hunting, activity analysis, and intelligence, and real-time curbing among other activities [14].

- **Zero Trust Architecture:** Traditional security techniques like perimeter security are no longer effective mainly because people work and interact from anywhere. Zero trust is a technique where one doesn't trust either outer or internal networks and verifies every user and device trying to enter one's network. ZTA helps organizations improve their shield and consequently reduces the need for being afraid of backward attacks and insider threats.
- **Deception Technologies:** Deception technologies are proactive security approaches that involve the management of deceptive servers, endpoints, and data to attract and deter aggressors. By effective acting dead, organizations can curb threats and get poison data and learn activities, techniques, and procedures. With deceptions, organization reduces the time taken to identify adversaries hidden in singly approved through real-time and decoys.
- **Inadequacy of Traditional Signature-Based Approaches:** Traditional signature-based approaches to cybersecurity are unable to detect and remediate unknown and rapidly evolving threats, including polymorphic malware and Zero-day exploits. Behavioral analytics and machine learning apply artificial intelligence and data analytics technology to identify anomalous behavior patterns representing cyber threats. They collect and correlate millions of data from security component and correlate dissimilar security occurrences to pinpoint suspected activities, enhance and prioritize alerts, and quicken the situation's resolution [15].
- **Threat Intelligence Sharing and Collaboration:** Cyber dangers are dynamic and continually changing, and thus, organizations should adopt the most recent threat intelligence and assault techniques. Intelligence sharing and corporate collaboration offer firm platforms for actionable intelligence and bulk indicators and attack indicators sharing. Sectors in this field where the business is dominant include government agencies, cybersecurity software vendors, and international agencies. They can increase their understanding of the environment, while their protection measures and counter-attacking cyber threats. The comparison of various security measures is given in Figure 10.6.

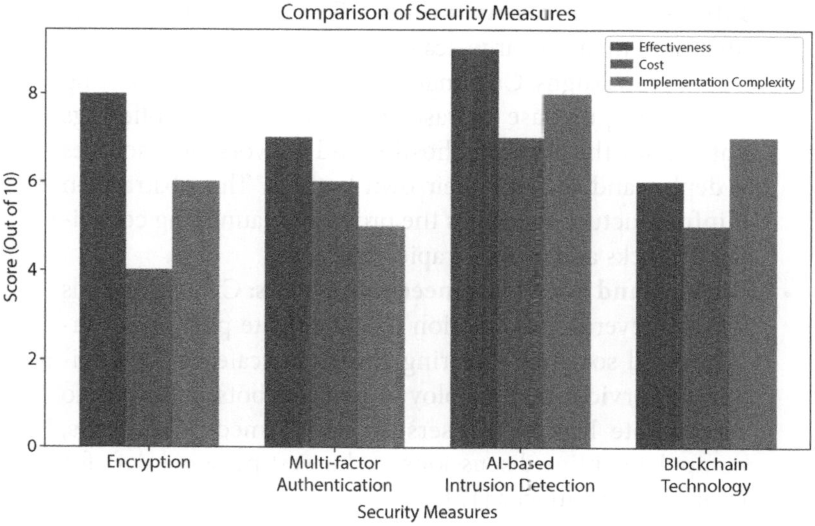

Figure 10.6 Comparison of various security measures.

10.8 Rise of Cyber Assaults as a Service: Automating Criminal Activities

10.8.1 Introduction to Cyber Assaults as a Service

One prominent trend in this landscape is the emergence of "cyber assaults as a service," where malicious actors offer tools, resources, and expertise for conducting cyberattacks in exchange for financial gain. This phenomenon represents a commodification of cybercrime, enabling even non-technical individuals to engage in illicit activities with minimal effort [16].

10.8.2 Automation of Criminal Activities

Cyber assaults as a service rely heavily on automation to streamline and scale criminal operations. This automation manifests in several key aspects:

- **Toolkits and Malware-as-a-Service (MaaS):** Criminals can purchase or rent ready-made malware toolkits and services from underground marketplaces. By outsourcing the development and maintenance of malware to specialized vendors, cybercriminals can launch sophisticated attacks without the need for advanced technical skills.

- **Botnets and Infrastructure-as-a-Service (IaaS):** Botnets often used to tackle large-scale attacks such as DDoS attacks or spam campaigns. Criminals can rent access to pre-existing botnets or purchase infrastructure-as-a-service offerings that provide the necessary hosting and networking resources to deploy and manage their own botnets. This abstraction of infrastructure simplifies the process of launching coordinated attacks and enables rapid scalability.
- **Phishing and Social Engineering Services:** Cybercriminals can also leverage automation to orchestrate phishing campaigns and social engineering attacks at scale. Social engineering services may employ automated bots or scripts to impersonate legitimate users on social media platforms, manipulate online discussions, or harvest personal data for use in targeted attacks [17].

10.8.3 Impact and Implications

The rise of cyber assaults as a service and the automation of criminal activities have profound implications for cybersecurity and society at large:

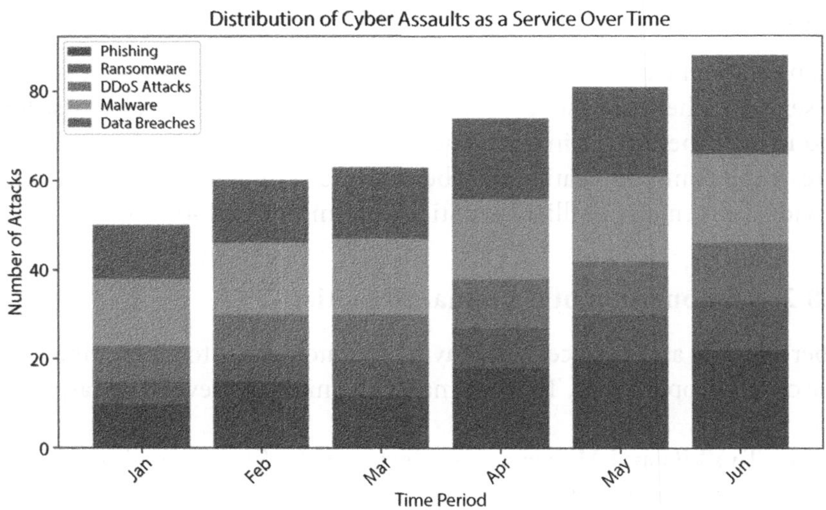

Figure 10.7 Distribution of cyber assaults as a service upon time.

- **Increased Accessibility:** Automation lowers the barrier to entry for cybercrime, enabling a wider range of individuals and groups to engage in illicit activities. This democratization of cybercrime democratizes cybercrime, leading to a proliferation of threats and challenges for defenders.
- **Economic Incentives**: The commercialization of cybercrime creates lucrative revenue streams for both cybercriminals and service providers. The profitability of cyber assaults as a service motivates innovation and competition in underground markets, driving further advancements in attack techniques and evasion strategies. Also, the distribution of cyber assaults as a service upon time is given in Figure 10.7.

10.9 Evolving Threat Landscape: Understanding Modern Cyber Attacks

10.9.1 Types of Modern Cyber Attacks

- **Trends and Patterns in Modern Cyber Attacks:** Several trends and patterns characterize the evolution of modern cyber-attacks:
- **Economic Motivations:** While nation-states remain active players in the cyber domain, cyber-attacks motivated by financial gain have become more prevalent. Ransomware attacks, in particular, have emerged as a lucrative revenue stream for cybercriminals, fueling a thriving underground economy.
- **Globalization of Threats:** The interconnected nature of the internet and digital economy has facilitated the globalization of cyber threats, enabling threat actors to operate across borders and target organizations and individuals anywhere in the world. Nation-state-sponsored cyber-attacks, in particular, pose significant geopolitical challenges and require international cooperation to address effectively.

10.9.2 Implications for Cybersecurity Defense

Understanding the evolving threat landscape is essential for developing effective cybersecurity defense strategies:

- **Threat Intelligence Sharing:** Enhancing situational awareness and enabling proactive defense against evolving cyber threats can be achieved through the sharing of threat intelligence and collaboration with industry peers, government agencies, and cybersecurity vendors. Information-sharing platforms, sector-specific Information Sharing and Analysis Centers (ISACs), and public-private partnerships are pivotal in this effort.
- **Investment in Cyber Resilience:** Cyber resilience involves not only preventing cyber-attacks but also preparing for and effectively responding to incidents when they occur. Organizations should invest in robust incident response capabilities, contingency planning, and cyber insurance to minimize the impact of cyber-attacks and ensure business continuity [18]. Figure 10.8, deploy Evolving threat landscape: Understanding Modern Cyber Attacks.

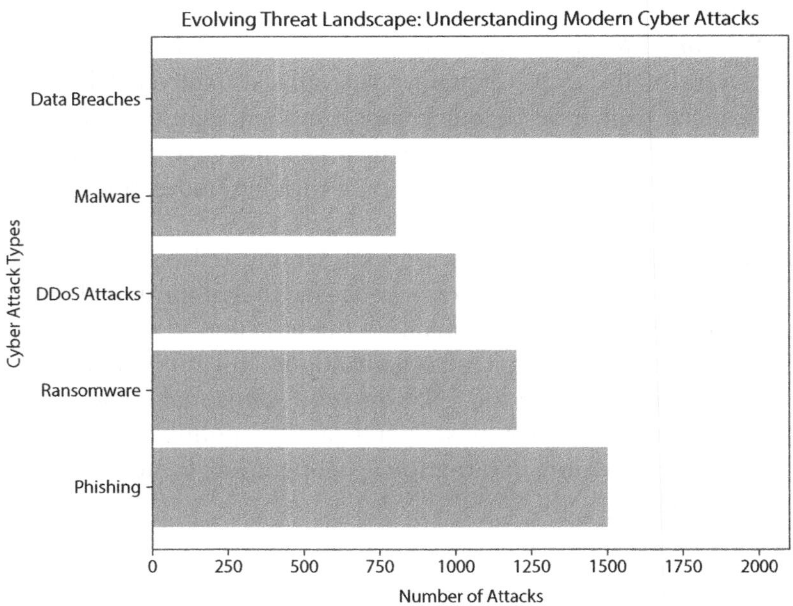

Figure 10.8 Evolving threat landscape: understanding modern cyberattacks.

10.10 Beyond Conventional Security Measures: The Need for Advanced Defense

The Need for Advanced Defense" underscores the necessity of evolving cybersecurity strategies beyond traditional approaches to effectively counter modern cyber threats. Here's a comprehensive explanation:

10.10.1 Challenges with Conventional Security Measures

- **Reactive Nature:** Conventional security measures typically operate on signature-based detection systems, which react to known threats based on predefined patterns or signatures. This reactive approach leaves systems vulnerable to zero-day exploits and novel attack methods that evade signature-based detection.
- **Limited Visibility:** Traditional security measures may lack comprehensive visibility into network traffic, user behavior, and system activity, making it challenging to detect subtle indicators of compromise or anomalous behavior indicative of a security breach.
- **Inability to Adapt:** Conventional security measures often lack the agility and adaptability required to keep pace with

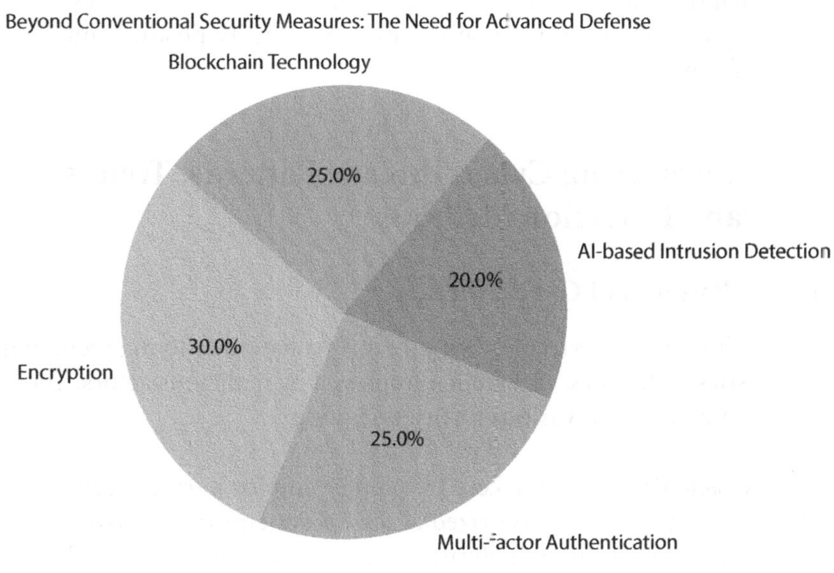

Figure 10.9 Conventional security measures vs. advanced security measures.

rapidly evolving cyber threats. Static security controls and rule-based policies may fail to address emerging threats or adequately respond to dynamic attack vectors. Figure 10.9, clearly explores the Conventional Security measures vs. advanced security measures.

10.10.2 The Evolution of Advanced Defense

In response to the limitations of conventional security measures, organizations are increasingly turning to advanced defense strategies that leverage innovative technologies, threat intelligence, and proactive mitigation tactics.

- **Continuous Monitoring and Response:** Advanced defense entails continuous monitoring of security events, system logs, and network activity to identify and respond to security incidents promptly. Automated response mechanisms, such as threat hunting, incident triage, and remediation workflows, enable organizations to mitigate threats in real-time and minimize the impact of security breaches.
- **Adaptive Security Controls:** Advanced defense solutions employ adaptive security controls that dynamically adjust security policies and enforcement based on changing threat conditions, risk profiles, and business requirements. By adapting defenses to evolving threats and vulnerabilities, organizations can maintain a resilient security posture and effectively mitigate cyber risks [19].

10.11 Uncovering Cyber Threats: Patterns, Trends, and Detection Methods

10.11.1 Patterns of Cyber Threats

Understanding the patterns of cyber threats involves identifying recurring characteristics, behaviors, and tactics employed by malicious actors. These patterns can manifest in various forms, including:

- **Attack Vectors:** Attackers frequently employ various techniques to gain unauthorized access to systems or networks, including phishing, malware infections, SQL injection, and exploiting unpatched vulnerabilities.

- **Malware Families:** Classification of malicious software into families based on similarities in code structure, functionality, or behavior. Examples include ransomware, Trojans, worms, and spyware.
- **Targeting Trends:** Patterns in the selection of targets by threat actors, such as specific industries, geographic regions, or types of organizations. Analyzing targeting trends can provide insights into the motives and objectives of attackers.
- **Trends in Cyber Threats:** Tracking trends in cyber threats involves monitoring changes, developments, and shifts in the cyber threat landscape over time.
- **Rise of Ransomware:** The proliferation of ransomware attacks targeting organizations of all sizes, from small businesses to large enterprises and critical infrastructure providers.
- **Nation-State-Sponsored Attacks:** Increasing prevalence of cyber-attacks attributed to nation-state actors, motivated by political, economic, or military objectives. Nation-state-sponsored attacks often involve sophisticated tactics and target government agencies, military organizations, or strategic industries.
- **Supply Chain Attacks:** Growing trend of targeting third-party vendors, suppliers, or service providers to compromise

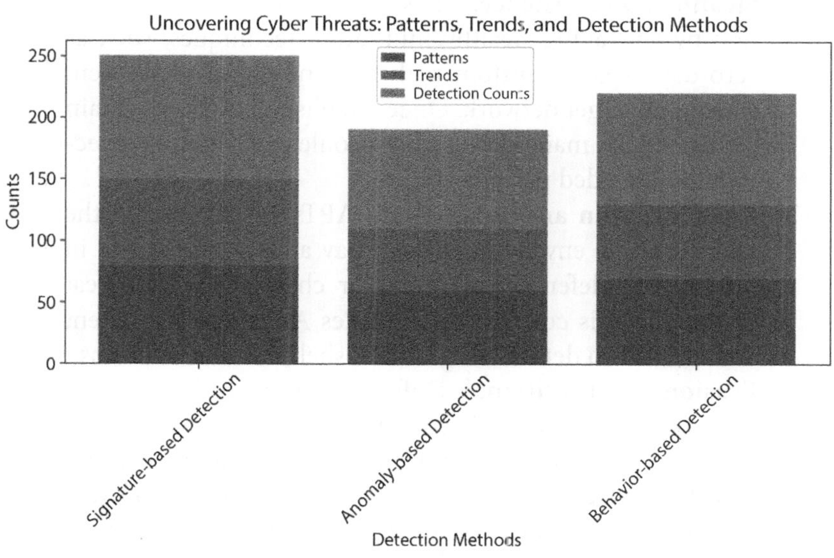

Figure 10.10 Various cyber threats: Patterns, trends and detection methods.

the security of their customers or partners. Supply chain attacks exploit trust relationships to gain access to high-value targets. Figure 10.10 provides the Various cyber threats such as Patterns, Trends and Detection methods.

10.12 Addressing Advanced Persistent Threats: Challenges and Solutions

10.12.1 Introduction to Advanced Persistent Threats (APTs)

Advanced Persistent Threats (APTs) are highly sophisticated and covert cyber-attacks carried out by experienced threat actors, who often have substantial resources and strong incentives, such as nation-states or well-funded criminal groups. These attacks generally involve a sustained and focused effort to penetrate a specific organization or network, with the goal of stealing sensitive information, disrupting operations, or fulfilling strategic objectives.

10.12.2 Challenges Posed by APTs

APTs present unique challenges for cybersecurity defenses due to their advanced tactics, techniques, and procedures (TTPs), including:

- **Stealth and Persistence:** APTs are designed to evade detection by leveraging stealthy infiltration techniques, such as zero-day exploits, custom malware, and lateral movement within the target network. Once established, APTs maintain persistence by maintaining a low profile and avoiding detection for extended periods.
- **Customization and Adaptation:** APTs are tailored to the specific target environment and may adapt their tactics in response to defensive measures or changes in the threat landscape. This customization makes APTs highly resilient and difficult to detect using off-the-shelf security solutions.
- **Evasion of Traditional Defenses:** Advanced Persistent Threats (APTs) frequently circumvent conventional security measures like firewalls, antivirus programs, and intrusion detection systems. They achieve this by exploiting software vulnerabilities, using social engineering tactics, or posing as legitimate users or processes. This evasion strategy

complicates the detection and mitigation of APTs for organizations relying solely on traditional security controls.

10.12.3 Solutions for Addressing APTs

Effectively addressing APTs requires a multi-faceted approach that combines advanced technologies, proactive threat intelligence, and robust incident response capabilities. Key solutions include:

- **Continuous Monitoring and Threat Hunting:** Adopting a proactive approach to threat detection through continuous monitoring and threat hunting allows organizations to actively search for signs of APT activity within their networks. This involves analyzing network traffic, system logs, and security alerts to identify indicators of compromise (IOCs) and anomalous behavior that may indicate the presence of an APT.
- **Intelligence Sharing:** Partnering with industry peers, government agencies, and cybersecurity vendors to exchange threat intelligence and insights on Advanced Persistent Threats (APTs) improves situational awareness. This collaborative approach helps organizations understand the tactics, techniques, and procedures used by attackers. Leveraging shared intelligence can refine defensive strategies, boost threat detection capabilities, and support more effective incident response.
- **Incident Management and Containment:** Creating comprehensive incident response plans is essential for swiftly identifying, containing, and addressing APTs. This includes defining roles and responsibilities, establishing escalation procedures, and regularly conducting tabletop exercises and drills to ensure preparedness for effective APT response.
- **Adaptive Security Controls:** Implementing adaptive security controls that dynamically adjust security policies and enforcement based on threat intelligence, risk assessments, and contextual factors can help organizations adapt their defenses to evolving APTs. This adaptive approach allows organizations to prioritize resources, implement targeted countermeasures, and mitigate the risks posed by APTs more effectively.

References

1. Kasowaki, L. and Kaan, M., The Evolving Threatscape: Understanding and Navigating Cybersecurity Risks, EasyChair, 2024.
2. Thakur, M., Cyber security threats and countermeasures in digital age. *J. Appl. Sci. Educ. (JASE)*, 4, 1, 1–20, 2024.
3. Bhortake, J., Securing the Digital Realm: Navigating Cyber Threats, Risks, and Resilience.
4. Chisty, N.M.A., Baddam, P.R., Amin, R., Strategic Approaches to Safeguarding the Digital Future: Insights into Next-Generation Cybersecurity. *Eng. Int.*, 10, 2, 69–84, 2022.
5. Safitra, M.F., Lubis, M., Fakhrurroja, H., Counterattacking cyber threats: A framework for the future of cybersecurity. *Sustainability*, 15, 18, 13369, 2023.
6. Kumar, S., Gupta, U., Singh, A.K., Singh, A.K., Artificial intelligence: revolutionizing cyber security in the digital era. *J. Comput. Mech. Manage.*, 2, 3, 31–42, 2023.
7. Shah, V., Machine Learning Algorithms for Cybersecurity: Detecting and Preventing Threats. *Rev. Espanola de Documentacion Cientifica*, 15, 4, 42–66, 2021.
8. Manoharan, A. and Sarker, M., Revolutionizing Cybersecurity: Unleashing the Power of Artificial Intelligence and Machine Learning for Next-Generation Threat Detection, 2023, DOI: https://www.doi. org/10.56726/IRJMETS32644.
9. Camacho, N.G., The Role of AI in Cybersecurity: Addressing Threats in the Digital Age. *J. Artif. Intell. Gen. Sci. (JAIGS)*, 3, 1, 143–154, 2024. ISSN: 3006-4023.
10. Kasowaki, L. and Alyan, M., Cybersecurity 101: a Comprehensive Guide to Protecting Your Digital World, EasyChair, 2023.
11. An, A., The Evolution of Cyber security Threats in the Digital Age. *Int. J. Bus. Manage. Visuals ISSN 3006-2705*, 5, 2, 22–29, 2022.
12. Babu, C.V.S., Adaptive AI for Dynamic Cybersecurity Systems: Enhancing Protection in a Rapidly Evolving Digital Landscap, in: *Principles and Applications of Adaptive Artificial Intelligence*, pp. 52–72, IGI Global, Hershey, PA, 2024.
13. Al-Mansoori, S. and Salem, M.B., The role of artificial intelligence and machine learning in shaping the future of cybersecurity: trends, applications, and ethical considerations. *Int. J. Soc. Anal.*, 8, 9, 1–16, 2023.
14. Kasowaki, L. and Kuzey, A., Threat Intelligence: Understanding and Mitigating Cyber Risks, 2024.
15. Azaan, S. and Elsa, J., The Rise of Automated Accounting: Navigating the Digital Landscape, EasyChair, 2024.
16. Raparthi, M., Dodda, S.B., Maruthi, SH., Examining the use of Artificial Intelligence to Enhance Security Measures in Computer Hardware, including

the Detection of Hardware-based Vulnerabilities and Attacks. *Eur. Econ. Lett. (EEL)*, 10, 1, 60–68, 2020.

17. Shah, A., Cybercrime Chronicles: Exploring the Evolving Landscape of Challenges in the Digital Era, 2024.
18. Balyan, S., Jangir, H., Tripathi, S.N., Tripathi, A., Jhang, T., Pandey, P., Seeding a Sustainable Future: Navigating the Digital Horizon of Smart Agriculture. *Sustainability*, 16, 2, 475, 2024.
19. Jimmy, F.N.U., Cyber security Vulnerabilities and Remediation Through Cloud Security Tools. *J. Artif. Intell. Gen. Sci. (JAIGS) ISSN 3006-4023*, 2, 1, 196–233, 2024.

11

Defense Strategies for Cyber-Physical Systems

Rajendran Thanikachalam[1]*, T. Nithya[2], Balaji Sampathkumar[3] and J. Mangayarkarasi[4]

[1]Department of Computer Science and Engineering, Vel Tech Rangarajan Dr. Sagunthala R&D Institute of Science and Technology, Chennai, Tamil Nadu, India
[2]Department of Computer Science and Engineering, Rajalakshmi Institute of Technology, Chennai, Tamil Nadu, India
[3]Department of Computer Science and Engineering, Akshaya College of Engineering and Technology, Coimbatore, Tamil Nadu, India
[4]Department of Artificial Intelligence and Machine Learning, Prathyusha Engineering College, Thiruvallur, India

Abstract

Cyber-Physical Systems (CPS) integrate computing devices, sensors, and physical components across critical domains, posing unique security challenges. This chapter elucidates advanced defense strategies crucial for safeguarding CPS against diverse threats. Anomaly detection, leveraging statistical and machine learning techniques, enables early threat identification by discerning deviations from normal behavior. Secure communication protocols, fortified with encryption and authentication mechanisms, shield data exchanges from unauthorized access. Machine learning-driven defenses predict and mitigate threats in real-time, enhancing CPS security adaptability. Additionally, resilience techniques like redundancy and self-healing mechanisms bolster system robustness. The Zero Trust model ensures strict identity verification and continuous monitoring, revolutionizing CPS security. Integrating intensive training empowers personnel to recognize and mitigate cyber risks effectively. Case studies exemplify the practical application of these strategies across industrial control systems, smart grids, and healthcare infrastructure. Addressing emerging challenges, such as novel attack vectors and ethical considerations, necessitates collaborative efforts. This chapter

**Corresponding author*: tlrajen@gmail.com

K. Ananthajothi, S. N. Sangeethaa, D. Divya, S. Balamurugan and Shen-Lung Peng (eds.) Securing Cyber-Physical Systems: Fundamentals, Applications and Challenges, (225–248) © 2025 Scrivener Publishing LLC

underscores the imperative of advanced defense strategies, offering insights for practitioners to fortify CPS resilience amidst evolving threats.

***Keywords*:** Resilience techniques, anomaly detection, zero trust model, emerging threats, anomaly detection, intensive training

11.1 Introduction

Cyber-Physical Systems (CPS), comprising interconnected computing devices, sensors, and physical components, play a pivotal role in various domains, including critical infrastructure, healthcare, and industrial automation. Ensuring the security of these systems is crucial due to their integration with the physical world, where cyber threats can result in tangible physical repercussions. CPS faces a myriad of threats, ranging from traditional cyber-attacks like malware and phishing to more sophisticated threats targeting the interconnected nature of these systems. These threats expose vulnerabilities in the system, potentially leading to disruptions, data breaches, or even physical harm [1]. The chapter delves into the sophisticated landscape of safeguarding CPS through advanced defense strategies. As the fusion of cyber and physical elements becomes ubiquitous, ensuring the security of these systems against diverse threats has become increasingly complex.

The Figure 11.1 depicts advanced defense strategies for Cyber-Physical Systems (CPS) encompasses a multifaceted approach aimed at fortifying these interconnected systems against evolving threats. These strategies leverage cutting-edge technologies and methodologies to ensure the resilience and security of CPS components. Anomaly detection serves as a foundational defense mechanism, employing statistical and machine learning techniques to identify deviations from normal system behavior, enabling early threat identification. Secure communication protocols, integrating encryption, authentication mechanisms, and resilient frameworks, safeguard data exchanges, shielding against unauthorized access or manipulation. Machine learning-driven defenses harness the power of AI algorithms to predict and counteract potential threats in real-time, bolstering CPS security by continuously adapting to emerging risks. Additionally, resilience techniques such as redundancy, diversity, and self-healing mechanisms bolster system robustness, ensuring continuity despite adversarial activities. Zero Trust Model is a security approach that assumes no trust in any user or device inside or outside the network perimeter. This model revolutionizes CPS security by enforcing strict identity verification, micro-segmentation, and continuous monitoring. Integrating an intensive training and awareness strategy empowers personnel to recognize and

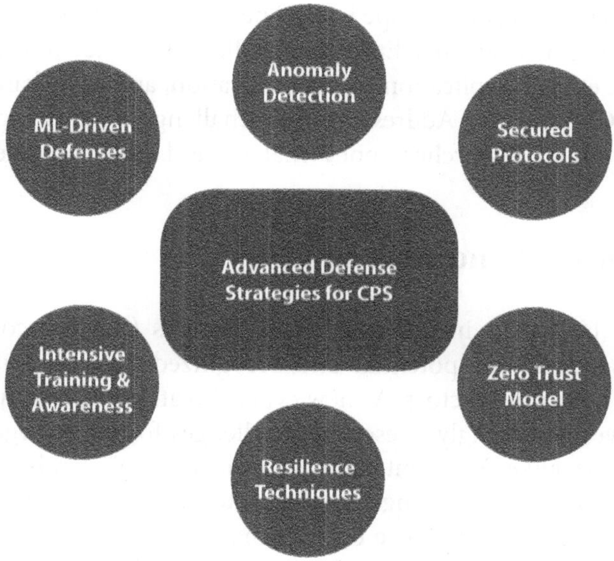

Figure 11.1 Advanced defense strategies for cyber-physical systems (CPS).

mitigate cyber risks effectively. These advanced defense strategies, amalgamating diverse methodologies, provide a comprehensive shield against cyber threats targeting the intricate interplay between cyber and physical components within CPS, thereby significantly fortifying these critical systems' resilience.

Illustrative case studies demonstrate the practical application of advanced defense strategies in various CPS domains, including industrial control systems, smart grids, and healthcare infrastructure. Industrial control systems, pivotal in manufacturing and critical infrastructure, highlight the successful implementation of defense strategies to secure complex operational processes. Smart grid systems exemplify how these strategies fortify energy infrastructure against cyber threats, ensuring uninterrupted power supply and grid stability. Furthermore, healthcare systems and medical devices illustrate the criticality of defense mechanisms in protecting patient data and ensuring the safety and integrity of healthcare operations. These case studies underscore the practicality and effectiveness of anomaly detection, secure communication protocols, machine learning-driven defenses, and resilience techniques in mitigating threats within distinct CPS environments. By showcasing real-world successes and challenges, this section provides valuable insights for practitioners, offering tangible examples of how advanced defense strategies can be tailored and applied to fortify the security posture of various CPS, paving the way for enhanced resilience and protection against evolving threats.

The evolving threat landscape in CPS necessitates continuous innovation in defense mechanisms. Emerging challenges include novel attack vectors, the ethical implications of AI integration, and legal frameworks governing CPS security. Addressing these challenges requires collaborative efforts among researchers, policymakers, and industry stakeholders.

11.2 Threat Landscape in CPS

The threat landscape in Cyber-Physical Systems (CPS) encompasses a dynamic spectrum of potential and recognized cybersecurity threats, influenced by various factors. As new cyber threats emerge daily, the landscape evolves accordingly, presenting challenges for users, organizations, and industries alike. Key contributors to this dynamic landscape include the proliferation of increasingly sophisticated tools and attack methods, as well as the growing reliance on information technology products and services, including Software-as-a-Service (SaaS) offerings. Moreover, networks facilitating the distribution of cybercrime profits, such as the dark web, contribute to the complexity of the threat landscape. Factors such as the availability of skills, personnel, and finances for cyberattacks, alongside external events like global pandemics or financial crises, further shape the threat landscape. Additionally, the rapid development of software with added functionality and the emergence of new hardware, such as Internet of Things (IoT) devices, introduce new vulnerabilities and attack vectors. The threat landscape varies depending on context, influenced by factors like the value of sensitive information, the level of information security measures in place, and geopolitical considerations. Understanding and mitigating these dynamic threats are crucial for effectively safeguarding CPS against potential risks and vulnerabilities.

Cyber-physical systems vulnerabilities and risks have become a critical concern in various industries, especially in critical infrastructures like power grids and transportation systems. The integration of control systems with new information technologies has introduced uncertainties not only from the physical world but also from the cyber components of the system ((2015) (IEEE)). The vulnerabilities of the software deployed in these systems expose them to potential risks and threats from attackers, as evidenced by incidents like the Stuxnet worm targeting Siemens SCADA systems [2]. Unmanned aerial vehicles (UAVs) have also seen rapid adoption across industries, with the aerospace industry facing new risks and vulnerabilities due to technological advancements [3]. The need to investigate and assess the security of UAVs in cyberphysical architectures is crucial to ensure the industry is prepared to address security challenges effectively. A methodology for automating the analysis of security threats in cyber-physical systems has been developed, focusing on structuring information about system architecture and potential risks [4]. By highlighting concepts and properties using an ontological approach, the methodology identifies threats, vulnerabilities, and attacks relevant to the system's characteristics, aiding in the development of effective security recommendations. In the context of distribution grids with distributed energy resources (DERs), a comprehensive risk assessment framework for cyberphysical security has been proposed, considering dynamic DER characteristics and communication systems vulnerabilities [5]. The framework models attack scenarios and quantifies attack impacts, providing insights into securing grid-edge DERs effectively. Furthermore, the need for security metrics in industrial cyberphysical systems (ICPSs) has been highlighted, with a systematic methodology proposed to gather, filter, and validate security metrics specific to ICPSs [6]. This approach aims to measure the security of ICPSs from various perspectives, addressing the evolving cyber-threat landscape and the interconnected nature of digital assets. Overall, the literature review underscores the importance of addressing cyberphysical systems vulnerabilities and risks through comprehensive risk assessment frameworks, automated security threat analysis methodologies, and tailored security metrics for specific industries and systems. Researchers can leverage these insights to enhance their understanding and mitigation strategies for cyberphysical security challenges.

Cyber-physical attacks represent a multifaceted threat landscape, encompassing techniques that exploit vulnerabilities across digital and physical domains, thereby posing significant risks to critical infrastructure and organizational assets. There are six common types of cyber-physical attacks, targeting the software, hardware, and network components of organizations.

- Network-based attacks exploit vulnerabilities within an organization's network infrastructure, compromising systems through weak access controls or insufficient intrusion detection mechanisms. Eavesdropping attacks intercept sensitive data transmitted over insecure networks, while replay attacks enable unauthorized access by replaying intercepted data.
- Software-based attacks target vulnerabilities within software applications or systems, exploiting weaknesses in code or configuration to gain unauthorized access or disrupt

operations. Data injection attacks manipulate system behavior by injecting malicious code, while denial of service attacks overwhelm systems with excessive requests, causing disruption.

- Hardware-based attacks compromise systems and gain unauthorized access for leveraging vulnerabilities in physical components like processors or USB devices. These vulnerabilities may arise from design flaws, manufacturing defects, or outdated firmware, emphasizing the importance of robust hardware security measures.
- Zero-day attacks exploit unknown vulnerabilities in software or hardware systems, posing significant risks due to the absence of available patches or fixes, leaving organizations vulnerable to exploitation.
- Side-channel attacks exploit unintended information leakage during system operation, such as power consumption or electromagnetic emissions, to infer sensitive data,

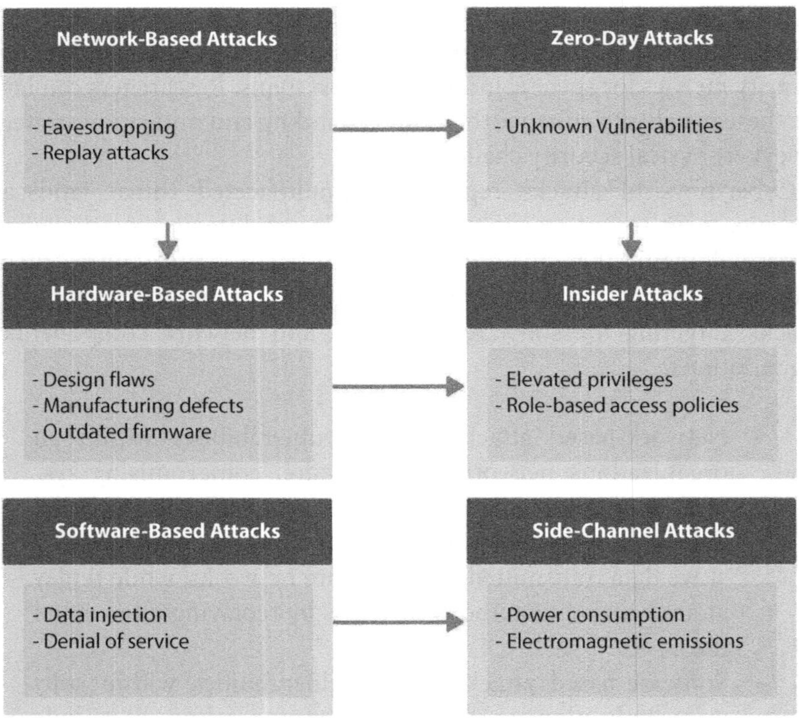

Figure 11.2 Threat landscape in cyber-physical systems (CPS).

highlighting the importance of mitigating unintentional information disclosure.

- Insider attacks involve malicious actions by employees with elevated privileges, emphasizing the need for stringent access control measures and role-based access policies to mitigate internal threats.

Figure 11.2 depicts the threat landscape in cyber-physical systems. The diagram includes six common types of cyber-physical attacks, targeting various components of organizations, along with arrows to illustrate connections and dependencies among these threats. Each box contains a brief description of the attack type and specific examples.

11.3 Advanced Defense Strategies

The growing presence of cyber-physical systems (CPS) – where physical components seamlessly integrate with digital controls – introduces a new layer of vulnerability. These systems, while powerful, become prime targets for cyberattacks due to their interconnectedness. Traditional security measures designed for standalone systems are no longer sufficient.

To combat this, advanced defense strategies are crucial. Security must be prioritized throughout a CPS's lifecycle, from design to operation. Real-time monitoring with advanced analytics is needed to detect and contain cyberattacks. Segmenting networks and implementing robust firewalls can minimize damage. Additionally, building inherently cyber-resilient infrastructure, with features like redundancy and fail-safes, becomes essential.

The global nature of CPS necessitates international collaboration. Sharing threat intelligence, best practices, and coordinating responses to attacks are vital. By acknowledging these vulnerabilities and proactively implementing advanced defenses, we can safeguard critical infrastructure, military preparedness, and navigate the complexities of a cyber-physical world. In this chapter will discuss various resilient defense strategies.

11.3.1 Anomaly Detection in CPS

Safeguarding the Interconnected Infrastructure Within the burgeoning realm of cyber-physical systems (CPS), anomaly detection plays a pivotal role in ensuring system integrity and security. CPS seamlessly integrate physical components with computational processes, forming a complex interconnected web. This interconnectedness necessitates robust methods for identifying deviations from normal behavior (anomalies) that could signify potential cyberattacks or internal malfunctions. The importance of continuous monitoring for timely detection of cyberattacks. Early identification of threats is crucial for mitigating potential damage and ensuring the overall security of CPS [7].

Anomaly detection in CPS involves the meticulous monitoring of sensor data, data streams, and system performance. Traditional anomaly detection algorithms face challenges in real-time data streams, leading to the development of new approaches. Studies have explored methods like deep learning algorithms, autoencoder-based prediction models, SFOM, HC techniques, and GPU-based algorithms for anomaly detection in sensor data. These methods aim to identify abnormal events, faults, outliers, and anomalies in sensor data streams efficiently. Utilizing machine learning algorithms on big data platforms like Apache Kafka enhances the detection of anomalies over streaming data, providing valuable insights for decision-making in various domains. Deviations from established baselines or normal patterns can then be flagged for further investigation. This proactive approach allows for early identification and mitigation of threats, safeguarding critical infrastructure and optimizing operational efficiency. Cloud-edge coordinated approach with Improved Online SARIMA for continuous anomaly detection in Industrial Cyber-Physical Systems. Utilizes edge alarms, cloud analysis, feature extraction, and CNN classifier for precise identification of attack types [8].

The arsenal of anomaly detection techniques employed within CPS security protocols is multifaceted. Statistical analysis plays a key role in establishing baselines and identifying statistically improbable deviations. Machine learning algorithms offer powerful tools for learning normal system behavior and flagging outliers. Additionally, custom anomaly detection models can be tailored to specific CPS architectures and functionalities. Behavior analysis and machine learning techniques are utilized for anomaly detection in cyber-physical systems, with a focus on real-world datasets and evaluation metrics for efficiency assessment [9].

By leveraging these diverse techniques, researchers and engineers can fortify the security posture of CPS. Continuous advancements in anomaly detection will be paramount as CPS technology continues to evolve and permeate critical infrastructure sectors.

11.3.2 Secure Communication Protocols

Cyber-Physical Systems (CPS) rely on robust and secure communication protocols to ensure the integrity, confidentiality, and availability of data exchanged between interconnected physical and computational components. This analysis explores prominent protocols that offer varying levels of security for CPS communication:

- Transport Layer Security (TLS) and Secure Sockets Layer (SSL): These cryptographic protocols establish a secure communication channel, ensuring data privacy, integrity, and mutual authentication between applications. TLS, the successor to SSL, is widely employed for secure web browsing (HTTPS) and other network communications.
- IPsec (Internet Protocol Security): This suite of protocols operates at the network layer, encrypting, authenticating, and ensuring data integrity for IP packets. IPsec offers a comprehensive security solution for communication between network devices.
- Secure Shell (SSH): SSH is a workhorse for secure remote access and file transfer. It encrypts data transmission and provides robust user and host authentication mechanisms.
- Message Queuing Telemetry Transport (MQTT) and Constrained Application Protocol (CoAP): These lightweight messaging protocols are popular choices for resource-constrained devices in CPS and Internet-of-Things (IoT) environments. MQTT can be secured with TLS, while CoAP leverages Datagram Transport Layer Security (DTLS) for secure communication over UDP.
- DTLS (Datagram Transport Layer Security): This variant of TLS caters to real-time applications and resource-constrained environments within CPS and IoT. DTLS ensures secure communication over unreliable datagram protocols like UDP.
- WirelessHART Security and Zigbee Security: These protocols, designed for industrial automation and home automation respectively, integrate security features like encryption, authentication, and secure key management to safeguard communication within wireless sensor networks.

The Figure 11.3 outlines a protocol stack for Cyber-Physical Systems (CPS), highlighting the network functional layers and their corresponding protocols or mechanisms. At the top, the Application Layer includes COAP (Constrained Application Protocol) and MQTT (Message Queuing Telemetry Transport), along with UDP (User Datagram Protocol),

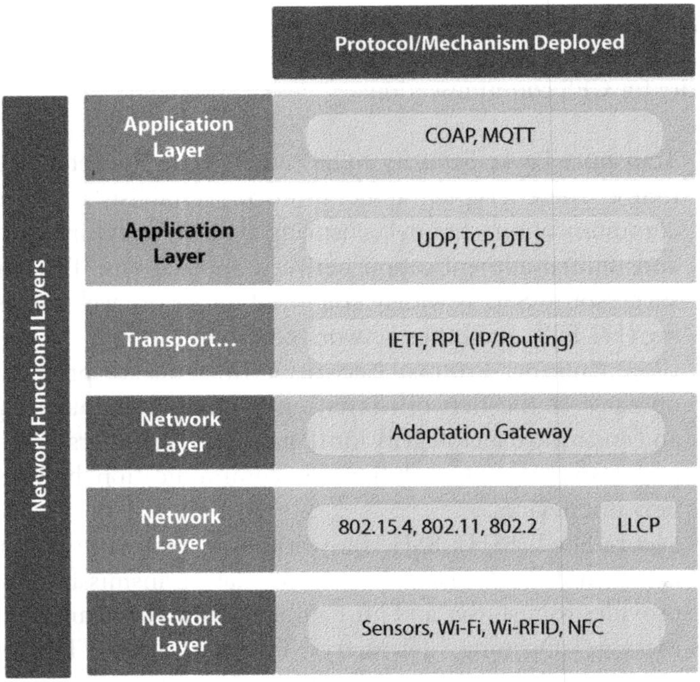

Figure 11.3 Protocols deployed in network layers.

TCP (Transmission Control Protocol), and DTLS (Datagram Transport Layer Security). The Transport Layer features standards the IETF (Internet Engineering Task Force) and RPL (Routing Protocol for Low-Power and Lossy Networks) set for IP and routing. The Network Layer is divided into three segments: the first involves an Adaptation Gateway, the second includes protocols such as IEEE 802.15.4 (Low-Rate Wireless Personal Area Networks), IEEE 802.11 (Wi-Fi), IEEE 802.2 (Logical Link Control), and LLCP, and the third encompasses components like sensors, Wi-Fi, Wi-RFID (Radio-Frequency Identification), and NFC (Near Field Communication). This stack illustrates the comprehensive communication framework and protocols to ensure efficient CPS operations.

Protocol Factors:

The selection of a security protocol for a CPS should be guided by a careful consideration of factors such as:

- Security Requirements: The specific security needs of the CPS application (confidentiality, integrity, or both) will influence the choice of protocol.

- Computational Resources: For resource-constrained devices, lightweight protocols like CoAP with DTLS may be preferred.
- Real-time Performance: Protocols like DTLS cater to real-time applications where low latency is crucial.
- Interoperability: Standardized protocols like TLS and IPsec facilitate communication between disparate CPS components from different vendors.
- Future research directions in CPS communication security could involve:
- Lightweight encryption algorithms optimized for resource-constrained devices.
- Post-quantum cryptography solutions to address the growing threat from quantum computers.
- Secure key management strategies specifically tailored to the dynamic nature of CPS deployments.

11.3.3 Machine Learning-Driven Defenses

Modern Cyber-Physical Systems (CPS) would not be comprehensive without machine learning-driven defensive mechanisms, which provide preventive threat detection, real-time response, and adaptive protection techniques to combat evolving cyber dangers. This study offers a thorough examination of the most recent developments in machine learning methods as they relate to CPS security, with an emphasis on real-time systems created and implemented to meet particular defensive goals.

Intrusion Detection and Prevention:
In CPS networks, real-time detection and prevention of intrusions are achieved through the use of machine learning models, which include deep learning and ensemble techniques. To detect abnormalities, existing threat signatures, and malicious conduct, these models examine network traffic, patterns of communication, and system logs. This allows for prompt mitigation and reaction.

Behavioral Analysis and Adaptive Security Controls:
The behavioral examination of CPS components and users is conducted by the use of deep learning algorithms, which allow for the real-time detection of normal behavior and aberrations that may indicate aberrant system behavior or insider threats. Adaptive security controls improve resilience and flexibility by dynamically modifying security settings, authentication

methods, and access regulations in response to real-time threat intelligence and system activity. The adaptive security control against false data injection attacks in nonlinear cyber-physical systems, utilizing state observers, neural networks, and time-varying symmetry barrier functions for protection [10]. Data-Driven-Based Event-Triggered Control with Model-Free Adaptive Control and Predictive Compensation enhances security in nonlinear CPSs against jamming attacks, ensuring tracking error boundedness using I/O data only [11]. A Deep Convolutional Network Model (DCNM) for active security control in cyber-physical systems that are subject to attacks known as denial-of-service (DoS), which can target both channels from the controller to the actuator and from the controllers to the sensor [12].

Anomaly Detection and Predictive Maintenance:

For anomaly detection in CPS, supervised, semi-supervised, and unsupervised learning techniques are used. These algorithms analyze sensor data and control processes in real-time, looking for abnormalities that might be signs of equipment failures or cyberattacks. In order to predict probable failures, enhance maintenance schedules, and improve system dependability, real-time predictive maintenance models make use of previous data as well as sensor readings. The authors proposed a new approach called deep graph stream support vector data description (SVDD) for anomaly detection, which first uses a transformer to preserve both short and long temporal patterns of monitoring data in temporal embeddings [13]. A deep bidirectional gated recurrent unit and variational autoencoder (BiGRU-VAE) model for anomaly detection in cyber-physical systems, achieving high accuracy in detecting abnormalities, aiding in predictive maintenance [14]. Digital Twin-based Anomaly Detection method LATTICE enhances security in cyber-physical systems by incorporating curriculum learning, outperforming ATTAIN and other detectors by up to 2.367% in F1 score [15].

Threat Intelligence and Response:

In CPS contexts, machine learning techniques are used for real-time analysis of threat intelligence feeds, security alerts, and incident data. Examples of these algorithms include natural language processing and anomaly detection. These algorithms provide quick incident response, forensic investigation, and decision-making to successfully mitigate cyberattacks by correlating, prioritizing, and contextualizing security events.

The continuous development of machine learning-driven defensive mechanisms in CPS by combining research findings and real-world applications. This gives stakeholders the tools they need to successfully reduce cyber risks and protect vital infrastructure from new threats.

11.3.4 Zero Trust Model for CPS

Zero Trust (ZT) model represents a burgeoning paradigm aimed at establishing secure resource access through meticulously defined policies. Central to the ZT framework is the principle of 'never trust, always verify,' wherein access to resources necessitates explicit authorization, even within ostensibly trusted operational domains. A set of zero-trust architectural patterns for cyber-physical systems is proposed to improve the system security posture based on the specific system requirements, such as confidentiality, integrity, and availability. Utilizing AADL modeling language for system security improvement [16].

The Figure 11.4 shows the foundational principles of Zero Trust encompass seven distinct pillars:

- Device: Concentrates on validating the trustworthiness of all access-seeking devices through metadata scrutiny and ongoing verification processes aligned with organizational access protocols.
- Network: Encompasses micro-segmentation strategies, exhaustive traffic inspection mechanisms, and data flow encryption protocols aimed at thwarting the lateral propagation of threats within the network infrastructure.

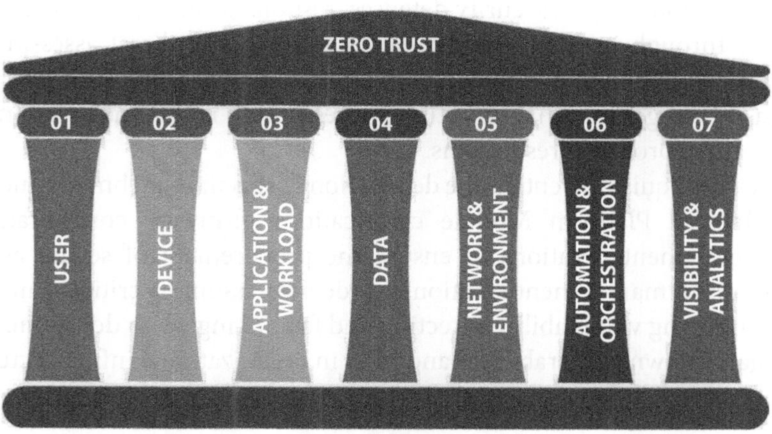

Figure 11.4 Seven pillars of zero trust model.

- Application: Prioritizes the establishment of secure application access protocols contingent upon user authentication, device integrity validation, and the sensitivity profile of the application in question.
- Data: Encompasses data classification methodologies, encryption protocols, and access monitoring mechanisms tailored to safeguard sensitive data assets.
- Identity: Directs attention towards implementing robust authentication mechanisms, least privilege access policies, and continuous surveillance of user interactions within the system.
- Visibility: Mandates comprehensive network, device, and user activity monitoring capabilities to facilitate timely threat detection and response initiatives.
- Analytics: Involves the utilization of sophisticated analytics frameworks and threat intelligence resources to preemptively identify and address potential security vulnerabilities.
- These pillars collectively underpin the Zero Trust security paradigm, accentuating the importance of perpetual monitoring, access governance, and threat mitigation strategies in fortifying the overall cybersecurity posture.

Organizations are urged to customize Zero Trust (ZT) principles to their unique requirements instead of adopting a standardized approach, taking into account variables such as mission objectives, asset safeguarding imperatives, and existing architectural frameworks to optimize implementation effectiveness. The ZT device component prioritizes the augmentation of cybersecurity defenses, responses, and operational capabilities through iterative enhancements and ongoing threat assessments. Recommendations are furnished for devising ZT roadmap strategies that align with organizational objectives, necessitating meticulous scrutiny to ascertain appropriate resolutions.

Device acquisition entails the delineation of specific benchmarks including Trusted Platform Module certifications, firmware configurations, and component iterations to ensure the procurement of secure assets. Centralized management solutions for devices assume a critical function in automating vulnerability detection and facilitating patch deployment to mitigate known vulnerabilities and risks in organizational infrastructure.

A Case Study - Zero Trust Architecture with Microsoft services:

The modern enterprise technology landscape has been transformed by the growing use of cloud-based services, mobile computing, the Internet of Things (IoT), and bring your own device (BYOD) policies. Traditional security architectures that depend on network firewalls and virtual private networks (VPNs) to control and restrict access to corporate resources are now inadequate for a workforce that frequently needs to access applications and resources outside conventional corporate network boundaries. The shift towards using the internet as the primary network and the continuous evolution of security threats have driven Microsoft to adopt a Zero Trust security model internally. Although this journey began several years ago, it is expected to continue evolving in the future.

Figure 11.5 below presents a simplified reference architecture for Microsoft's Zero Trust implementation. Key components of this approach include Intune for device management and security policy configuration, Microsoft Azure Active Directory (Azure AD) conditional access for device health validation, and Azure AD for maintaining user and device inventory.

The system operates by using Intune to push configuration requirements to managed devices. These devices then generate a health statement, which is stored in Microsoft Azure AD. When a user requests access to a resource, the device's health state is verified as part of the authentication process with Azure AD [17].

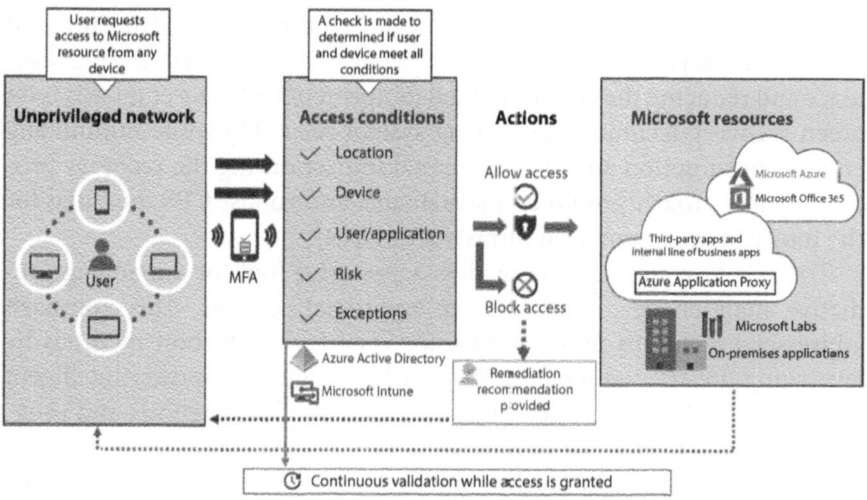

Figure 11.5 Microsoft's internal zero trust architecture [17].

11.3.5 Resilience Techniques for CPS

The concept of resilience in cyber-physical systems (CPS) is crucial for ensuring the robustness and reliability of critical functionalities amid unforeseen disruptions. These disruptions can arise from natural disasters, technological malfunctions, or deliberate cyberattacks. CPS inherently integrate computational and physical processes, making them vital across sectors such as energy, transportation, healthcare, and manufacturing. The complexity and interconnectedness of these systems mean that disturbances can propagate rapidly, potentially leading to significant operational failures.

Achieving resilience requires designing systems that can anticipate, withstand, recover from, and adapt to adverse conditions. This necessitates a multi-pronged approach, including robust system architecture, real-time monitoring, and adaptive response strategies. Redundancy and diversification within system components can mitigate single points of failure, while sophisticated monitoring tools can detect anomalies and initiate corrective actions before they escalate into critical issues.

Self-healing Cyber-Physical Systems (SH-CPS) can harness implicit redundancy to adapt structurally without the explicit duplication of components. This form of redundancy allows the system to utilize inherent capabilities for adaptation, eliminating the need for direct replication of components. Through the principles of inheritance and decomposition, implicit guarantees are embedded, thereby ensuring the dependability and robustness of the system [18].

Green resilience in cyber-physical systems (CPS) can be achieved by utilizing a collaborative artificial intelligence system (CAIS). The proposed solution employs game theory to strike a balance between enhancing resilience and reducing the environmental footprint of CPS. The emphasis is on green recovery techniques, ensuring system reliability while minimizing energy consumption and environmental impact during the recovery process. This approach promotes a sustainable and robust CPS, essential for the future of interconnected infrastructure [19].

Transfer learning has emerged as a powerful tool for enhancing predictive maintenance capabilities in industrial settings. This approach addresses limitations inherent to traditional fault detection methods by leveraging pre-trained models. Transfer learning can empower intelligent systems to perform not only fault detection but also diagnosis and prognosis within the predictive maintenance framework. However, for effective adoption in real-world industrial applications, it is crucial to address key challenges associated with this technique [20].

Robust System Design:
The robust system design for Cyber-Physical Systems (CPS) aims to ensure that these systems maintain their functionality amidst various disturbances and perturbations. This robustness is crucial in fields such as automotive, aeronautics, medical devices, and smart infrastructure, where CPS are integral. The primary goal is to sustain system performance and correctness, even when faced with unforeseen events and parameter variations.

Key strategies for achieving robustness in CPS include game-theoretical approaches, compositional control design, and hybrid dynamic models. Game theory provides a framework to balance the control system's robustness against disturbances with minimal energy consumption. This method models the controller as a cost minimizer and the disturbances as cost maximizers, leading to a minimax control strategy. Compositional control design involves creating controllers for individual subsystems that can interact while preserving their safety and performance guarantees. This approach addresses the complexities of decentralized control systems, ensuring that each subsystem can handle uncertainties independently while contributing to the overall system's robustness. Hybrid dynamic models combine continuous-time dynamics for physical processes with discrete-time dynamics for cyber interactions, offering a comprehensive view of CPS operations. This approach integrates optimal control design for the physical layer with defense mechanisms at the cyber layer, ensuring robust and resilient system performance.

Overall, designing robust CPS requires interdisciplinary methods, combining insights from control theory, computer science, and engineering to develop systems that can adapt to and recover from a wide range of challenges, ensuring reliability and efficiency in critical applications.

Moreover, resilience is a dynamic capability that evolves with the changing threat landscape. This requires continuous evaluation and improvement, incorporating the latest technological advancements and insights from past incidents. By prioritizing resilience, organizations can protect their CPS against a wide range of disruptions, ensuring operational continuity and reliability even under extreme circumstances. This proactive approach is essential for maintaining trust and stability in an increasingly interconnected and interdependent world.

11.3.6 Intensive Training and Awareness

Employee training and awareness are crucial for fortifying the cyber-physical perception layer of a system. Equipping personnel at all levels with knowledge of evolving cyber threats, best practices for secure interactions, and relevant security policies enhances the system's ability to detect and prevent potential attacks. Comprehensive cyber security training programs empower employees to recognize suspicious activities within the cyber domain that could impact the physical components of CPS. This includes identifying phishing attempts, social engineering tactics, and anomalous network behaviors that might compromise system integrity.

Comprehensive Training Process:
To protect enterprise resources against cyberattacks, comprehensive training for internal employees is essential. This training should encompass a variety of key areas to ensure a well-rounded understanding and preparedness.

- First, employees should be educated on cybersecurity fundamentals. This includes understanding basic cyber threats such as phishing, malware, social engineering, and ransomware. It is crucial to explain how these threats operate and the potential consequences of falling victim to them. Training employees to identify and respond to these threats is a foundational step in building a resilient workforce.
- Safe online practices are another vital component of the training. Employees should be taught the importance of strong passwords and multi-factor authentication. They need to recognize and avoid suspicious emails, attachments, and unsafe websites. Additionally, it is important to discuss prudent social media use and data sharing practices to prevent inadvertent exposure to cyber threats.
- Secure use of company resources should also be a focus. Employees must be instructed on proper data handling procedures to prevent information leaks. They should be educated on company policies regarding email and internet usage, and the importance of reporting suspicious activities immediately. Training should also cover how to recognize and counter social engineering attempts that target company resources.
- To reinforce these lessons, phishing simulations can be conducted. These simulated attacks help assess and improve employee response to phishing attempts. Feedback and additional training based on simulation results are essential to continually enhance awareness and preparedness.

- Training delivery methods should be diverse to cater to different learning preferences. Interactive online modules offer flexible and accessible training through online platforms, incorporating quizzes and simulations to enhance engagement. In-person training sessions with security experts can facilitate live Q&A and scenario-based learning, solidifying understanding through discussion.
- Regular updates and reinforcement of key security principles are crucial. Providing ongoing training updates keeps employees informed about new threats and tactics. Utilizing email reminders, posters, and internal communication channels can help reinforce these principles consistently.
- Tailoring training to different roles within the organization ensures that the specific needs and risk levels of various departments are addressed. Role-specific training programs can focus on the types of threats and data employees encounter in their daily tasks.
- Finally, creating a culture of security awareness is essential. Promoting a company culture that prioritizes cybersecurity and encourages open communication about security concerns helps reinforce the importance of these practices. Recognizing and rewarding employees who demonstrate responsible cybersecurity practices can further enhance this culture.

By integrating these elements, enterprises can significantly enhance their workforce's ability to identify and prevent cyberattacks, thereby safeguarding their resources.

Strategies to Conduct Training:

To effectively safeguard enterprise resources against cyberattacks, a multipronged approach to cybersecurity training is essential. This section explores various strategies that can be implemented.

- Interactive Online Modules: These modules offer flexibility and accessibility, allowing employees to learn at their own pace *via* online platforms. Gamified exercises, quizzes, and simulations can be incorporated to maintain engagement. This self-paced approach caters to diverse learning styles and accommodates busy schedules.

- In-Person Training Sessions: These sessions provide opportunities for in-depth knowledge sharing by cybersecurity experts. Hands-on exercises and scenario-based learning solidify key concepts. Group discussions promote collaborative learning and experience exchange, fostering problem-solving skills.
- Phishing Simulations: Realistic scenarios mimicking real-world phishing attempts test and refine employee awareness and response capabilities. Detailed feedback on simulation results helps identify areas for improvement and guides further training. Regular testing ensures employees remain vigilant against evolving phishing techniques.
- Role-Specific Training: Tailored content is crucial to address the specific needs and risk profiles of different departments and roles. Relevant case studies and examples pertinent to daily tasks and data handling are employed. This approach emphasizes the types of cyber threats most likely to impact each role, ensuring practical and applicable knowledge.
- Regular Updates and Reinforcement: Continuous education is paramount. Ongoing training updates equip employees with knowledge of new threats, tactics, and best practices. Email reminders, internal newsletters, and posters serve as effective channels for reinforcing key security principles. Periodic refresher courses ensure important concepts are retained and employees stay updated on the latest cybersecurity landscape.
- Gamification: This approach leverages game elements like points, leaderboards, and rewards to make training more engaging and competitive. Cybersecurity challenges or quests provide opportunities for recognition and incentivize participation. Interactive scenarios simulate real-world cyber incidents, testing employee responses in a controlled environment.
- Mobile Learning: This method enables on-the-go training with mobile-friendly modules accessible through smartphones or tablets. Microlearning offers short, focused sessions that can be easily integrated into daily routines. Push notifications can serve as reminders for upcoming training or deliver quick cybersecurity tips.
- Mentorship and Peer Learning: Pairing less experienced employees with cybersecurity-savvy mentors fosters

guidance and support. Peer learning groups enable knowledge sharing, discussions on security incidents, and learning from each other's experiences. Establishing a community of practice encourages ongoing discussions and knowledge exchange on cybersecurity topics.

By strategically integrating these diverse approaches, organizations can develop a comprehensive and impactful cybersecurity training program. This empowers employees with the knowledge, vigilance, and response capabilities necessary to safeguard enterprise resources from cyberattacks.

11.3.7 Conclusion and Future Directions

This chapter has provided an in-depth analysis of defense strategies for cyber-physical systems (CPS) against a dynamic cyber threat landscape. We explored advancements in anomaly detection, secure communication protocols, machine learning-based defenses, and the Zero Trust model. Additionally, the importance of resilience techniques and comprehensive training programs was emphasized. These multifaceted approaches contribute to the robustness and reliability of CPS.

Future CPS defense necessitates the integration of AI and IoT for enhanced predictive threat modeling and autonomous response systems. Quantum-resistant cryptographic algorithms are essential to counter the rise of quantum computing. Standardized protocols and real-time threat intelligence sharing will be paramount for collaborative defense mechanisms. Human-machine collaboration can be further strengthened through innovative interfaces and decision-support systems. Furthermore, robust regulatory frameworks and stringent security standards are crucial. Finally, developing adaptive resilience techniques for unknown threats involving continuous monitoring and dynamic risk assessment is vital.

References

1. Aslan, O., Aktuğ, S.S., Ozkan-Okay, M., Yilmaz, A.A., Akin, E., A comprehensive review of cyber security vulnerabilities, threats, attacks, and solutions. *Electronics*, *12*, 6, 1333, 2023, https://doi.org/10.3390/electronics12061333.
2. Fouda, R.M., Security vulnerabilities of cyberphysical unmanned aircraft systems, in: *IEEE Aerospace and Electronic Systems Magazine*, Institute of Electrical and Electronics Engineers IEEE, USA, 2018, September, https://doi.org/10.1109/maes.2018.170021.

3. Basan, E., Gritsynin, A., Shulika, M., Kryuchkov, V., Automation of the Process of Analysis of Security Threats in Cyber-Physical Systems. *Voprosy kiberbezopasnosti A.L. Makarenko GI*, 4, 35–47, 2021, https://doi.org/10.21681/2311-3456-2021-4-35-47.
4. Gao, X., Ali, M., Sun, W., A Risk Assessment Framework for Cyber-Physical Security in Distribution Grids with Grid-Edge DERs. *Energies*, 17, 1587, 2024, https://doi.org/10.3390/en17071587.
5. Gori, G., Rinieri, L., Melis, A., Al Sadi, A., Callegati, F., Prandini, M., A Systematic Analysis of Security Metrics for Industrial Cyber–Physical Systems. *Electronics*, 13, 1208, 2024, March 25, MDPI AG https://doi.org/10.3390/electronics13071208.
6. Keenan, C., Maier, H.R., van Delden, H., Zecchin, A.C., Bridging the Cyber–Physical Divide: A Novel Approach for Quantifying and Visualising the Cyber Risk of Physical Assets. *Water*, 16, 637, 2024, February 21, MDPI AG, https://doi.org/10.3390/w16050637.
7. Tushkanova, O., Levshun, D., Branitskiy, A., Fedorchenko, E., Novikova, E., Kotenko, I., Detection of cyberattacks and anomalies in cyber-physical systems: Approaches, data sources, evaluation. *Algorithms*, 16, 2, 85, 2023.
8. Tao, Y., Weijie, H., Qiang, Y., Wenhai, W., Cloud-edge coordinated traffic anomaly detection for industrial cyber-physical systems. *Expert Syst. Appl.*, 233, 120668, 2023, https://doi.org/10.1016/j.eswa.2023.120668.
9. Jeffrey, N., Tan, Q., Villar, J., Using Ensemble Learning for Anomaly Detection in Cyber–Physical Systems. *Electronics.*, 13, 1391, 2024, 10.3390/electronics13071391.
10. Baoling, M., Hao Duo, W., Yan-Jun, L., Lei, L., Adaptive Security Control against False Data Injection Attacks in Cyber-Physical Systems. *IEEE J. Emerging Sel. Top. Circuits Syst.*, 13, 743–751, 2023, https://doi.org/10.1109/jetcas.2023.3253483.
11. Wang, Y., Qiu, X., Zhang, H., Xie, X., Data-Driven-Based Event-Triggered Control for Nonlinear CPSs Against Jamming Attacks, in: *IEEE Transactions on Neural Networks and Learning Systems*, vol. 33, pp. 3171–3177, July 2022, https://doi.org/10.1109/TNNLS.2020.3047931.
12. Meganathan, R., Manjunath, B.,., Anand, R., Murugesh, V., Jaganathan, S., Suriyan, K., Security Establishment Using Deep Convolutional Network Model in Cyber-physical Systems, 2023, https://doi.org/10.21203/rs.3.rs-2888758/v1.
13. Azim, E., Wang, D., Fu, Y., Deep Graph Stream SVDD: Anomaly Detection in Cyber-Physical Systems, 2023.
14. Alguliev, R.M., Sukhostat, L.V., Mammadov, A., *Anomaly.* Detection in Cyber-Physical Systems based on BiGRU-VAE, 2022, https://doi.org/10.1109/AICT55583.2022.10013581.
15. Xu, Q., Ali, S., Yue, T., Digital Twin-based Anomaly Detection with Curriculum Learning in Cyber-physical Systems. *ACM Trans. Soft. Eng. Methodol.*, 32, 1–32, 2023, https://doi.org/10.1145/3582571.

16. Hasan, S., Amundson, I., Hardin, D., Zero Trust Architecture Patterns for Cyber-Physical Systems, 2023, SAE technical paper series, https://doi.org/10.4271/2023-01-1001.
17. Microsoft, Implementing a zero trust security model at Microsoft, in: *Inside Track*, 2024, June 11, https://www.microsoft.com/insidetrack/blog/implementing-a-zero-trust-security-model-at-microsoft/.
18. Randolph, L., Vrizlynn, L., Thing, L., Enhancing Cyber-Resilience in Self-Healing Cyber-Physical Systems with Implicit Guarantees, 2023, arXiv.org, https://doi.org/10.48550/arXiv.2305.08335.
19. Patri, S.K., Green Resilience of Cyber-Physical Systems, 2022, https://doi.org/10.1109/issrew55968.2022.00048.
20. Azari, M.S., Francesco, F., Santini, S., Improving Resilience in Cyber-Physical Systems based on Transfer Learning, 2022, https://doi.org/10.1109/CSR54599.2022.9850282.

12

Cybersecurity in the Era of Artificial Intelligence: Challenges and Innovations

Ashwini A.[1]*, H. Sehina[2] and Banu Priya Prathaban[3]

[1]*Department of Electronics and Communication Engineering, Vel Tech Rangarajan Dr. Sagunthala R&D Institute of Science and Technology, Avadi, Chennai, Tamil Nadu, India*
[2]*PSN College of Engineering and Technology, Tirunelveli, Tamil Nadu, India*
[3]*Department of Networking and Communications, School of Computing, College of Engineering and Technology, SRM Institute of Science and Technology, SRM Nagar, Kattankulathur, Kancheepuram, Chennai, Tamil Nadu, India*

Abstract
Artificial intelligence (AI) and cyber-security have a mutually advantageous relationship that has become a crucial axis on which security and privacy stand in the digitally modern landscape. Cyber-security assessments are significantly impacted by two closely linked fields: post-quantum cyber-security and quantum computing. Given that quantum computers may pose a danger to traditional cryptographic systems, post-quantum security aims to develop hashing and encryption algorithms that are resistant to attacks by these machines. A review process was conducted on 116 papers that were found using the keywords "Cyber-security," "Artificial Intelligence," "machine learning," and "Deep learning" from two research databases: Web of Science and Scopus. From 2005 until the present, the models that aided in the research are discussed. Discussions about AI-powered cyber security showcase innovation by showing how AI can adjust security settings in real-time and transform secure communication. The conclusion of this chapter highlights the significant and revolutionary role that AI has played in the evolution of block chain technology and the cryptography landscape, emphasizing how important it is to handle both issues and advancements to safeguard the digital realm of the near future.

**Corresponding author*: a.aswiniur@gmail.com

K. Ananthajothi, S. N. Sangeethaa, D. Divya, S. Balamurugan and Shen-Lung Peng (eds.) Securing Cyber-Physical Systems: Fundamentals, Applications and Challenges, (249–268) © 2025 Scrivener Publishing LLC

Keywords: Artificial intelligence, block chain, cyber-security, digital world, encryption, machine learning, quantum computing, deep learning algorithm

12.1 Introduction to Cybersecurity Analysis

In the modern era where digital connectivity is pervasive, doing in-depth cyber security analysis is becoming essential. This leads to an endless flow of data that seeps into day-to-day existence. The increasing frequency and sophistication of cyber assaults puts individuals, companies, and nations at significant risk. A thorough analysis of the most current advancements in cryptography and possible areas for improvement is set up by the interesting historical backdrop and evolution of artificial intelligence and cyber-security. This chapter is mainly concentrated in providing an in depth view of how cyber security has developed, and its innovations with the challenges aspect. This acts as the key point in the start of shift from the cyber threat perspective with the primary focus in safeguarding the assets at digital forum. Numerous developments are made in machine learning platforms with the significant use of AI in the novel framework of cybersecurity [1]. This study inn using the application based networking systems to verify the flaws and the network breaches related to security. Thus for protecting the data which are personal to an individual or a firm, accuracy and safety being a key concern, a continued system of operation is performed that addresses the key areas in terms of integrity, accessibility and also discretion factors.

The performance of the Quantum computers are remarkably smart and good when compared to the traditional networking systems. These are also termed as the "quantum supremacy," as it proves to be a challenge in all digital realm conditions. This possibility is mainly due to cloud advancements based on AI and Internet of Things (IoT), ensuring the safety and security at the constant rate. This contributes to the development in research undergoing constant improvement in technology and emerging risk with the careful examination factors. It forms an interconnection between the privacy and the cyber security characteristics exploring various advancements in monitoring the personal information's. Though there are various innovations, it also possess several challenges and risk factors. Concerns with respect to ethical values, privacy with the risks associated to the working of the quantum devices that are examined before it is executed in to real world. This statement proves the nominal requirement for governing such a robust system that balances the safety and entrepreneurship.

The five categories of cyber security where the research is mainly focused are given in Figure 12.1.

Cyber security based artificial intelligence (AI) provides various instances and the implementations which provides confidentiality that in turn provides the balance of AI benefits. This focus on sensitive data preserving with the research and development in the field of AI and encryption fields. As increasing numbers of data-driven AI apps are created, issues about the privacy of people's data including financial, private, medical, and psychological information are becoming more and more prevalent. Differential privacy is a popular technique to secure specific data points through introducing noise to query replies. This method's effectiveness and utility are always being improved. Because homomorphic encryption allows computation on encrypted data, it maintains privacy. This kind of innovation is currently being built for use in practical applications through ongoing research.

AI that protects privacy is essential for clinical research and diagnostics that maintain patient safety. A significant difficulty is achieving a mutually agreeable compromise between information confidentiality and the effectiveness of AI models. It's still difficult to ensure privacy at scale, particularly for extensive applications [2]. For privacy-preserving techniques and technologies to become widely used, they must be made simple to use. It is necessary to implement AI systems, but the process is difficult due to such a vast number of data protection laws regularly appearing all over the world. A possible solution to alleviate some of the tensions that may come with the possibilities of AI while at the same time ensuring privacy is to link encryption with privacy-preserving AI. The following is suggested to

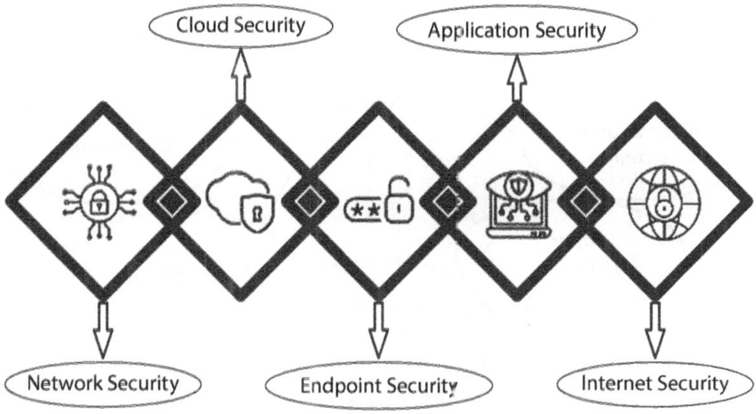

Figure 12.1 Types of cyber-security.

adapt themselves to new challenges in support of ethical and responsible AI, while doing research in this area is in evolution. In conclusion, we may state that the detailed explanation of the Security Analysis is helpful to grasp the main concepts and practices to apply to liberate the security of the development of the digital world and the much more interdependent society or economy.

12.2 Need for AI in Cybersecurity

AI must be incorporated into cyber security since incidents are on the rise and new forms of attacks are being developed every day. The requirement for employing AI in cyber security is illustrated in Figure 12.2. Because AI is more effective and faster in identifying threats than previous generations, can respond to situations automatically, and analyze the behavior, it is useful in the prevention of cyber-attacks [3]. All these abilities are especially useful when the scammers are using increasingly sophisticated and flexible strategies. Still, one of the main objectives is to design and establish the encryption methods that are safe from quantum attacks. As AI's

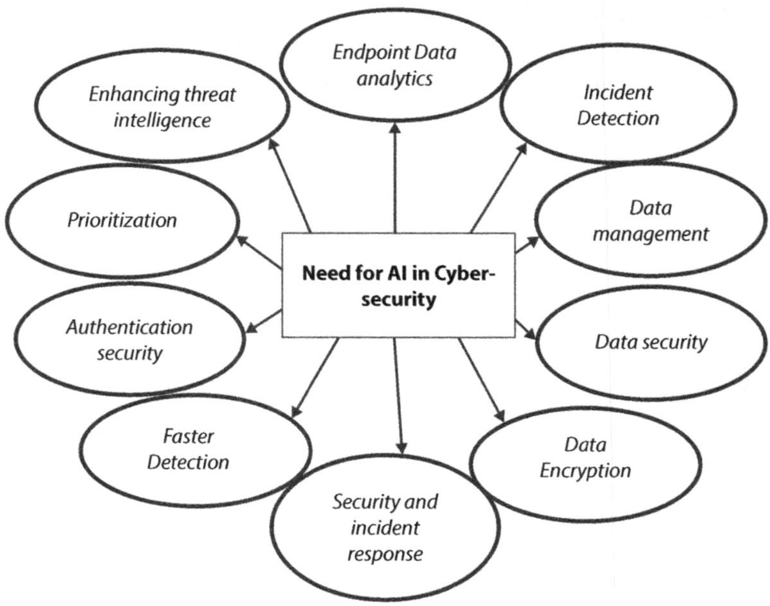

Figure 12.2 Need for AI in cyber-security.

capabilities increase, worries about its possible application in cryptanalysis are also growing.

Common encryption technique Shor's technique, which suggests that quantum computers could be able to defeat present cyber-security measures, depends on the challenging task of factoring huge numbers. Grover's method is quadratically faster than traditional methods that shorten the optimal key's length for encryption that is symmetrical. Lattice-based security is a common post-quantum cyber-security method. The foundation of hexagonal-based systems is the complexity of lattice theory-related problems, which are thought to be immune to quantum attacks. Another strategy is to build encrypted networks that are immune to quantum faults by utilizing error-correcting codes [4]. Hashing-based cyber-security is thought to be quantum-resistant and can be used to create secure digital certificates and other cryptographic fundamentals. In order to find potential weaknesses in post-quantum security online systems and to constantly adjust to new threats, analysts are engaged in continuing research projects. The use of AI and cyber security together for algorithmic learning that protects privacy will increase dramatically. There will be more advancements in the domains of federated learning, differential privacy, and safe multi-party computation. Research on block chain technology and cryptocurrency security will continue to be at the forefront. Persistent hurdles include enhancing transaction privacy, addressing scalability issues, and improving consensus mechanisms. Secure key distribution and management will require AI-driven solutions.

12.3 Current Cybersecurity Techniques

Together, cyber security strategies address the challenges posed by a dynamic threat landscape, resulting in a more proactive, flexible, and successful cyber-security posture. Following are some popular AI-based cyber safety techniques:

- *Behavioral Analysis:* Through analysis of behaviors, AI is able to identify prevalent system and user action patterns [5]. Obstacles from those trends could indicate possible weaknesses in security, allowing for the swift detection of variations that may indicate averse implementation.
- *Machine Learning for Threat Detection:* Big data sets are assessed using predictive algorithms, which search for similarities related to recognized and unidentified risks.

This makes the ability to identify unwanted conduct, such as infections and fraudulent activities, using features that have been acquired.

- *Predictive Analytics:* Predictive analytics is a tool that AI models use to find emerging trends and patterns in prior data to foresee hazards in the future [6]. Organizations that adopt a plan of action have the ability anticipate issues and act in advance of they get stronger.
- *Natural Language Processing (NLP):* A form of text data is monitored and studied for warning signs of attacks using the method of natural language processing (NLP), which examines and understands how people speak. It is also important to recognize when social engineering techniques are being used and to employ email security.
- *User and Entity Behavior Analytics (UEBA):* UEBA solutions employ machine learning to create profiles of normal usage patterns. Any deviations from these characteristics, including abnormal access schedules or actions by trusted individuals, may result in warnings that require careful examination.
- *Adversarial Machine Learning (AML):* Creating systems with artificial intelligence that can fend off intruders is the aim of AML [7]. This is important because hackers may attempt to take control of AI-powered systems, and AML techniques aim to make algorithms more adaptive.
- *Network Traffic Analysis:* An AI system scans the network's activity for signs of suspicious activities. Networks activity detection of anomalies helps identify possible security threats, including breaches and data extraction.
- *Autonomous Response:* The use of AI is utilized for identifying unusual activity in network interactions. Networking activity identification allows for easy to recognize probable security issues, such as attacks and data harvesting.
- *Cognitive Security Operations:* Safety Operation Centers utilize neural networks together with developments in artificial intelligence to strengthen surveillance of threats and reaction to incidents [8]. This involves using AI to sort through massive quantities of protected data, classify alarms, and assists investigators in making conclusions.
- *Privacy-Preserving AI:* Particularly in the medicine and financial industries, safeguarding privacy AI techniques—like

homomorphic passwords and cooperative learning—are utilized to help ensure certain personal information used by algorithms stays confidential and safe.

- *Block Chain for Cyber Security:* Experts are looking into using the technology of block chain and artificially intelligent technology (AI), but not nearly AI, for greater internet safety. When linked with the technology's distributed and irreversible structure, AI will provide reliable inspection and resilience against several hazards.

12.4 Role of AI in Cybersecurity

- AI algorithms monitor user activity, log files, and network traffic in real-time.
- Instantly detects irregularities, fraudulent communications, both known and unknown malware, and other dubious activities.
- Quickly recognizes deviations from established patterns and triggers alerts for timely investigation.
- It offers timely and proactive control of emerging risks before they escalate.
- AI-powered autonomous response systems respond to cyber security issues automatically.
- By isolating affected systems and performing remedial measures rapidly, it lessens the impact of threats.
- Facilitates the prompt detection of potential security problems, including but not limited to invasions and data exfiltration.
- Rapidly assesses and prioritizes warnings, assisting analysts in taking prompt action in response to incidents. Real-time safe authorization and online threat protection are now feasible through the combination of block chain technology and artificial intelligence.
- The volume of data gathered in digital ecosystems necessitates advanced analytics, and AI's capacity to sift through massive datasets makes it feasible to spot anomalies that could indicate security breaches [9].
- Because artificial intelligence machine learning algorithms are constantly evolving to learn from new threats, artificial learning has dynamic safety mechanisms that can adapt to changing assault strategies.

12.5 Challenges in AI Enhanced Cybersecurity

While integrating AI into cyber security has many advantages, there are drawbacks as well. The following are the main difficulties with cyber security boosted by AI:

Adversarial Attacks: Adversarial attacks entail the misleading introduction of carefully constructed input data to manipulate AI algorithms [10]. AI algorithm flaws can be exploited by cybercriminals. Inaccurate or altered findings from compromised AI models could result in security lapses.

Insufficient Training Data: Large and varied datasets are necessary for AI models to be trained effectively. It can be difficult to get enough labeled data in cyber security, particularly for uncommon or novel threats. Insufficient training data could make it more difficult for the model to identify novel or emerging cyber threats.

Over-Reliance on AI: When AI is overused without human supervision, blind spots and misunderstandings may result. For a danger assessment to be accurate, human perception and contextual knowledge are frequently essential. The efficacy of cyber security precautions may be compromised if AI is used exclusively. This could lead to false positives or negatives.

Explainability and Transparency: A lot of AI models, especially models based on deep learning, are thought of as "black boxes" because of their intricate topologies [11–13]. It is difficult to comprehend how these models come to particular conclusions. Regarding explainability issues, it complicates the evaluation of model outputs, which increases skepticism about the credibility of AI-based cyber security decisions.

Resource Intensity: Sophisticated AI models can require a lot of resources to train and implement in real time. This covers the amount of energy used, the computational power, and the specialist knowledge. Businesses with less funding may find it difficult to successfully adopt and manage AI-driven cyber security solutions [14].

Integration with Existing Systems: It can be challenging to smoothly integrate AI with the current cyber security infrastructure. Interoperability problems and incompatibilities between legacy systems might occur. Inadequate integration can lead to coverage gaps, inefficiencies, and trouble synchronizing reaction to security incidents.

False Positives and Negatives: AI models might generate inaccurate positives, which are non-dangers which move, or incorrect adverse effects, that are actual hazards that are detected. Striking an equilibrium which reduces both types of faults is complicated. False negatives may result in unnoticed hacking, but a lot of false alarms could lead to notify fatigue.

Regulatory Compliance: Employing AI while complying with various privacy regulations and regulations can be difficult, especially as these requirements are open to change. Compliance could result in implications for law in along with undermining the image of an enterprise.

To overcome those obstacles, more research is needed as is partnership among defense and AI specialists, as well as an obligation to ethical and responsible AI use in the realm of cyber-security [15–17].

12.6 Quantum Computing and Post Quantum Computing in Cybersecurity

The emergence of quantum computers has had an enormous impact on the field of cyber-security, requiring the use of unique mechanisms for securing personal information as well as to the utilization of earlier cryptographic techniques. The use of quantum computing raises multiple risks due to its ability to break commonly utilized encrypted public-key schemes. In one instance, if completed on a sufficiently powerful nano computer, Shor's algorithm could correctly factor massive amounts, endangering the dependability underlying cryptography systems [18]. The cyber-security community must stay informed since this has implications for secure financial transactions, secure communications, and data protection. Table 12.1 shows the standardization algorithm of the post quantum cyber-security phenomenon.

For an actual example, that quantum computing becomes possible and can quickly factor huge quantities. This capacity would compromise the protection of online transactions by making public-key cryptography,

Table 12.1 Post quantum cyber-security with standardization algorithms.

Year	Standardization algorithms
1998	2-Qubit Computer
2000	5-Qubit Computer & 7-Qubit Computer
2006	12-Qubit Computer
2008	28-Qubit Computer
2017	58-Qubit Computer
2018	49-Qubit Computer & 72-Qubit Computer
2019	128-Qubit Computer
2021	127-Qubit Quantum Processor

which is extensively used, susceptible. With present cryptography techniques, an opponent with a quantum computer might decrypt intercepted communication. This emphasizes how important it is for businesses to create and use quantum-resistant cryptography methods in order to get ready for the quantum future. Lattice-based cryptography, hash-based digital signatures, and other forms of post-quantum cryptography are being investigated as possible remedies to the vulnerabilities brought forth by quantum computing [19–22]. Post-quantum cryptography techniques must be included into practical cyber security procedures as the quantum threat develops in order to maintain the integrity and secrecy of critical digital assets.

In cyber security, post-quantum computing is a calculated reaction to the possible danger that quantum computers could offer to current cryptography methods. Popular public-key encryption methods like RSA and ECC run the risk of being effectively cracked by quantum methods like Shor's as quantum computers develop. The creation and application of cryptographic methods resistant to assaults from both traditional and quantum computers constitute post-quantum cryptography. Real-time scenarios demonstrate the need for following quantum cryptography approaches to safeguard digital messages and data against anticipated quantum assaults in the future [23, 24]. Consider the protection of private financial data through the application of lattice-based cryptography. One of the greatest solutions for post-quantum security is lattice-based encryption since it is impervious to quantum attacks. Even with the advent of cryptography based on post-quantum techniques in useful applications, organizations may ensure the privacy and reliability of data by taking proactive steps to protect their digital assets.

12.7 AI Powered Encryption Analysis

AI encryption technique is a special cyber security tactics which helps to bring a prime use of encryption analysis. These are capable of doing the real time encryption through the development and analyzing of the codes which analyses the shortcomings through AI. Advanced privacy laws are enacted using these machine learning capabilities [25, 26]. A practical example for such as encrypted protocol analysis is done by means of the transport-level security (TLS).

Figure 12.3 illustrates the need for AI imposed on the computer programs. This tool enables the efficiency and the stability of the cryptographic tools that identifies the disparities, which identifies the dangers indicating the patterns for such encrypted data values. Thus when a different unusual pattern in found on the encryption ranges within a business entities, the AI system delivers an alarm signal thus enhancing the security. Moreover, it provides a nominal range of adaptation and recognizing the encryption based strategies for its effective defense on cyber security threat systems. Thus the factor of crypt analysis provides a nominal improvement in the field of digital communication and fully supports for the measurement of security in such dynamic digital world.

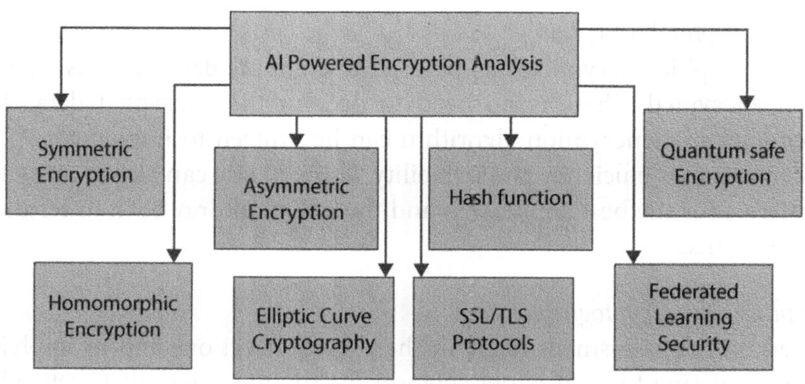

Figure 12.3 Need for AI in cyber-security.

Symmetric Encryption:
Using the advantageous model of the AI algorithms synchronous methods of encryption are evaluated based on the key administration processes which enhances the blocking ability when there is an attack by a vector. This helps in identification of the patterns that contributes to the weaker zones where the symmetric keys can be used effectively.

Asymmetric Encryption:
RSA is the most common techniques of encryption where the AI plays an important role. This helps in solving the mathematical problems that are complex in nature. When the flaws are identified, it is distributed and generated using the keys and machine learning concepts. This increasing the evaluation security

Hash Functions:
Artificial intelligence-driven analysis is necessary to assess hash functions' long-term dependability [27]. Given their ability to detect collision patterns and issues with hash algorithms, machine learning models may be helpful in locating potential weaknesses that might compromise data integrity.

Quantum-Safe Encryption:
AI can help with benchmarks and analysis of quantum-safe encryption algorithms as post-quantum cryptography develops. Machine learning frameworks can assist in selecting and implementing strong cryptography techniques by assessing their susceptibility to both classical and quantum attacks.

Homomorphic Encryption:
Homomorphic encryption can be used to compute data that has already been encrypted. There is no need to decrypt the encrypted data. The homomorphic encryption algorithm can be utilized to implement AI in order to test its efficiency and reliability. Using it, one can also identify the scenarios for the best application and the potential drawback in terms of performance.

Elliptic Curve Cryptography (ECC):
Based on the assessment made in the previous sections and by applying AI-engineering tools, it is possible to state the following: ECC reliability can be discussed considering the complexity of the mathematical calculations with an elliptic curve [28]. It is possible to apply machine learning

to the identification of any deviations with regards to key generation and curve selection to ensure that embedded code encryption remains strong.

SSL/TLS Protocols:
SSL/TLS protocol analysis, commonly deployed in securing internet applications, employed strong AI in its predictive measures. Artificial intelligence and machine learning can use encrypted network data and then recognize a range of discrepancies and create an initial stage of potential threats and weak points.

Federated Learning Security:
Chatbot In the context of AI confidentiality keep information intact during interactive learning, like federated learning and analysis carried out by AI. Like with other types of computing frameworks, to guarantee privacy, encryption methods that learning models may assess are used in federated learning. AI in encryption analysis leads to an enhancement in scrutinizing the performance of cryptographic methodologies and assists in adapting security measures in response to threats and vulnerabilities [29]. It further shows how an imperative part AI is in the improvement of encryption systems across a spectrum of fields in the dynamic cyber security domain.

12.8 Adaptive Cybersecurity

Adaptive cyber security is a systematic model of cyber security that emphasize process, product, and personnel security with frequent threat detection and responding. Their action methodology involves the employment of modern technological devices and upcoming strategies aimed at detecting the cyber threat and responding to it in real time. Key components of adaptive cyber security are as follows, with an illustration:

Real-Time Monitoring:
Feature: Continual real-time monitoring of system activity, user behavior, and network traffic is a requirement of adaptive cyber security.
Example: Anomaly detection tools, which instantly identify and respond to suspicious activity by monitoring web traffic patterns in real-time, may be used by an adaptive cyber security system.

Behavioral Analysis:

Feature: To find common structures and user behavior patterns, adaptive cyber security uses behavioral analysis.

Example: An adaptive cyber security technology called Action Analytics may detect patterns of access or strange login timings and other anomalies that might point to a security issue. It learns from regular usage and recognizes it.

Machine Learning and AI Integration:

Feature: Artificial intelligence (AI) and machine learning together enable improved danger detection, pattern recognition, and dataset analysis.

Example: An agile cyber system can employ AI algorithms to evaluate historical data and find new cyber threat patterns in order to identify and avoid new attack vectors.

By combining these components, adaptive cyber security ensures that businesses can effectively counter new and complex attack techniques while providing a proactive and flexible defense against the ever-changing cyber threat landscape.

12.9 Overall Analysis of AI in Cybersecurity

Machine learning is an essential component in cyber security analysis that has fundamentally altered how enterprises detect, assess, and mitigate online threats [30]. Algorithms for artificial intelligence (AI), particularly those that use machine learning, are very good at sorting through massive amounts of data and finding patterns that could point to security risks. Behavioral analysis, which allows for the rapid detection of irregularities or suspicious activity and the identification of conventional user and system behavior, is one of the most crucial components of AI-driven cyber security. By using previous data to foresee potential dangers, predictive analytics gives enterprises a proactive approach to defense. Adversarial machine learning fortifies AI models against sophisticated attacks intended to modify their functionality. Machine learning (AI) is utilized by automatic response systems to neutralize hazards in real time and by analyzers of network traffic to identify anomalies that may show security incidents. AI-powered cognitive security operations improve the effectiveness of

Security Operations Centers by helping analysts make decisions and giving warnings priority. AI methods that protect privacy, like federated learning, guarantee the safe processing of private information while it's being analyzed. The dynamic and adaptable properties of AI have become essential for bolstering cyber security defenses because they provide a flexible and effective way to address the always changing threat scenario.

12.10 Privacy Preserving AI and Cybersecurity

A key paradigm in cyber security is privacy-preserving AI, which tackles the delicate balance that needs to be struck between realizing the potential of artificial intelligence and safeguarding individuals' personal information is shown in Figure 12.4. Concerns about data privacy are growing as more businesses utilize AI for applications related to cyber security [31]. To ensure that personal data is secure during analysis, artificial intelligence techniques like federated learning and homomorphic encryption are crucial. Federated learning allows AI models to be constructed across disparate platforms without transferring raw data, therefore protecting the security of participant contributions.

Because homomorphic compression allows operations on protected data without requiring its first decryption, it allows for the secure and intelligent assessment of private data. It appears that such method is useful in protection usages in areas that require the protection of financial and personal information including the medical and finance fields. Patients' information can be protected, yet integration of secrecy-preserving AI tools into IT security projects will provide firms with better analytics and threat identification. This tactic helps in building a user confidence as it also adhere to prescribed standard of privacy.

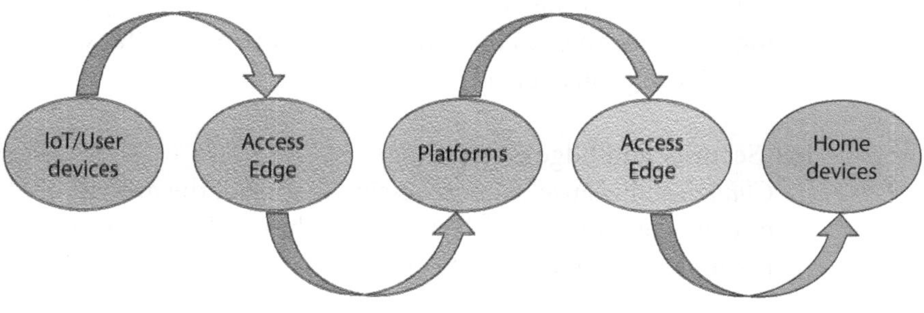

Figure 12.4 Privacy preserving AI and cyber security.

12.11 Future Directions and Research Challenges

Matters concerning cyber security and technology present a shifting paradigm which is both full of possibilities as well as challenges, especially given the emergence and integration of Artificial Intelligence (AI). As machine learning develops, the following crucial topics should be investigated and given more thought about in order to improve privacy protocols:

Adversarial AI and Countermeasures:
Challenge: When it comes to the interaction of AI models, conflict of interest could be harmfully devastating. Such efforts have to direct their efforts towards the development of robust algorithms that cannot be gamed.
Direction: Studying adversarial attacks and finding practical countermeasures to strengthen the antecedent intelligence-security layer.

Explainable AI in Security:
Challenge: Many AI models lack transparency, which makes it challenging to comprehend and trust the results they provide in cyber security.
Direction: In order to help security professionals better comprehend and interpret neural networks used in cyber situations, research initiatives should focus on improving their explainability.

Quantum-Safe Cryptography:
Challenge: The traditional cryptography algorithms are under threat from the emergence of quantum computing. To create and standardize post-quantum cryptography methods, research is necessary.
Direction: Ongoing research and development of cryptographic techniques that are safe from quantum attacks in order to protect data.

IoT Security and Edge Computing:
Challenge: Because data processing is spread, the growth of edge computing and Network of Things (IoT) equipment presents new security challenges.

Direction: The main goals of research should be to secure edge computing infrastructures, address specific vulnerabilities, and create adaptive cyber security solutions for IoT environments.

Secure AI Model Sharing:

Challenge: Cyber security collaborative AI models might need exchanging private data. It is quite difficult to ensure safe sharing methods without sacrificing privacy.

Direction: Investigating methods such as secure multi-party computation and federated learning to facilitate cooperative model training while protecting the confidentiality of shared data.

Human-Centric Security:

Challenge: Achieving a balance between the benefits of AI-driven automation and human-centric security is imperative. Understanding human factors in cyber security encounters and decisions is an ongoing challenge.

Direction: Research should concentrate on centered on people cybercrime design which take user actions, ideas, and interactions into account in order to increase the effectiveness of AI-based security systems.

Ethical AI in Cyber security:

Challenge: The ethical considerations of AI-driven cyber security are critical to prevent exploitation and biased outcomes.

Direction: It is important to delve into foundations for moral artificial intelligence in cybersecurity, with an emphasis on discrimination, justice, and accountability in algorithms and decision-making processes.

Resilience against Advanced Persistent Threats (APTs):

Challenge: APTs continues to advance in complexity. Creating robust defenses against complex and enduring threats is a major scientific issue.

Direction: Examining cutting-edge methods for APT detection, avoidance, and reaction, such as adaptable cyber security and powered by AI deceiving technologies.

Cyber security research in the current age requires interdisciplinary and cooperative research in order to address some of these issues. In this way, future approaches to the security of online infrastructure will be more trustworthy, flexible, and privacy-aware to solve these problems and protect online infrastructure from new point attacks.

12.12 Conclusion

Cyber security investment by Intelligent machines (AI) is a growing field that presents both innovation and great challenge. This book chapter has explored the integration of safety and AI and the interactive aspects as well as tensions that this link entails. From this chapter, the complexity of safeguarding computer networks has been illustrated; these entail the issues of quantum-safe encrypted data, moral issues in artificial-driven data protection, threats posed by adversarial AI, and access requirements. Thus, it is possible to see that the application of AI in the context of reactions has the potential to be very useful; this is proven by such things as dynamic defense methods based on AI, as well as safeguarding privacy AI, AI for the security recognition, and evaluation of reactions. Ethical AI and joint investigation are going to be important if a multi-layered cyber defense mechanism can be developed to ward off new threats that today's cyber security cannot detect, mitigate, or prevent with ease due to the point of technological convergence. This chapter also proves that there is a need for candid debate and research to ensure the future of communication in an AI world.

References

1. Kumar, S., Gupta, U., Singh, A.K., Singh, A.K., Artificial intelligence: revolutionizing cyber security in the digital era. *J. Computers Mech. Manage.*, 2, 3, 31–42, 2023.
2. Farooq, M. and Khan, M.H., Artificial Intelligence-Based Approach on Cybersecurity Challenges and Opportunities in The Internet of Things & Edge Computing Devices. *Int. J. Eng. Comput. Sci.*, 12, 07, 25763–25768, 2023.
3. Kaur, R., Gabrijelcic, D., Klobucar, T., Artificial intelligence for cybersecurity: Literature review and future research directions. *Inf. Fusion*, 97, 101804, 2023.
4. Bharadiya, J., Machine Learning in Cybersecurity: Techniques and Challenges. *Eur. J. Technol.*, 7, 2, 1–14, 2023.

5. Lone, A.N., Mustajab, S., Alam, M., A comprehensive study on cybersecurity challenges and opportunities in the IoT world. *Secur. Privacy*, 6, 6, e318, 2023.
6. Rangaraju, S., AI Sentry: Reinventing Cybersecurity Through Intelligent Threat Detection. *EPH-International J. Sci. Eng.*, 9, 3, 30–35, 2023.
7. Dapel, M.E., Asante, M., Dike Uba, C., Agyeman, M.O., Artificial Intelligence Techniques in Cybersecurity Management, in: *Cybersecurity in the Age of Smart Societies: Proceedings of the 14th International Conference on Global Security, Safety and Sustainability, London, September 2022*, vol. 241–255, 2023.
8. Michael, K., Abbas, R., Roussos, G., AI in Cybersecurity: The Paradox. *IEEE Trans. Technol. Soc.*, 4, 2, 104–109, 2023.
9. Gama, F. and Magistretti, S., Artificial intelligence in innovation management: A review of innovation capabilities and a taxonomy of AI applications. *J. Prod. Innov. Manage.*, 2023. https://doi.org/10.1111/jpim.12698.
10. Ashwini, A.S., Quadruple spherical tank systems with automatic level control applications using fuzzy deep neural sliding mode FOPID controller. *J. Eng. Res.*, 2023, Preprint. https://doi.org/10.1016/j.jer.2023.09.022.
11. Muneer, S.M., Bux Alvi, M., Farrakh, A., Cyber Security event detection using machine learning technique. *Int. J. Comput. Innov. Sci.*, 2, 2, 42–46, 2023.
12. Ashwini, A., Purushothaman, K.E., Rosi, A., Vaishnavi, T., Artificial Intelligence based real-time automatic detection and classification of skin lesion in dermoscopic samples using DenseNet-169 architecture. *J. Intell. Fuzzy Syst.*, 45, 4, 1–16, 2023, Preprint.
13. Humied, I.A., Improving Cybersecurity Systems using Artificial Intelligence Techniques, 2023.
14. Bonfanti, M.E., Artificial intelligence and the offence-defence balance in cyber security, in: *Cyber Security: Socio-Technological Uncertainty and Political Fragmentation*, vol. 64–79, Routledge, London, 2022.
15. Wiafe, I., Koranteng, F.N., Obeng, E.N., Assyne, N., Wiafe, A., Gulliver, S.R., Artificial intelligence for cybersecurity: a systematic mapping of literature. *IEEE Access*, 8, 146598–146612, 2020.
16. Abdullahi, M., Baashar, Y., Alhussian, H., Alwadain, A., Aziz, N., Capretz, L.F., Abdulkadir, S.J., Detecting cybersecurity attacks in internet of things using artificial intelligence methods: A systematic literature review. *Electronics*, 11, 2, 198, 2022.
17. Saeed, S., Altamimi, S.A., Alkayyal, N.A., Alshehri, E., Alabbad, D.A., Digital transformation and cybersecurity challenges for businesses resilience: Issues and recommendations. *Sensors*, 23, 15, 6656, 2023.
18. Ashwini, A. and Kavitha, V., Automatic Skin Tumor Detection Using Online Tiger Claw Region Based Segmentation–A Novel Comparative Technique. *IETE J. Res.*, 69, 97, 1–9, 2021.

19. Kuzlu, M., Fair, C., Guler, O., Role of artificial intelligence in the Internet of Things (IoT) cybersecurity. *Discover Internet Things*, 1, 1–14, 2021.
20. Schmitt, M., Securing the Digital World: Protecting smart infrastructures and digital industries with Artificial Intelligence (AI)-enabled malware and intrusion detection. *J. Ind. Inf. Integr.*, 36, 100520, 2023.
21. Prasad, R., Rohokale, V., Prasad, R., Rohokale, V., Artificial intelligence and machine learning in cyber security. *Cyber Security Lifeline Inf. Commun. Technol.*, 231–247, 2020.
22. Chehri, A., Fofana, I., Yang, X., Security risk modeling in smart grid critical infrastructures in the era of big data and artificial intelligence. *Sustainability*, 13, 6, 3196, 2021.
23. Milson, S. and Yusef, O., *Dark Web Chronicles: Unveiling Cybersecurity's Unseen Frontiers*, p. 11708, EasyChair, 2024.
24. Ashwini, A. and Murugan, S., Automatic Skin Tumour Segmentation Using Prioritized Patch Based Region–A Novel Comparative Technique. *IETE J. Res.*, 66, 1–12, 2020.
25. Sayfiddinov, A., Issues of Liability for Violations of the Rules for Safe and Secure Use of Artificial Intelligence. *Science-Conference.com*, 1, 1, 1–11, 2024.
26. Ferlin, A.A. and Rosi, V., Iot based object perception algorithm for urban scrutiny system in digital city. *2023 International Conference on Circuit Power and Computing Technologies (ICCPCT)*, pp. 1788–1792, 2023.
27. Kaur, N., Sahay, S., Dixit, S., Role of Artificial Intelligence (AI)-aided Internet of Things (IoT) Technologies in Business and Production, in: *Advanced IoT Technologies and Applications in the Industry 4.0 Digital Economy*, pp. 29–41, CRC Press, Boca Raton, 2024.
28. Ashwini, A., Purushothaman, K.E., Priya, B., Prathaban, M., Jenath, P., Automatic Traffic Sign Board Detection from Camera Images Using Deep learning and Binarization Search Algorithm. *2023 International Conference in recent advances in Electrical, Electronics, Ubiquitous Communication and Computational Intelligence (RAEEUCCI)*, IEEE, 2023.
29. Khan, I.U.K.U., Ouaissa, M., Ouaissa, M., Abou El Houda, Z., Fazal Ijaz, M. (Eds.), *Cyber Security for Next-Generation Computing Technologies*, CRC Press, Boca Raton, 2024.
30. Younis, H.A., Elfadil Eisa, T.A., Nasser, M., Sahib, T.M., Noor, A.A., Alyasiri, O.M., Salisu, S., Hayder, I.M., Younis, H.AK., A Systematic Review and Meta-Analysis of Artificial Intelligence Tools in Medicine and Healthcare: Applications, Considerations, Limitations, Motivation and Challenges. *Diagnostics*, 14, 1, 109, 2024.
31. John, J. and Sukumaran, S., Machine Learning for Cyber Security Threat Detection: A Comprehensive Model. *J. Environ. Sci. Technol.*, 3, 1, 1–11, 2024.

13

Safeguarding the Virtual Realm: Assessing Cyber Security Challenges and Innovations in Today's World

Rajaram P.[1]*, Rajasekar Rangasamy[2], R. C. Karpagalakshmi[3], J. Lenin[4] and S. Muthulingam[5]

[1]School of Computer Science and Engineering, Galgotias University, Greater Noida, Uttar Pradesh, India
[2]Computer Science and Engineering, Alliance School of Advance Computing, Alliance University, Bengaluru, India
[3]Computer Science and Information Technology, Alliance College of Engineering and Design, Alliance University, Bangalore, India
[4]Computer Applications, School of Advance Computing, Alliance University, Anekal, Bengaluru, India
[5]Computer Science and Engineering, Alliance University, Anekal, Bengaluru, India

Abstract
In today's digital age, a vast array of government, social, cultural, economic, and commercial activities occur online, involving individuals, NGOs, and government agencies. The frequency of cyber-attacks and the risks associated with wireless technologies are major concerns for businesses and governments globally. Protecting sensitive information from cyber threats has become a significant challenge due to our reliance on electronic technologies. Cybercriminals often target businesses with the intent of causing financial harm, though some attacks have political or military objectives as well. These threats include computer viruses, data breaches, and disruptions to data distribution services. In response, organizations implement various strategies to prevent or mitigate the impact of cyber-attacks. Given the constantly evolving nature of cyber threats, cybersecurity initiatives must stay abreast of the latest technological developments. Researchers worldwide have proposed diverse strategies, ranging from exploratory to operational, to address these

**Corresponding author*: rajaramnov82@gmail.com

K. Ananthajothi, S. N. Sangeethaa, D. Divya, S. Balamurugan and Shen-Lung Peng (eds.) Securing Cyber-Physical Systems: Fundamentals, Applications and Challenges, (269–294) © 2025 Scrivener Publishing LLC

evolving threats. This study aims to provide a comprehensive evaluation of the current state of cybersecurity by examining the challenges, limitations, and benefits of these strategies. It explores emerging cyber-attack trends, evaluates standard security frameworks, and covers the ongoing evolution of cybersecurity, making it a valuable resource for IT and cybersecurity professionals.

Keywords: Data distribution services (DDS), cyber-attacks, cyber threats

13.1 Introduction

In our modern era, where digital interactions permeate every aspect of daily life, maintaining strong cybersecurity is more important than ever. The digital age, characterized by extraordinary technological progress and highly interconnected systems, presents vast opportunities for innovation. However, it also introduces significant risks, particularly in the form of cyber-attacks. This blog post delves into the current cybersecurity landscape, addressing the challenges we encounter and outlining strategies to protect our digital future [1]. The rapid advancement of digitalization has fundamentally transformed our lifestyles, work environments, and communication methods. Technologies have become essential components of our everyday lives. Despite their numerous benefits, these advancements have significantly increased the potential attack surface for cyber threats. As our world becomes more interconnected, the number of vulnerabilities rises, demanding a proactive and adaptable approach to cybersecurity [2].

Cyber adversaries employ these tools to exploit vulnerabilities and compromise sensitive information. This evolving threat landscape requires individuals and organizations to continuously update and enhance their cybersecurity measures to stay ahead of potential attacks. The motivations behind cyber-attacks vary widely, encompassing financial gain, information theft, ideological reasons, and even state-sponsored cyber warfare. To effectively counter these threats, it is imperative to understand the constantly evolving tactics employed by cybercriminals. In response to these dynamic threats, both organizations and individuals must adopt proactive defense measures. A comprehensive cybersecurity strategy includes continuous monitoring, advanced threat detection, and rigorous vulnerability management. These elements are crucial for identifying and addressing potential security issues before they can be exploited.

Ensuring compliance with international cybersecurity regulations is pivotal for establishing a strong defense posture. These regulations offer a structured framework for implementing effective cybersecurity practices, thereby bolstering overall security measures. To further emphasize, embracing

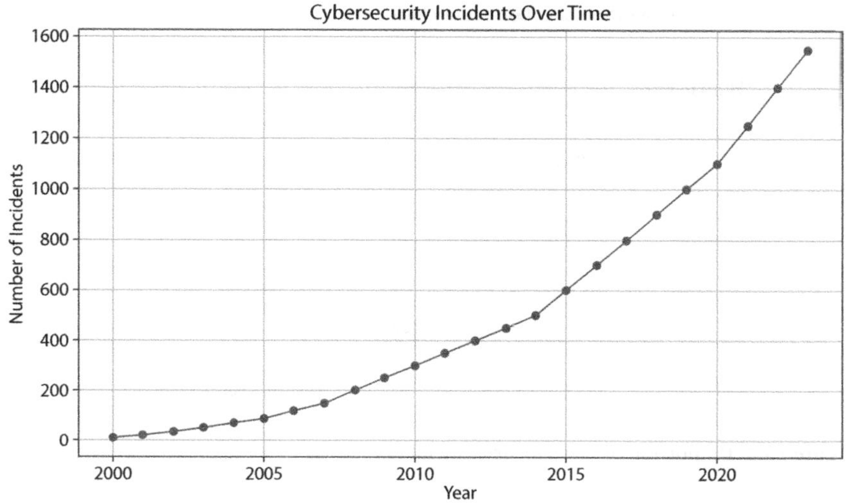

Figure 13.1 Cybersecurity incident growth over two decades.

technological breakthroughs. A behavioral analytics system that is powered by artificial intelligence, for example, can spot abnormalities and possible breaches of security by analyzing patterns and recognizing activities that are not typical [3]. Employing adaptive defense strategies that harness these technologies enables organizations to anticipate and thwart attacks, offering a significant advantage in the cybersecurity landscape. Moreover, collaborative efforts such as threat intelligence sharing and international cooperation are essential for creating a united front against global cyber threats. By working together, organizations and nations can enhance their collective security and better prepare for potential attacks. While technological solutions are indispensable, the human element remains a crucial factor in cybersecurity. By understanding and mitigating social engineering tactics, and by improving human resilience against cyber threats, individuals can significantly contribute to the overall defense strategy. Figure 13.1 clearly explains the cybersecurity incident growth over two decades.

Anticipating future trends is vital for preparing against emerging cyber threats. As technology progresses, cybercriminals continuously refine their tactics to exploit new vulnerabilities. Future cybersecurity will be shaped by advancements in quantum computing, the development of adaptive security architectures, and the ongoing innovation in defense strategies. In the ever-evolving digital landscape, securing our digital future is a shared responsibility among individuals, organizations, and policymakers. By gaining a thorough understanding of the current cyber threat environment and

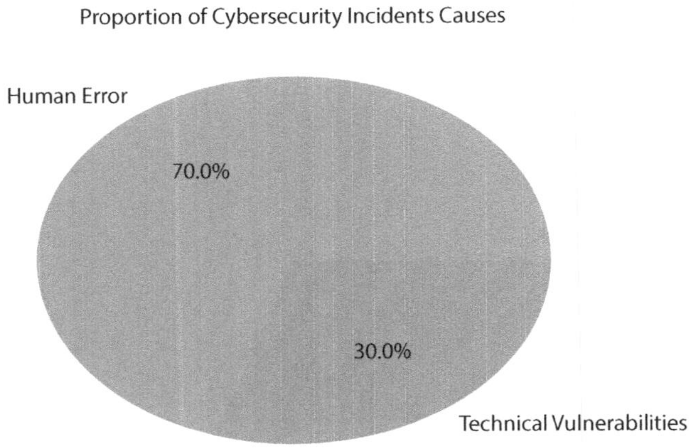

Figure 13.2 Proportion of cybersecurity incidents causes.

implementing sophisticated defense mechanisms, we can better protect our digital assets. Additionally, fostering a culture of cybersecurity awareness is crucial. Figure 13.2 clearly given the proportion of cybersecurity incidents causes over the periods.

Advanced technologies like quantum computing promise to revolutionize cybersecurity, offering both new defenses and new threats. Adaptive security architectures will enable systems to respond in real-time to attacks, providing a more robust defense against increasingly sophisticated cybercriminals. Continuous innovation in these areas will be essential to stay ahead of potential threats. Moreover, collaboration is key. Threat intelligence sharing and international cooperation can strengthen our defenses, creating a united front against global cyber threats. By pooling resources and knowledge, we can develop more effective strategies to combat cybercrime [4]. Ultimately, ensuring a secure digital future requires a multi-faceted approach. This includes leveraging advanced technologies, adhering to regulatory standards, promoting international collaboration, and enhancing human awareness and education. By staying informed and vigilant, we can collectively safeguard the digital realm, creating a safer online environment for future generations. Let's work together to protect our digital world.

13.2 Understanding the Motivations Behind Cyber Attacks: Financial, Political, and Military Goals

As a result of the advent of the digital age, cyberattacks have become a very significant risk for individuals, organizations, and governmental entities.

For the purpose of building effective cybersecurity tactics, it is vital to demonstrate an understanding of the motives underlying these attacks. It is possible to classify the principal motivations into three broad categories: monetary, political, and defense-related. Each of these categories has a unique set of objectives and ramifications.

Financial Motivations

Financial gain remains the most common motivation for cyber-attacks. Cybercriminals target individuals, businesses, and financial institutions to steal money, sensitive information, or intellectual property [5]. Key methods include:

- **Ransomware** is a type of cyberattack in which the perpetrators encrypted the data of the victim and then demand payments in exchange for decrypting the data. Significant global losses equal to billions of dollars were caused by high-profile incidents such as the WannaCry and CryptoLocker assaults, which distinguish themselves from other attacks.
- **Phishing and Spear Phishing:** These are two types of schemes that entail deceiving individuals into giving confidential data, such as their login information or details about their bank accounts. As a means of increasing their chances of success, perpetrators frequently assume the identity of reputable organizations.
- **Credit Card Fraud:** Cybercriminals employ various methods like skimming, cloning, and exploiting vulnerabilities in e-commerce platforms to unlawfully obtain and misuse credit card information.
- **Financial Institution Attacks:** Targeted and sophisticated assaults on banks and financial systems can result in significant financial losses. For instance, the 2016 Bangladesh Bank heist exemplifies such attacks, wherein hackers absconded with $81 million through the SWIFT banking network.

Political Motivations

Political motivations often drive state-sponsored cyber-attacks and hacktivist activities. These attacks aim to influence political outcomes, disrupt government operations, or propagate ideological messages [6], which was clearly shown in Figure 13.3. Key aspects include:

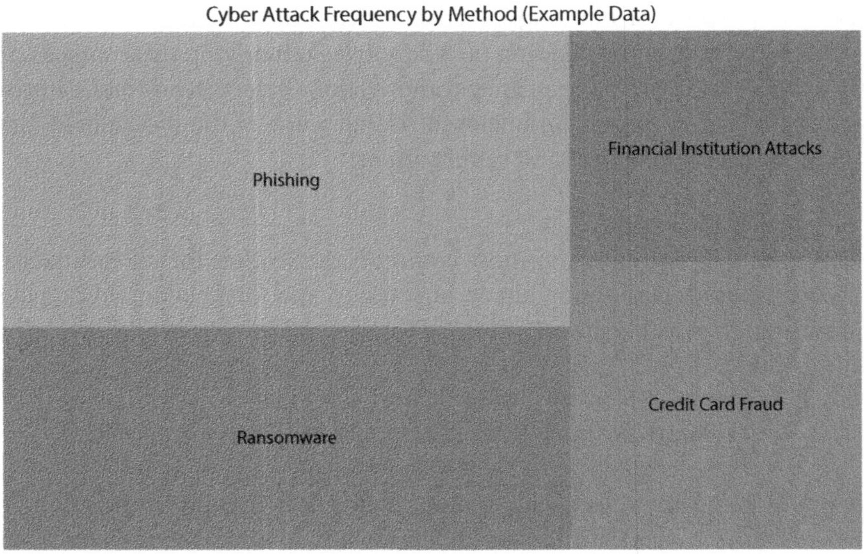

Figure 13.3 Cyber-attack frequency by method.

- **Espionage:** State actors infiltrate foreign government networks to steal sensitive information, gather intelligence, or gain strategic advantages.
- **Disruption:** Cyber-attacks are used to disrupt political processes or operations. For instance, the 2016 DNC email leak during the U.S. presidential election aimed to influence the electoral process.
- **Propaganda:** Hacktivists and state actors use cyber platforms to spread propaganda and influence public opinion.
- **Activism:** Hacktivist groups, such as Anonymous, launch cyber-attacks to support political causes, protest government actions, or expose perceived injustices. These attacks can range from website defacements to more complex operations.

Military Motivations

Cyber-attacks driven by military objectives are often state-sponsored and aim to weaken adversaries' defense capabilities, gather intelligence, or prepare for physical warfare [7], Figure 13.4 clearly emphasizes the cloud of propaganda messages. Key elements include:

Figure 13.4 Word cloud of propaganda messages.

- **Cyber Warfare:** State-sponsored cyber units target critical infrastructure, military networks, and communication systems of adversaries.
- **Intelligence Gathering:** Military cyber espionage involves infiltrating enemy networks to collect strategic information, disrupt operations, or gain insights into military capabilities and plans. China's alleged cyber activities against U.S. defense contractors highlight the significance of cyber espionage in modern warfare.
- **Preparation for Kinetic Warfare:** Cyber operations can be used to disrupt or disable enemy defense systems in preparation for physical military actions. This tactic ensures a strategic advantage and reduces the effectiveness of the adversary's response capabilities.
- **Psychological Operations:** Cyber-attacks can also serve to demoralize or mislead enemy forces and civilian populations. Disinformation campaigns and psychological operations (PSYOPs) conducted through cyber means aim to create confusion and weaken the morale of the adversary.

Understanding the diverse motivations behind cyber-attacks—financial, political, and military—is crucial for developing targeted cybersecurity measures and strategies. Financially motivated cybercriminals focus on immediate monetary gain, often through ransomware and phishing attacks. Politically motivated attackers, including state actors and hacktivists, aim to influence political processes, disrupt operations, and propagate

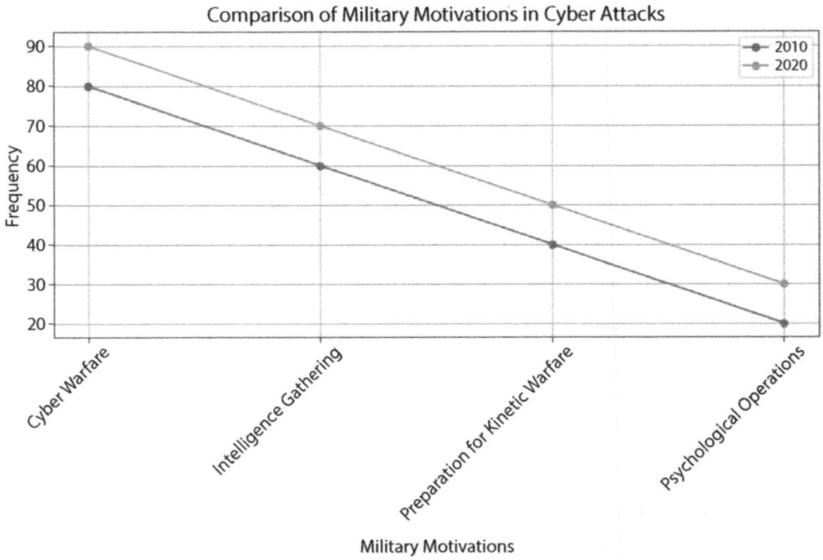

Figure 13.5 Comparison of military motivations in cyber-attacks.

ideologies. Militarily motivated cyber operations seek to gather intelligence, disrupt enemy capabilities, and prepare for physical conflicts. By recognizing these motivations, cybersecurity professionals and policymakers can better anticipate threats and implement comprehensive defenses. Figure 13.5 provides the comparison of military motivations in cyber-attacks.

13.3 Types of Cyber Threats: From Viruses to Data Breaches

This section delves into various cyber threats, from traditional viruses to sophisticated data breaches, shedding light on their characteristics, impacts, and mitigation strategies [8].

Viruses and Malware:

- Infecting computers and replicating themselves in order to propagate to other systems is the primary function of viruses, which are harmful software programs. Because they frequently attach themselves to legal files or applications, they have the potential to corrupt data, cause the system to crash, and provide unauthorized access.

- Malware that replicates itself and spreads across computer systems and networks without the assistance of a human being is known as a worm. Worms are able to swiftly spread and wreak extensive damage because they take use of flaws in the protocols and software that are used by networks.
- Trojan horses: By granting attackers unauthorized access to infected computers, they make it possible for them to steal data, conduct surveillance, or further corrupt the system.
- Ransomware is a type of malicious software that encodes files or locks down computers, which have severe repercussions for individuals, businesses, and vital infrastructure.

Phishing and Social Engineering:

- **Spear Phishing:** Targeted at specific individuals or organizations, spear phishing attacks leverage personalized information to increase success rates. Highly convincing emails exploit social connections or organizational hierarchies to deceive recipients.
- **Manipulation in Cybersecurity:** This involves using manipulative techniques to exploit human psychology in order to deceive individuals into revealing sensitive information or taking actions contrary to their best interests. Methods include pretexting, baiting, and various forms of psychological manipulation, focusing more on influencing behavior than on exploiting technical vulnerabilities.

Data Breaches and Insider Threats:

- **Data Breaches:** Instances involving unauthorized access to sensitive or confidential information, leading to its exposure, theft, or misuse. These breaches can stem from various causes, such as system vulnerabilities, inadequate security controls, or malicious insider activities.
- **Insider Threats:** Risks emanating from individuals within an organization who misuse their access privileges or deliberately breach security policies for personal gain or malicious intents. These threats may involve employees, contractors, or partners abusing their entrusted access to sensitive data, resulting in data breaches, theft of intellectual property, or acts of sabotage [9].

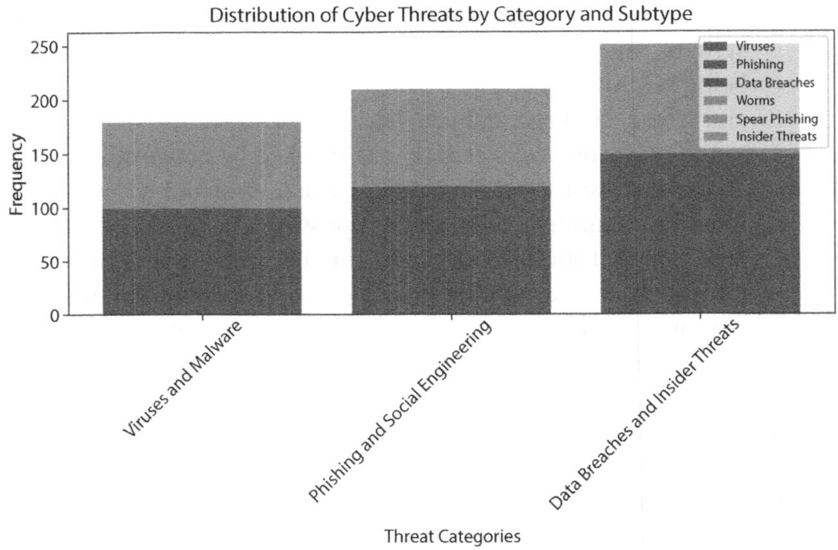

Figure 13.6 Various distribution of cyber threats by category and subtype.

From viruses and malware to phishing attacks and data breaches, organizations are able to create proactive defense plans and implement adequate controls to limit risks and secure their digital assets if they have a thorough awareness of the characteristics and implications of all the different cyber threats, which was given in Figure 13.6. Effective cybersecurity demands a holistic approach that addresses both technical vulnerabilities and human elements, stressing the significance of ongoing vigilance, education, and collaboration in combating cyber threats.

13.4 Impact of Cyber Attacks on Businesses and Governments: Financial and Operational Consequences

Cyber-attacks have become a widespread threat to businesses and governments alike, causing disruptions in operations, compromising sensitive information, and leading to considerable financial damage. Recognizing the extensive impact of these attacks is essential for developing robust cybersecurity strategies and minimizing their adverse effects. This section delves into the significant repercussions of cyber-attacks on organizations and governmental bodies, emphasizing the financial and operational challenges that arise from these incidents [10].

Financial Consequences:

- **Direct Financial Losses:** It is common for cyberattacks to result in direct financial losses, such as the theft of finances, the payment of extortion, and the destruction of infrastructure and individual goods. It is possible for these losses to reach to millions of dollars for businesses, which includes the price of remediation, litigation costs, and regulatory fines. Government agencies may also incur significant expenses in restoring critical services, compensating affected parties, and enhancing cybersecurity infrastructure.
- **Indirect Financial Costs:** Beyond immediate financial losses, cyber-attacks impose indirect costs on businesses and governments, such as loss of revenue due to operational disruptions, decline in customer trust and loyalty, and decreased market value. These intangible losses can have long-term repercussions, impacting competitiveness, investor confidence, and brand reputation.

Operational Consequences:

- **Disruption of Operations:** Cyber-attacks disrupt normal business and government operations, causing downtime, delays in service delivery, and interruption of essential functions. For businesses, operational disruptions can result in missed deadlines, loss of productivity, and inability to fulfill customer orders, leading to reputational damage and loss of market share. Governments may face challenges in providing critical services, enforcing regulations, and maintaining public trust and confidence.
- **Damage to Infrastructure:** Infrastructure damage is a common consequence of cyber-attacks, particularly in the case of targeted attacks. Breaches of infrastructure systems can lead to physical damage, loss of control over critical assets, and compromise of public safety. The WannaCry ransomware attack, for instance, disrupted operations at numerous healthcare facilities worldwide, highlighting the vulnerability of essential infrastructure to cyber threats.

Mitigation Strategies:

- **Invest in Comprehensive Cybersecurity Measures:** It's imperative for businesses and governments to allocate resources towards robust cybersecurity measures. This includes implementing advanced intrusion detection systems, fortified endpoint protection software, encryption technologies to secure sensitive data, and comprehensive employee training programs. By adopting a proactive stance towards cybersecurity, organizations.
- **Strengthen Incident Response Capabilities:** Building effective incident response plans and protocols is paramount in minimizing the impact of cyber-attacks. Businesses and governments should prioritize regular drills, simulations, and tabletop exercises to assess and refine their response capabilities. These exercises enable organizations to swiftly detect, contain, and recover from cyber incidents, thereby reducing downtime, financial losses, and reputational damage.
- **Enhance Cooperation and Knowledge Exchange:** Fostering collaboration and sharing information between businesses, government agencies, and cybersecurity professionals is crucial in combating cyber threats. By creating a cooperative

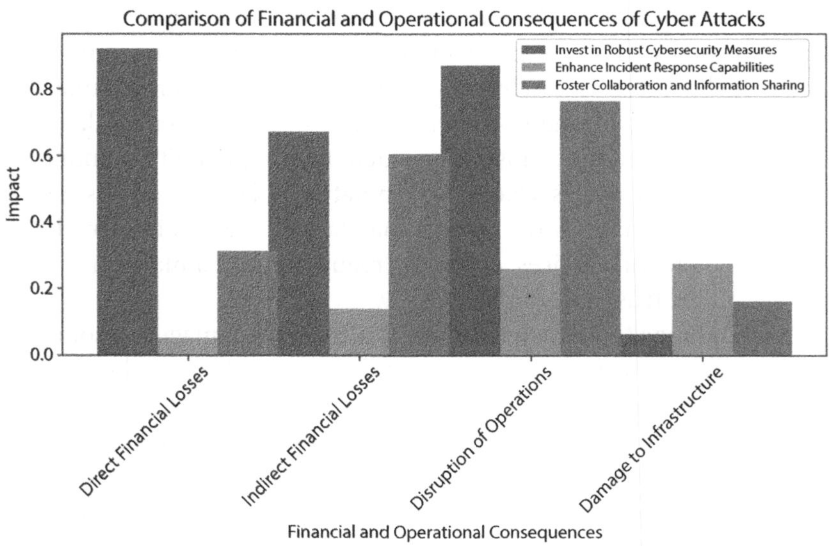

Figure 13.7 Financial vs. operational consequences of cyber-attacks.

environment, organizations can trade valuable threat intelligence, disseminate best practices, and gain insights from previous incidents. This united approach strengthens overall defenses and improves responses to cyber-attacks, thereby reducing their financial and operational repercussions on a larger scale [11]. Figure 13.7 provides the consequences of cyber-attacks over operational vs financial.

Cyber-attacks present considerable financial and operational threats to both businesses and governments, highlighting the necessity for proactive cybersecurity practices and robust incident response strategies. By understanding the multifaceted impact of cyber-attacks and implementing comprehensive mitigation strategies, organizations can safeguard their assets, preserve their operational continuity, and protect the interests of stakeholders against evolving cyber threats.

13.5 Strategies for Cyber Security: Prevention, Detection, and Response

In the modern digital world, robust cybersecurity strategies are essential for protecting sensitive data, maintaining operational stability, and defending against harmful cyber threats. This section explores crucial cybersecurity strategies, emphasizing measures for prevention, detection, and response to effectively manage the risks associated with cyber-attacks [12].

Prevention:
Prevention strategies entail proactive measures intended to diminish the likelihood of cyber-attacks and reinforce defense mechanisms against potential threats. These encompass:

- To prevent unauthorized users from accessing systems and data, it is necessary to implement stringent controls on access and verification measures.
- For the purpose of addressing known vulnerabilities and security problems, it is necessary to perform routine software and system updates and patches.
- Using encryption methods to protect sensitive data while it is both in transit and while it is stored, thereby preventing unauthorized access and interception of the data.

- The implementation of antivirus programs, intrusion detection systems (IDS), and intrusion prevention technologies (IPS) for the purpose of monitoring network traffic and detecting and blocking hostile actions in real time in a timely manner.

Detection: Detection strategies concentrate on identifying and promptly responding to cyber threats and security incidents to minimize their impact. Key detection measures include:

- Carrying out security audits, vulnerability scans, and penetration tests on a regular basis in order to proactively detect vulnerabilities and flaws in computer systems and networks.
- Putting in place protocols and procedures for detecting and responding to emergencies in order to facilitate the rapid identification, evaluation, and management of security breaches and incidents.
- Making use of threat intelligence feeds as well as data sharing platforms in order to keep up with evolving threats and attack patterns, and modifying defense measures in accordance with these developments.

Response: Response strategies involve efficiently addressing security incidents and breaches to mitigate their impact, restore normal operations, and prevent future occurrences [19]. These encompass:

- Developing and implementing incident response plans and playbooks outlining roles, responsibilities, and procedures for responding to security incidents and breaches.
- Establishing incident response teams comprising individuals with specialized skills in cybersecurity, forensic analysis, legal, and communications to coordinate response efforts and manage the incident lifecycle.
- Conducting post-incident analysis and lessons learned sessions to identify gaps, weaknesses, and areas for improvement in incident response processes and procedures.
- Maintaining transparent communication with stakeholders, including employees, customers, partners, regulators, and law enforcement, to provide timely updates and information about security incidents and their resolution.

Effective cybersecurity necessitates a multi-layered approach encompassing prevention, detection, and response strategies to mitigate the evolving threats posed by cyber-attacks. Increasing their resistance to cyber assaults and protecting their critical resources and operations accomplished by organizations through the implementation of preventative measures for avoiding incidents, the utilization of cutting-edge technologies to perform early threat detection, and the establishment of robust incident handling capabilities.

13.6 Evolving Threat Landscape: Keeping Pace with Emerging Cyber Threats

In the rapidly changing digital world, the landscape of cyber threats is continuously shifting due to technological progress, changes in attack strategies, and the growing sophistication of cybercriminals. This section examines how cyber threats are evolving and underscores the importance for organizations to stay alert and flexible to effectively address new and emerging risks [13].

Rapid Technological Advancements: The rapid advancement of technology, including innovations in artificial intelligence (AI), the Internet of Things (IoT), cloud computing, and mobile tech, has greatly broadened the potential attack surface. These developments create new vulnerabilities that cybercriminals can target. Additionally, emerging technologies such as quantum computing and 5G networks present both exciting opportunities and significant challenges for cybersecurity, introducing new capabilities and complexities that could be exploited by malicious actors.
Sophistication of Cyber Threats: Cyber threats have grown increasingly sophisticated and diverse, spanning traditional malware and phishing attacks to advanced persistent threats (APTs), ransomware, and supply chain attacks. To avoid being detected, infiltrate networks, and obtain sensitive information for different reasons such as financial gain, espionage, or causing disruption.
Expanding Attack Surface: The proliferation of connected devices, remote work environments, and digital ecosystems has considerably expanded the attack surface. This expansion provides cybercriminals with numerous opportunities to exploit vulnerabilities and target individuals, businesses, and critical infrastructure. Remote access technologies, third-party services, and cloud-based applications create new entry points for attackers to

infiltrate networks and compromise systems, necessitating the implementation of robust security measures and risk mitigation strategies.

Adapting Security Posture: To effectively tackle the continuously changing cyber threat landscape, organizations must adopt a proactive and flexible approach to cybersecurity. It is important to consistently evaluate and enhance their security measures in order to effectively manage changing risks and vulnerabilities. It involves making investments in cutting-edge detection and reaction capabilities, utilizing risk intelligence and statistical analysis to detect and address emerging threats, and improving communication and knowledge exchange with other business colleagues and cybersecurity experts.

Embracing a Culture of Security: It is essential to foster an environment of security awareness in order to empower staff as well as stakeholders to identify and address cyber threats with efficiency. It is crucial for organizations to give utmost importance to security awareness training and education programs. These initiatives should focus on promoting best practices, raising risk awareness, and establishing incident response protocols. By doing so, organizations can enhance their resilience and minimize the impact of human errors in cyber-attacks [14].

Given the constantly changing nature of threats, it is crucial for organizations to maintain a watchful, flexible, and forward-thinking approach

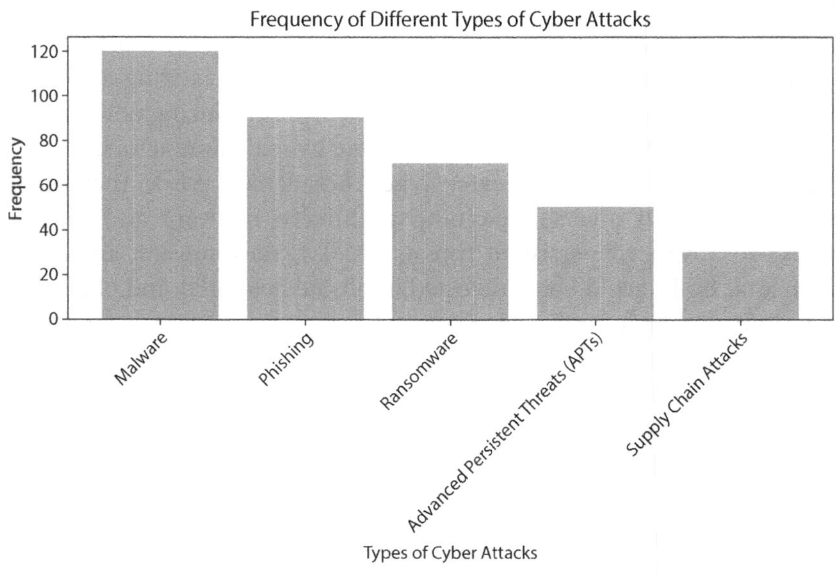

Figure 13.8 Frequency of several types of cyber-attacks.

to cybersecurity. By embracing technological advancements, improving detection and mitigation features, and fostering a strong culture of security understanding, organizations can proactively stay on top of emerging online dangers and safeguard their valuables, operations, and credibility in an ever-evolving digital landscape, which was given in Figure 13.8.

13.7 Exploring Global Cyber Security Initiatives: Collaborative Efforts and Best Practices

In our increasingly interconnected world, cyber threats now cross geographical and sectoral boundaries, posing growing challenges to the global community. To tackle these issues effectively, collaboration and adherence to best practices in cybersecurity have become essential. This section examines important initiatives, partnerships, and best practices in cybersecurity, emphasizing the critical role of cooperation and knowledge-sharing in reducing cyber risks [15].

Global Collaborative Efforts:
International collaborative initiatives unite governments, private sector entities, academia, and non-governmental organizations (NGOs) to foster cooperation, share information, and build capacity in cybersecurity on a global scale. It plays pivotal roles in facilitating multilateral dialogues, policy discussions, and joint initiatives aimed at addressing cyber threats and promoting cyber resilience.

Information Sharing Platforms:
Information sharing platforms serve as conduits for exchanging threat intelligence, best practices, and cybersecurity insights among stakeholders, facilitating timely detection and response to cyber threats. Organizations to collaborate, share threat data, and coordinate response efforts, ultimately strengthening the collective resilience against cyber threats.

Cybersecurity Capacity Building:
Cybersecurity capacity building initiatives aim to enhance the resilience of individuals, organizations, and nations against cyber threats through education, training, and skill development programs.

International organizations, governments, and industry stakeholders invest in capacity building efforts, such as cybersecurity awareness campaigns, professional certifications, and technical training workshops.

Best Practices and Standards:
Best practices and cybersecurity standards provide guidelines and frameworks for organizations to establish robust cybersecurity policies, procedures, and controls.

Initiatives such as the NIST Cybersecurity Framework, ISO/IEC 27001, and the European Union Agency for Cybersecurity (ENISA) guidelines offer comprehensive frameworks for risk management, governance, and compliance, enabling organizations to align their cybersecurity efforts with international best practices and standards.

Global cybersecurity initiatives, collaborative efforts, and established best practices are crucial for boosting cyber resilience, facilitating information exchange, and fortifying defenses against cyber threats worldwide. By fostering collaboration, sharing knowledge, and adopting international best practices and standards, the global community can collectively address cyber threats, safeguard critical infrastructure, and ensure a secure and resilient cyberspace for all stakeholders [16].

13.8 Cyber Security Frameworks: Origins, Evolution, and Effectiveness

Cybersecurity frameworks serve as fundamental structures for organizations to establish, implement, and manage effective cybersecurity programs. They offer guidance, best practices, and standardized approaches for assessing, managing, and mitigating cyber risks. This section delves into the origins, evolution, and effectiveness of cyber security frameworks, emphasizing their importance in bolstering cyber resilience and advocating a proactive stance toward cybersecurity.

Origins of Cyber Security Frameworks:

- The need for standardized cybersecurity methods became clear with the advancement of digital technologies and the increasing complexity of cyber threats in the late 20th century.
- Initial cybersecurity frameworks, including the Trusted Computer System Evaluation Criteria (TCSEC) and the Information Technology Infrastructure Library (ITIL), established fundamental security requirements, controls, and practices across different areas.

Evolution of Cyber Security Frameworks:

- The evolution of cyber security frameworks has been propelled by technological advancements, shifts in the threat landscape, and the growing acknowledgment of cybersecurity as a critical business concern.
- Frameworks like the NIST Cybersecurity Framework, ISO/IEC 27001, and the PCI DSS have emerged as widely recognized standards for addressing cybersecurity risks, management, and conformity [17].

Key Cyber Security Frameworks:

- The NIST Cybersecurity Framework (framework provides organizations with a voluntary way to evaluate and enhance their information security position by utilizing industry standards and best practices.
- ISO/IEC 27001 is a worldwide standard that provides guidelines for organizations to establish and maintain a system for managing information security (ISMS). It focuses on the necessities for establishing and continually strengthening the system to ensure the security of information.
- The CIS Controls were developed by the Centre for Internet Security (CIS) and provide a prioritized list of measures for cybersecurity defense. These controls are based on real-world risks and weaknesses, ensuring effective protection.

Effectiveness of Cyber Security Frameworks:

- Cyber security frameworks equip organizations with structured methodologies to identify, assess, and mitigate cyber risks, empowering them to fortify resilience against evolving threats and regulatory mandates.
- Through the adoption of cyber security frameworks, organizations can streamline compliance endeavors, enhance security posture, and refine risk management practices.
- Nonetheless, the efficacy of cyber security frameworks hinges on their implementation, customization to organizational requisites, and continual monitoring and evaluation to ensure alignment with evolving threats and business imperatives.

- Cyber security frameworks have progressed from nascent standards to comprehensive frameworks that provide organizations with structured methodologies for cybersecurity risk management and compliance.

13.9 Emerging Trends in Cyber Security: AI, Blockchain, and IoT Solutions

In the ever-evolving realm of cybersecurity, emerging trends significantly influence the future landscape of cyber defense.

Artificial Intelligence (AI) in Cybersecurity:

- AI is revolutionizing cybersecurity by improving threat detection, automating responses, and augmenting human capabilities.
- By employing machine learning algorithms, AI scrutinizes extensive datasets in real-time to pinpoint patterns, anomalies, and potential security threats, thereby enabling proactive defense strategies.
- AI-powered security solutions adapt to evolving threats, forecast attack trends, and prioritize alerts, empowering organizations to mitigate risks more effectively and respond swiftly to security incidents [18].

Blockchain Technology for Enhanced Security:

- Blockchain technology provides decentralized and resistant platforms for protecting sensitive data, transactions, and digital assets.
- The unchangeable nature of blockchain records guarantees data integrity and transparency, reducing the risks of data manipulation, fraud, and unauthorized access.
- Blockchain applications in cybersecurity include secure identity management, decentralized authentication, and reliable data sharing between trusted entities, which diminishes dependence on centralized systems and reduces single points of failure.

Internet of Things (IoT) Security Solutions:

- The rapid increase in IoT devices brings about new security challenges, such as weaknesses in devices and concerns regarding the privacy of data.
- IoT security solutions employ various measures to ensure the safety of IoT devices, systems, and information transmissions. These measures include authentication, encryption, and accessibility control mechanisms.
- By implementing strong security protocols, regularly assessing vulnerabilities, and using particular safety precautions for IoT devices, you can reduce the risks that accompany deployments of IoT devices, protect vital systems, and keep sensitive data safe.

Understanding and embracing emerging trends in cybersecurity—such as AI-driven threat intelligence, blockchain-enabled security solutions, and robust IoT security measures. By embracing these trends, organizations can fortify their cyber resilience, mitigate risks effectively, and cultivate a secure digital environment. Embracing innovation in cybersecurity empowers organizations to adapt to changing threat landscapes and construct.

13.10 Challenges and Limitations of Current Cyber Security Approaches

In today's interconnected digital world, cyber security stands as a critical pillar safeguarding our data, infrastructure, and privacy. However, this realm is not without its challenges. As technology advances, so too do the tactics and sophistication of cyber threats. This section aims to delve into the multifaceted challenges and limitations encountered by current cyber security approaches [19].

Sophistication of Cyber Attacks: Cyber-attacks have evolved from simple malware to intricate, multi-stage assaults orchestrated by highly skilled threat actors. Techniques like ransomware, where attackers encrypt victims' data until a ransom is paid, or advanced persistent threats (APTs), where adversaries stealthily infiltrate networks for long-term espionage or sabotage, demonstrate the growing sophistication. These attacks often exploit vulnerabilities in software, human psychology through social engineering, or weaknesses in network defenses, making them difficult to detect and mitigate.

Complexity of IT Infrastructures: Modern IT infrastructures have become more intricate, incorporating a wide range of applications. Although these innovations bring significant advantages, they also increase the vulnerability, giving adversaries more opportunities to exploit. In addition, navigating security in this complex environment can be quite challenging, as organizations face difficulties in implementing uniform policies and ensuring complete protection. Moreover, managing security across this intricate landscape becomes a formidable task, with organizations struggling to enforce consistent policies and ensure comprehensive protection [20].

Shortcomings of Traditional Security Measures: Conventional security measures, which were once effective, now encounter limitations in countering advanced threats. These tools face challenges over the malware variants and zero-day exploits. Additionally, their focus on perimeter defense proves inadequate in defending against insider threats or attacks originating from compromised internal systems.

Resource Constraints and Budgetary Limitations: Many organizations, particularly smaller enterprises and non-profit entities, face resource constraints when it comes to cyber security. Limited budgets restrict investments in essential security tools, skilled personnel, and incident response capabilities. Balancing the need for cyber resilience with competing business priorities presents a challenging dilemma for decision-makers striving to allocate resources effectively.

Regulatory Compliance and Legal Challenges: The regulatory landscape surrounding cyber security continues to evolve, with stringent mandates like GDPR and HIPAA imposing strict requirements on data protection and privacy. Achieving and maintaining compliance is a complex undertaking, compounded by the diverse regulatory frameworks across industries and jurisdictions. Non-compliance not only incurs hefty fines but also tarnishes reputations and erodes customer trust.

Global Nature of Cyber Threats: Cyber threats transcend geographical boundaries, with attackers operating from remote locations to target entities worldwide. This global nature complicates efforts to combat cybercrime, as jurisdictional differences and geopolitical tensions hinder international cooperation. Collaborative initiatives and information-sharing mechanisms are vital in fostering a collective defense against cyber adversaries.

Emerging Technologies and Evolving Threat Landscape: As technologies like artificial intelligence (AI) and quantum computing reshape

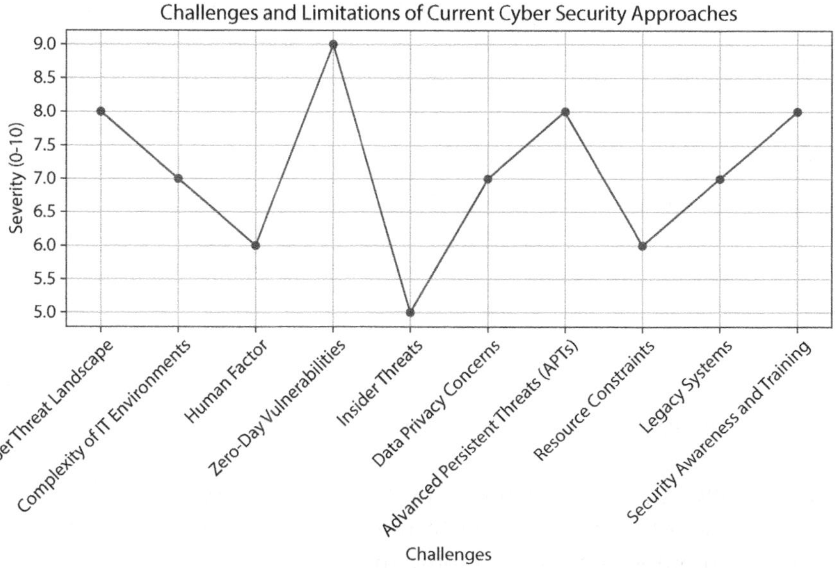

Figure 13.9 Numerous challenges and limitation of cyber security approaches.

various fields, they bring both new opportunities and cybersecurity challenges. AI can improve security by enabling automated detection and response to threats, yet it also has the potential to be used by attackers for more advanced assaults. Meanwhile, quantum computing threatens existing encryption methods, necessitating proactive strategies to update and enhance security measures [21]. Figure 13.9 given different challenges and limitations of cyber security approaches.

13.11 Future Directions in Cyber Security Research and Development

The landscape of cybersecurity is at a critical juncture, marked by rapid technological advancements and increasingly sophisticated threats reshaping our digital world. Looking forward, it's crucial to anticipate forthcoming challenges and proactively implement measures to safeguard our digital assets. This section delves into emerging trends and areas of focus within cybersecurity research and development (R&D), aiming to foster innovation and resilience against evolving threats.

Privacy-Enhancing Technologies and Data Protection: Amid heightened privacy concerns and stringent regulatory requirements, privacy-enhancing

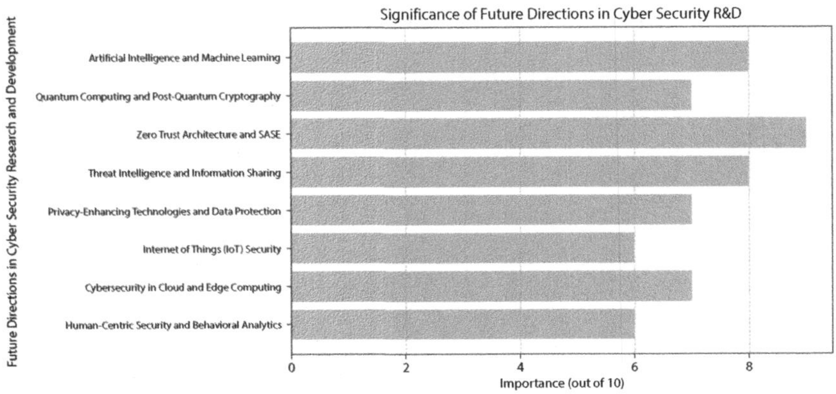

Figure 13.10 Significance of future direction in cyber-attacks.

technologies (PETs) are gaining prominence as essential tools for safeguarding sensitive data. Various techniques, such as differential confidentiality, homomorphic cryptography, and secure multi-party computation, allow organizations to perform analytics while ensuring the privacy of data. Furthermore, innovations in decentralized identity management and privacy-preserving analytics empower individuals to maintain control over their personal information within digital ecosystems. Figure 13.10 shown the Significance of future direction in cyber-attacks.

Cybersecurity in Cloud Computing and Edge Computing: It introduce unique security considerations, necessitating tailored approaches to risk management and threat mitigation. Organizations must implement robust security controls for cloud infrastructure, containerized applications, and serverless architectures. Cloud-native security solutions and DevSecOps practices facilitate seamless integration of security into the software development lifecycle, ensuring continuous protection against evolving threats.

Human-Centric Security and Behavioral Analytics: While technological advancements are pivotal in cyber defense, human factors remain central to security outcomes. Behavioral analytics and user-centric security measures can detect insider threats and phishing attacks by analyzing behavior patterns and identifying anomalies. Security awareness training, coupled with gamification techniques and behavior-based authentication, empowers individuals to actively participate in cyber defense efforts.

13.12 Conclusion

This research underscores the profound impact of the internet on diverse aspects of modern society and the growing concerns surrounding cyber security in today's interconnected world. With government entities, businesses, NGOs, and individuals increasingly reliant on electronic technology, the vulnerability to cyber threats becomes more pronounced. The research highlights the multifaceted nature of cyber-attacks, which range from financially motivated schemes to those driven by political or military agendas. Various threats, including computer viruses, data breaches, and disruptions to data distribution services, underscore the breadth and complexity of cyber security challenges.

This research offers a thorough evaluation of the current cybersecurity landscape by exploring the challenges, limitations, and potential advantages of various strategies. It investigates emerging cyber-attack trends and assesses established security frameworks, highlighting the progression of cybersecurity practices. Additionally, the study covers the evolving aspects of cybersecurity, including new trends, technological advancements, and ongoing issues. This resource is particularly valuable for IT and cybersecurity professionals, providing crucial insights into current conditions and offering strategies to tackle the complex and dynamic nature of cyber threats. Ultimately, the study aims to equip stakeholders with the knowledge and tools necessary to effectively navigate the intricate realm of cybersecurity.

References

1. Zaid, T. and Garai, S., Emerging Trends in Cybersecurity: A Holistic View on Current Threats, Assessing Solutions, and Pioneering New Frontiers. *Blockchain Healthcare Today*, 7, 2024.
2. Oyewole, A.T., Okoye, C.C., Ofodile, O.C., Ugochukwu, C.E., Cybersecurity risks in online banking: A detailed review and preventive strategies applicatio. *World J. Adv. Res. Rev.*, 21, 3, 625–643, 2024.
3. Rao, P.S., Gopi Krishna, T., Rao Muramalla, V.S.S., Next-gen Cybersecurity for Securing Towards Navigating the Future Guardians of the Digital Realm. *Int. J. Progressive Res. Eng. Manage. Sci. (IJPREMS)*, 3, 178–190, 2023.
4. Javaid, M., Haleem, A., Pratap Singh, R., Suman, R., Towards insighting cybersecurity for healthcare domains: A comprehensive review of recent practices and trends. *Cyber Secur. Appl.*, 1, 100016, 2023.
5. Gupta, S., Kumari, S., Sugandh, U., Protecting Children's Data from Cybersecurity Attacks to Prevent Child Sexual Abuse: A Techno-Legal Approach, in: *2023 International Conference on Communication, Security and Artificial Intelligence (ICCSAI)*, IEEE, pp. 1–7, 2023.

6. Sriram, S., Manikandan, J., Hemalatha, P., Leema Roselin, G., A chatbot mobile quarantine app for stress relief, in: *2021 International Conference on System, Computation, Automation and Networking (ICSCAN)*, IEEE, pp. 1–5, 2021.
7. Lad, S.S. and Adamuthe, A.C., Malware Classification with Improved Convolutional Neural Network Model. *Int. J. Comput. Netw. Inf. Secur. (IJCNIS)*, 12, 6, 30–43, 2020.
8. Sarker, I.H., *AI-Driven Cybersecurity andThreat Intelligence: Cyber Automation, Intelligent Decision-Making and Explainability*, Springer Nature, Switzerland, 2024.
9. Al-Hashem, N. and Saidi, A., The psychological aspect of cybersecurity: understanding cyber threat perception and decision-making. *Int. J. Appl. Mach. Learn. Comput. Intell.*, 13, 8, 11–22, 2023.
10. Nilaiswariya, R., Manikandan, J., Hemalatha, P., Improving scalability and security medical dataset using recurrent neural network and blockchain technology, in: *2021 International Conference on System, Computation, Automation and Networking (ICSCAN)*, IEEE, pp. 1–6, 2021.
11. Manoharan, A. and Sarker, M., *Revolutionizing Cybersecurity: Unleashing the Power of Artificial Intelligence and Machine Learning for Next-Generation Threat Detection*, vol. 1, 2023, DOI: https://www. doi. org/10.56726/IRJMETS32644.
12. Camacho, N.G., The role of ai in cybersecurity: Addressing threats in the digital age. *J. Artif. Intell. Gen. Sci. (JAIGS)*, 3, 1, 143–154, 2024, ISSN 3006-4023.
13. Smith, J. and Evan, C., *The Virtual Vanguard: Understanding the Advantages of Internet Banking in Today's Financial World*, EasyChair, United Kingdom, 2024.
14. Familoni, B.T., Cybersecurity challenges in the age of AI: theoretical approaches and practical solutions. *Comput. Sci. IT Res. J.*, 5, 3, 703–724, 2024.
15. Shackelford, S.J., "Protecting intellectual property and privacy in the digital age: the use of national cybersecurity strategies to mitigate cyber risk. *Chap. L. Rev.*, 19, 445, 2016.
16. Thammareddi, L., Agarwal, S., Bhanushali, A., Patel, K., Venkata, S., Analysis On cybersecurity threats in modern banking and machine learning techniques for fraud detection, 2023.
17. Alayli, S., Factors Influencing the Establishment of Clothing Retailers in the Metaverse: The Role of Metaverse Technology as a Mediator. *Dutch J. Finance Manage.*, 5, 1, 22281, 2023.
18. Jones, A. and Ashenden, D., Risk management for computer security: Protecting your network and information assets, Elsevier, United Kingdom, 2005.
19. Bokhari, S.A.A. and Myeong, S., The influence of artificial intelligence on e-Governance and cybersecurity in smart cities: A stakeholder's perspective. *IEEE Access*, 11, 69783–69796, 2023.
20. Jimmy, F., Emerging Threats: The Latest Cybersecurity Risks and the Role of Artificial Intelligence in Enhancing Cybersecurity Defenses. *Valley Int. J. Digital Lib.*, 1, 564–574, 2021.
21. Smith, J. and Thomas, R., *Cyber Cash: Exploring the Edge of Internet Banking in Today's Digital Landscape*, EasyChair, United Kingdom, 2024.

14

Predicting Android Ransomware Attacks Using Categorical Classification

A. Pandiaraj[1]*, N. Ramshankar[2], Mathan Kumar Mounagurusamy[1], Karakanapati Mrudhula[3], P. Lahari Sai[3] and Lekkala Likhitha[3]

[1]*Department of Computing Technologies, Faculty of Engineering and Technology, SRM Institute of Science and Technology, Kattankulathur, Chennai, India*
[2]*Department of Computer Science and Engineering, Saveetha Engineering College, Tamil Nadu, India*
[3]*Department of Computer Science and Engineering, RMD Engineering College, Kavaraipettai, Chennai, India*

Abstract

Android ransomware has become a significant cybersecurity threat, posing serious risks to mobile devices and users' data. To effectively combat this growing menace, predictive models that preserve detect and thwart ransomware attacks in real-time are crucial. This investigate depicts an unusual method for predicting Android ransomware attacks using categorical classification techniques. Data pre-processing is performed to extract and transform essential features from Android applications. Subsequently, the categorical classification model is instructed on a labeled dataset comprising both benign and ransomware applications. The research discoveries demonstrate the effectiveness of the suggested method in predicting Android ransomware attacks with high accuracy. The model shows promising results in identifying malicious applications, thus providing a proactive defense against ransomware threats on Android devices. By implementing categorical classification techniques, the proposed system enables timely identification and mitigation of potential threats, contributing to a safer and more secure mobile ecosystem.

Keywords: Android ransomware, cybersecurity, predictive modeling, categorical classification, mobile devices, data preprocessing, android applications, permissions

**Corresponding author*: pandi.mnmjain@gmail.com

K. Ananthajothi, S. N. Sangeethaa, D. Divya, S. Balamurugan and Shen-Lung Peng (eds.) Securing Cyber-Physical Systems: Fundamentals, Applications and Challenges, (295–308) © 2025 Scrivener Publishing LLC

14.1 Introduction

Android devices are ubiquitous and versatile, enabling communication, entertainment, productivity, and navigation. Android apps continuously evolve, integrating new features over time. Ransomware attacks involve malicious software that encrypts business files, making them inaccessible. The particularly troubling aspect of ransomware is its indiscriminate nature; it targets anyone with a digital presence, regardless of location, industry, or status. From greater concerns to small corporations, government interventions to health care contributors, no one is exempt.

The techniques used by cybercriminals to spread ransomware are getting more and more complex. They use social engineering techniques, take advantage of software flaws, and even cooperate in secret forums to hone their methods. Because of this, ransomware attacks are becoming more frequent and severe, which poses a danger to everyone's cybersecurity.

When analyzing ML-built Automaton malware revealing techniques that leverage characteristics from fixed code investigation, we examine two primary directions of advancement. Firstly, the acquiring procedure alterations from being decoration-driven to facts-driven, reducing reliance on manually crafted features.

Categorization-based approaches isolate raw series of Application programming Interfaces or operation codes directly from binary code, eliminating the need for complex feature engineering. These methods often utilize the success of DL techniques, in NLP tasks but tend to ignore the control-flow information crucial for program analysis. Additionally, many approaches association diverse attributes to enhance the robustness of downriver classifiers. For example, Arp *et al.* integrate different feature sets in the feature galaxy, while Kim *et al.* suggest using multimode realizing to jointly train distinctive characteristics. However, these patterns often treat separate characteristic sets independently, failing to consider the underlying relationships during preprocessing. As a result, current feature representation methods struggle to capture sufficient relationships, which can impair the execution of downriver in behavior modeling [13].

Roughly prevailing studies elucidate ML decisions by examining the weights assigned to individual features, such as distinctive Application programming Interface or authorizations. For example, SVM influences with the significance of its decoration-based attributes. However, only a few NN-constructed detection techniques grant significant descriptions. The challenge of explainability is a fundamental issue with NN-based techniques. Current explanation methods do not investigate the reason behind mechanism issues, making it difficult to recognize hateful code snatches within malware.

We exploit GNN methods for inductive chart-level grouping and introduce a fragment demonstration method called BSS to demonstrate tricky behaviors in Automaton application. The explanation perception is that mischievous code is often fulfilled in multiple clips across vulnerable Application programming Interface. To isolate characteristics, we exclude behavior possessions similar strings and resourcefulness files, focusing instead on three robust properties: call graph, opcode, and permissions. Noting that malware typically exhibits at tiniest one mischievous behavior, while benevolent apps do not, we recommend an application subgraph demise to facilitate the semi-supervised guidance activity [12].

Detecting harmful software (malware) on Android phones is tough, especially when dealing with real-world situations. Also, it's important to understand why a detection system flags something as harmful. So, the researchers created a system called MSDROID to tackle these challenges. It's good at handling real-world circumstances and provides clear rationalizations for its decisions.

We evaluated the performing of MSDROID on a dataset of 81,790 Automaton application collected around six years. MSDROID achieved an accuracy of 97.82%, demonstrating its superiority over state-of-the-art methods by up to 9.15%.

14.2 Background Study

Connolly, L.Y. *et al.*, This paper, we're going to talk about how machine learning can help us catch ransomware and stop it from wreaking havoc. We'll also take a look at some of the biggest ransomware attacks that happened in 2022, including how much money the attackers demanded. This will help us understand the problem better and come up with better solutions in the future [1].

Al-Qurishi, Hossain, M.S., *et al.*, This paper, researchers are looking into how we can better predict and prevent ransomware attacks on these industrial systems. They're exploring different ideas and approaches, like working closely with both cybersecurity experts and people who know a lot about ICS and SCADA systems. By teaming up and sharing knowledge, they hope to come up with better ways to keep these critical systems safe from ransomware attacks in the future [2].

Android, App resources overview, 2020 Imagine you have a security system for your computer that's like a guard checking for bad guys. Right now, this guard uses a method called signature-based detection, which is like recognizing known criminals by their faces. But the problem is, this method can't catch new or disguised bad guys very well. So, researchers are turning to machine learning, which is like teaching the guard to spot suspicious behavior rather than just recognizing faces. Based on their study, they came up with recommendations for the best ways to use machine learning to detect malware. This can help improve computer security and could also be a establishing point for imminent investigation in this area [3].

Android, App resources overview, 2020 In this paper, researchers decided to focus on what the app does while it's running. They used something called System calls, which are like actions or requests the app makes to the phone's system. They set up a special environment to run these apps safely, kind of like a test lab, and then they let the malware do its thing. They kept an eye on all the actions the app took and recorded them. After that, they fed all this data into distinct machine learning demonstrates, like K-NN and DT, which are like smart programs that can learn from data. They found that these models were pretty good at spotting malware and even figuring out what family it belonged to. So, it's like having a smart guard that can tell if a shady character is up to no good on your Android phone [4].

A.P *et al.* developed cross-domain transfer discovering processes for feature-based sentiment analysis. Traditional methods involve training classifiers on aspects from a source province and pertaining them to a target domain, which can lead to inconsistencies. To address this, the Cross-domain method was proposed. This method includes a label breeding procedure for feature lineage from unrelated networks, using morphological attributes as a bridge for the transfer. Experimental results on both labeled and unlabeled data demonstrated that this approach outperforms existing methods [6].

Ray and Chakrabarti proposed a deep knowledge approach for extracting aspects from textual content and evaluating user sentiment. They combined this deep knowledge approach with an instruction-based method, leading to improvements in both the attribute descent development and emotion grading. The technique accomplished an overall accuracy of 0.87, superior the accuracy of presented methods and establishing its effectiveness [7].

Jagdale *et al.* focused on analyzing product criticisms using machine learning procedures They began by selecting several online stages, including Facebook, Twitter, Amazon, and others significantly influence invention sales and supply valuable customer criticisms. They acquired a dataset from Amazon containing reviews of products such as cameras, mobile phones, laptops, tablets, televisions, and video reconnaissance techniques.

The study utilized machine learning to analyze both positive and negative customer reviews, testing procedures such as SVM and Naive Bayes [8].

Machine learning-built Automaton malware recognition learning can be divided into 2 major approaches: stable investigation and dynamical investigation. Stable investigation involves extracting evidence from the Android Package Kit (APK) installation profile to gather details about the manifest, agreements, Application programming Interface calls, intentions, and more [5]. In contrast, dynamical analysis monitors an request's behavior—such as logical mistakes, combined remembrance usage, scheme call, and progressions—while it runs in a sandpile or inaccessible environment. While stable analysis is advantageous due to its lack of ecological setup requirements and shorter execution time, dynamic investigation offers resilience against code obfuscation techniques [9].

Rejwana Islam *et al.* [15] introduced a machine learning collaborative model that combines several algorithms—RF, K-NN, Multi-Layer Perceptron, DT, SVM, and Logistic Regression to categorize twelve main malware classes within a newly issued dataset comprehending a large gathering of both caring and hateful applications. The research also presents a healthy-structured data organization technique companionable with multiple dynamical analysis attribute sets. Successful outlier handling and feature grading processes destroyed 60.2% of the features, even with a substantial error boundary. To further reduce the feature set, PCA was employed, selecting only 45 principal components out of the original 141 features. This reduction in complexity improved model accurateness by 0.8%. In conditions of concert, the recommended subjective polling combination prototypical outperforms all individualistic reproductions in the initial coating, the outmoded mainstream polling prototypical, and relevant studies involving the classification of at least 12 classes. Future work will utilize this technique to other freshly available datasets to evaluate its effectiveness.

M. S. Hossain *et al.* [16] propose a new Automaton ransomware revealing technique established on transfer investigation to focus existing restrictions. This method employs PSO to choose traffic characteristics. Using these selected features, data traffic is classified with DT and RF classifiers. The study examines ransomware cyberattacks in two scenarios: first, identifying ransomware traffic, and second, distinguishing specific types of malware traffic from caring traffic. The particle swarm optimization assisted attribute selection significantly enhances the accuracy of the classifiers. The RF classifier achieves the highest performance in distinguishing ransomware, while the DT excels at identifying exclusive ransomware types. The accurateness enhancements are 2.26% and 3.7% in the first and second situations, correspondingly. The recommended method reduces

56.01% to 91.95% of the attributes and converges rapidly, reaching an optimal value in about ten iterations.

14.3 Scope

The compass of prognosticating Android ransomware attacks using categorical brackets with machine learning is extensive, encompassing the development of a sophisticated system capable of the early discovery and categorization of implicit pitfalls. This approach seeks to assess the threat associated with Android operations, furnishing a visionary defense medium to keep users from the addition of ransomware incidents. The rigidity of the model is pivotal, allowing it to constantly evolve and learn from ransomware tactics, icing sustained efficacy over time. By minimizing false cons, the system aims to maintain stoner trust and help gratuitous dislocations in normal app operations. Integration into the broader Android security ecosystem, scalability to handle different app geography, and adherence to sequestration norms further define the compass, establishing a holistic strategy to robustly address the complex challenges posed by ransomware in the mobile terrain.

14.4 Experimentation

A. Data Wrangling

During data wrangling, we first load the data, then assess its cleanliness, and proceed to prune and hygienic the dataset for investigation. Ensure each step is documented thoroughly and that all cleaning decisions are well justified.

B. Data Collection

The dataset gathered for prediction is separated into a instructing set and an assessment set, naturally using a 7:3 ratio. The records exhibit, constructed using RF, Logistic Regression, DT algorithms, and SVC, is concerned to the guiding set, and established on the examination result accurateness truthfulness set expectation was performed.

C. Data Pre-processing

Data pre-processing is a critical stage in ML used to estimate the mistake frequency of an ML demonstrate, aiming to approximate the actual mistake frequency of the dataset. While validation approaches may not be required if the facts capacity is sufficiently sizeable to represent the inhabitants, practical-world scenarios often involve operating with data tests that might not be fully representative. Pre-processing helps identify missing values, duplicate values, and data types, whether they are categorical or numerical. The facts trial is used to grant a detached estimate of a prototypical fit on the guiding dataset piece pitching the typical excitable factors.

Incorporating the authorization dataset into the representation association can introduce bias into the evaluation process. Although the authorization set is used to estimate a given simulation, it is often employed for repeated valuation. ML experts use these facts to adjust the demonstrate with hyperparameters. Data gathering, investigation, and management of data contents insides and organization can be time-consuming. All through the conduct of data detection, it reliefs to identify your facts and its parcels, which will assistance you decide the procedure to use to make your pattern [14].

Several data visualization responsibilities using Python's library primarily emphasis on handling missing values, which is crucial for quickly cleaning data. It requires less time to draw data and further explore and model the data.

D. Data Validation Process

The leading objective of facts wiping is to identify and rectify mistakes and inconsistencies, thereby improving data quality for analytics and decision-making. A validation dataset, a subset of data withheld during model training, is used to estimate the representation's performing and fine-tune its parameters. This approach optimizes the use of validation and test datasets for model evaluation. The logistic regression procedure uses a straight reckoning with autonomous predictors to forecast a consequence, which can series from -ve infinity to +ve infinity. This algorithm is designed for classifying categorical data, and its effectiveness is measured by its predictive accuracy, often compared to other models to achieve the effective results.

True Positive Rate (TPR) = True Positive/ (True Positive + False Negative)

False Positive rate (FPR) = False Positive/ (False positive + True Negative)

The proportionality of all predictions that are accurate, indicating how often the representation accurately identifies both shirkers and non- shirkers.

Accurateness is the most intuitive metric, representing the ratio of accurately guessed annotations to the total interpretation. One possibly will guess that a high accurateness indicates the prototype is performing well.

Precision is the proportion of optimistic projections that are precise.

$$\text{Precision} = \text{True Positive}/(\text{True Positive} + \text{False Positive})$$

Precision is the ratio of accurately guessed positive annotations to the total guessed positive interpretation. These metric responses the problem: of all commuters labeled as survived, how much subsisted? High strictness corresponds to a low false +ve rate. We achieved a precision of 0.788, which is relatively good.

Recall is the percentage of actual +ve values that are accurately guessed, indicating the percentage of concrete dodgers that the template will accurately guess.

$$\text{Recall} = \text{TruePositive}/(\text{TruePositive} + \text{FalseNegative})$$

Recall thoughtfulness is the rate of perfectly guessed +ve reflections to all annotations in the genuine "yes" class.

The F1 Score is the prejudiced median of Recall and Precision, taking both false positive and false negatives into account. While it may not be as straightforward as accurateness the F1 Score is generally more beneficial, particularly with an irregular class division. Accurateness works best when the costs of false positives and false negatives are related.

General Formula:

$$\text{F- Measure} = 2\text{TruePositive} / (2\text{TruePositive} + \text{FalsePositive} + \text{FalseNegative})$$

F1- Score Formula:

$$\text{F1 Score} = 2 * (\text{Recall} * \text{Precision}) (\text{Recall Precision})$$

14.5 Methodology

While addressing the tricky of malware discovery and family prediction, categorization algorithms play a pivotal role. As identified, malware detection fits into the binary classification category, where the goal is to distinguish between malicious (malware) and benign software. On the other hand, malware family prediction extends into multiclass classification territory since it involves categorizing malware samples into one of several predefined families based on their characteristics, behavior, or origin.

A. Decision Trees

Decision Trees are non-linear extrapolative demonstrates used for both categorization and worsening assignments in supervised learning scenarios. For malware detection, a decision tree could use features like file size, the presence of certain API calls, or network activity to decide if a file is benign or malware. For family prediction, it can further classify a malware sample into specific families based on more detailed attributes.

DTs are implemented in supervised learning scenarios, where the algorithm is instructed on a labeled dataset, requiring that the stored data (X) is accompanying with subsequent output labels (Y). They have categorized structure, comprising of intersections where respectively node act for a judgment based on an attribute of the input data. The predictor function, denoted as h: X→Y, represents the plotting from input space (X) to the output space (Y) based on the learned decision rules [11].

B. Artificial Neural Networks

Neural networks are employed in ransomware detection as part of machine learning-based cybersecurity solutions. The utilize of neural networks allows for the creation of sophisticated models that can learn patterns and features from large datasets, enabling them to identify potentially malicious behavior associated with ransomware.

The rectified linear unit initiation meaning is described as $f(x) = max(0,x)$ It announces non-segment to the demonstrate by outputting the entered precisely if it is +ve; otherwise, it outputs zero.

$$f(x) = \frac{1}{1+e^{-x}}$$

Artificial neurons are equated to logistic regression. In the context of neural networks, neurons are the basic processing units that perform computations. The overall structure of the neural network involves passing input features through multiple layers with ReLU activation functions, and finally, using a sigmoid activation function in the output layer for binary classification.

C. Support Vector Machine

The primary goal of using SVMs in ransomware detection is to create a model that can effectively distinguish between benign and malicious software based on features extracted from the data. The binary classification for the decision function and the optimal hyperplane can be described as follows. For a binary classification problem, where we have two classes, let's denote them as -1 and +1. The determination function for a linear.

Support Vector Machine can be defined as

$$f(x)sign = (\sum_{i=1}^{n} w_i \cdot x_i + b)$$

Here,

- $f(x)$ is the determination task that guesses the class label for the input direction.
- w_i *are* weights associated with each feature.
- b is the preference designate.
- sign is the meaning those outputs +1 if the dispute is +ve, -1 if -ve, and 0 if zero.

The most favorable hyperplane is the one that maximizes the boundary, which is the separate connecting the hyperplane and the closest records spot from either class. The equation of the hyperplane can be expressed as

$$\sum_{i=1}^{n} w_i \cdot x_i + b = 0$$

In Figure 14. 1:

- The blue circles symbolize data points from one class (e.g., benign software).
- The red squares symbolize data points from another class (e.g., ransomware).
- The constant dark line is the optimal hyperplane found by the SVM. This hyperplane maximizes the boundary, which is

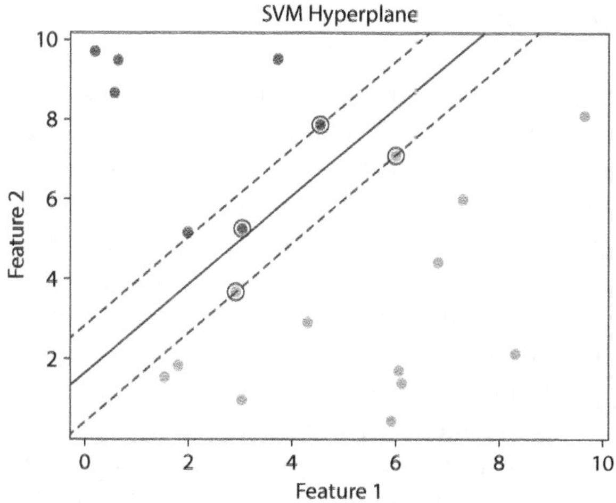

Figure 14.1 SVM hyperplane.

the gap relating the hyperplane and the neighboring records point from whichever class.

- The dashed lines flanking the hyperplane indicate the support directions, which are the nearest data points to the hyperplane and play a crucial role in determining the optimal hyperplane.

D. Random Forests

Random Forests is a powerful ML algorithm that can be effectively used for ransomware detection. This ensemble ascertaining method piece together various decision trees throughout the exercising phase and determines the final output based on the majority class (for classification) or the mean prediction (for regression) of the distinct trees [10].

- Ensemble Learning: RF combines the strengths of multiple decision trees, making them robust and less prone to over fitting.
- Feature Importance: RF can afford discernments into which shows contribute the most to the categorization, aiding in the interpretability of the model.
- Non-Linearity Handling: RF can detention complex non-linear relations in the data, which is favorable for detecting sophisticated ransomware patterns.

14.6 Conclusion

In conclusion, predicting Android ransomware attacks through categorical classification emerges as a pivotal strategy for bolstering mobile security. By deploying advanced machine learning models, the system achieves early detection and risk assessment, prioritizing user protection against the ever-changing ransomware landscape. The commitment to minimizing false positives ensures a user-friendly experience without compromising security. The model's adaptability to new threats and seamless integration into the Android security ecosystem underscore its proactive stance. As the mobile app environment evolves, the scalability of this approach proves essential, ensuring a resilient defense against emerging risks. Overall, the application of categorical classification in predicting Android ransomware marks a significant advancement in fortifying the platform against cyber threats, showcasing the efficacy of machine learning in safeguarding mobile ecosystems.

References

1. Connolly, L.Y., Wall, S.D., Lang, M., Oddson, B., An empirical study of ransomware attacks on organizations: an assessment of severity and salient factors affecting vulnerability. *J. Cybersecur.*, 6, tyaa023, 2020. https://doi.org/10.1093/cybsec/tyaa023.
2. Al-Qurishi, Hossain, M.S., AlRubaian, M.A., Rahman, S.M.M., Alamri, A., Leveraging analysis of user behavior to identify malicious activities in large-scale social networks. *IEEE Trans. Ind. Inf.*, 14, 2, 799–813, 2018.
3. Android, App resources overview, 2020, https://developer.android.com/guide/topics/resources/providingresources,2020.
4. Global Mobile OS Market Share 2023—Statista, Available online: https://www.statista.com/statistics/272698/global-marketshare-held-by-mobile-operating-systems-since-2009/, 2023.
5. Aljabri, M. and Mohammad, R.M.A., Click fraud detection for online advertising using machine learning. *Egypt. Inform. J.*, 24, 299, 341–350, 2023.
6. A., P., C., S., XXXS., P., Sentiment analysis on newspaper article reviews: contribution towards improved rider optimization-based hybrid classifier. *Kybernetes*, 51, 1, 348–382, 2021, https://doi.org/10.1108/K-08-2020-0512.
7. Ray, P. and Chakrabarti, A., A mixed approach of deep learning method and rule-based method to improve aspect level sentiment analysis. *Appl. Comput. Inf.*, 18, 1/2, 163–178, 2019. https://doi.org/10.1016/j.aci.2019.02.002.

8. Jagdale, R.S., Shirsat, V.S., Deshmukh, S.N., Sentiment analysis on product reviews using machine learning techniques, in: *Cognitive informatics and soft computing*, pp. 639–647, Springer, Singapore, 2019.
9. Musikawan, P., Kongsorot, Y., You, I., So-In, C., An enhanced deep learning neural network for the detection and identification of android malware. *IEEE Internet Things J.*, 10, 8560–8577, 2023, https://ieeexplore.ieee.org/document/9845349.
10. Pandiaraj, A., Ramshankar, N., Venkatesan, R., Unlocking the Power of Long Short-Term Memory Networks: A Text Classification Approach, *2023 14th International Conference on Computing Communication and Networking Technologies (ICCCNT)*, pp. 1–6, 2023, doi: 10.1109/ICCCNT56998.2023.10308054.
11. Suhasini, S., Pandiaraj, A., Ramshankar, N., Exploration of Pretrained Models used in Automatic Speech Recognition System: A Review and Analysis. *2023 6th International Conference on Recent Trends in Advance Computing (ICRTAC)*, pp. 150–157, 2023, doi: 10.1109/ICRTAC59277.2023.10480839.
12. Tiwari, N., Gupta, I., Sethi, D., Marwaha, S., Jha, V., A Review on Ransomware Detection in Android Using Feature Selection and Machine Learning. *2024 International Conference on Intelligent Systems for Cybersecurity (ISCS)*, pp. 01–06, 2024.
13. Radhakrishna, T. and Majd, N.E., Edge Computing Ransomware Detection in IoT Using Machine Learning. *2024 International Conference on Computing, Networking and Communications (ICNC)*, pp. 244–248, 2024.
14. Pandiaraj, A., Prakash, S.L., Gopal, R., Kanna, P.R., Ganesh, Generating Art and Music Using Deep Neural Networks, in: *Artificial Intelligent Techniques for Wireless Communication and Networking*, Kanthavel, R., Ananthajothi, K., Balamurugan, S., R.K. (Eds.), 2022, https://doi.org/10.1002/9781119821809.ch7.
15. Islam, R., Tian, R., Batten, L., Versteeg, S., Classification of Android malware using dynamic analysis with ensemble machine learning, recursive feature selection, and PCA. *Internet Things Cyber-Phys. Syst.*, 3, 100–111, 2023.
16. Hossain, M.A., Hasan, T., Ahmed, F., Cheragee, S.H., Kanchan, M.H., Haque, M.A., Towards superior android ransomware detection: An ensemble machine learning perspective. *Cyber Security and Applications*, 3, 100076, 2025.

15

Defense Strategies for Cognitive Cyber-Physical Systems in Machine Learning Domain

M. Karthiga[1], N. Sangavi[1*], V. R. Kiruthika[1], S. N. Sangeethaa[1], P. Ananthi[2] and S. Vaanathi[3]

[1]*Department of CSE, Bannari Amman Institute of Technology, Sathyamangalam, Erode, Tamil Nadu, India*
[2]*Department of CSD, Kongu Engineering College, Erode, Tamil Nadu, India*
[3]*Department of AIDS, Bannari Amman Institute of Technology, Sathyamangalam, Erode, Tamil Nadu, India*

Abstract

Cognitive Cyber Physical Systems merge physical processes with computational intelligence and bring about special challenges and security concerns. Therefore, it is important that the most robust strategies of defense be implemented in order to protect these systems against potential cyber-attacks. Defense mechanisms for Cognitive CPS include Security by Design, Encryption and Authentication, Network Security, Anomaly Detection, Update and Patch Management, Physical Security Measures, Incident Response and Recovery, Regulatory Compliance, User Education and Awareness, Continuous Monitoring, Supply Chain Security, Redundancy and Resilience, Collaboration and Information Sharing, and Privacy Protection. The system of optimal strategies developed, under both cyber and physical defense, is comprehensive for Cyber-Physical Systems with integrated losses in both domains. This paper shows approach in view of interdependence of elements in the cyber-physical system to make an enhancement in the system's overall resiliency. Embedded in the approach is a systematic procedure for the choice of strategies, following the evaluation of potential losses incurred in both the cyber and the physical aspects, and optimizing the strategy of defense to minimize the integrated impact. Equally, it is resource-efficient and integrates with the system architecture, considering that

**Corresponding author*: sangavin@bitsathy.ac.in

K. Ananthajothi, S. N. Sangeethaa, D. Divya, S. Balamurugan and Shen-Lung Peng (eds.) Securing Cyber-Physical Systems: Fundamentals, Applications and Challenges, (309–342) © 2025 Scrivener Publishing LLC

it is compliant with regulations. We have elaborated on the attacks associated with machine learning such as dataset and model poisoning, privacy violation, membership inference, and runtime interference together with the proposed defense mechanisms designed to counter many threats. Furthermore, we have discussed the challenges and the problems associated with ML security in CPS deployment, which includes the accuracy and failure of security mechanisms. User education, continuous monitoring, and scalability complete the criteria so as to make sure that a full-proof and effective defense system is in place. The methodology has been tested and validated through simulations and case studies which yield valuable information on the process of an effective defense strategy planning for CPS.

Keywords: Cognitive cyber physical systems, machine learning, encryption, authentication, supply chain security, anomaly detection, physical security measures

15.1 Introduction

The recent change from localized networks to extensive systems such as Internet have been facilitated the emergence of CPS. These systems integrate cyber and physical components to continuous monitor and control physical processes in real-time. CPS has gained increasing importance in various sectors, including manufacturing, healthcare, transportation, and smart cities. Automation has introduced a new era characterized by the convergence of self-driving cars and agricultural systems with CPS. The networking architecture is also vital for the systems to work harmoniously and effectively, ensuring the collaboration between the physical world and cyber part of systems. The network design, thus, should be extremely reliable, of low latency, and have high data transfer capacity to meet instant operational needs. In a similar vein, most of the CPS systems incorporate redundancies, failover mechanisms, and load balancing in order to efficiently assure service availability during design [1]. In this regard, CPS has to consider several variables, including interconnection, flexibility, security, and dependability. The framework has to allow users and investors privacy. In addition, it has to be scalable, reliable, and safety operation characteristics. It is also mandatory for the system to connect with different systems and scale greater workloads at much ease and without suffering a decrease in its performance level. It is essential to use a broad approach that effectively addresses these challenges in the planning and implementation phases in order for CPS to operate correctly. However, the security issue remains a top priority for the CPS systems as they are exposed to hackers, which may have consequences that cause harm [2, 3]. Adversarial forces can penetrate CPS connections to hold influence over material processes and thus poses security and stability risks. Now, the design of networks of CPS is very important with mechanisms for security that will guarantee total elimination of any risk caused by unauthorized access or attacks. The major components in the process involve IDS, encryption mechanisms, and accessibility control mechanisms [4]. Cyber-Physical Systems are applied in the sectors of smart homes, healthcare, and transportation systems. Although they have wide applications, security and privacy in CPS face a big challenge because of some potential attacks, such as malware injections, man in the middle attack, outflow of confidential information, and unacceptable modification of input information. ML models find their applications in CPS oriented software applications to derive meaningful information with sensors. Accuracy is very important in these models; hence, the different possible attacks in the system could lead to the deformation of its output, which is a wrong result [5]. ML is a computational discipline that uses techniques to train systems on how to perform different tasks to automate workload without necessarily providing explicit steps for each operation. This field has found applications in various sectors, like healthcare, agriculture, and prediction of disasters. It, in turn, can be further combined and applied in different areas such as IoT, CPS, cybersecurity, computer vision, image processing, robotics, natural language processing, and more. That is, ML has many functionalities, which enables the increase of capabilities in CPS for better efficiency and improved reliability in a host of applications. Since ML security is relevant to this work, the understanding stages of ML tasks could be worthwhile. A typical ML task mainly split into 2 phases: (1) Training phase, and (2) Deployment phase.

- Training Phase: In the Training Phase, data initially is collected from trustworthy and authentic sources as a first phase of the training task. The data is thoroughly preprocessed prior to analysis which incorporates cleaning, enhancing, and partitioning to filter out the anomalies and gaps in the records. Further, the dataset is assessed for the category labels and features along with the interrelation between the features. The data is divided into classes to model and validate the number of variable traits and attribute predictions. Feature engineering is a method by which the output can be predicted using an equation that must be applied to the value of a quantity. In order to train ML models, the selected training ML model is fed with data to get trained with the relevant information and potential patterns of the same to compute and establish forecasting metrics. Testing is performed to assess the efficiency of the model for predictions, and test data are taken into account. Then, the process involves tuning hyperparameters to obtain the greatest iteration of ML method and after reaching adequate accuracy, the finalization of the model is performed.

- Deployment Phase : The integrated finalized model is put in this phase on the application or the system is selected with respect to new unseen data. This is the step of implementation, which would be completed in the way of integrating the model with the application and, from that, continuously monitoring is carried out to retain the accurateness of the model. Maintenance also includes periodic updates with the most recent data and retraining if necessary to sustain the performance of the model. Data security is a systematic approach taken toward preserving the information and private data from different risks, such as unauthorized entry, usage, modification, examination, and destruction of data. CIATriad is a framework that guarantees the security of data on the CPS and has key techniques such as privacy, reliability, and accessibility. The first and most important among them is privacy; sometimes, this is also referred to as confidentiality. This can be implemented by restricting access to information and saving it from unauthorized modifications or malicious parties. One way of achieving this is through crypto techniques, for example, encryption using public keys and safety tokens. One is data integrity also known as integrity that further ensures reliability and accuracy of data. Ensuring that usefulness of data is maintained, and that use can be guaranteed in achieving another objective is a commonly implemented principle. This objective can be realized by applying several methods one of them being through versions and access control, through hashing and compliance checking, and maintenance of the data checks. The last would be availability; it guarantees easy use and access of the data by whoever might need them. it ensures regular maintenance by utilizing information storage systems; host surveillance, duplication of storage, solutions to program malfunctions, and application of backup rules are effective methods to mitigate the risks of Denial of Service (DoS) or Distributed DoS attacks (DDoS). The following are essential features involved in domain of safety of information. However, all this should consider other crucial features such as identification, access control, permission, forward secrecy, backward secrecy, and information freshness. In this paper, investigates the intricacies that arise with ML security particularly concerned with CPS. ML security also deals with cyber methods to incorporate protection of integrity and secrecy of an ML module from a cyber-assault. The system uses various defensive techniques to reduce possible attacks that would, in turn lead to the exposure of secure data. Further, it helps contain possible disasters linked to incorrect predictions of the outcomes. With the widespread utilization of ML and its effects on the software used in millions' daily lives, it is crucial to protect our significant data and make sure the deployment of services that rely on the safety of ML runs smoothly. An ML deployment process has to include the application of safeguards against harmful actions. Ensuring security for our machine learning process is important. Correct data training is essential in dealing with private information. The continuous challenges of securing various sorts of information, not to mention preserving ML activities, have become increasingly important due to the substantial increase of technology and large amounts of data advancements.

15.1.1 Background and Motivation

Numerous methods in safe communication had been a reply to the surge in demand the interactions among physical and cyber space within Cyber-Physical Systems. Such kind of networks' safety has been guaranteed so that they run both appropriately and securely by analyzing the safety of communications, thus being able to realize weak points and in this way make the system even more secure. Such security may be enhanced with these measures, further ensuring reliability, safety, and confidence of users and clients in optimal service delivery. The increased concern has put the level of safety in communication methods via CPS that it analyzes to ensure that potential dangers or attacks are minimized. Machine Learning security operates through utilization of many cyber techniques to save the confidentiality and isolation of ML systems against numerous threats and assaults. The model employs preventive measures to mitigate the risk of attacks, protecting sensitive data from potential breaches and reducing the likelihood of providing incorrect results or forecasts. The overarching objective of the survey was to absorb findings from studies on ML security in CPS. Currently, many application domains utilize such interaction environments, including, but not limited.

In the area of ML, models practiced to make predictions about certain occurrences. The literature review has revealed that ML models are weak to various attacks, including modifying the existing dataset, Manipulating the model biases , privacy breaches, runtime disruption, and other membership inference attacks. Given widespread utilization of ML, it is imperative to save the models from potential threats. Therefore, our focus is directed towards understanding the diverse forms of attacks associated with ML models. The mechanisms underlying these attacks had been examined, together with potential preventive measures. The results of this endeavor will prove advantageous for researchers in enhancing the security and resilience of ML [13, 14].

Mechanisms for these attacks have also been studied, and mechanisms to mitigate them. The results of this will be useful for researchers to make the ML secured and increased robustness.

15.1.2 Challenges in CPS Defense

15.1.2.1 Resource Constraints and Real-Time Demands: Security in a Tight Spot

- Limited Resources: A majority of CPS devices, especially those deployed within industrial control systems, have limited computational power, memory size, and battery life. Deploying conventional security mechanisms could be costly and put extra burden on the already overstrained systems [15].
- Real-time Constraints Demand Efficiency: CPS often work in real-time environments where even slight lag can have catastrophic impacts. Security countermeasures have to be designed efficiently with minimum system latency [6].

15.1.2.2 Data Security and Privacy: Balancing Protection with User Rights

- Protecting Sensitive Data: CPS stores a tremendous amount of critical information. It contains industrial control information and even personal health documents. This data has to be saved from illegal access, tampering, or theft [7].

- Privacy Concerns in a Data-Driven World: The far-reaching data collection associated with CPS raises privacy concerns. There is a need for a delicate balance between the security requirements and user privacy. It is this challenge that researchers are working hard to develop robust anonymization and data protection techniques for [8].

15.1.2.3 *Human Factors and Insider Threats: The Weakest Link*

- Human Error: A Persistent Threat: Human error continues to be a major cause of incidents in cybersecurity. In CPS, operational carelessness and inadequate training on the part of operators bring about vulnerabilities that attackers can exploit [9].
- Insider Threats: A Breach from Within: Malicious insiders having legal access to a CPS pose a massive threat. Insider threat mitigation requires efficient access control and extensive record of surveillance on suspicious activities [10].

15.1.2.4 *Evolving Threats: A Never-Ending Battle*

- Zero-Day Attacks: The Unforeseen Threat: Attackers keep on looking for new strategies to get attack wins on existing vulnerabilities. The threat landscape keeps changing, and that translates to the evolving need for monitoring, continuous vulnerability assessments, and quick incident responses [11].
- Supply Chain Attacks: A Web of Vulnerability: The largest supply chains that CPS own may as well introduce vulnerability. An adversary attacking a software or hardware supplier can easily gain access to a large number of CPS deployments [12].

These challenges underscore the complexity of securing CPS.

15.2 Literature Review

CPS are transforming many fields, but their intricate fusion of physical and cyber worlds demand strong security aspects. Utilizing cloud computing and big data in health care applications and employing game theory concepts are discussed too.

1. Securing CPS: Challenges and Solutions

CPS issues have been widely studied from various aspects. Hasan *et al.* [16] targeted current security challenges smart grids are being able to face by means of analyzing protocols and the link between technology, communication protocols, and security standards. These authors give good advice on how one could try to improve security in smart grids.

Intrusion response systems can also be important for protecting CPS from cyber-attacks. Bashendy *et al.* reviewed current intrusion response systems in place and identified RL-based techniques as a promising solution for CPS security [17]. This review will evaluate the latest research work in this area of securing ML tasks from diverse attacks and assuring data privacy. Authors address existing challenges that involve protecting Machine Learning-based Software Systems (MLBSS) [18]. Their aim is to give a full range of security for MLBSS, comprising its risks, available procedures, and expected research work. They further proposed a framework for analyzing these attacks [19–21]. Papernot emphasized the need to secure model integrity and privacy of ML models, discussing possible threats and offering a framework to get privacy-preserving ML [22, 23].

2. Beyond Security: Collaboration with Cloud and Big Data for Healthcare

The healthcare sector stands to benefit significantly from integration of CPS, Cloud Computing, and Big Data. Gupta and Singh [24] emphasized discussing inherent challenges in healthcare and emphasizing potential of CPS to address them through advancements in technology.

3. Game Theory and Resilience Assessment

Tushar *et al.* [25] explored applicability of game theory to CPS, suggesting that various game-theoretic approaches can be suitable for different CPS types. Additionally, Cassottana *et al.* [26] proposed a unique approach for assessing resilience of CPS based on the disruption incidence analysis. They completed a case study for illustrate impact of disruptions on CPS resilience.

4. AI for Enhanced Security

Deep RL offers promising avenues for enhancing CPS security. Rupprecht and Wang [27] focused on applying deep RL algorithms for CPS tasks requiring motor control and resource allocation. While Chen *et al.* provides an effective survey on the adversarial attacks in RL, their work lacked details on potential attacks and comparative studies on existing solutions for machine learning attacks.

5. Machine Learning Security and Privacy: A Growing Research Landscape
ML has become ubiquitous, driving advancements in various fields. However, security and privacy of these powerful models are emerging concerns. This review will highlight recent research efforts to secure ML tasks against diverse attacks and preserve the privacy of data. Difficulties in the protection of Machine Learning-based Software Systems are discussed by authors in [28]. Their objective is to present a detailed survey of MLBSS security, which involves risks, existing procedures, and potential future study areas. They also proposed a framework for analyzing these attacks in [29]. Papernot [30] emphasized the need to secure model integrity and privacy of ML models, discussing possible threats and offering a framework to get privacy-preserving ML. Xue *et al.* viewed many types of security procedure to counter possible attacks for both Neural Network and other than Neural Network models. They even proposed a novel technique to address some of the major security vulnerabilities. Extending this, Liu *et al.* gave an extensive classification of threats against ML models during their training and deployment [31]. They also discussed the available defenses and what needs further attention in research. It is important to embed measures, both corrective and preventive, to minimize possible threats. There is a high necessity to adopt robust security, like encryption, authentication, and many other authorization methods, to be able to ward off potential cyber vulnerabilities [32].

Evtimov *et al.* [34] also proposed an adversarial data generation attack and the efficiency of this attack to manipulate road sign classification models. Papernot *et al.* further explored other security and privacy threats of ML models which are as follows: Adversarial attacks were further elaborated in terms of how they can be performed with complete and limited knowledge of the model. Guo *et al.*'s work and Yang *et al.*'s work showed that the ML models applied in network flow and IDS are vulnerable to adversarial attacks. Song and Shmatikov and Carlini *et al.* discussed attacks that target the classifiers based on machine learning and the natural language generation models used with chatbots and predictive keyboards. These attacks could endanger the privacy of users seeing that; models, tend to memorize user's input. Ateniese *et al.* showed how to actually conduct an attack to establish a relationships to another classifier and gain information regarding the training set. Liu *et al.* offered the state-of-the art findings about the security threats in DL and described the possible adversarial actions at development and deployment periods

According to Rigaki and Garcia, there are two main classifications regarding previous research works on privacy attacks on ML models on the basis of the attacker's knowledge of the model, which are: Researchers such as; Gu *et al.* employed real case scenarios to assess the ML models' weaknesses and potential attacks based thereon. Tramer *et al.* proposed model extraction attacks and it proves that, the integrity of deployed ML models can be violated using prediction APIs or queries. Their research demonstrated how a model might be obtained even if only the class labels are available. Fredrikson *et al.* introduced model inversion attacks where an evil individual seeks to obtain the training data or the users' data by either the manipulation of the model parameters or through model API. Subsequently, Hidano *et al.* extended this study by showing the feasibility of inversion attacks without utilizing the model's any non-sensitive attributes as well as without affecting the model's performance.

6. Privacy-Preserving Techniques and Countermeasures
Al-Rubaie and Chang discussed privacy concerns in ML systems and reviewed potential approaches like homomorphic encryption and garbled circuits for building privacy-preserving models. They also explored countermeasures such as access restrictions and authentication for ML APIs. This review highlights the growing body of research in ML security and privacy. As ML adoption continues to expand, robust security measures and privacy-preserving techniques are crucial for building trust and ensuring the responsible use of this powerful technology.

15.3 CPS Security Fears

The intersection of cyber and physical threats in CPS security culminates in cyberphysical risks, a pressing concern that necessitates immediate attention. Alguliyev *et al.* highlight that their study primarily focuses on cyber pressures, as they pose a significant risk to Industrial IoT security due to vulnerabilities introduced by advanced metering infrastructure and SCADA issues. Cyber-attacks are becoming easier to execute from any device, unlike physical attacks that require physical presence and specific tools. The impact of these attacks is amplified by smart meter's susceptibility to remote threats. Therefore, without sufficient defensive measures and preventive strategies, mitigating and resisting cyber-attacks becomes challenging, a sentiment echoed by Metke and Ekl. The study by Ajiboye *et al.*, examines current security issues, flaws, and techniques for attacking networks and AMI data. In addition, it examines available security solutions and suggests directions for further study, with an emphasis on enhancing security effectiveness while cutting down on communication delays.

CPS systems are also vulnerable to a range of threats, including wireless exploitation, wireless jamming or deauthentication waves, surveillance, remote access, information disclosure, unauthorized access, interception, GPS exploitation, and information-gathering. These threats have potential to cause severe consequences such as industrial espionage, financial losses, and black-outs. Moreover, these threats violate ethical norms and compromise privacy and data confidentiality, integrity, and availability. Physical threats, encompassing physical loss, damage, and maintenance issues, pose a significant risk to CPS security. Substations are less secure and more susceptible to disruption and sabotage, even if power-generating stations are heavily fortified. The most alarming scenario is when a malicious attacker disrupts multiple substations, potentially leading to a complete blackout of large urban areas for several hours. Self healing systems that detect faults or disruptions, contain the issue, and notify relevant management system can help mitigate the risks posed by physical threats to CPS. However, to prevent aggressive theft or physical tampering, it is still crucial to enhance backup capacity for critical components and fortify access controls, authentication, and authorization systems, including password-based, biometric, and access card systems.

15.3.1 Vulnerabilities Posed in CPS

Industrial espionage, alternatively referred to as active assaults or reconnaissance, focuses on exploiting weaknesses inside Critical Infrastructure Protection Systems (CPS) in order to attain a competitive advantage. The identification and mitigation of these vulnerabilities are of utmost importance in order to enhance security, and vulnerability assessment plays a pivotal role in facilitating this procedure. There are three primary categories of CPS vulnerabilities that commonly arise: network vulnerabilities, platform vulnerabilities, and management vulnerabilities. Several aspects, such as assumptions and isolation, growing interconnection, various system characteristics, USB usage, unethical behaviour, espionage activities, system homogeneity, and the existence of suspicious persons, influence the formation of these vulnerabilities. Cyber vulnerabilities represent a substantial classification within the realm of CPS vulnerabilities, comprising the hazards linked to commonly employed standard protocols like TCP/IP and ICCP, which frequently exhibit insufficient security measures. Furthermore, the widespread occurrence of malicious software, including Stuxnet, Duqu, RED October, Gauss, Shamoon, Mahdi, and the Slammer Worm, amplifies the susceptibility of computer systems to cyber threats.

Wireless communications across short distances and open/wireless protocols such as Ethernet are highly vulnerable to a range of assaults, including man in the middle attacks, sniffing, eavesdropping, wiretapping, war dialing, botnets, Trojan attacks, rootkit attacks, and replay attacks. Wireless communications over long distances are also susceptible to intrusion and eavesdropping. SQL injection continues to be a prominent vulnerability in the online realm, enabling unauthorized individuals to get access to server databases. Medical equipment that depends on wireless communications is susceptible to various types of assaults, including jamming, replay, and modification attacks. Smart grid power systems that utilize protocols such as ICS, DNP3, and Modbus have comparable vulnerabilities as a result of their architectural resemblances. In order to guarantee the safety and security of CPS, it is crucial to regularly conduct vulnerability assessments to discover and address any existing vulnerabilities It is very important to take corrective and preventive measures to reduce any possible risks. Taking into account the fact that strong security measures, such as encryption, authentication, and any authorization methods, can be used in protecting from cyber vulnerabilities, it is highly essential to incorporate them.

15.4 Secure Approaches for CPS: In Terms of Technology and Attack Perspectives

With this context, there is a need to put more emphasis on the execution of high-level security operations within CPS because of the increase in cyber-attacks targeting these systems. In this regard, the subsequent section elaborates on several security approaches for Cyber-Physical Systems, with their division into two subsections, namely: those that hinge on the perspectives of attack and those that hinge on the domains of technology.

15.4.1 Security Strategies for Various Aspects of Attacks

The Phenomenon of Eavesdropping Attacks

One of the ways of cyber-attack is eavesdropping, the act of secretly listening to people's communication in a bid to steal data. This is made possible by several means, such as sniffing, packet capture, or wiretapping. Several mechanisms have been proposed to mitigate eavesdropping in CPS. Ju *et al.* proposed a new strategy in which millimeter-wave and physical layer methods are applied to strengthen the level of confidentiality in ad hoc networks. In a related work, Zhou *et al.* proposed a decoding schedule to minimize errors subject to energy constraints. In another work, Golchha *et al.* offered a method for key and digital signature generation using Lattice-based techniques. Furthermore, several other technologies have been proposed: deep learning, long-range key generation, intrusion detection systems (IDS), artificial intelligence (AI), and blockchain.

Phishing Attack

Phishing, in which fraudulent means are applied to get a person's personal details, is another element that brings a lot of risk to the security and safety of CPS. The challenge requires the adoption of a lot of solutions. Ji *et al.* presented a procedure for assessing threats to safety and security in Cyber-Physical Systems (CPS). This consists of attack route models and analysis of safety relevant variables. Rosado *et al.* explained the methodology of a risk analysis on CPS using the MARISMA and eMARISMA models. Another method includes the Intrusion Detection Systems (IDS), blockchain, machine learning, feature selection, and deep learning approaches.

Denial of Service (DoS) and Distributed Denial of Service (DDoS) attack

Denial of Service (DoS) and Distributed Denial of Service (DDoS) attacks severely threaten Cyber-Physical Systems (CPS) to the extent that most of them may lead to infrastructure breakdown. To deal with these attacks, robust security measures are supposed to be adopted. Machine learning and deep learning, in combination with the techniques of threshold and Intrusion Detection System (IDS), are promising methods of solutions for the same.

Malware Attacks

Malware poses considerable threats to CPS, with the potential to inflict major harm on vital infrastructure. Access control, intrusion detection, anomaly detection, and regular software updates are among the detection and mitigation measures employed in the field. Methods such as SOFS-OGCNMD, which focuses on detecting malware, together with ensemble learning, deep learning, artificial intelligence, trust-based techniques, and cryptography, play a crucial role in tackling malware threats. The various security attacks with respect to its approaches are detailed in below Figure 15.1.

Customized security measures are essential in CPS circumstances where standard operating systems are not available. Robust physical security measures, such as lockable enclosures and tamper-evident seals, are required in response to physical assaults. The importance of redundancy in sensing and cryptographic verification of sensor data is underscored by the presence of sensor spoofing or manipulation threats. Hardware-based timekeeping systems and robust protocols are necessary to address time synchronization concerns. The mitigation of side-channel attacks can be achieved by implementing physical shielding, minimizing leakage, and

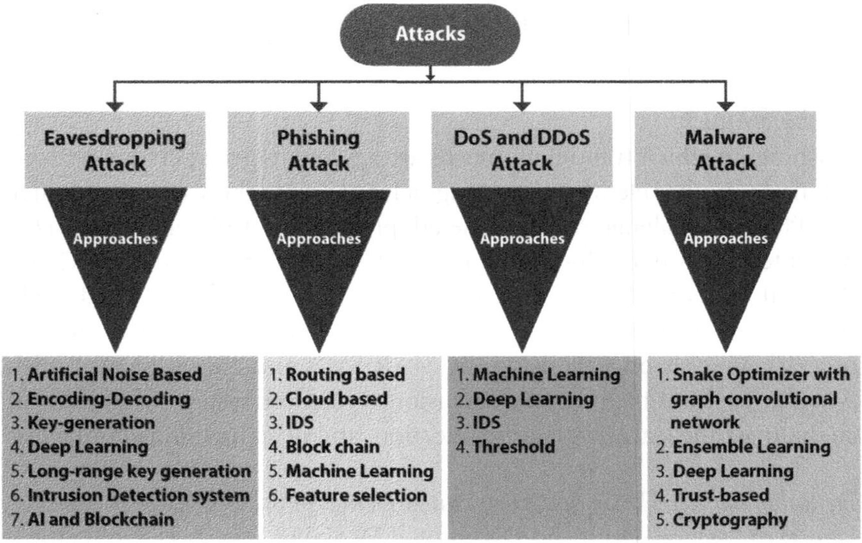

Figure 15.1 Security attacks and their approaches.

utilizing cryptographic safeguards. In order to mitigate vulnerabilities in wireless communication and the supply chain, it is imperative to implement rigorous supply chain security protocols, encryption techniques, authentication mechanisms, and secure communication protocols. In order to effectively prevent fail-operational attacks, zero-day exploits, and social engineering approaches, it is crucial to implement redundancy, fail-safe systems, continuous monitoring, timely patching, and extensive training programs. The aforementioned customized approaches provide strong defense mechanisms against a wide range of threats, specifically designed to handle the distinctive features of CPS environments that lack traditional operating systems.

15.5 Issues and Concerns for Ml Protection for CPS

In the domain of ML security, it is imperative to acknowledge and tackle several potential concerns and obstacles in order to guarantee the resilience of implemented procedures within cyber-physical systems (CPS). The security of deployed mechanisms is crucial for the successful execution of machine learning models. In the event that these models are compromised, the overall performance of the system is adversely affected. Security preservation in machine learning models can be ensured through a variety of mechanisms: from sound authentication schemes, efficient access control schemes—certificate-based and certificateless—to intrusion detection schemes. Accuracy in ML tasks is highly important. This will be less accurate, however, in the case of poor data preprocessing or incorrect selection of machine learning techniques. This means that careful consideration should be made in terms of data pretreatment and choice of machine learning algorithms that are tailored according to the specific scenario and datasets at hand. This is a really critical issue, despite the utilization of many protection procedures, given that there are so many zero-day vulnerabilities that hackers exploit.

Zero-day attacks can therefore stop or disrupt the functioning of machine learning models for the same reason. Therefore, it is very important to implement efficient IDS, which uses a hybrid anomaly detection technique with both signature-based and anomaly-based detection. The ML security ecosystem involves a variety of machine-learning techniques and security computations: from encryption and digital authentication to stability, each of which with its constraints and limits, all impacting interoperability. The importance of ensuring that there is compatibility across the different algorithms cannot be overstated, since it must be carefully thought through and integrated to tackle possible interoperability challenges.

Obsolescence: This raises questions about the potential obsolescence of some machine learning methods, safety computations, and communication-related technology. The only way this can be fixed is through continued periodic updates to support the changes in technology. This will imply the phasing out of old tools and technologies in favor of modern substitutes that will make machine-learning tasks resilient. We discussed a number of issues and challenges for the security of ML in cyber-physical systems within this section. These include mechanisms for secure deployment, worries related to accuracy, potential failure of security mechanisms, challenges associated with interoperability, and the challenge of getting outdated. In the following section, we present the various types of attacks on machine learning models and describe the countermeasures that can be employed to resist such attacks.

15.5.1 ML Model Attacks and the Relevant Measures for Prevention

This section goes over the broad categories that attacks on ML models can broadly be divided into. These include dataset poisoning attacks which can either be real-time or during training, model poisoning attacks, privacy breach, model inversion attacks, and runtime disruption attacks. Figure 15.2 illustrates pictorially the possible weak links in a machine learning pipeline. These mentioned points serve as the focal sites of interference intending to disrupt the operations and breach privacy, leading towards an alteration in the correctness of the model. Now, let's explain the details of each category:

- Dataset Poisoning Attack: In this kind of attack, adversaries intentionally inject examples that are biased in datasets, intending the predictions to be inaccurate from the focused model.
- Model Poisoning Attack: In this type of attack, it is an integrity and model functioning attack, the manipulations of internal mechanisms of a model and change in the parameter.
- Attacks on Privacy Breach: These types of attacks focus to finally compromise the privacy and confidentiality of the user's sensitive data to gain useful information from the model. This raises huge risks to data security and privacy.
- Runtime Disruption Attack: The runtime disruption attacks occur when unauthorized users attack the running machine learning workflow by interrupting the model's ability to produce the right and good predictions when it is running. There can be a system crash or misleading results from the model.

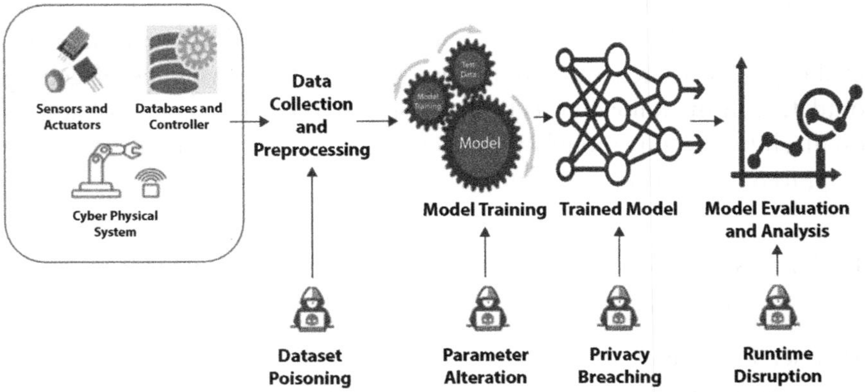

Figure 15.2 Attack checkpoints during ML process flow.

These attack categories take the form of several techniques whose objective is to compromise the integrity, confidentiality, and utility of the machine learning models. In the following sections, we discuss each type of attack in more detail and the techniques, their possible impact, and mitigation strategies to minimize the negative effect.

15.5.1.1 *Dataset Poisoning Attacks*

Dataset poisoning attacks are the diversified strategies of adversaries used to penetrate the training and testing data that eventually disrupt normal operation for machine learning activities. Adversaries use adversarial instances to target sources of data, be it in a server or a data lake acting as a repository for raw data and images. The exposure of different sources of data opens the door to the implementation of modified data, and thus affects the model's performance. Finally, these modifications yield inaccurate outputs that the classifier makes, and this can have grave consequences, for instance, classifying a patient's health state as normal while the reality is that the patient has a severe disease. Figure 15.3 describes the effects and impacts of dataset poisoning attacks on a machine learning

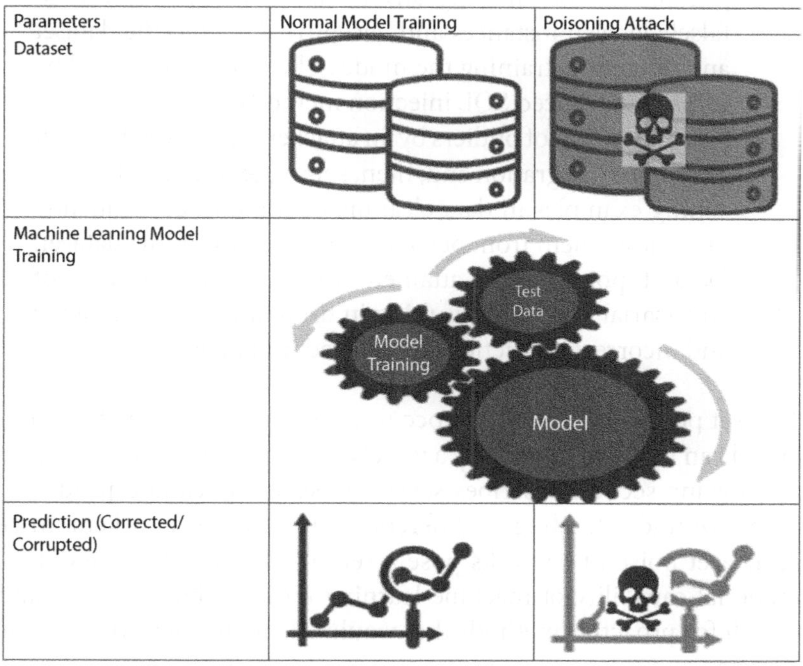

Figure 15.3 Dataset poisoning attack – a sample.

model. It shows how the inclusion of poisoned data—for example, adversarial examples—weakens the classifier's capabilities in building precise and trustworthy predictions. Adversarial examples constitute one of the main challenges to machine learning because they destroy the capacity of classifiers to make correct predictions even in test and training phases. To effectively mitigate such attacks, there is a dire need to understand them comprehensively from the attacker's perspective.

Dataset Poisoning Attack Mechanism

This section explains in detail the methodology of dataset poisoning attacks, enumerating the steps that an attacker can take to execute a dataset poisoning attack:

- The first aspect of the attacker's strategy is to study the machine learning environment, with emphasis on identifying the data lake or warehouse where the training data is maintained or accessed.
- This process involves detecting breach points in the data flow and after that, changing the regular input data flow with adversarial samples.
- The process of injecting adversarial instances pertains to falsely labeled instances and deceptive data into the dataset and, therefore, training the model. This is often achieved by utilizing advanced SQL injection methods.
- The prevention of outliers by an attacker is achieved through a seamless integration and, then, subsequent removal of poisoning examples in data cleaning operations, consequently preventing them from becoming outliers within the dataset.
- Dataset poisoning is attained with a proper number of adversarial examples resulting in dropping model accuracy and incorrect predictions for labeled input data.

Dataset poisoning attacks can occur in the data at training time or real data and can be characterized by a variety of techniques used in the attack. The following section describes several types of attack and produces an informative understanding of different tactics used by attackers. In general, dataset poisoning attacks pose a serious threat to the integrity and operational capability of machine learning models; thus, it is demanded to search for proactive methods that would efficiently identify and reduce these assaults.

Algorithm: Dataset Poisoning Assault Mechanism

```
function DatasetPoisoningAttack(MLi, N, Thresh):

  for i = 1 to N:  # Loop through all deployed models (MLi)
    adversary = AnalyzeEnvironment(MLi)  # Analyze the ML environment
    breachPoints = adversary.IdentifyBreachingPoints()  # Identify breaching points

    for point in breachPoints:
      adversaryExample = adversary.GenerateAdversaryExample(point)  # Generate adversary example

      # Train the model with the adversary example
      MLi.Train([adversaryExample])

      # Prevent adversary example from being identified as outlier
      adversary.MaskOutlier(adversaryExample, MLi)

    # Check if dataset poisoning is successful
    if MLi.EvaluateAccuracy() < Thresh:  # Compare accuracy with threshold
      print(f"Model {i} is poisoned! Accuracy: {MLi.EvaluateAccuracy()}")
      break  # Stop attacking this model if successful
```

15.5.1.2 Black-Box Attack

A black box attack is a scenario in which an attacker cannot see the inner mechanism, functions, parameters, and internal design of the intended machine learning model fully according to the configuration illustrated in Figure 15.4. But the attacker can inspect the feedback or prediction results through analysis, given the adversarial samples. Current research endeavors have been primarily directed on the execution of black box attacks on machine learning models, resulting in a notable misclassification rate of adversarial instances. As an illustration, the misclassification rate of

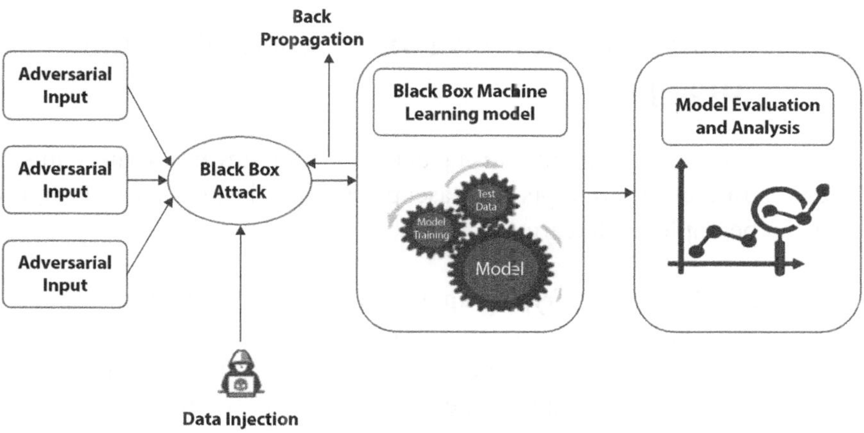

Figure 15.4 Black-box attack – a sample.

84.24% was attained by the researchers through the introduction of adversarial instances into a model. Subsequently, the misclassification rate rose to 96.19% following the calibration process on a model hosted on Amazon Web Services. Black box attacks have also included strategies such as poisoning to generate backdoor instances.

15.5.1.3 White Box Attack

White box attacks, as opposed to black box attacks, provide the attacker with the ability to access the parameters and internal mechanisms of the model.

15.5.1.4 Backdoor Attacks

Backdoor attacks are by far the most widely practiced activity in machine learning, especially on Convolutional Neural Network (CNN) models. Such adversarial data are manipulated in such a way that during model training, a stimulus is activated, hence leading to an input being misclassified when it wasn't misclassified before. Multiple defense strategies have been proposed to mitigate backdoor attacks. These include the activation cluster methodology, deterministic test-time augmentation technique, and a hybrid approach that uses fine-tuning and pruning. Additionally, researchers have proposed methodologies to effectively mitigate dataset poisoning attacks. Methodologies recommended by Aladag *et al.* and Steinhardt *et al.* encompass distinct techniques aimed at addressing the adverse effects of dataset poisoning on machine learning models.

15.6 Countermeasures Against Dataset Poisoning Attempts

It is necessary to implement a strong detection and prevention mechanism to counterattack the attempts of dataset poisoning. The possible techniques that can be implemented are:

- *Application of Cryptography Techniques*: To identify any malicious data injection, developers might make use of symmetric and asymmetric key cryptography techniques. Cryptographic approaches can be utilized to identify outliers within the dataset, hence facilitating the detection procedure.

- *Training an Outlier Catcher*: An outlier detection and an ML model may be developed simultaneously. Because it deviates from typical prediction trends during deployment, this detector aids in the filtering of any data that is considered to be tainted.
- *Tokenization of Particular Data*: Certain data sets, along with the predictions they provide, may be tokenized and kept apart during training. These tokens can be compared during deployment to find any irregularities that might point to an assault.
- *Keeping an Eye Out for Discrepancies*: If the accuracy difference between the training and deployment phases surpasses a certain threshold, it may indicate a possible data poisoning attack that could occur during deployment.
- *Using Generative Models Based on Artificial Neural Networks*: Using generative models based on artificial neural networks in tandem with machine learning models can yield extra verification. Data poisoning incidents can be cross-verified with pre-computed accuracy scores.

15.6.1 Simulated Poisoning Incidents

Model poisoning attacks are conducted by malicious agents who modify parameters to produce wrong output for a given input. This interference can cause the sensitivity limit to deviate, leading to over-fitting or under-fitting of the classifier. The process for conducting the model poisoning attacks are as follows;

Model Poisoning Assault Method

- *Finding Redundancy in the Classifier*: By interacting with the machine learning environment, attackers might find redundancies in the classifier and gain information about possible weaknesses.
- *Training Process Alteration*: Attackers have the ability to alter the training process in order to produce false outputs and publish misleading results, so compromising the model's integrity.

- *Manipulation of Hyperparameters*: Attackers may manipulate the hyperparameters in order to cause the model to fit too closely or too little, which could cause problems for the model during testing.
- *Dynamic Variable Alteration*: Because algorithm parameters can be changed dynamically and are frequently hard-coded, using the method without protection can make attacks more effective.

These safeguards are essential for maintaining the reliability and honesty of artificial intelligence systems by comprehending and lessening the effects of model poisoning assaults.

15.6.2 Countermeasures Against Model Poisoning Incidents

Several precautions can be put in place to lessen the risks caused by model poisoning attacks:

- *Rehashing of Predictive Labeling and Restrictions*: Using hashing methods, users can insert their own hash and vectorize constraints and predictive labels while building a ML classifier.
- *Modify Hash - Hyperparameter Tweaking*: To make sure that any changes to the model are identified and handled, administrators have the ability to modify the classifier's hash over the hyperparameter adjustment stage.
- *Validation of Hash During Delivery*: In order to spot any disparities that would point to possible model modifications, the hash of model that was used can be checked with predicted hash at the process of deployment.
- *Blockchain Execution*: In a secured network context, blockchain technology can be used to store and validate the classifier's hash value, adding an extra degree of protection against potential attacks.

15.7 Vulnerability to Privacy

Users' personal data and machine learning algorithms' mechanisms might get to exposed by various methods, such as unsecured files, lack of encrypted flows during the training and application stages of the

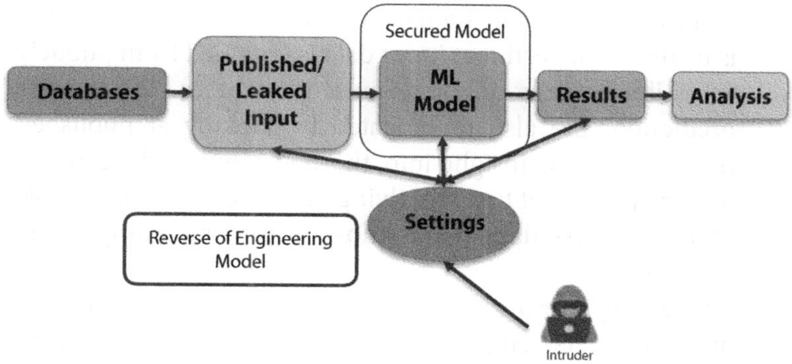

Figure 15.5 API calls based privacy breach on ML model – a sample scenario.

application. Papernot *et al.* emphasized the need for protection for the user's sensitive data by privacy solutions and drew attention to the privacy hazards associated with ML workflows. These techniques certainly change the model the by using noise generation techniques to randomize its behavior in order to provide differential privacy. Additionally, if ML models trained via publicly accessible APIs, which reveal the inner workings of the model, confidential user, data may be jeopardized. By building a dummy ML model, that is exact replicas of the target model and using API calls to obtain edge-case data and prediction outputs, attackers can take advantage of this vulnerability. The behavior of the model helps to understand by comparing this data with the expectations of the goal model. A sample scenario of the privacy breach represented in Figure 15.5. Then, the attacker can take the results issued to build a working machine-learning model that behaves like the target model. One can carry out a number of attacks, including membership inference attacks, using this dummy model.

15.7.1 Process of Reverse Engineering and API Calls Disclosing Sensitive Data

The following actions are involved in revealing sensitive data through reverse engineering and API calls, which is considered a privacy breach attack:

- *Comprehending the Problem Statement*: To determine the target data and results, the machine learning (ML) task's problem statement must first be understood.

- *Data Gathering and Analysis*: Because server authorization is insufficient, pertinent input data is obtained from publicly accessible sources or compromised databases. The model's predictions are also investigated by looking at published results. Gaining insight into the behaviour and decision-making process of the underlying model requires an analysis of the recovered data. This is known as understanding model intuition.
- *Reverse Engineering*: Using the learned insights, an effort is made to reverse engineer the parameters and functionality of the model in order to produce a dummy machine learning model with approximate parameters.
- *Using the fake Model*: Next, to retrieve user data and private information, the fake model is applied to publicly available input resources.
- *Optimization*: To improve the speed of the fake model, API calls are optimized on the original model to fetch particular outputs based on particular input arguments. Steer clear of popular settings that users may trigger in order to avoid discovery.
- Techniques derived from the area of cryptography and in particular from the so-called homomorphic encryption have been used to safeguard data and the model. Also, Ma *et al.* has suggested ways and methods on how the differential privacy can be utilized to train models with minimized privacy loss and, on the same note, Abadi *et al.* has also come up with ways and means of minimizing privacy loss. The privacy schemes were incorporated by Mohassel and Zhang in a distribution context, in the framework of a two server model where the data owners split their data to two non interactant servers for model training using secure two parties computation, in two-party scenarios where protected privacy is mandatory within a federated context.
- To enhance proper implementation of security measures, it is crucial to understand the maneuver of disclosing confidential information through API calls and reverse engineering, which are elements of the privacy breach attack. The steps for the mechanism of the security breach and the specific process of the reverse engineering is shown in Algorithm 2. Another way of launching this attack is through membership inference attacks; details are provided below.

Algorithm: Privacy Breach Attack Mechanism

```
function PrivacyBreachAttack(MLi, N):

  for i = 1 to N:  # Loop through all deployed models (MLi)
    adversary = AnalyzeModelEnvironment(MLi)  # Analyze model and environment

    # Attempt to uncover the training dataset (may not always be successful)
    dataset = adversary.TryUncoverTrainingData(MLi)

    if dataset is None:
      print(f"Failed to uncover training data for model {i}")
      continue  # Move on to the next model if data retrieval fails

    # Analyze the training data to understand model behavior
    adversary.AnalyzeTrainingData(dataset)

    # Simulate a dummy model to interact with the target model
    dummyModel = adversary.CreateDummyModel(MLi)

    # Craft inputs for the dummy model to extract private information
    craftedInputs = adversary.CraftPrivacyProbingInputs(dataset, dummyModel)

    # Use the dummy model to interact with the target model (MLi)
    inferredInformation = adversary.InferPrivateInformation(MLi, craftedInputs)

    # Verify if the inferred information reveals user privacy breach
    if adversary.VerifyPrivacyBreach(inferredInformation):
      print(f"Privacy breach detected for user {i} with information: {inferredInformation}")
    else:
      print(f"No privacy breach detected for model {i}")
```

15.8 Membership Inference Assaults

By inserting personal data into the model workspace and examining its use during model training, membership inference attacks take advantage of flaws in machine learning models. Because the disclosure of membership data jeopardizes confidentiality and presents a number of privacy hazards, this attack scenario poses serious privacy concerns. To quantify and formalize membership inference attacks, researchers have presented a number of attack techniques that give information on potential weaknesses and defenses. Stacey *et al.* carried out extensive membership inference attacks on a variety of datasets, exposing weaknesses, and going over federated learning-related concerns. Milad *et al.* quantified membership inference attacks in both federated and white-box scenarios. In order to evaluate the influence on opponent knowledge, Sablayrolles *et al.* investigated Bayesian learning using noise-injected training data. They also suggested risk-reduction strategies including cropping and rounding. Moreover, in black-box circumstances, researchers have countered membership inference assaults by introducing noise into the dataset, which successfully thwarts inference attempts. Another defensive strategy is to train an autoencoder, which uses adversarial learning to improve defense against certain attacks by focusing confidence scores from the target model on distinct patterns. Figure 15.6 details the membership inference assault scenario.

Furthermore, generative models have been used with differential privacy algorithms to lessen the model's memorization and prevent membership inference attacks. A membership inference attack goes through the following steps:

- The data that needs to be determined for membership status is initially sourced by the invader.
- After that, the target model is reverse-engineered to produce a dummy model.
- After that, the dummy model receives the intended data record in order to make predictions.
- The invader gains the intuition to determine whether the particular data instance was included in the training dataset by contrasting the predictions made by the target model and the dummy model.
- Either way, the membership status of the data instance is violated during this operation.

This kind of attack is alarming on the aspects of privacy and stresses the need to introduce better safeguard measures for Machine Learning models to prevent leakage of information. Therefore, more efforts and funding should be laid down on research and development of prevention strategies to effectively combat the said vulnerabilities.

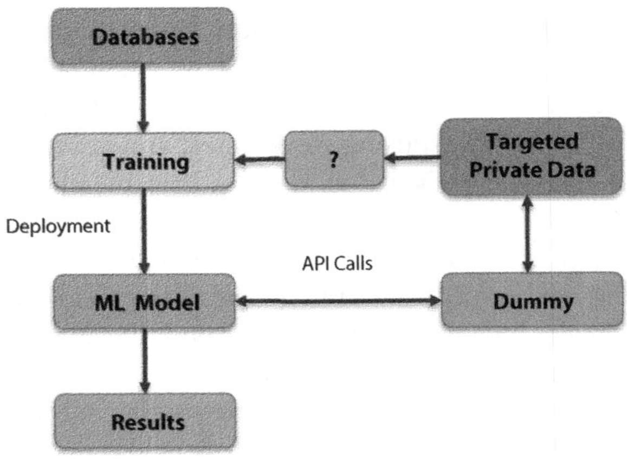

Figure 15.6 Membership inference assault – a sample scenario.

15.9 Runtime Disruption Assault

Malicious actors use runtime disruption attacks to stall or impede machine learning activities. These attacks usually try to remotely disrupt the machine learning process's regular functioning by focusing on the server during the deployment phase. By taking advantage of weaknesses in the system, hackers breach the runtime server through methods such as SQL injection, denial-of-service (DoS), and phishing. Such interruptions can result in downtime and resource waste, which is especially important in industries like government and healthcare where any interruption or breach can have serious repercussions. Decentralization of the machine learning workspace has been suggested as a defense against these threats.

Big data virtualization techniques are covered by Alaasam *et al.* These techniques can be included into machine learning jobs to improve security. Furthermore, distributed machine learning can be implemented using blockchain-based techniques, which protect the confidentiality and integrity of both users and models. Parallel computing approaches are used as a defense against runtime disruption attacks, shielding machine learning tasks running on actual data from interruptions caused by attacks. With this technique, sub-units that are in charge of particular tasks receive

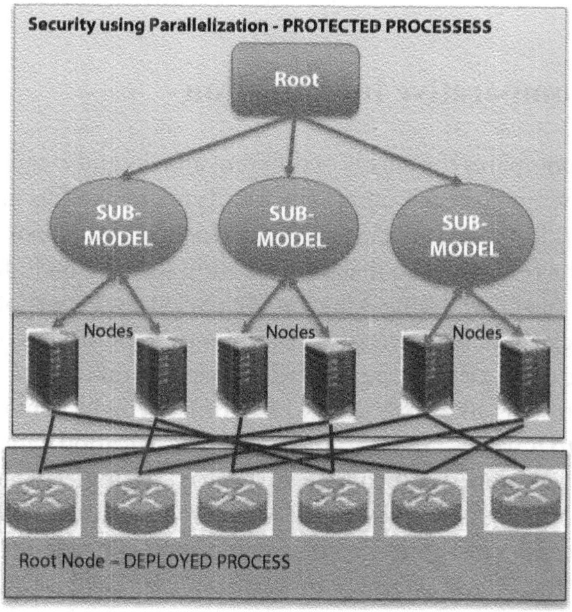

Figure 15.7 Protecting ML tasks from runtime disruption assault from parallelization.

instructions from a master node that holds the learned model. These subunits process data and produce outputs in accordance with instructions from the master node. They are further subdivided into racks and numerous slave nodes. The machine learning task is self-sufficient even in the case of an attack because numerous computers are working on the same unit of data. The master node aggregates various results to provide redundancy and integrity so that tasks are completed seamlessly—even in the event of an assault.

The decentralization of machine learning workload to protect the system against disruption attacks on deployed models is shown in Figure 15.7. It shows a model that has been split up into several machines that each carry out different prediction tasks. The architecture's sub-models are grouped into clusters, and each cluster assigns duties to computers based on the master or root node notion. Other racks can carry out computing activities in the event of a disruption assault at the rack level, guaranteeing continued execution with longer computational times. This method shows how to protect machine learning activities from server attacks using a rack-awareness algorithm.

We have looked at a number of machine learning model threats in this area, including dataset poisoning, model poisoning, and privacy violations. We've also talked about ways to lessen these attacks. We will next contrast the effects of various attacks and give specifics about their defenses.

15.10 Comparative Investigation

This section compares the effects of different attacks and evaluates how well defenses work against each other. The four types of assaults are as follows: inference attacks, access attacks, privacy breaches, and poisoning attacks.

Some of the first issues in machine learning security include adversarial and dataset poisoning. Using Amazon Web Services, Papernot *et al.* developed an attack that uses adversarial samples to trick models, obtaining an accuracy rate of 96.19% on the MNIST dataset. Kurakin *et al.* showed how minor adjustments like contrast and brightness might contaminate photos, leading to a 98.0% adversarial data misclassification rate. These ideas were further developed to produce adversarial examples. Data poisoning was used by Chen *et al.* to establish a targeted backdoor attack that had a 97.90% success rate. Only five poisoned samples needed to be injected in order for the attack accuracy to surpass 99%. Defense tactics against dataset poisoning have been examined and contrasted by, who conducted a comparative study after reviewing a number of publications. An attack known as the "r-attack" and a defense method known as "TRIM," which turned out to be an incredibly quick defense mechanism, were presented by Jagielski *et al.* The deep-KNN assault was introduced by Gupta *et al.* It successfully separated locations by applying the KNN method, and the defense was able to obtain a 91% accuracy score. Another defense strategy, was tested against a variety of attacks. It showed resilience in some poisoned defense situations, with accuracy ratings as high as 93%.

This comparative analysis demonstrates how machine learning security assaults are changing and how defense methods have advanced in tandem. Researchers are still working to create ways to lessen these risks and protect machine learning systems against data poisoning and hostile manipulation through thorough study and experimentation.

As pointed out by Gu backdoor assaults have been demonstrated by getting triggers into the dataset which resulted in a mislabeling rate of 0. to be 56% and its success rate never dropped below 99%. Indirect way of labeling is poison, while the backdoor attacks covert with average success rate of 90 percent. Lorenz *et al.* launched backdoor attacks on black-box and white-box models reducing the accuracy to 90 percent. These forms of attacks utilizing inserted poisoned data affected the accuracy by performing indirect attacks, which caused the average to be lowered to 8. 8%. Some defense methods used are; the deterministic test-time augmentation proposed by Weber *et al.* it provides robustness with a test accuracy of 98. 6%, it is claimed that fine-tuning and pruning defenses, proposed by Liu and his colleagues, provide a 97.7%.

Privacy threats formed the core of our study and the defenses against them were critical in our analysis. Sablayrolles *et al.* proposed a study regarding membership inference attacks demonstrating that assaults on black-box and white-box models can be performed with 79% accuracy. 5% they increased up to 90% with data augmentation. Referential realism-absent augmentation defenses, such as cropping or rounding, is at 8%. Actually, Milad *et al.* were able to obtain 74% using flaws in stochastic gradient descent. 3% attack accuracy that was later increased to 82. The cost was estimated to be 1% of the total constructs in a federated arrangement. This enabled them to get membership inference data leaks. According to Stacey *et al.*, the use of decision tree model gave a 95 percent accuracy to predict knee OA statuses. Obtain up to 74% accuracy rate whilst launching membership inference attacks on a set of diverse ML models, using the "Purchases- 100 dataset".

Many inference defenses is called, like MemGuard by Yang *et al.* that has a 50.8% attack accuracy against black-box inference attacks on the "Texas100 dataset." Another line of defense was to train an autoencoder, which resulted in a 15% decrease in membership inference attack accuracy but a four-fold increase in model inversion error with just a 0.4% reduction in classification accuracy. Other privacy threats were found, such as the model inversion attack, which has a 74.1% success rate in disclosing private information. With less estimating errors than in certain regression models, Wang and Gong were able to steal the hyperparameters of a model. Zhang *et al.* outperformed previous techniques by up to 75% when they reconstructed models using publically accessible data, attaining attack accuracies of 76% (black-box knowledge highest on CelebA dataset) and 80% (white-box knowledge highest on MNIST dataset). Papernot *et al.*'s integration of differential privacy techniques and homomorphic encryption [34] were two privacy protection strategies, but with a 1.3% accuracy drop in the overall model on the MNIST dataset with differential privacy. Using a two-server architecture as the distributed framework, Mohassel and Zhang constructed privacy techniques with 98.62% accuracy on the MNIST dataset.

This section gives an account of relative harm and protection methods of poisoning, backdoor, and inference attacks. In the last section, we give a brief concluding remark of the study and suggest the possible future studies.

15.11 Conclusion and Future Research Directions

To be in brief, the significant potentials of Cyber-Physical Systems (CPS) has resulted as notable progress across diverse sectors. Nevertheless, the utilization of sensor data and cloud computing in networks also presents possible security vulnerabilities, including the possibility of data breaches and unauthorized modifications. In order to fully use the advantages of CPS while guaranteeing security, it is imperative to solve these flaws. A range of machine learning security attacks were delineated, encompassing dataset and model poisoning, privacy breaches, membership inference, and runtime disruptions. Additionally, defense strategies were proposed to alleviate these potential risks. In addition, we deliberated on the difficulties and concerns related to machine learning security in CPS deployments, including the precision and malfunction of security methods.

In the future, it is recommended that future study priorities the utilization of deep learning techniques, such as "Generative adversarial networks (GANs)", in order to augment the resilience of cybersecurity measures. The investigation of the efficacy of federated learning in mitigating threats during the deployment of machine learning tasks, as well as the development of lightweight security methods, are significant domains of research. The establishment of standardized evaluation standards and the effective management of heterogeneous data are imperative for the advancement of machine learning security. In addition, it is necessary to conduct thorough testing and validation of security schemes in order to guarantee comprehensive safeguarding against potential vulnerabilities in machine learning models that are deployed within cyber-physical systems (CPS) environments.

References

1. Kumar, P., Kumar, R., Srivastava, G., Gupta, G.P., Tripathi, R., Gadekallu, T.R., Xiong, N.N., Developed a privacy-preserving and secure framework using blockchain-based machine learning for IoT-driven smart cities. *IEEE Trans. Network Sci. Eng.*, 8, 3, 2326–2341, 2021.
2. Pundir, S., Wazid, M., Singh, D.P., Das, A.K., Rodrigues, J.J., Park, Y., Conducted a survey on intrusion detection protocols in wireless sensor networks integrated with IoT, discussing future challenges. *IEEE Access*, 8, 3343–3363, 2019.
3. Wazid, M., Das, A.K., Shetty, S., Gope, P., Rodrigues, J.J., Explored security issues, challenges, and future research directions in 5G-enabled IoT communication. *IEEE Access*, 9, 4466–4489, 2020.
4. Hou, Y., Garg, S., Hui, L., Jayakody, D.N.K., Jin, R., Hossain, M.S., Proposed an enhanced data security access control mechanism in mobile edge computing. *IEEE Access*, 8, 136119–136130, 2020.
5. Ghosh, U., Chatterjee, P., Tosh, D., Shetty, S., Xiong, K., Kamhoua, C., Presented an SDN-based framework for securing and optimizing performance in information-centric cloud networks, in: *2017 IEEE 10th International Conference on Cloud Computing (CLOUD)*, pp. 749–752, 2017.
6. Sun, G., Cong, Y., Dong, J., Wang, Q., Lyu, L., Liu, J., Investigated data poisoning attacks on federated machine learning. *IEEE Internet Things J.*, 9, 13, 11365–11375, 2021.
7. Sisejkovic, D., Merchant, F., Reimann, L.M., Leupers, R., Developed deceptive logic locking techniques for protecting hardware integrity against machine learning attacks. *IEEE Trans. Comput. Aided Des. Integr. Circuits Syst.*, 41, 6, 1716–1729, 2021.
8. Zheng, H., Ye, Q., Hu, H., Fang, C., Shi, J., Discussed protecting the decision boundary of machine learning models using differentially private perturbation. *IEEE Trans. Dependable Secure Comput.*, 19, 3, 2007–2022, 2020.
9. More, S., Singla, J., Verma, S., Ghosh, U., Rodrigues, J.J., Hosen, A.S., Ra, I.H., Presented a security-assured CNN-based model for reconstructing medical images on the IoT healthcare platform. *IEEE Access*, 8, 126333–126346, 2020.

10. Luo, Z., Zhao, S., Lu, Z., Xu, J., Sagduyu, Y.E., Studied learning-empowered attacks in cooperative spectrum sensing within the realm of AI. *IEEE Trans. Mob. Comput.*, 21, 5, 1892–1908, 2020.
11. Rao, A., Carreón, N., Lysecky, R., Rozenblit, J., Proposed a probabilistic threat detection method for managing risks in cyber-physical medical systems. *IEEE Software*, 35, 1, 38–43, 2017.
12. Kordestani, M. and Saif, M., Reviewed observer-based attack detection and mitigation strategies for cyber-physical systems. *IEEE Syst. Man Cybern. Mag.*, 7, 2, 35–60, 2021.
13. Giraldo, J., Sarkar, E., Cardenas, A.A., Maniatakos, M., Kantarcioglu, M., Conducted a comprehensive survey on security and privacy in cyber-physical systems. *IEEE Des. Test*, 34, 4, 7–17, 2017.
14. Humayed, A., Lin, J., Li, F., Luo, B., Surveyed the security landscape of cyber-physical systems. *IEEE Internet Things J.*, 1802–1831, 2017.
15. Hasan, M.K., Habib, A.A., Shukur, Z., Ibrahim, F., Islam, S., Razzaque, M.A., Reviewed standards, protocols, constraints, and recommendations for cyber-physical and cyber-security systems in smart grids. *J. Network Comput. Appl.*, 209, 1033540, 2023.
16. Bashendy, M., Tantawy, A., Erradi, A., Surveyed intrusion response systems for cyber-physical systems comprehensively. *Comput. Secur.*, 124, 102984, 2023.
17. Kim, S., Park, K.J., Lu, C., Analyzed network security for cyber-physical systems from threats to resilient design. *IEEE Commun. Surv. Tutor.*, 24, 3, 1534–1573, 2022.
18. Agrawal, N. and Kumar, R., Provided a decade-wide survey on the security perspective of industrial cyber-physical systems. *ISA Trans.*, 130, 10–24, 2022.
19. Berman, D.S., Buczak, A.L., Chavis, J.S., Corbett, C.L., Surveyed deep learning methods for cybersecurity. *Information*, 10, 4, 122, 2019.
20. Dasgupta, D., Akhtar, Z., Sen, S., Provided a comprehensive survey on machine learning in cybersecurity. *J. Def. Model. Simul.*, 19, 1, 57–106, 2022.
21. Rosenberg, I., Shabtai, A., Elovici, Y., Rokach, L., Discussed adversarial machine learning attacks and defense methods in the cybersecurity domain. *ACM Comput. Surv. (CSUR)*, 54, 5, 1–36, 2021.
22. Kamilaris, A. and Prenafeta-Boldú, F.X., Surveyed deep learning applications in agriculture. *Comput. Electron. Agric.*, 147, 70–90, 2018.
23. Gupta, N., Huang, W.R., Fowl, L., Zhu, C., Feizi, S., Goldstein, T., Dickerson, J., Discussed strong baseline defenses against clean-label poisoning attacks, 2019.
24. Tushar, W., Yuen, C., Saha, T.K., Nizami, S., Alam, M.R., Smith, D.B., Poor, H.V., Surveyed cyber-physical systems from a game-theoretic perspective. *IEEE Access*, 11, 9799–9834, 2023.

25. Cassottana, B., Roomi, M.M., Mashima, D., Sansavini, G., Reviewed models and methods for resilience analysis of cyber-physical systems. *Risk Anal.*, 43, 11, 2359–2379, 2023.
26. Rupprecht, T. and Wang, Y., Surveyed deep reinforcement learning in Markovian cyber-physical systems, discussing common problems and solutions. *Neural Networks*, 153, 13–36, 2022.
27. Chen, H. and Babar, M.A., Surveyed security threats, practices, and challenges in machine learning-based software systems, 2023.
28. Barreno, M., Nelson, B., Joseph, A.D., Tygar, J.D., Discussed the security aspects of machine learning. *Mach. Learn.*, 81, 121–148, 2010.
29. Papernot, N., Provided a comprehensive overview of security and privacy in machine learning, 2018, available on arXiv preprint arXiv:1811.01134.
30. Xue, M., Yuan, C., Wu, H., Zhang, Y., Liu, W., Reviewed threats, countermeasures, and evaluations in machine learning security. *IEEE Access*, 8, 74720–74742, 2020.
31. Liu, Q., Li, P., Zhao, W., Cai, W., Yu, S., Leung, V.C., Surveyed security threats and defensive techniques in machine learning from a data-driven perspective. *IEEE Access*, 6, 12103–12117, 2018.
32. Auernhammer, K., Kolagari, R.T., Zoppelt, M., Discussed accountability issues in machine learning attacks at SafeAI@ AAAI, 2019.
33. Eykholt, K., Evtimov, I., Fernandes, E., Li, B., Rahmati, A., Xiao, C., Song, D., Presented robust physical-world attacks on deep learning visual classification. *IEEE Conf. Comput. Vision Pattern Recognit.*, 1625–1634, 2018.
34. Papernot, N., McDaniel, P., Sinha, A., Wellman, M.P., Provided a comprehensive overview of security and privacy in machine learning. *2018 IEEE European Symposium on Security and Privacy (EuroS&P)*, pp. 399–414, 2018.

16

Cyber-Physical Systems: Challenges, Opportunities, Security Solutions

Gopinathan S.[1*], S. Babu[2] and P. Shanmugam[3]

[1]*Department of Artificial Intelligence and Data Science, Sri Sai Ram Institute of Technology, West Tambaram, Chennai, India*
[2]*Department of Computing Technologies, SRM Institute of Science and Technology, Kattankulathur, Chennai, India*
[3]*Department of Computer Science and Engineering, Rajalakshmi Engineering College, Chennai, India*

Abstract

Cyber-Physical Systems (CPSs) have become a focal point of research, drawing the interest of numerous scholars. It emphasizes the challenges researchers face in formulating a suitable formalism that transcends mere networking and information technology, aiming to seamlessly integrate information and knowledge into physical objects. It further provides a synthesis of critical security and protection considerations, offering actionable directions to enhance the availability and security of smart grids. The Digital Transformation (DT) is characterized by the migration of from administrative processes to solutions for IT, ushering in substantial changes throughout an organization. However, the global impetus of digital transformation is accelerated by developing technologies like cloud computing, blockchain, data analytics and big data, and artificial intelligence, concurrently heightening cyber security risks for businesses navigating this transformative journey.

The vast amount of sensor data from both individuals and corporations has become an enticing target for cybercriminals and state-sponsored espionage. This has resulted in a significant surge in both the number of potential vulnerabilities and the actors posing threats. Industry 4.0's perspective on cyber-physical systems (CPS) hold considerable promise for driving the digital transformation of industrial value creation. These systems seamlessly integrate various technological approaches, such as big data analysis and artificial intelligence, thereby improving

**Corresponding author*: gopinath.ai@sairamit.edu.in

K. Ananthajothi, S. N. Sangeethaa, D. Divya, S. Balamurugan and Shen-Lung Peng (eds.) Securing Cyber-Physical Systems: Fundamentals, Applications and Challenges, (343–368) © 2025 Scrivener Publishing LLC

the instantaneous observation and management of manufacturing processes.The development of Cyber-Physical Systems (CPS) has been greatly influenced by advancements in the networking and computation sectors. The widespread adoption of CPSs has introduced new security challenges, given the proliferation of intrusions, threats, and attacks. Consequently, the security of CPS is highly precarious. Conducting a thorough examination of CPS security requirements and employing techniques for risk assessment can be really important in enhancing and fortifying security measures.

***Keywords*:** Cyber-physical system, digital transformation, cyber-security, industry 4.0

16.1 Cyber-Physical Systems

16.1.1 Introduction

The integration of digital tools into everyday life, such as calculators and the internet, has revolutionized how humans exchange information. This has eliminated the limitations of time and location, making information exchange more convenient. As communication relies heavily on computational processes, the complexity of computing has evolved to meet the demands of rapid development. This includes the intricate processing of data into meaningful information. The speed of computation is closely tied to technological advancements. These advancements also result in changes in the size of devices, sensors, and actuators. It's now common to have computing devices the size of a credit card, whereas just a few decades ago, the same tools could be as large as a lecture hall.

Cyber-Physical Systems (CPS) are systems in which networks and integrated computers monitor and regulate physical mechanisms, and where the interaction between computing and physical processes is fundamental. As shown in Figure 16.1 the hardware such as actuators, sensors, and embedded systems, as well as a variety of proprietary, commercial, and software products for control and monitoring, come together to form CPS. Scalability, promptness, fault tolerance, independence, distributed management, and control are among the essential characteristics of CPS. The diversity of the essential components makes security in CPS more difficult. Safety and privacy protection are hampered by the CPS elements' complexity and diversity [1]. It becomes difficult to identify vulnerabilities and threats because of the complex interactions inside CPS. It is time-consuming to locate, evaluate, and monitor breaches on various CPS devices. It is essential to have a deep awareness of threats, vulnerabilities, and intrusions while building defence systems.

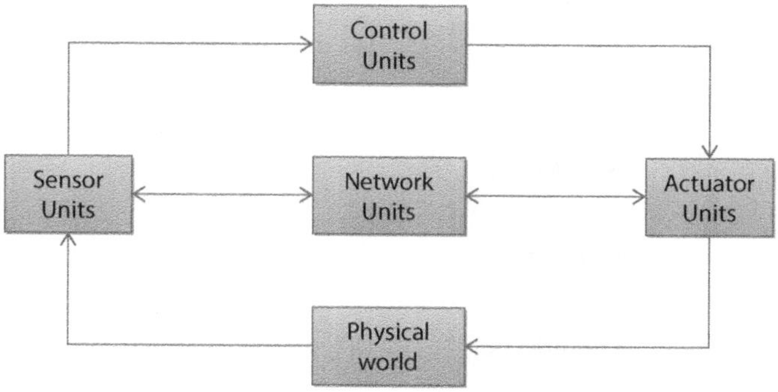

Figure 16.1 Cyber-physical system model.

CPS dependability can be negatively impacted by sporadic breakdowns. Reliability criteria, which include liveness, function optimisation, safety, and closed-loop stability, are designed to guarantee the stability of functional objectives. security rules main objective is to safeguard CPS against online threats. Information availability, security, integrity, and confidentiality are important security factors. The credibility of the system depends on maintaining data integrity, particularly when it comes to data that is gathered and transmitted by control units, actuators, and sensors. Availability is the ability to access and use the system upon request; one significant issue is denial-of-service (DoS) assaults [2]. Maintaining the privacy of information from unauthorised users requires maintaining confidentiality. Strong secrecy safeguards in a CPS can successfully block unusual efforts to access data streams between tiers. Preventive measures are crucial in this scenario, even though secrecy alone might not be able to combat every threat.

16.1.2 Present Issues on Cyber Security

Cybersecurity entails understanding various cyber threats and applying defense strategies or countermeasures to ensure the availability, reliability, and confidentiality of digital or IT systems. Figure 16.2 depicts the vulnerabilities in the cyber physical system. Malware is commonly recognized by cybersecurity professionals as the main tool used by malicious actors to compromise efforts in preventing cyberattacks. Malware is the term for this large class of assaults that are usually put on a system without the owner's knowledge. It consists of malware like as viruses, worms, Trojan horses, spyware, and bot executables. These may propagate across systems through

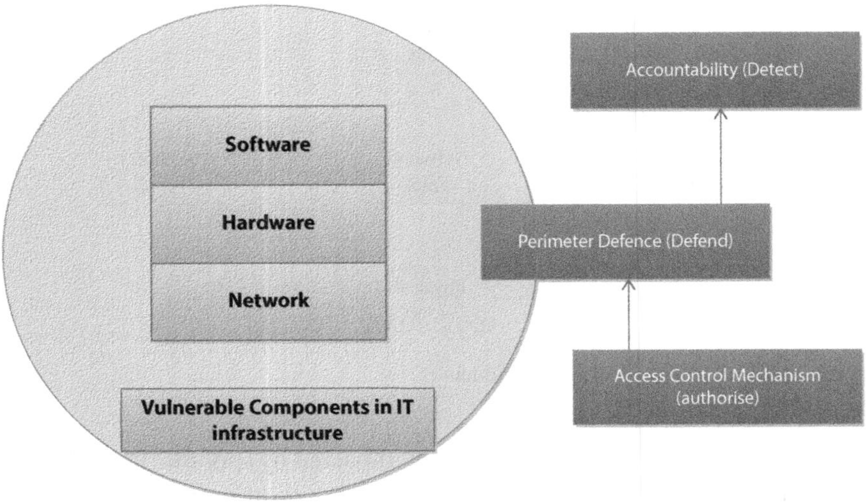

Figure 16.2 Vulnerabilities in cyber-physical system.

a variety of means, including tricking users into opening dubious files or luring them to malicious websites.

Malware can attach itself to a USB drive that is placed into an infected computer in more specific cases of infection, and it can then spread to every machine that the device is subsequently connected to. Malware may spread through devices and equipment that have computational logic and embedded systems. A gadget can become infected with malware at any point in its existence. End users, servers, network hardware like routers and switches, and process control systems like SCADA are just a few of the systems it may target. Malware's growing frequency and sophistication are two of the biggest issues with the Internet nowadays.

16.1.2.1 Phishing Exploits

These instances accounted for 32% of verified data breaches, according to Verizon's most recent data breach report. With the intention of gaining sensitive information like usernames, passwords, social security numbers, and credit card data, the assaults trick victims into thinking they are communicating with a reliable individual via email, text, and increasingly over the phone.

16.1.2.2 *Internet of Things Ransomware*

The Internet of Things includes a range of network-connected devices, like service sensors and home appliances. While these devices, such as refrigerators and climate control systems, typically don't hold sensitive information themselves, they can be targeted by hackers aiming to access backend systems, such as those in power supply and communication facilities, by taking control of these devices.

16.1.2.3 *Strengthened Regulation of Data Privacy*

In order to enforce adherence to stricter international standards and to improve the rights of European individuals to privacy protection, the General Data Protection Regulation (GDPR) was established in May 2018 and carries substantial financial penalties for non-compliance.

16.1.2.4 *Cyberattacks Using Mobile Technology*

With mobile devices becoming integral to both personal and professional aspects of our lives, recent RSA research has revealed that fraudulent mobile transactions surged to 80% in 2018, reflecting a significant rise in mobile app fraud since 2015. Consequently, people's awareness of and concern about these risks has also heightened.

16.1.2.5 *A Higher Allocation of Resources to Automation*

Automation technology is increasingly adopted by organizations, as it allows overburdened cybersecurity teams to focus on more complex challenges rather than routine, often repetitive tasks. According to a recent Ponemon Institute survey, 50% of respondents plan to implement security automation in their organizations, and 79% are already using security automation tools and frameworks. In this context, the primary approach to data protection provides the most robust defense against cyberattacks, such as database fraud and other threats that can impact a company. While automation can boost productivity, it is still essential to have knowledge and expertise to mitigate the risk of cyberattacks.

16.1.3 CPS –Applications and Research Areas

Noteworthy uses for cyber-physical systems are shown in Figure 16.3.

a. Smart Grids

To increase sustainability, trustworthiness, and efficiency in electrical grid modernization, CPS technologies are employed. They make it possible for energy production, distribution, and transmission systems to be monitored, controlled, and optimised in real time.

b. Autonomous Automobiles

By combining actuators, sensors, algorithms for control, and communication networks, CPS is essential to the invention of autonomous automobiles. These systems allow autonomous vehicles to see their surroundings, decide what to do, and drive safely.

c. Smart Health System

Applications of CPS in healthcare include drug delivery systems, medical imaging systems, wearable technology for monitoring patients at home, and smart prostheses. These solutions make it easier to provide effective and individualised healthcare.

d. The Industrial Internet of Things (IIoT)

To improve productivity, quality, and safety in automated factories and manufacturing processes, CPS technologies are widely deployed. Manufacturing machinery and process optimisation, predictive maintenance, and real-time monitoring are made possible by IIoT.

e. Smart Cities

CPS integrates actuators, sensors, and networks of communication to monitor and control several urban systems, including waste management, electricity, transportation, and water. This makes it easier to create the infrastructure of smart cities.

f. Agricultural Automating

CPS uses for agriculture include drones, sensor networks, autonomous tractor models, remote sensing, and precision farming methods. These solutions lessen resource use, improve crop yields, and lessen their negative effects on the environment.

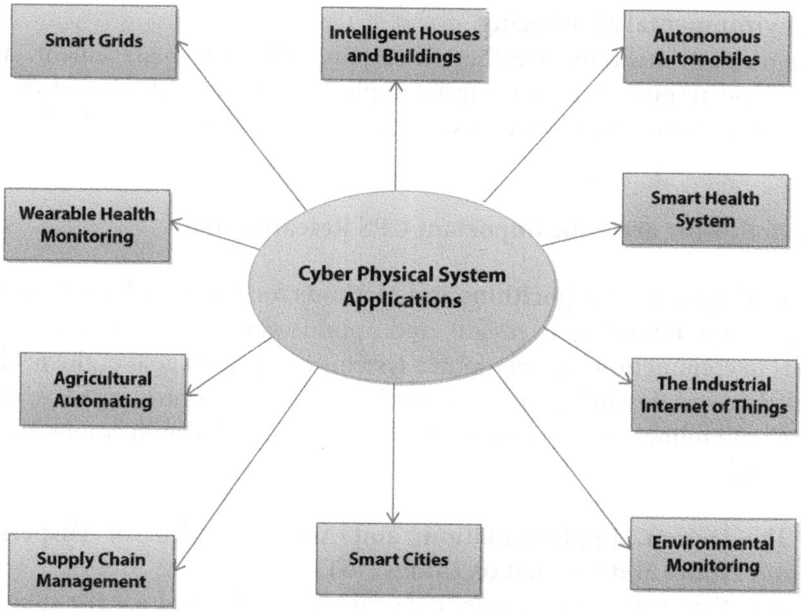

Figure 16.3 CPS applications.

g. Wearable Health Monitoring

Wearable's with CPS functionality, like as smart watches, activity trackers, and medical sensors monitor heart rates and other vital parameters, and other health-related information. They enable people to regularly monitor their health and help in the early identification of medical issues.

h. Intelligent Houses and Buildings

Home automation systems employ CPS technologies to remotely operate and keep an eye on a variety of appliances and equipment. In both residential and commercial buildings, these systems improve comfort, security, and energy efficiency.

i. Supply Chain Management

Real-time tracking of commodities, predictive maintenance for automobiles, and dynamic route optimisation to reduce costs and delays are all made possible by CPS technologies.

j. Environmental Monitoring

Applications including weather forecasting, disaster management, and water and air quality monitoring are implemented using CPS-based sensor networks. These systems offer useful data for policy-making and scientific study.

The following are some important CPS Research areas:

1. Development of Algorithms and Methods for the Real Time System

Real-time monitoring, oversight, and optimisation of mechanical operations in conjunction with computer systems is the main goal of the field of real-time systems and control. Research on feedback control systems, real-time scheduling, and optimisation techniques for CPS applications are all included.

2. The Design, Implementation, and Administration of Dispersed Sensor Nodes and Internet of Things (IoT)

Devices that gather and transfer data from the real world are the subjects of study in sensor networks and IoT. This covers subjects including sensor data fusion, location methods, and energy-efficient communication protocols.

3. Hardware Design and Embedded Systems

CPS's research on embedded systems focuses on creating software and hardware platforms that are optimised for low-power devices, real-time operation in contexts with limited resources. This covers studies on energy-efficient computing, sensor interfaces, and microcontroller designs.

4. Cybersecurity and Privacy

The main goals of CPS cybersecurity research are to safeguard sensitive data's integrity and privacy while defending networked systems against online attacks. This entails researching cryptographic methods designed specifically for CPS applications, detection of intrusion systems, and secure communication protocols.

5. Artificial Intelligence and Machine Learning for CPS

Research in AI and Machine Learning examines how these methods can be used in CPS for tasks like autonomous decision-making, predictive maintenance, and anomaly detection. Creating artificial intelligence algorithms that acquire information from sensory data and control physical systems in an adaptive manner is one way to do this.

6. Interaction between Humans and Cyber-Physical Systems
This field of study looks into how people connect with cyber-physical systems as well as how to create user interfaces that make control and monitoring easier. It comprises studies on person-in-the-loop CPS architectures, user experience layout, and psychological factors.

7. Networked and Distributed CPS
Research on networked CPS concentrates on coordinating several interconnected systems to accomplish global goals while taking local limits into account. This covers things like multi-agent systems, coordinated procedures for networked CPS deployments, and distributed consensus techniques.

8. Energy Efficiency and Sustainability
By creating methods for maximising resource utilisation, lowering carbon footprints, and enhancing the general ecological impact of cyber-physical systems, CPS research addresses issues related to energy efficiency and sustainability.

9. Safety and Reliability
Including tolerance for faults processes, reliability analysis, and security-critical system design approaches, assuring the safety as well as dependability of cyber-physical structures is an important topic of research.

10. Applications Across Disciplines
CPS research frequently entails cooperation between several fields, such as robots, healthcare, transportation, energy efficiency, and smart cities in particular. Multidisciplinary study investigates the application of CPS concepts to particular problems in these fields.

16.2 Cyber Security Challenges

The effectiveness of CPS relies heavily on its capacity to swiftly handle and transmit data in real-time across an intricate network of systems, all the while ensuring security. Table 16.1 outlines the key hurdles hindering the advancement of CPS development.

Table 16.1 Challenges for cyber-physical systems.

Challenge	Description
Diversity	Establishing uniform data formats across a range of different origins.
Coherence	The capability to unify all individual subsystems into a singular entity.
Compatibility	Systems need to communicate through shared platforms.
Security	Safeguarding confidential information and systems from malicious intrusions.

16.2.1 Social Media Role in Cyber-Security

As society becomes more interconnected through social media in an increasingly connected world, companies face the challenge of safeguarding personal information. Social media platforms significantly impact cyber security and pose considerable threats to personal data. With the rising adoption of social media among individuals, the risk of cyber-attacks escalates [3]. The allure of social media makes people susceptible to hackers who use it as a means to acquire sensitive information. Despite the risks associated with social media, businesses cannot afford to cease its usage due to its vital role in publicity. Instead, they need proactive solutions to detect and address threats promptly. However, companies must acknowledge the importance of analyzing information, especially in social media conversations, and implementing adequate security measures to mitigate risks. This involves establishing policies and leveraging suitable technologies to manage social media effectively.

16.2.2 Cyber-Security Methods

16.2.2.1 Access Management and Passphrase Protection

The use of usernames and passwords has long been a fundamental method of safeguarding our information and is often considered one of the initial steps in cyber security.

16.2.2.2 Verification of Data

Before downloading documents, it's crucial to authenticate their origin and ensure they haven't been tampered with, verifying that they come from trusted and reliable sources. Typically, this authentication process is carried out by antivirus software installed on devices. Therefore, having effective antivirus software is essential for protecting devices from viruses.

16.2.2.3 Malicious Software Detectors

This software typically checks all system files and documents for harmful viruses or malicious code. A few examples of dangerous software that is commonly referred to as "malware" are Trojan horses, worms, and viruses.

16.2.2.4 Network Security Barriers

A firewall, whether software or hardware-based, acts as a protective barrier against hackers, viruses, and worms attempting to access your computer via the Internet. It monitors all incoming and outgoing messages on the internet, analysing each one and preventing those that fail to meet pre-defined security standards from passing through. Therefore, firewalls are instrumental in identifying and blocking malware.

16.2.2.5 Antimalware

software Antivirus Software refers to a computer application designed to identify, prevent, and respond to dangerous software, such as worms and viruses [4]. The majority of antivirus programs incorporate an auto-update functionality, allowing the software to download profiles of newly identified viruses, enabling it to promptly scan for and detect these newly discovered threats. Antivirus software is considered an essential and indispensable requirement for every system.

16.3 Integration of Physical and Digital

Protecting technical systems from cyber-attacks should be an organization's top priority since bad actors might take advantage of holes in digital infrastructures. The implementation of authentication, encryption, and access control measures is vital in strengthening cybersecurity and protecting networks and data from malicious activities and unauthorised access. Furthermore, companies ought to consider obtaining cyber insurance in order to provide monetary protection against possible damages resulting from successful cyberattacks. It's crucial to raise employee awareness about cybersecurity threats, as informed employees are more likely to practice reliable information security behaviours [5]. The frequency of cyber attacks has surged, necessitating that businesses understand cybersecurity threats and adopt comprehensive mitigation strategies. These assaults usually seek to disrupt regular corporate operations, extort financial rewards, or gain access to, change, or delete sensitive information. The word "cybersecurity" refers to a broad range of techniques used to safeguard computers and networks against theft, data loss, and unauthorised access.

There is an increasing trend of rising cybersecurity costs and cybercrimes worldwide. Cybersecurity breaches have financial consequences that extend beyond the organisations who are the targets; they can affect industries that experience lower profitability and higher insurance costs. Protecting intellectual property, satisfying customer expectations, reducing customer attrition, improving brand image, gaining access to secure vendor networks, maintaining firm reputation, and minimising industry-wide impact are just a few benefits of investing in cybersecurity. Numerous frameworks, such as Lee's risk management framework, emphasise the significance of assessing the cost-effectiveness of cybersecurity investments and continuously improving cybersecurity processes. The National Institute of Standards and Technology (NIST) Cybersecurity Framework is widely used by organisations for risk management; however, it does not have a specific section for cost-benefit analysis.

16.3.1 Materials and Procedures

We describe our approach in this part, which comprised performing in accordance with the below mentioned criteria [15]. Our procedure, which makes use of the Google Scholar database, is shown in Figure 16.4. In order

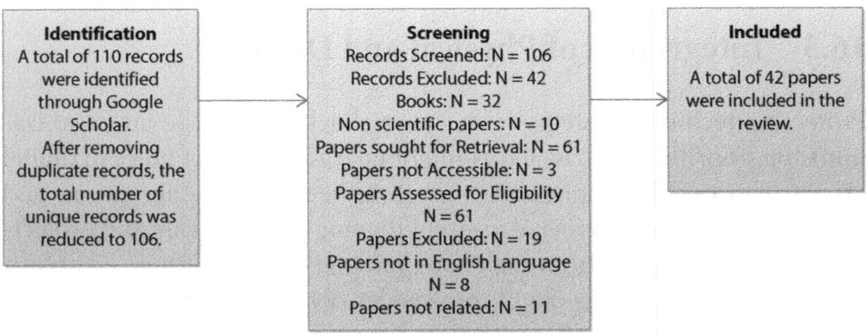

Figure 16.4 A visual representation of our systematic literature review process is depicted in the PRISMA diagram.

to gather primary research pertinent to our subject—which is the nexus between cybersecurity and business—we utilised targeted keywords.

We searched using variations of phrases like (digital conversion also cybersecurity), (digital conversion also business transformation), (digital conversion also protection), (digital conversion also cybersecurity), and (digitization) also security. We used inclusion criteria, which stipulated that articles have to be relevant to cybersecurity and digital business and published between 2019 and 2023, in order to guarantee the applicability of our findings. On the other hand, exclusion criteria, such as language limitations (i.e., papers written outside of English), unrelated subjects, and review papers, were utilised to weed out irrelevant publications. We meticulously evaluated every Google Scholar result in relation to these standards. Finding pertinent studies required going through a quality evaluation stage where we first skimmed through titles and language (English or not), then verified the material was related to our investigation. The number of publications chosen following this rigorous screening procedure is shown in Figure 16.4.

16.3.2 Applications

16.3.2.1 Financial Sector

The financial industry is essential in the economy, and numerous empirical studies conducted in various geographical contexts shed light on its vulnerabilities. In Bangladesh, Zografopoulos *et al.* examined the funding division and emphasized the importance of developing cybersecurity systems to identify money laundering transactions, which can have adverse effects on economic development. The integration of modern technologies presents significant opportunities for enhancing security within Almudaires and Almaiah looked at important issues that credit card companies faced in the banking industry and offered solutions to improve their cybersecurity procedures [6].

16.3.2.2 Health Division

Cybersecurity in the healthcare sector is centred on protecting patient privacy and guaranteeing the security of medical equipment. Adopting a secure digital transformation plan helps improve healthcare organisations' governance. Garcia-Perez *et al.* emphasised how important it is to manage the digital transformation of healthcare systems by using a cybersecurity perspective. Based on observations made by UK senior management during the COVID-19 pandemic, their study highlighted the necessity of creating a comprehensive framework. This framework should take into account the advancement of cybersecurity knowledge, efficient risk management, and recognition of the complex organisational and systematic relationships within the industry. These components are essential for promoting digital sustainability and resilience in the healthcare sector, and they have consequences for management strategies as well as research projects.

16.3.2.3 Business Sector

Business organizations exhibit significant heterogeneity, which is reflected in the diverse technological systems they deploy. Advanced technologies such as the Internet of Everything offer potential avenues for enhancing cybersecurity measures within organizations. Gonchar offered suggestions for improving financial stability in the digital age that were both theoretical and applicable. Their study examined how digital technologies affected entrepreneurial activity in Ukraine and found that, although there were differences depending on a company's size and industry, information and communication technology were increasingly being adopted by firms. A technique for assessing a nation's degree of technological change within this framework was also presented in the article, with the goal of streamlining the examination of factors associated with innovation and entrepreneurship.

16.3.2.4 Industry Sector

Industry 5.0 promotes the development of solutions for intelligent production that rely on using Internet of Things technologies. Industrial organisations can improve their security with a range of technical innovations, such as digital twins, automated control rooms, automated attack detection, and zero trust architecture. Osak and Buzina looked into techniques for evaluating the security and flexibility of power systems in changing environments brought about by changes in industrial norms and digital transformation, such as the popularity of electric cars and renewable energy sources. The writers covered the fundamentals of automatically controlling energy systems during digital transition while accounting for variations in various electrical installation types [7].

16.4 Digital Threats to Physical Systems

Software-based systems' threat models frequently fail to account for the potential for physical access or assume that physical security will always be maintained. Threat actors can, however, physically access Cyber-Physical Systems (CPS) components and hack devices via a variety of hardware interfaces or network channels, particularly if the system is dispersed over numerous locations and lacks appropriate physical security measures. Thus, putting in place physical controls in addition to logical controls is essential for drawing limits of trust. There aren't many thorough descriptions in the literature of how these boundaries are established in CPS, taking into account both logical and physical security assumptions [8]. Furthermore, they don't explain in detail how assumptions about the system and environment under discussion connect to concerns about trust boundaries. When performing threat modelling studies inside known frameworks and standards, this gap is very important. Moreover, the interaction between the virtual and actual worlds demands attention because some cyberattacks can require physical security prerequisites.

Strong threat enumerations structures are absent from threat modelling methodologies such as STRIDE, even beyond their system models. As such, the skill of those participating is frequently critical to the efficacy of threat elicitation. To improve threat enumeration quality and lessen reliance on highly skilled specialists, It is necessary to create a knowledge base in the form of threat databases, attack lists/taxonomies, or vulnerability databases. By amassing information from many projects and integrating it into a knowledge base, security personnel may consistently enhance their procedures. Furthermore, any attempt at semi- or fully-automated threat modelling would require this framework. However, the integration of a knowledge base into the threat elicitation stage has not been investigated in any of the field's previous studies.

16.4.1 Threats Prioritization

During the phase of selecting security requirements, it could be necessary to acknowledge and accept other hazards while concentrating solely on tackling high-priority ones due to time and resource constraints. A popular definition of risk is the result of combining impact and likelihood. In our specific situation, we don't have enough information—such as operating systems, protocols, and product vendors—or precise standards to determine whether dangers are likely at this early stage [9]. Nonetheless, carrying out an impact assessment—which might be predicated on recognised repercussions and anticipated losses. Thus, in order to rank the risks in our case study, Instead of doing a risk assessment, we chose to conduct an effect assessment. At first, the energy expert was largely responsible for determining the priority levels for losses. These findings were then linked to the effects of threats and, eventually, to the threats themselves. As such, our three-stage impact evaluation process is as follows: 1) Loss prioritisation; 2) threat consequence prioritisation; and 3) threat selection and prioritisation.

16.4.2 Selection of Security Requirements

Making the right security requirement selection is critical during the critical threat modelling phase. To do this, consult the extensive list of security requirements found in the international standard IEC 62443, which is designed especially for Industrial Automation and Control Systems (IACS). Table 16.2 outlines the Levels of security in IEC-62443. Software Application Requirements (SAR), Host Device Requirements (HDR), Embedded Device Requirements (EDR) or Network Device Requirements (NDR), and Component Requirements (CR), if applicable across all component types, are the categories into which IEC 62443-4-2 divides

Table 16.2 Levels of security in IEC-62443.

Levels of security	Description
LS 1	Prevent unintentional exposure or listening in that could reveal information without authorization.
LS 2	Stop information from being unintentionally revealed to a party that is actively looking for it using simple methods, little resources, rudimentary knowledge, and low motivation.
LS 3	Stop information from being disclosed without authorization to a party that is actively looking for it, has moderate resources, specialised knowledge of Industrial Automation and Control Systems (IACS), and is not very motivated.
LS 4	Stop information from being disclosed without authorization to a party that is actively looking for it, has a lot of resources, is highly motivated, and has specialised knowledge of Industrial Automation and Control Systems (IACS).

Table 16.3 Selected security needs for danger T-82.

Threat ID	Requirements
T_82	CR 1.2 - Identification and authentication of software processes and devices. CR 1.2 RE (1) - Distinctive identification and authentication. CR 6.2 - On-going surveillance.

requirements for various system components. These specifications are derived from seven core categories: control over identification and authentication, control over use, integrity of the system, confidentiality of data, restricted data flow, prompt event response, and resource availability [10]. The standard also assigns a security level (SL) based on the capabilities of the attacker; more sophisticated attacks, usually linked to state-sponsored actors, are assigned SL 4.

We concentrate on SL 1, SL 2, and SL 3 needs for our purposes; SL 4 criteria are not included because they are too advanced for us to handle at this time. In order to address risks that have been identified, our team of cybersecurity professionals carefully chose pertinent security needs. After then, an outline of the standard and these needs were given to the whole team. After that, the group discussed and evaluated whether the chosen requirements could actually be met.

For example, special security measures were proposed to counter the critical spoofing threat T_82 that targets the Server process, wherein a threat agent tries to impersonate the server. Table 16.3 outlines the selected security needs for danger T-82. To prevent spoofing attacks, one such requirement, CR 1.2 and its improvement RE (1), encourages the server process to authenticate itself to other components. To further strengthen overall security measures, CR 6.2 recommends using continuous monitoring technologies to quickly identify and report IP spoofing instances.

16.5 Industry 4.0 Security

In 2009, a nuclear enrichment facility had difficulties due to a virus instance known as Stuxnet that altered the speeds of the centrifuges. This malware demonstrated the possibility of cyberattacks as tools in networked physical workplaces by propagating autonomously across production networks and through removable devices in isolated networks. This emphasises the continuous conflict that exists between companies trying to protect their equipment and hackers taking advantage of holes in it.

Striking a balance between countering external threats and realising the cyber risks that come with companies adopting more connected, smart technology for innovation, transformation, and strategic decision-making is crucial [11]. It's imperative to mitigate and manage these new risks well. The advent of Industry 4.0, marked by increased connection and artificial intelligence, increases the stakes. The objective of Industry 4.0 is to transform the industrial sector by integrating intelligent and linked systems, flexible supply chains, and customised goods and services. It also presents new cyberthreats, though, for which the sector could not be sufficiently ready. As Industry 4.0 advances through the integration of operational technology (OT) and information technology (IT) in industrial value chains, a comprehensive strategic strategy to cyber risk must be developed.

16.5.1 Classification of Cyber-Physical Systems and their Pertinent Themes within the Framework of Industry 4.0

Within the context of Industry 4.0, the classification divides the knowledge gained from Cyber-Physical Systems (CPS) literature into 10 distinct areas. These sections address a number of topics, such as the definition and wider background of industrial CPS, as well as the potential benefits and challenges associated with their implementation. It also examines the requirements, guiding principles, and related technologies of industrial CPS, highlighting the socio-technical nature of these systems. It also outlines the industrial CPS's architecture and how it affects the creation of industrial value. Lastly, it looks at how industrial CPS might help with partnership formation and cross-organizational integration.

The fundamental characteristics of Cyber-Physical Systems (CPS) are applicable to both industrial and non-industrial environments [12]. There are two categories for these traits: self-characteristics and general traits. Connectivity and modularity are two general features that emphasise the adaptability of industrial CPS, which can be tailored to meet different needs and scenarios through the use of modular architecture and standardised interfaces. Timely implementation and verification of system modifications are guaranteed by real-time functionality and traceability. Self-characteristics highlight CPS's considerable autonomy by enabling them to control system states, respond to external and internal stimuli on their own, and exhibit resilience.

The specific industrial context within which these systems operate distinguishes them as industrial CPS. Referred to widely as Industry 4.0 in the literature, this term originates from a German governmental funding initiative and symbolizes digitized and interconnected industrial value creation. Anchoring industrial CPS within the Industry 4.0 framework underscores the inherent innovation potential and relevance of this concept.

16.5.2 The Digital Supply System

The supply chain is crucial for manufacturing organizations as it governs the flow of materials into production and the distribution of finished or semi-finished products to consumers. To meet consumer demand effectively, many global companies rely on demand forecasts, employing advanced analytics to understand and predict buying patterns. With the advent of Industry 4.0 technologies, there's a shift towards digital supply networks (DSNs), integrating intelligent, interconnected platforms and devices throughout the supply chain. This evolution promises improved material and product flow, resource utilization, and better alignment with customer needs. However, this increased connectivity also introduces cyber vulnerabilities that need careful consideration at every stage of design and operation to mitigate significant risks [13].

16.5.2.1 The Data Sharing Hazards Associated with the Digital Supply System

One anticipated result of the evolution of the Digital Supply Network (DSN) is the creation of a system that enables dynamic, real-time pricing of materials or goods based on customer demand relative to available supply. But creating a network this adaptable and responsive needs unfettered data exchange across all supply chain players. This is a serious problem since it means striking a careful balance between security and transparency for different types of data.To stop illegal access over the network, organisations need to deal with the challenge of protecting this data. Strong security measures must be implemented for a number of processes, including vendor acceptance, data exchange, and system access [14]. Not only could these procedures be secret, but they might also act as gateways to other corporate data. Figure 16.5 depicts the risks and wise decisions in cyber physical system. Furthermore, third-party risk management becomes more complex as a result of this increased connectedness. Two main areas are impacted when evaluating the cybersecurity threats related to interconnected DSNs:

Stage of the production life cycle	Safe, watchful, and robust classification	The necessity of cybersecurity	Objective
Digital Supply System	safe, watchful, and resilient.	Exchanging data	Maintain system integrity to prevent access to confidential or proprietary data.
	safe, watchful, and resilient.	Processing of vendors	When processes cannot be validated, keep your faith intact.

Figure 16.5 Risks and wise decisions.

- **Data Sharing:** Ensuring secure data exchange while maintaining transparency.
- **Vendor Processing:** Managing risks related to vendors' involvement in the network

Addressing these challenges requires thoughtful strategies and a holistic approach to cybersecurity in the age of Industry 4.0.

16.5.2.2 Data Sharing: Granted Access to Information for More Parties

Certainly, organizations navigating the complexities of a Digital Supply Network (DSN) must carefully weigh the balance between data sharing and security. Here are some considerations:

a. Selective Data Sharing:
Organizations should deliberate on which data to share openly and which to protect. For instance, suppliers within a specific DSN might be competitors in other contexts. Consequently, they may be hesitant to disclose certain types of data, such as pricing or proprietary material information.

b. Privacy and Regulatory Constraints:
Suppliers could also be subject to regulations that restrict the type of information they can share. Striking a balance between transparency and compliance is crucial.

c. Risk of Partial Data Exposure:
Opening up only part of the data could inadvertently provide access to other sensitive information. Vigilance is necessary to prevent unauthorized access by those with malicious intent.

In this intricate landscape, organizations must find ways to foster collaboration while safeguarding proprietary data and maintaining cybersecurity across the supply network.

16.5.3 Cybersecurity Challenges in Industry 4.0

Although the manufacturing sector ranks as the second-most targeted industry for cyber attacks, it is trailing behind in implementing adequate security measures. Smart factories encounter comparable vulnerabilities to other networks, such as susceptibility to exploitation, malware infections, denial of service (DoS) attacks, device breaches, and various typical attack techniques. The increased attack surface of smart factories poses challenges for detecting and defending against cyber threats, especially with the rise of the Internet of Things (IoT), which could result in significant physical ramifications [15]. In the era of Industry 4.0, organizations encounter several new security challenges:

- Each device that is linked has the potential to cause harm.
- Manufacturing systems, such as Industrial Control Systems (ICS), are particularly vulnerable to cyberattacks because of their special weaknesses.
- Industry 4.0 expands the attack surface by integrating systems that were previously isolated.
- System upgrades are often implemented incrementally due to the complexity of systems.
- The manufacturing sector lacks stringent compliance standards compared to other industries.
- Visibility across separate systems and isolated environments is limited.
- The asymmetrical nature of the battle between defenders and attackers is evident.Attackers just need to target the weakest link in an organization's enormous attack surface, despite the fact that organisations must secure a wide range of technologies [16].

Table 16.4 Prioritization of fundamental security objectives differs between cyber-physical systems (CPS) and traditional IT systems.

Hierarchy	Cyber physical system	IT systems
High	Accessibility	Secrecy
Medium	Authenticity	Authenticity
Low	Secrecy	Accessibility

16.6 Evaluation of Risk for CPS

Evaluation of risk and management show a crucial part in the development of Cyber-Physical Systems (CPS). Initially, developers focused primarily on safety concerns in CPS development. Safety risks in CPS arise from interactions with the environment, within the system itself, and with authorized users. Table 16.4 shows the Prioritization of fundamental security objectives differs between cyber-physical systems (CPS) and traditional IT systems. The Confidentiality, Integrity, and Availability (CIA) trio, represents the core security objectives for both CPS and traditional IT systems [17]. However, unlike IT systems, availability takes precedence in CPS. While these core goals are essential for both CPS and IT systems, their significances differ. Safety and availability in CPS are geared towards maintaining a secure state below a predetermined appropriate cutoff point.

16.6.1 Safety Risk Assessment Standards

Process industries place a high priority on safety, which is addressed by standards like IEC 61508. In order to assess the dependability of safety-related systems, this standard defines metrics such as Safety Integrity Level (SIL) and Safe Failure Fraction (SFF). It uses a risk-based methodology to determine which SIL is suitable for systems that perform safety utilities. Although A fundamental safety standard is IEC 61508. for many businesses, some industries, like the process industry, have their own standards, like ISA 84 / IEC 61511. IEC 61508 and ISA 84 / IEC 61511 both demand the measurement of successful risk mitigation, usually represented by SIL, ascertained by threat and risk examination in conjunction with predetermined risk recognition principles.

16.6.2 Approaches for Safety Risk Evaluation in CPS

Identification of belongings, study of liabilities, and estimation of possible damages are all part of risk assessment and management. In general, there are two types of risk assessment methodologies: qualitative and quantitative. While quantitative evaluation provides exact risk estimates for systems, qualitative assessment depends on the knowledge and expertise of experts. Diverse approaches are at hand for carrying out safety risk assessments in Cyber-Physical Systems (CPS), underscoring the continuous progress in CPS safety procedures.

16.6.2.1 Analysis of Fault Trees

One of the earliest methods for assessing safety risk was fault tree analysis analysis of fault trees, which is now frequently used for hazard and risk assessment in Cyber-Physical Systems (CPS). Visualising probable normal and faulty events that could result in the top-level undesirable event is the main goal of analysis of fault trees. The fault tree is made up of nodes, which stand for undesirable system events, gates, which show links between nodes (like AND or OR gates), and edges, which show the undesirable events' course through the system. the procedure for building a simple fault tree with "fire" as the top undesirable event by utilising AND and OR gates [18].

16.6.2.2 Failure Modes and Impacts Evaluation (FMIE)

FMIE is a systematic approach involving teams to analyze system safety by identifying, evaluating, and scoring potential failures and their impacts. It assesses how a component might fail (failure mode) and scores the leniency of these failure modes. The Risk Precedence Number is a key component of quantitative FMIEscrutiny, calculated by multiplying leniency, possibility of incidence, and recognition probability. Grunske *et al.* introduced a probabilistic version of FMIE to identify failure modes with probabilities exceeding tolerable hazard rates. FMIE typically occurs during the primary design stage of the system life cycle.

16.6.2.3 The Menace and Operability Approach

It is a System Hazard Scrutinyprocedure that is commonly employed to investigate both operability issues and risks inside a system. Potential departures from the design parameters are identified, along with the consequences for system performance. By identifying risks and operational issues, the analysis assists in determining how a progression might depart from its original strategy and reach a defect or inaccuracy condition.

16.6.2.4 Model-Centred Engineering

To validate requirements and guarantee CPS safety, It entails creating interactiveprototypes of real-time structures. First, system safety is taken into account, and characteristics of the physical world, computer systems, and cyber-physical interactions are extracted. After that, these characteristics are examined in abstract models in order to assess anticipated characteristics and confirm safety standards.

16.6.2.5 Master Logic Illustration with Objective Tree - Accomplishment Tree

A function-based architecture for dependability and menacescrutiny, Itcontains of a Master Logic Illustration (MLI), aAccomplishment Tree (AT), and a Objective Tree (OT). While accomplishment trees and MLI use the Boolean physical, and fuzzy logic to denote objects and relationships, it represents attributes as functions and goals. This paradigm may describe fuzzy, physical, and logical links in complicated physical systems.

16.6.2.6 System Theoretical Accident Model and Procedures (STAMP) is the Foundation for System Theoretic Process Analysis, a Hazard Analysis Method

Particularly suitable for complex systems with software-intensive components. STAMP treats the system as a hierarchical control structure and identifies accident scenarios by analyzing interactions within this structure. It focuses on causations of hazards rather than distinguishing hazards themselves, providing systematic guidance for achieving better results.

References

1. Khalil, S.M., Bahsi, H., Ochieng' Dola, H., Korõtko, T., McLaughlin, K., Kotkas, V., Threat modeling of cyber-physical systems-a case study of a microgrid system. *Comput. Secur.*, 124, 102950, 2023.
2. Alcaraz, C. and Lopez, J., Digital twin: A comprehensive survey of security threats. *IEEE Commun. Surv. Tutorials*, 24, 3, 1475–1503, 2022.

3. Mostaani, A., Vu, T.X., Sharma, S.K., Nguyen, V.-D., Liao, Q., Chatzinotas, S., Task-oriented communication design in cyber-physical systems: A survey on theory and applications. *IEEE Access*, 10, 133842–133868, 2022.
4. Humayun, M., Industry 4.0 and cyber security issues and challenges. *Turk. J. Comput. Math. Educ. (TURCOMAT)*, 12, 10, 2957–2971, 2021.
5. Cova, G., Cyber risk assessment of cyber-physical system for renewable energy application, 2020.
6. Tantawy, A., Abdelwahed, S., Erradi, A., Shaban, K., Model-based risk assessment for cyber physical systems security. *Comput. Secur.*, 96, 101864, 2020.
7. Lozano, C.V. and Vijayan, K.K., Literature review on cyber physical systems design. *Procedia Manuf.*, 45, 295–300, 2020.
8. Walker-Roberts, S., Hammoudeh, M., Aldabbas, O., Aydin, M., Dehghantanha, A., Threats on the horizon: Understanding security threats in the era of cyber-physical systems. *J. Supercomputing*, 76, 2643–2664, 2020.
9. Zografopoulos, I., Ospina, J., Liu, X., Konstantinou, C., Cyber-physical energy systems security: Threat modeling, risk assessment, resources, metrics, and case studies. *IEEE Access*, 9, 29775–29818, 2021.
10. Lyu, X., Ding, Y., Yang, S.-H., Safety and security risk assessment in cyber-physical systems. *IET Cyber-Phys. Syst.: Theor. Appl.*, 4, 3, 221–232, 2019.
11. Bartocci, E., Deshmukh, J., Donzé, A., Fainekos, G., Maler, O., Ničković, D., Sankaranarayanan, S., Specification-based monitoring of cyber-physical systems: a survey on theory, tools and applications. *Lect. Runtime Verification Introductory Adv. Top.*, 10, 135–175, 2018.
12. Northern, B., Burks, T., Hatcher, M., Rogers, M., Ulybyshev, D., Vercasm-cps: Vulnerability analysis and cyber risk assessment for cyber-physical systems. *Information*, 12, 10, 408, 2021.
13. Bordel, B., Alcarria, R., Robles, T., Martín, D., Cyber–physical systems: Extending pervasive sensing from control theory to the Internet of Things. *Pervasive Mob. Comput.*, 40, 156–184, 2017.
14. Culot, G., Fattori, F., Podrecca, M., Sartor, M., Addressing industry 4.0 cybersecurity challenges. *IEEE Eng. Manage. Rev.*, 47, 3, 79–86, 2019.
15. Hussain, A., Mohamed, A., Razali, S., A review on cybersecurity: Challenges & emerging threats, in: *Proceedings of the 3rd International Conference on Networking, Information Systems & Security*, pp. 1–7, 2020.
16. He, H. and Yan, J., Cyber-physical attacks and defences in the smart grid: a survey. *IET Cyber-Phys. Syst.: Theor. Appl.*, 1, 1, 13–27, 2016.
17. Tonge, A.M., Kasture, S.S., Chaudhari, S.R., Cyber security: challenges for society-literature review. *IOSR J. Comput. Eng.*, 2, 12, 67–75, 2013.
18. Rajasekharaiah, K.M., Dule, C.S., Sudarshan, E., *IOP Conf. Ser.: Mater. Sci. Eng.*, 981, 2, 022062, 2020.

Index

Access management, 353
Adaptive control strategies, 70, 73
Adaptive security controls, 235
Adaptive security measures, 110, 112, 121, 129
Adversarial attacks, 256
Adversary capabilities, 67–68
Agricultural automation, 350
Android ransomware, 295
Anomaly detection, 74, 225–227, 231–232, 236, 245, 309, 321
Antivirus software, 353
Artificial intelligence, 25, 27, 28, 29, 30, 31, 32, 36, 38, 39, 40, 41, 42, 43, 45, 46, 47, 48, 50, 52, 53, 58, 60, 61, 62, 87, 95, 96, 100, 101, 102, 105, 110, 112, 114, 118, 119, 120, 121, 125, 126, 127, 128, 129, 133, 134, 139, 144, 151, 152, 153, 154, 178, 180, 182, 185, 189, 190, 201, 204, 208, 213, 217, 221, 249, 279, 280, 281, 285, 287, 291, 293
Artificial intelligence in CPS, 351
Artificial neural network, 303
Artificial noise, 99, 100, 101, 102
Attack surfaces, 68–69
Authentication, 309, 322
Authentication mechanisms, 72
Automation in cybersecurity, 348
Autonomous automobiles, 349
Autonomous connected vehicles, 1, 2, 3, 4, 5, 6, 7, 8, 14, 15, 17, 18, 19, 21, 22, 23
Autonomous response systems, 69, 71

Behavioral analysis, 235
Big data, 29, 31, 199–200, 276, 281, 289
Blockchain, 199–200, 277, 282, 283, 290, 321, 322
Blockchain protocol, 186, 187, 188, 192, 194
Body area networks, 166, 167
BSS, 296

Challenges and security, 345
Cloud computing, 199, 200, 215, 221, 276, 279, 285, 289, 291
Cloud platforms, 219, 221, 278, 286, 288, 291
Cloud-integrated CPS, 75
Cognitive base station, 3, 4, 7, 8, 9, 11, 12, 13
Cognitive cyber physical security, 110, 111, 112, 114, 115, 117, 119, 121, 125, 126, 127, 128, 129, 130
Cognitive cyber-physical systems (CCPS), 1, 3, 4, 22, 23, 25, 26, 27, 28, 29, 30, 31, 32, 33, 34, 36, 37, 38, 39, 40, 41, 42, 43, 45, 46, 47, 48, 51, 55, 56, 60, 61, 62, 87, 88, 89, 90, 92, 93, 94, 95, 96, 97, 98, 99, 102, 103, 104, 105, 133, 134, 135, 136, 137, 138, 139, 141, 143, 144, 151, 152, 153, 154, 309–310, 313
Cognitive cybersecurity, 177, 178, 181, 183, 189, 192, 194
Cognitive decision-making, 181, 184, 192, 194
Cognitive feedback loops, 66–67

Cognitive radio networks, 3, 7, 8, 11, 12, 13
Control architecture, 68
Controller area network, 6
CPS model, 345
Cross-disciplinary applications, 351
Cryptanalysis, 253
Cryptographic techniques, 72–73
Cryptography, 312, 321, 329
Cyber attacks, 111, 113, 117, 121, 127, 128, 129, 199, 200, 204, 206, 207, 212, 217, 218, 221, 270, 272, 275, 277, 280, 282, 284, 286, 289, 309, 312, 320
Cyber layer, 66–68
Cyber threats, 199–200, 219–222, 269–272, 278–285
Cyberattacks using mobile technology, 348
Cyber-physical systems (CPS), 157, 158, 159, 160, 161, 163, 169, 172, 173, 177, 179, 183, 190, 192, 194, 225–228, 230–233, 235, 240–241, 245, 309–339
Cyber-physical threats, 359
Cybersecurity, 1, 4, 5, 14, 21, 46, 47, 59, 61, 62, 89, 94, 95, 96, 105, 106, 133, 136, 137, 138, 143, 153, 154, 249, 269–273, 276–283, 295
Cybersecurity and privacy, 351

Data fusion, 71
Data injection attacks, 6, 8
Data mining, 31, 35, 40
Data preprocessing, 295, 300
Data privacy, 110, 111, 114, 122, 123, 127, 128, 204, 205, 209, 212, 217, 277, 278, 279, 286, 289, 292
Data privacy regulations (GDPR), 347
Data sharing and security, 362
Data validation, 301
Data verification, 353
Data visualization, 301
Dataset poisoning, 311, 324–326, 336
DDoS, 199–200
Decision tree, 298, 299, 303
Deep learning, 29, 30, 31, 39, 40, 45, 46, 61, 62, 179, 185, 213, 217, 221, 232, 235, 281, 285, 287, 312, 321, 336
Differential privacy, 330–332, 338
Digital connectivity, 250
Digital supply systems, 361
Digital transformation, 200, 201, 204, 271, 274, 277, 279, 283, 287
Digital transformation in business, 355
Digital twin, 236
Dynamic context monitoring, 182, 188, 193

Eavesdropping, 320–321
E-commerce, 203, 204, 210, 273
Embedded sensors, 67–68
Embedded systems and hardware design, 351
Encryption, 259, 309, 322
Encryption fields, 251
Encryption protocols, 73
Energy efficiency and sustainability, 351
Energy management, 68
Ensemble learning, 305
Environmental monitoring, 350

F1 score, 302
Failure modes and impacts evaluation (FMIE), 365
Fault analysis, 90, 91
Fault tree analysis, 365
Federated learning, 333, 339

General Data Protection Regulation, 114, 115
GNN, 296

Health Insurance Portability and Accountability Act, 113, 115
Healthcare applications, 33, 34, 38, 41, 42
Healthcare Data Protection, 178, 188, 192

Healthcare ecosystems, 178, 179, 188, 194
Homomorphic encryption, 331, 338
Human interaction with CPS, 351

IDS (Intrusion Detection System), 311, 321
Improved medical cyber-physical systems, 166, 167, 168, 169
Industrial control systems (ICS), 26, 27, 28, 29, 31, 225, 227
Industrial Internet of Things (IIoT), 89, 90, 106, 349
Industry 4.0, 45, 46, 49, 50, 51, 52, 53, 59, 60, 61, 62, 88, 96
Integrated clinical environment, 118, 124, 128
Integrity, 250
Intelligent cyber-physical systems, 47, 49, 50, 53, 54, 56, 58, 59, 60, 61, 62
Intelligent houses and buildings, 350
Intelligent machines, 266
Intelligent transportation system, 3, 6
Intensive training and awareness, 226, 241
Internet of Things, 26, 27, 28, 29, 30, 33, 34, 35, 36, 37, 38, 39, 40, 41, 87, 88, 93, 94, 95, 96, 102, 103, 105, 109, 110, 111, 112, 113, 114, 115, 117, 118, 121, 126, 127, 128, 129, 130, 133, 134, 135, 136, 137, 138, 139, 142, 143, 144, 152, 153, 154, 177, 180, 183, 185, 190, 192, 194
Internet of Things Ransomware, 347
Internet of Vehicles, 2, 12
Intrusion detection and prevention, 235
Intrusion detection system, 46, 48, 49, 50, 51, 53, 56, 58, 59, 60, 61, 62, 74
IoT and sensor node management, 350

KNN, 298, 299

Local binary patterns, 182
Logistic regression, 300

Machine learning (ML), 2, 3, 17, 18, 32, 38, 39, 40, 41, 42, 43, 45, 46, 47, 48, 61, 62, 110, 111, 118, 127, 128, 133, 134, 135, 136, 137, 138, 140, 141, 143, 144, 152, 153, 154, 161, 173, 199, 200, 262, 280, 281, 287, 290, 309–339
Machine learning in CPS, 74–75
Machine learning-driven defenses, 225–227, 235
Malware, 199–200, 208–214
Malware attacks, 321–322
Malware detection, 353
Medical cyber physical system, 116, 117, 118, 119, 120, 121, 122, 123, 124, 125, 128, 157, 158, 161, 162, 169, 172, 173, 179, 180, 182, 183, 190, 194
Membership inference attack, 309, 333–334, 338
Micro-segmentation, 226, 237
Model inversion, 330–331, 338
Model poisoning, 324, 328–330
Model-centered engineering, 366
MSDROID, 296
Mult arm bandit, 9, 14, 15

Natural language processing, 254
Network security, 1, 4
Network security (Firewalls), 353
Networked and distributed CPS, 351
NLP, 296

Object classification, 3, 9
Outlier detection, 329

Parallelization, 335–336
Partial least square, 182
Patient controlled analgesia, 165, 166, 169, 170
Phishing, 199, 204, 205, 213, 273–275, 283, 284
Phishing attack, 321
Phishing exploits, 347

Physical layer, 66
Physical layer security, 97, 99, 100, 101, 102, 105
Physical system, 90, 91, 97
Post quantum, 253
Precision, 302
Predictive analysis, 254
Predictive maintenance, 236, 240
Primary user, 3, 9, 12, 13
Privacy breach, 311, 324, 330
Privacy preserving, 251
PSO, 299

Quality of service, 25, 33, 41, 43, 92, 96, 97, 98, 100, 105, 161
Quantum attacks, 252
Quantum computers, 250

Random forests, 305
Ransomware, 204, 205, 209, 211, 273, 274, 275, 277, 283, 284, 289
Ransomware attacks, 295–296
Real time monitoring, 261, 240
Real-time system algorithms, 350
Recall, 302
Regulatory compliance, 257
Reinforcement learning, 177, 178, 185, 186, 187, 189, 190, 192, 194
Remote work, 201, 203, 207, 274, 275, 278, 283, 290
Resilience mechanisms, 69–70
Resilience techniques, 225–227, 240, 245
Resilient security, 178, 189, 194
Risk assessment standards, 364
Runtime disruption, 324–325, 335–336

Safety and reliability, 351
SCADA systems, 66–67, 72
Secure communication, 313, 317
Secure communication protocols, 225–227, 232, 245
Security analysis, 252
Security requirement selection, 358
Security requirements, 69–72
Self-healing mechanisms, 225–226
Sensor-actuator network, 67–68
Signature-based detection, 298
Small and medium-sized enterprises, 140, 149, 150, 153, 154
Smart cities, 349
Smart grids, 225, 227, 348
Smart health system, 349
Smart healthcare systems, 109, 110, 112, 114, 115, 119, 128, 129, 130
Social media and cybersecurity, 352
Supply chain management, 350
Supply chain security, 309, 322
SVM, 296, 299, 304, 305
System hazard analysis (HAZOP), 366
System theoretic process analysis (STAMP), 366
System-theoretic accident and processes, 158
System-theoretic process analysis, 164, 170

Telemedicine, 203, 204, 210, 211, 278, 281, 284, 288
Threat detection, 110, 111, 121, 123, 128, 178, 185, 194
Threat intelligence, 231, 236, 238, 245
Threat modeling, 66–69
Threats prioritization, 357
Tokenization, 329
Traffic signs, 3, 9, 15, 16, 17, 18
Transport layer security (TLS), 233–234

Unified integration of information, uncertainty and control, 161

Vehicle-to-everything, 2
Vehicle-to-infrastructure, 2, 6
Vehicle-to-vehicle, 2
Vulnerabilities in CPS, 346

Wearable health monitoring, 350

Zero trust model, 225–226, 237, 245
Zero-day attacks, 315, 326

Also of Interest

Check out these published and forthcoming titles in the "Industry 5.0 Transformation Applications" series from Scrivener Publishing

Cyber-Physical Systems for Innovating and Transforming Society 5.0
Edited by Tanupriya Choudhury, Abhijit Kumar, Ravi Tomar, S. Balamurugan and Ankit Vishnoi
Forthcoming 2025. ISBN 978-1-394-19771-2

Distributed Time-Sensitive Systems
Edited by Tanupriya Choudhury, Rahul Kumar Singh, Ravi Tomar, S. Balamurugan, J. C. Patni
Published 2025. ISBN 978-1-394-19772-9

Generative Artificial Intelligence
Concepts and Applications
Edited by R. Nidhya, D. Pavithra, Manish Kumar, A. Dinesh Kumar, and S. Balamurugan
Published 2025. ISBN 978-1-394-20922-4

Intelligent Robots and Cobots
Concepts and Applications for Industry 5.0 Transformation
Edited by Ramasamy V., S. Balamurugan, and Sheng-Lung Peng
Published 2025. ISBN 978-1-394-19817-7

Smart Factories for Industry 5.0 Transformation
Edited by R. Nidhya, Manish Kumar, S. Karthik, Rishabh Anand and S. Balamurugan
Published 2025. ISBN 978-1-394-19995-2

Optimized Computational Intelligence Driven Decision-Making
Theory, Application and Challenges
Edited by Hrudaya Kumar Tripathy, Sushruta Mishra, Minakhi Rout, S. Balamurugan and Samaresh Mishra
Published 2024. ISBN 978-1-394-24253-5

Welding Practices for Industry 5.0
Edited by Syed Quadir Moinuddin, Shaik Himam Saheb, Ashok Kumar Dewangan, Muralimohan Cheepu and S. Balamurugan
Published 2024. ISBN 978-1-394-17241-2

Metaverse and Immersive Technologies
An Introduction to Industrial, Business and Social Applications
Edited by Chandrashekhar A., Shaik Himam Saheb, Sandeep Kumar Panda, S. Balamurugan and Sheng-Lung Peng
Published 2023. ISBN 978-1-394-17454-6

www.scrivenerpublishing.com

Printed and bound by CPI Group (UK) Ltd, Croydon, CR0 4YY
17/09/2026
14964263-0005